THINKING,

FAST AND SLOW

THINKING, FAST AND SLOW

DANIEL KAHNEMAN

ALLEN LANE
an imprint of
PENGUIN BOOKS

ALLEN LANE

Published by the Penguin Group
Penguin Books Ltd, 80 Strand, London WC2R 0RL, England
Penguin Group (USA) Inc., 375 Hudson Street, New York, New York 10014, USA
Penguin Group (Canada), 90 Eglinton Avenue East, Suite 700, Toronto, Ontario,
Canada M4P 2Y3 (a division of Pearson Penguin Canada Inc.)
Penguin Ireland, 25 St Stephen's Green, Dublin 2, Ireland
(a division of Penguin Books Ltd)
Penguin Group (Australia), 250 Camberwell Road, Camberwell,
Victoria 3124, Australia (a division of Pearson Australia Group Pty Ltd)
Penguin Books India Pvt Ltd, 11 Community Centre,
Panchsheel Park, New Delhi – 110 017, India
Penguin Group (NZ), 67 Apollo Drive, Rosedale, Auckland 0632, New Zealand
(a division of Pearson New Zealand Ltd)
Penguin Books (South Africa) (Pty) Ltd, 24 Sturdee Avenue,
Rosebank, Johannesburg 2196, South Africa

Penguin Books Ltd, Registered Offices: 80 Strand, London WC2R 0RL, England

www.penguin.com

First published in the United States of America by Farrar, Straus and Giroux 2011
First published in Great Britain by Allen Lane 2011
4

Copyright © Daniel Kahneman, 2011

The moral right of the author has been asserted

Grateful acknowledgment is made for permission to reprint the following previously
published material: "Judgment Under Uncertainty: Heuristics and Biases" from *Science,
New Series*, Vol. 185, No. 4157, copyright © 1974 by Amos Tversky and Daniel Kahneman.
Reprinted by permission of *Science*. "Choices, Values, and Frames" from *The American
Psychologist*, copyright © 1983 by Daniel Kahneman and Amos Tversky.
Reprinted by permission of the *American Psychological Association*.

Grateful acknowledgment is made for permission to reprint the following images:
Image on page 19 courtesy of Paul Ekman Group, LLC. Image on page 57 from "Cues of
Being Watched Enhance Cooperation in a Real-World Setting" by Melissa Bateson, Daniel
Nettle, and Gilbert Roberts, *Biology Letters* (2006); reprinted by permission of *Biology
Letters*. Image on page 100 from *Mind Sights* by Roger N. Shepard (New York:
W.H. Freeman and Company, 1990); reprinted by permission of Henry Holt and Company.
Image on page 300 from "Human Amygdala Responsivity to Masked Fearful Eye Whites"
by Paul J. Whalen et al., *Science* 306 (2004). Reprinted by permission of *Science*.

Printed in Great Britain by Clays Ltd, St Ives plc

A CIP catalogue record for this book is available from the British Library

Hardback ISBN: 978–1–846–14055–6
Trade paperback ISBN: 978–1–846–14606–0

www.greenpenguin.co.uk

MIX
Paper from
responsible sources
FSC
www.fsc.org   FSC™ C018179

Penguin Books is committed to a sustainable
future for our business, our readers and our
planet. This book is made from paper certified
by the Forest Stewardship Council.

In memory of Amos Tversky

CONTENTS

PART III. OVERCONFIDENCE

PART IV. CHOICES

PART V. TWO SELVES

THINKING,
FAST AND SLOW

INTRODUCTION

Every author, I suppose, has in mind a setting in which readers of his or her work could benefit from having read it. Mine is the proverbial office water-cooler, where opinions are shared and gossip is exchanged. I hope to enrich the vocabulary that people use when they talk about the judgments and choices of others, the company's new policies, or a colleague's investment decisions. Why be concerned with gossip? Because it is much easier, as well as far more enjoyable, to identify and label the mistakes of others than to recognize our own. Questioning what we believe and want is difficult at the best of times, and especially difficult when we most need to do it, but we can benefit from the informed opinions of others. Many of us spontaneously anticipate how friends and colleagues will evaluate our choices; the quality and content of these anticipated judgments therefore matters. The expectation of intelligent gossip is a powerful motive for serious self-criticism, more powerful than New Year resolutions to improve one's decision making at work and at home.

To be a good diagnostician, a physician needs to acquire a large set of labels for diseases, each of which binds an idea of the illness and its symptoms, possible antecedents and causes, possible developments and consequences, and possible interventions to cure or mitigate the illness. Learning medicine consists in part of learning the language of medicine. A deeper understanding of judgments and choices also requires a richer vocabulary than is available in everyday language. The hope for informed gossip is that there are distinctive patterns in the errors people make. Systematic errors are known as biases, and they recur predictably in particular circumstances. When the handsome and confident speaker bounds onto the stage, for example, you can anticipate that the audience will judge his comments more favorably than he deserves. The availability of a diagnostic label for this bias—the halo effect—makes it easier to anticipate, recognize, and understand.

When you are asked what you are thinking about, you can normally answer. You believe you know what goes on in your mind, which often consists of one conscious thought leading in an orderly way to another. But that is not the only way the mind works, nor indeed is that the typical way. Most impressions and thoughts arise in your conscious experience without your knowing how they got there. You cannot trace how you came to the belief that there is a lamp on the desk in front of you, or how you detected a hint of irritation in your spouse's voice on the telephone, or how you managed to avoid a threat on the road before you became consciously aware of it. The mental work that produces impressions, intuitions, and many decisions goes on in silence in our mind.

Much of the discussion in this book is about biases of intuition. However, the focus on error does not denigrate human intelligence, any more than the attention to diseases in medical texts denies good health. Most of us are healthy most of the time, and most of our judgments and actions are appropriate most of the time. As we navigate our lives, we normally allow ourselves to be guided by impressions and feelings, and the confidence we have in our intuitive beliefs and preferences is usually justified. But not always. We are often confident even when we are wrong, and an objective observer is more likely to detect our errors than we are.

So this is my aim for watercooler conversations: improve the ability to identify and understand errors of judgment and choice, in others and eventually in ourselves, by providing a richer and more precise language to discuss them. In at least some cases, an accurate diagnosis may suggest an intervention to limit the damage that bad judgments and choices often cause.

ORIGINS

This book presents my current understanding of judgment and decision making, which has been shaped by psychological discoveries of recent decades. However, I trace the central ideas to the lucky day in 1969 when I asked a colleague to speak as a guest to a seminar I was teaching in the Department of Psychology at the Hebrew University of Jerusalem. Amos Tversky was considered a rising star in the field of decision research—indeed, in anything he did—so I knew we would have an interesting time. Many people who knew Amos thought he was the most intelligent person they had ever met. He was brilliant, voluble, and charismatic. He was also blessed with a perfect memory for jokes and an exceptional ability to use them to make a point. There was never a dull moment when Amos was around. He was then thirty-two; I was thirty-five.

Amos told the class about an ongoing program of research at the University of Michigan that sought to answer this question: Are people good intuitive statisticians? We already knew that people are good intuitive grammarians: at age four a child effortlessly conforms to the rules of grammar as she speaks, although she has no idea that such rules exist. Do people have a similar intuitive feel for the basic principles of statistics? Amos reported that the answer was a qualified yes. We had a lively debate in the seminar and ultimately concluded that a qualified no was a better answer.

Amos and I enjoyed the exchange and concluded that intuitive statistics was an interesting topic and that it would be fun to explore it together. That Friday we met for lunch at Café Rimon, the favorite hangout of bohemians and professors in Jerusalem, and planned a study of the statistical intuitions of sophisticated researchers. We had concluded in the seminar that our own intuitions were deficient. In spite of years of teaching and using statistics, we had not developed an intuitive sense of the reliability of statistical results observed in small samples. Our subjective judgments were biased: we were far too willing to believe research findings based on inadequate evidence and prone to collect too few observations in our own research. The goal of our study was to examine whether other researchers suffered from the same affliction.

We prepared a survey that included realistic scenarios of statistical issues that arise in research. Amos collected the responses of a group of expert participants in a meeting of the Society of Mathematical Psychology, including the authors of two statistical textbooks. As expected, we found that our expert colleagues, like us, greatly exaggerated the likelihood that the original result of an experiment would be successfully replicated even with a small sample. They also gave very poor advice to a fictitious graduate student about the number of observations she needed to collect. Even statisticians were not good intuitive statisticians.

While writing the article that reported these findings, Amos and I discovered that we enjoyed working together. Amos was always very funny, and in his presence I became funny as well, so we spent hours of solid work in continuous amusement. The pleasure we found in working together made us exceptionally patient; it is much easier to strive for perfection when you are never bored. Perhaps most important, we checked our critical weapons at the door. Both Amos and I were critical and argumentative, he even more than I, but during the years of our collaboration neither of us ever rejected out of hand anything the other said. Indeed, one of the great joys I found in the collaboration was that Amos frequently saw the point of my vague ideas much more clearly than I did. Amos was the more logical thinker, with an orientation to theory and an unfailing sense of direction. I was more intuitive and rooted in the psychology of perception, from which we borrowed many ideas. We were sufficiently similar to understand each other easily, and sufficiently different to surprise each other. We developed a routine in which we spent much of our working days together, often on long walks. For the next fourteen years our collaboration was the focus of our lives, and the work we did together during those years was the best either of us ever did.

We quickly adopted a practice that we maintained for many years. Our research was a conversation, in which we invented questions and jointly examined our intuitive answers. Each question was a small experiment, and we carried out many experiments in a single day. We were not seriously looking for the correct answer to the statistical questions we posed. Our aim was to identify and analyze the intuitive answer, the first one that came to mind, the one we were tempted to make even when we knew it to be wrong. We believed—correctly, as it happened—that any intuition that the two of us shared would be shared by many other people as well, and that it would be easy to demonstrate its effects on judgments.

We once discovered with great delight that we had identical silly ideas about the future professions of several toddlers we both knew. We could identify the argumentative three-year-old lawyer, the nerdy professor, the empathetic and mildly intrusive psychotherapist. Of course these predictions were absurd, but we still found them appealing. It was also clear that our intuitions were governed by the resemblance of each child to the cultural stereotype of a profession. The amusing exercise helped us develop a theory that was emerging in our minds at the time, about the role of resemblance in predictions. We went on to test and elaborate that theory in dozens of experiments, as in the following example.

As you consider the next question, please assume that Steve was selected at random from a representative sample:

An individual has been described by a neighbor as follows: "Steve is very shy and withdrawn, invariably helpful but with little interest in people or in the world of reality. A meek and tidy soul, he has a need for order and structure, and a passion for detail." Is Steve more likely to be a librarian or a farmer?

The resemblance of Steve's personality to that of a stereotypical librarian strikes everyone immediately, but equally relevant statistical considerations are almost always ignored. Did it occur to you that there are more than 20 male farmers for each male librarian in the United States? Because there are so many more farmers, it is almost certain that more "meek and tidy" souls will be found on tractors than at library information desks. However, we found that participants in our experiments ignored the relevant statistical facts and relied exclusively on resemblance. We proposed that they used resemblance as a simplifying heuristic (roughly, a rule of thumb) to make a difficult judgment. The reliance on the heuristic caused predictable biases (systematic errors) in their predictions.

On another occasion, Amos and I wondered about the rate of divorce among professors in our university. We noticed that the question triggered a search of memory for divorced professors we knew or knew about, and that we judged the size of categories by the ease with which instances came to mind. We called this reliance on the ease of memory search the availability heuristic. In one of our studies, we asked participants to answer a simple question about words in a typical English text:

Consider the letter K.
Is K more likely to appear as the first letter in a word OR as the third letter?

As any Scrabble player knows, it is much easier to come up with words that begin with a particular letter than to find words that have the same letter in the third position. This is true for every letter of the alphabet. We therefore expected respondents to exaggerate the frequency of letters appearing in the first position—even those letters (such as K, L, N, R, V) which in fact occur more frequently in the third position. Here again, the reliance on a heuristic produces a predictable bias in judgments. For example, I recently came to doubt my long-held impression that adultery is more common among politicians than among physicians or lawyers. I had even come up with explanations for that "fact," including the aphrodisiac effect of power and the temptations of life away from home. I eventually realized that the transgressions of politicians are much more likely to be reported than the transgressions of lawyers and doctors. My intuitive impression could be due entirely to journalists' choices of topics and to my reliance on the availability heuristic.

Amos and I spent several years studying and documenting biases of intuitive thinking in various tasks—assigning probabilities to events, forecasting the future, assessing hypotheses, and estimating frequencies. In the fifth year of our collaboration, we presented our main findings in *Science* magazine, a publication read by scholars in many disciplines. The article (which is reproduced in full at the end of this book) was titled "Judgment Under Uncertainty: Heuristics and Biases." It described the simplifying shortcuts of intuitive thinking and explained some 20 biases as manifestations of these heuristics—and also as demonstrations of the role of heuristics in judgment.

Historians of science have often noted that at any given time scholars in a particular field tend to share basic assumptions about their subject. Social scientists are no exception; they rely on a view of human nature that provides the background of most discussions of specific behaviors but is rarely questioned. Social scientists in the 1970s broadly accepted two ideas about human nature. First, people are generally rational, and their thinking is normally sound. Second, emotions such as fear, affection, and hatred explain most of the occasions on which people depart from rationality. Our article challenged both assumptions without discussing them directly. We documented systematic errors in the thinking of normal people, and we traced these errors to the design of the machinery of cognition rather than to the corruption of thought by emotion.

Our article attracted much more attention than we had expected, and it remains one of the most highly cited works in social science (more than three hundred scholarly articles referred to it in 2010). Scholars in other disciplines found it useful, and the ideas of heuristics and biases have been used productively in many fields, including medical diagnosis, legal judgment, intelligence analysis, philosophy, finance, statistics, and military strategy.

For example, students of policy have noted that the availability heuristic helps explain why some issues are highly salient in the public's mind while others are neglected. People tend to assess the relative importance of issues by the ease with which they are retrieved from memory—and this is largely determined by the extent of coverage in the media. Frequently mentioned topics populate the mind even as others slip away from awareness. In turn, what the media choose to report corresponds to their view of what is currently on the public's mind. It is no accident that authoritarian regimes exert substantial pressure on independent media. Because public interest is most easily aroused by dramatic events and by celebrities, media feeding frenzies are common. For several weeks after Michael Jackson's death, for example, it was virtually impossible to find a television channel reporting on another topic. In contrast, there is little coverage of critical but unexciting issues that provide less drama, such as declining educational standards or overinvestment of medical resources in the last year of life. (As I write this, I notice that my choice of "little-covered" examples was guided by availability. The topics I chose as examples are mentioned often; equally important issues that are less available did not come to my mind.)

We did not fully realize it at the time, but a key reason for the broad appeal of "heuristics and biases" outside psychology was an incidental feature of our work: we almost always included in our articles the full text of the questions we had asked ourselves and our respondents. These questions served as demonstrations for the reader, allowing him to recognize how his own thinking was tripped up by cognitive biases. I hope you had such an experience as you read the question about Steve the librarian, which was intended to help you appreciate the power of resemblance as a cue to probability and to see how easy it is to ignore relevant statistical facts.

The use of demonstrations provided scholars from diverse disciplines—notably philosophers and economists—an unusual opportunity to observe possible flaws in their own thinking. Having seen themselves fail, they became more likely to question the dogmatic assumption, prevalent at the time, that the human mind is rational and logical. The choice of method was crucial: if we had reported results of only conventional experiments, the article would have been less noteworthy and less memorable. Furthermore, skeptical readers would have distanced themselves from the results by attributing judgment errors to the familiar fecklessness of undergraduates, the typical participants in psychological studies. Of course, we did not choose demonstrations over standard experiments because we wanted to influence philosophers and economists. We preferred demonstrations because they were more fun, and we were lucky in our choice of method as well as in many other ways. A recurrent theme of this book is that luck plays a large role in every story of success; it is almost always easy to identify a small change in the story that would have turned a remarkable achievement into a mediocre outcome. Our story was no exception.

The reaction to our work was not uniformly positive. In particular, our focus on biases was criticized as suggesting an unfairly negative view of the mind. As expected in normal science, some investigators refined our ideas and others offered plausible alternatives. By and large, though, the idea that our minds are susceptible to systematic errors is now generally accepted. Our research on judgment had far more effect on social science than we thought possible when we were working on it.

Immediately after completing our review of judgment, we switched our attention to decision making under uncertainty. Our goal was to develop a psychological theory of how people make decisions about simple gambles. For example: Would you accept a bet on the toss of a coin where you win $130 if the coin shows heads and lose $100 if it shows tails? These elementary choices had long been used to examine broad questions about decision making, such as the relative weight that people assign to sure things and to uncertain outcomes. Our method did not change: we spent many days making up choice problems and examining whether our intuitive preferences conformed to the logic of choice. Here again, as in judgment, we observed systematic biases in our own decisions, intuitive preferences that consistently violated the rules of rational choice. Five years after the *Science* article, we published "Prospect Theory: An Analysis of Decision Under Risk," a theory of choice that is by some counts more influential than our work on judgment, and is one of the foundations of behavioral economics.

Until geographical separation made it too difficult to go on, Amos and I enjoyed the extraordinary good fortune of a shared mind that was superior to our individual minds and of a relationship that made our work fun as well as productive. Our collaboration on judgment and decision making was the reason for the Nobel Prize that I received in 2002, which Amos would have shared had he not died, aged fifty-nine, in 1996.

WHERE WE ARE NOW

This book is not intended as an exposition of the early research that Amos and I conducted together, a task that has been ably carried out by many authors over the years. My main aim here is to present a view of how the mind works that draws on recent developments in cognitive and social psychology. One of the more important developments is that we now understand the marvels as well as the flaws of intuitive thought.

Amos and I did not address accurate intuitions beyond the casual statement that judgment heuristics "are quite useful, but sometimes lead to severe and systematic errors." We focused on biases, both because we found them interesting in their own right and because they provided evidence for the heuristics of judgment. We did not ask ourselves whether all intuitive judgments under uncertainty are produced by the heuristics we studied; it is now clear that they are not. In particular, the accurate intuitions of experts are better explained by the effects of prolonged practice than by heuristics. We can now draw a richer and more balanced picture, in which skill and heuristics are alternative sources of intuitive judgments and choices.

The psychologist Gary Klein tells the story of a team of firefighters that entered a house in which the kitchen was on fire. Soon after they started hosing down the kitchen, the commander heard himself shout, "Let's get out of here!" without realizing why. The floor collapsed almost immediately after the firefighters escaped. Only after the fact did the commander realize that the fire had been unusually quiet and that his ears had been unusually hot. Together, these impressions prompted what he called a "sixth sense of danger." He had no idea what was wrong, but he knew something was wrong. It turned out that the heart of the fire had not been in the kitchen but in the basement beneath where the men had stood.

We have all heard such stories of expert intuition: the chess master who walks past a street game and announces "White mates in three" without stopping, or the physician who makes a complex diagnosis after a single glance at a patient. Expert intuition strikes us as magical, but it is not. Indeed, each of us performs feats of intuitive expertise many times each day. Most of us are pitch-perfect in detecting anger in the first word of a telephone call, recognize as we enter a room that we were the subject of the conversation, and quickly react to subtle signs that the driver of the car in the next lane is dangerous. Our everyday intuitive abilities are no less marvelous than the striking insights of an experienced firefighter or physician—only more common.

The psychology of accurate intuition involves no magic. Perhaps the best short statement of it is by the great Herbert Simon, who studied chess masters and showed that after thousands of hours of practice they come to see the pieces on the board differently from the rest of us. You can feel Simon's impatience with the mythologizing of expert intuition when he writes: "The situation has provided a cue; this cue has given the expert access to information stored in memory, and the information provides the answer. Intuition is nothing more and nothing less than recognition."

We are not surprised when a two-year-old looks at a dog and says "doggie!" because we are used to the miracle of children learning to recognize and name things. Simon's point is that the miracles of expert intuition have the same character. Valid intuitions develop when experts have learned to recognize familiar elements in a new situation and to act in a manner that is appropriate to it. Good intuitive judgments come to mind with the same immediacy as "doggie!"

Unfortunately, professionals' intuitions do not all arise from true expertise. Many years ago I visited the chief investment officer of a large financial firm, who told me that he had just invested some tens of millions of dollars in the stock of Ford Motor Company. When I asked how he had made that decision, he replied that he had recently attended an automobile show and had been impressed. "Boy, do they know how to make a car!" was his explanation. He made it very clear that he trusted his gut feeling and was satisfied with himself and with his decision. I found it remarkable that he had apparently not considered the one question that an economist would call relevant: Is Ford stock currently underpriced? Instead, he had listened to his intuition; he liked the cars, he liked the company, and he liked the idea of owning its stock. From what we know about the accuracy of stock picking, it is reasonable to believe that he did not know what he was doing.

The specific heuristics that Amos and I studied provide little help in understanding how the executive came to invest in Ford stock, but a broader conception of heuristics now exists, which offers a good account. An important advance is that emotion now looms much larger in our understanding of intuitive judgments and choices than it did in the past. The executive's decision would today be described as an example of the affect heuristic, where judgments and decisions are guided directly by feelings of liking and disliking, with little deliberation or reasoning.

When confronted with a problem—choosing a chess move or deciding whether to invest in a stock—the machinery of intuitive thought does the best it can. If the individual has relevant expertise, she will recognize the situation, and the intuitive solution that comes to her mind is likely to be correct. This is what happens when a chess master looks at a complex position: the few moves that immediately occur to him are all strong. When the question is difficult and a skilled solution is not available, intuition still has a shot: an answer may come to mind quickly—but it is not an answer to the original question. The question that the executive faced (should I invest in Ford stock?) was difficult, but the answer to an easier and related question (do I like Ford cars?) came readily to his mind and determined his choice. This is the essence of intuitive heuristics: when faced with a difficult question, we often answer an easier one instead, usually without noticing the substitution.

The spontaneous search for an intuitive solution sometimes fails—neither an expert solution nor a heuristic answer comes to mind. In such cases we often find ourselves switching to a slower, more deliberate and effortful form of thinking. This is the slow thinking of the title. Fast thinking includes both variants of intuitive thought—the expert and the heuristic—as well as the entirely automatic mental activities of perception and memory, the operations that enable you to know there is a lamp on your desk or retrieve the name of the capital of Russia.

The distinction between fast and slow thinking has been explored by many psychologists over the last twenty-five years. For reasons that I explain more fully in the next chapter, I describe mental life by the metaphor of two agents, called System 1 and System 2, which respectively produce fast and slow thinking. I speak of the features of intuitive and deliberate thought as if they were traits and dispositions of two characters in your mind. In the picture that emerges from recent research, the intuitive System 1 is more influential than your experience tells you, and it is the secret author of many of the choices and judgments you make. Most of this book is about the workings of System 1 and the mutual influences between it and System 2.

WHAT COMES NEXT

The book is divided into five parts. Part 1 presents the basic elements of a two-systems approach to judgment and choice. It elaborates the distinction between the automatic operations of System 1 and the controlled operations of System 2, and shows how associative memory, the core of System 1, continually constructs a coherent interpretation of what is going on in our world at any instant. I attempt to give a sense of the complexity and richness of the automatic and often unconscious processes that underlie intuitive thinking, and of how these automatic processes explain the heuristics of judgment. A goal is to introduce a language for thinking and talking about the mind.

Part 2 updates the study of judgment heuristics and explores a major puzzle: Why is it so difficult for us to think statistically? We easily think associatively, we think metaphorically, we think causally, but statistics requires thinking about many things at once, which is something that System 1 is not designed to do.

The difficulties of statistical thinking contribute to the main theme of Part 3, which describes a puzzling limitation of our mind: our excessive confidence in what we believe we know, and our apparent inability to acknowledge the full extent of our ignorance and the uncertainty of the world we live in. We are prone to overestimate how much we understand about the world and to underestimate the role of chance in events. Overconfidence is fed by the illusory certainty of hindsight. My views on this topic have been influenced by Nassim Taleb, the author of *The Black Swan*. I hope for watercooler conversations that intelligently explore the lessons that can be learned from the past while resisting the lure of hindsight and the illusion of certainty.

The focus of part 4 is a conversation with the discipline of economics on the nature of decision making and on the assumption that economic agents are rational. This section of the book provides a current view, informed by the two-system model, of the key concepts of prospect theory, the model of choice that Amos and I published in 1979. Subsequent chapters address several ways human choices deviate from the rules of rationality. I deal with the unfortunate tendency to treat problems in isolation, and with framing effects, where decisions are shaped by inconsequential features of choice problems. These observations, which are readily explained by the features of System 1, present a deep challenge to the rationality assumption favored in standard economics.

Part 5 describes recent research that has introduced a distinction between two selves, the experiencing self and the remembering self, which do not have the same interests. For example, we can expose people to two painful experiences. One of these experiences is strictly worse than the other, because it is longer. But the automatic formation of memories—a feature of System 1—has its rules, which we can exploit so that the worse episode leaves a better memory. When people later choose which episode to repeat, they are, naturally, guided by their remembering self and expose themselves (their experiencing self) to unnecessary pain. The distinction between two selves is applied to the measurement of well-being, where we find again that what makes the experiencing self happy is not quite the same as what satisfies the remembering self. How two selves within a single body can pursue happiness raises some difficult questions, both for individuals and for societies that view the well-being of the population as a policy objective.

A concluding chapter explores, in reverse order, the implications of three distinctions drawn in the book: between the experiencing and the remembering selves, between the conception of agents in classical economics and in behavioral economics (which borrows from psychology), and between the automatic System 1 and the effortful System 2. I return to the virtues of educating gossip and to what organizations might do to improve the quality of judgments and decisions that are made on their behalf.

Two articles I wrote with Amos are reproduced as appendixes to the book. The first is the review of judgment under uncertainty that I described earlier. The second, published in 1984, summarizes prospect theory as well as our studies of framing effects. The articles present the contributions that were cited by the Nobel committee—and you may be surprised by how simple they are. Reading them will give you a sense of how much we knew a long time ago, and also of how much we have learned in recent decades.

PART 1

TWO SYSTEMS

1

THE CHARACTERS OF THE STORY

To observe your mind in automatic mode, glance at the image below.

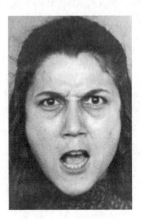

Figure 1

Your experience as you look at the woman's face seamlessly combines what we normally call seeing and intuitive thinking. As surely and quickly as you saw that the young woman's hair is dark, you knew she is angry. Furthermore, what you saw extended into the future. You sensed that this woman is about to say some very unkind words, probably in a loud and strident voice. A premonition of what she was going to do next came to mind automatically and effortlessly. You did not intend to assess her mood or to anticipate what she might do, and your reaction to the picture did not have the feel of something you did. It just happened to you. It was an instance of fast thinking.

Now look at the following problem:

$$17 \times 24$$

You knew immediately that this is a multiplication problem, and probably knew that you could solve it, with paper and pencil, if not without. You also had some vague intuitive knowledge of the range of possible results. You would be quick to recognize that both 12,609 and 123 are implausible. Without spending some time on the problem, however, you would not be certain that the answer is not 568. A precise solution did not come to mind, and you felt that you could choose whether or not to engage in the computation. If you have not done so yet, you should attempt the multiplication problem now, completing at least part of it.

You experienced slow thinking as you proceeded through a sequence of steps. You first retrieved from memory the cognitive program for multiplication that you learned in school, then you implemented it. Carrying out the computation was a strain. You felt the burden of holding much material in memory, as you needed to keep track of where you were and of where you were going, while holding on to the intermediate result. The process was mental work: deliberate, effortful, and orderly—a prototype of slow thinking. The computation was not only an event in your mind; your body was also involved. Your muscles tensed up, your blood pressure rose, and your heart rate increased. Someone looking closely at your eyes while you tackled this problem would have seen your pupils dilate. Your pupils contracted back to normal size as soon as you ended your work—when you found the answer (which is 408, by the way) or when you gave up.

TWO SYSTEMS

Psychologists have been intensely interested for several decades in the two modes of thinking evoked by the picture of the angry woman and by the multiplication problem, and have offered many labels for them. I adopt terms originally proposed by the psychologists Keith Stanovich and Richard West, and will refer to two systems in the mind, System 1 and System 2.

- *System 1* operates automatically and quickly, with little or no effort and no sense of voluntary control.

- *System 2* allocates attention to the effortful mental activities that demand it, including complex computations. The operations of System 2 are often associated with the subjective experience of agency, choice, and concentration.

The labels of System 1 and System 2 are widely used in psychology, but I go further than most in this book, which you can read as a psychodrama with two characters.

When we think of ourselves, we identify with System 2, the conscious, reasoning self that has beliefs, makes choices, and decides what to think about and what to do. Although System 2 believes itself to be where the action is, the automatic System 1 is the hero of the book. I describe System 1 as effortlessly originating impressions and feelings that are the main sources of the explicit beliefs and deliberate choices of System 2. The automatic operations of System 1 generate surprisingly complex patterns of ideas, but only the slower System 2 can construct thoughts in an orderly series of steps. I also describe circumstances in which System 2 takes over, overruling the freewheeling impulses and associations of System 1. You will be invited to think of the two systems as agents with their individual abilities, limitations, and functions.

In rough order of complexity, here are some examples of the automatic activities that are attributed to System 1:

- Detect that one object is more distant than another.
- Orient to the source of a sudden sound.
- Complete the phrase "bread and . . ."
- Make a "disgust face" when shown a horrible picture.
- Detect hostility in a voice.
- Answer to $2 + 2 = ?$
- Read words on large billboards.
- Drive a car on an empty road.
- Find a strong move in chess (if you are a chess master).
- Understand simple sentences.
- Recognize that a "meek and tidy soul with a passion for detail" resembles an occupational stereotype.

All these mental events belong with the angry woman—they occur automatically and require little or no effort. The capabilities of System 1 include innate skills that we share with other animals. We are born prepared to perceive the world around us, recognize objects, orient attention, avoid losses, and fear spiders. Other mental activities become fast and automatic through prolonged practice. System 1 has learned associations between ideas (the capital of France?); it has also learned skills such as reading and understanding nuances of social situations. Some skills, such as finding strong chess moves, are acquired only by specialized experts. Others are widely shared. Detecting the similarity of a personality sketch to an occupational stereotype requires broad knowledge of the language and the culture, which most of us possess. The knowledge is stored in memory and accessed without intention and without effort.

Several of the mental actions in the list are completely involuntary. You cannot refrain from understanding simple sentences in your own language or from orienting to a loud unexpected sound, nor can you prevent yourself from knowing that 2 + 2 = 4 or from thinking of Paris when the capital of France is mentioned. Other activities, such as chewing, are susceptible to voluntary control but normally run on automatic pilot. The control of attention is shared by the two systems. Orienting to a loud sound is normally an involuntary operation of System 1, which immediately mobilizes the voluntary attention of System 2. You may be able to resist turning toward the source of a loud and offensive comment at a crowded party, but even if your head does not move, your attention is initially directed to it, at least for a while. However, attention can be moved away from an unwanted focus, primarily by focusing intently on another target.

The highly diverse operations of System 2 have one feature in common: they require attention and are disrupted when attention is drawn away. Here are some examples:

- Brace for the starter gun in a race.
- Focus attention on the clowns in the circus.
- Focus on the voice of a particular person in a crowded and noisy room.
- Look for a woman with white hair.
- Search memory to identify a surprising sound.
- Maintain a faster walking speed than is natural for you.
- Monitor the appropriateness of your behavior in a social situation.
- Count the occurrences of the letter a in a page of text.
- Tell someone your phone number.
- Park in a narrow space (for most people except garage attendants).
- Compare two washing machines for overall value.
- Fill out a tax form.
- Check the validity of a complex logical argument.

In all these situations you must pay attention, and you will perform less well, or not at all, if you are not ready or if your attention is directed inappropriately. System 2 has some ability to change the way System 1 works, by programming the normally automatic functions of attention and memory. When waiting for a relative at a busy train station, for example, you can set yourself at will to look for a white-haired woman or a bearded man, and thereby increase the likelihood of detecting your relative from a distance. You can set your memory to search for capital cities that start with N or for French existentialist novels. And when you rent a car at London's Heathrow Airport, the attendant will probably remind you that "we drive on the left side of the road over here." In all these cases, you are asked to do something that does not come naturally, and you will find that the consistent maintenance of a set requires continuous exertion of at least some effort.

The often-used phrase "pay attention" is apt: you dispose of a limited budget of attention that you can allocate to activities, and if you try to go beyond your budget, you will fail. It is the mark of effortful activities that they interfere with each other, which is why it is difficult or impossible to conduct several at once. You could not compute the product of 17×24 while making a left turn into dense traffic, and you certainly should not try. You can do several things at once, but only if they are easy and undemanding. You are probably safe carrying on a conversation with a passenger while driving on an empty highway, and many parents have discovered, perhaps with some guilt, that they can read a story to a child while thinking of something else.

Everyone has some awareness of the limited capacity of attention, and our social behavior makes allowances for these limitations. When the driver of a car is overtaking a truck on a narrow road, for example, adult passengers quite sensibly stop talking. They know that distracting the driver is not a good idea, and they also suspect that he is temporarily deaf and will not hear what they say.

Intense focusing on a task can make people effectively blind, even to stimuli that normally attract attention. The most dramatic demonstration was offered by Christopher Chabris and Daniel Simons in their book *The Invisible Gorilla*. They constructed a short film of two teams passing basketballs, one team wearing white shirts, the other wearing black. The viewers of the film are instructed to count the number of passes made by the white team, ignoring the black players. This task is difficult and completely absorbing. Halfway through the video, a woman wearing a gorilla suit appears, crosses the court, thumps her chest, and moves on. The gorilla is in view for

9 seconds. Many thousands of people have seen the video, and about half of them do not notice anything unusual. It is the counting task—and especially the instruction to ignore one of the teams—that causes the blindness. No one who watches the video without that task would miss the gorilla. Seeing and orienting are automatic functions of System 1, but they depend on the allocation of some attention to the relevant stimulus. The authors note that the most remarkable observation of their study is that people find its results very surprising. Indeed, the viewers who fail to see the gorilla are initially sure that it was not there—they cannot imagine missing such a striking event. The gorilla study illustrates two important facts about our minds: we can be blind to the obvious, and we are also blind to our blindness.

PLOT SYNOPSIS

The interaction of the two systems is a recurrent theme of the book, and a brief synopsis of the plot is in order. In the story I will tell, Systems 1 and 2 are both active whenever we are awake. System 1 runs automatically and System 2 is normally in a comfortable low-effort mode, in which only a fraction of its capacity is engaged. System 1 continuously generates suggestions for System 2: impressions, intuitions, intentions, and feelings. If endorsed by System 2, impressions and intuitions turn into beliefs, and impulses turn into voluntary actions. When all goes smoothly, which is most of the time, System 2 adopts the suggestions of System 1 with little or no modification. You generally believe your impressions and act on your desires, and that is fine—usually.

When System 1 runs into difficulty, it calls on System 2 to support more detailed and specific processing that may solve the problem of the moment. System 2 is mobilized when a question arises for which System 1 does not offer an answer, as probably happened to you when you encountered the multiplication problem 17×24. You can also feel a surge of conscious attention whenever you are surprised. System 2 is activated when an event is detected that violates the model of the world that System 1 maintains. In that world, lamps do not jump, cats do not bark, and gorillas do not cross basketball courts. The gorilla experiment demonstrates that some attention is needed for the surprising stimulus to be detected. Surprise then activates and orients your attention: you will stare, and you will search your memory for a story that makes sense of the surprising event. System 2 is also credited with the continuous monitoring of your own behavior—the control that keeps you polite when you are angry, and alert when you are driving at night.

System 2 is mobilized to increased effort when it detects an error about to be made. Remember a time when you almost blurted out an offensive remark and note how hard you worked to restore control. In summary, most of what you (your System 2) think and do originates in your System 1, but System 2 takes over when things get difficult, and it normally has the last word.

The division of labor between System 1 and System 2 is highly efficient: it minimizes effort and optimizes performance. The arrangement works well most of the time because System 1 is generally very good at what it does: its models of familiar situations are accurate, its short-term predictions are usually accurate as well, and its initial reactions to challenges are swift and generally appropriate. System 1 has biases, however, systematic errors that it is prone to make in specified circumstances. As we shall see, it sometimes answers easier questions than the one it was asked, and it has little understanding of logic and statistics. One further limitation of System 1 is that it cannot be turned off. If you are shown a word on the screen in a language you know, you will read it—unless your attention is totally focused elsewhere.

CONFLICT

Figure 2 is a variant of a classic experiment that produces a conflict between the two systems. You should try the exercise before reading on.

Your first task is to go down both columns, calling out whether each word is printed in lowercase or in uppercase. When you are done with the first task, go down both columns again, saying whether each word is printed to the left or to the right of center by saying (or whispering to yourself) "LEFT" or "RIGHT."

LEFT			upper	
	left		lower	
right				LOWER
RIGHT			upper	
	RIGHT		UPPER	
	left			lower
LEFT				LOWER
	right		upper	

Figure 2

You were almost certainly successful in saying the correct words in both tasks, and you surely discovered that some parts of each task were much easier than others. When you identified upper- and lowercase, the left-hand column was easy and the right-hand column caused you to slow down and perhaps to stammer or stumble. When you named the position of words, the left-hand column was difficult and the right-hand column was much easier.

These tasks engage System 2, because saying "upper/lower" or "right/left" is not what you routinely do when looking down a column of words. One of the things you did to set yourself for the task was to program your memory so that the relevant words (*upper* and *lower* for the first task) were "on the tip of your tongue." The prioritizing of the chosen words is effective and the mild temptation to read other words was fairly easy to resist when you went through the first column. But the second column was different, because it contained words for which you were set, and you could not ignore them. You were mostly able to respond correctly, but overcoming the competing response was a strain, and it slowed you down. You experienced a conflict between a task that you intended to carry out and an automatic response that interfered with it.

Conflict between an automatic reaction and an intention to control it is common in our lives. We are all familiar with the experience of trying not to stare at the oddly dressed couple at the neighboring table in a restaurant. We also know what it is like to force our attention on a boring book, when we constantly find ourselves returning to the point at which the reading lost its meaning. Where winters are hard, many drivers have memories of their car skidding out of control on the ice and of the struggle to follow well-rehearsed instructions that negate what they would naturally do: "Steer into the skid, and whatever you do, do not touch the brakes!" And every human being has had the experience of *not* telling someone to go to hell. One of the tasks of System 2 is to overcome the impulses of System 1. In other words, System 2 is in charge of self-control.

ILLUSIONS

To appreciate the autonomy of System 1, as well as the distinction between impressions and beliefs, take a good look at figure 3.

This picture is unremarkable: two horizontal lines of different lengths, with fins appended, pointing in different directions. The bottom line is obviously longer than the one above it. That is what we all see, and we

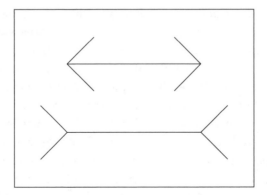

Figure 3

naturally believe what we see. If you have already encountered this image, however, you recognize it as the famous Müller-Lyer illusion. As you can easily confirm by measuring them with a ruler, the horizontal lines are in fact identical in length.

Now that you have measured the lines, you—your System 2, the conscious being you call "I"—have a new belief: you *know* that the lines are equally long. If asked about their length, you will say what you know. But you still *see* the bottom line as longer. You have chosen to believe the measurement, but you cannot prevent System 1 from doing its thing; you cannot decide to see the lines as equal, although you know they are. To resist the illusion, there is only one thing you can do: you must learn to mistrust your impressions of the length of lines when fins are attached to them. To implement that rule, you must be able to recognize the illusory pattern and recall what you know about it. If you can do this, you will never again be fooled by the Müller-Lyer illusion. But you will still see one line as longer than the other.

Not all illusions are visual. There are illusions of thought, which we call *cognitive illusions*. As a graduate student, I attended some courses on the art and science of psychotherapy. During one of these lectures, our teacher imparted a morsel of clinical wisdom. This is what he told us: "You will from time to time meet a patient who shares a disturbing tale of multiple mistakes in his previous treatment. He has been seen by several clinicians, and all failed him. The patient can lucidly describe how his therapists misunderstood him, but he has quickly perceived that you are different. You share the same feeling, are convinced that you understand him, and will be able to help." At this point my teacher raised his voice as he said, "Do not even *think* of taking on this patient! Throw him out of the office! He is most likely a psychopath and you will not be able to help him."

Many years later I learned that the teacher had warned us against psychopathic charm, and the leading authority in the study of psychopathy confirmed that the teacher's advice was sound. The analogy to the Müller-Lyer illusion is close. What we were being taught was not how to feel about that patient. Our teacher took it for granted that the sympathy we would feel for the patient would not be under our control; it would arise from System 1. Furthermore, we were not being taught to be generally suspicious of our feelings about patients. We were told that a strong attraction to a patient with a repeated history of failed treatment is a danger sign—like the fins on the parallel lines. It is an illusion—a cognitive illusion—and I (System 2) was taught how to recognize it and advised not to believe it or act on it.

The question that is most often asked about cognitive illusions is whether they can be overcome. The message of these examples is not encouraging. Because System 1 operates automatically and cannot be turned off at will, errors of intuitive thought are often difficult to prevent. Biases cannot always be avoided, because System 2 may have no clue to the error. Even when cues to likely errors are available, errors can be prevented only by the enhanced monitoring and effortful activity of System 2. As a way to live your life, however, continuous vigilance is not necessarily good, and it is certainly impractical. Constantly questioning our own thinking would be impossibly tedious, and System 2 is much too slow and inefficient to serve as a substitute for System 1 in making routine decisions. The best we can do is a compromise: learn to recognize situations in which mistakes are likely and try harder to avoid significant mistakes when the stakes are high. The premise of this book is that it is easier to recognize other people's mistakes than our own.

USEFUL FICTIONS

You have been invited to think of the two systems as agents within the mind, with their individual personalities, abilities, and limitations. I will often use sentences in which the systems are the subjects, such as, "System 2 calculates products."

The use of such language is considered a sin in the professional circles in which I travel, because it seems to explain the thoughts and actions of a person by the thoughts and actions of little people inside the person's head. Grammatically the sentence about System 2 is similar to "The butler steals the petty cash." My colleagues would point out that the butler's action actually explains the disappearance of the cash, and they rightly question whether the sentence about System 2 explains how products are calculated. My answer is that the brief active sentence that attributes calculation to System 2 is intended as a description, not an explanation. It is meaningful only because of what you already know about System 2. It is shorthand for the following: "Mental arithmetic is a voluntary activity that requires effort, should not be performed while making a left turn, and is associated with dilated pupils and an accelerated heart rate."

Similarly, the statement that "highway driving under routine conditions is left to System 1" means that steering the car around a bend is automatic and almost effortless. It also implies that an experienced driver can drive on an empty highway while conducting a conversation. Finally, "System 2 prevented James from reacting foolishly to the insult" means that James would have been more aggressive in his response if his capacity for effortful control had been disrupted (for example, if he had been drunk).

System 1 and System 2 are so central to the story I tell in this book that I must make it absolutely clear that they are fictitious characters. Systems 1 and 2 are not systems in the standard sense of entities with interacting aspects or parts. And there is no one part of the brain that either of the systems would call home. You may well ask: What is the point of introducing fictitious characters with ugly names into a serious book? The answer is that the characters are useful because of some quirks of our minds, yours and mine. A sentence is understood more easily if it describes what an agent (System 2) does than if it describes what something is, what properties it has. In other words, "System 2" is a better subject for a sentence than "mental arithmetic." The mind—especially System 1—appears to have a special aptitude for the construction and interpretation of stories about active agents, who have personalities, habits, and abilities. You quickly formed a bad opinion of the thieving butler, you expect more bad behavior from him, and you will remember him for a while. This is also my hope for the language of systems.

Why call them System 1 and System 2 rather than the more descriptive "automatic system" and "effortful system"? The reason is simple: "Automatic system" takes longer to say than "System 1" and therefore takes more space in your working memory. This matters, because anything that occupies your working memory reduces your ability to think. You should treat "System 1" and "System 2" as nicknames, like Bob and Joe, identifying characters that you will get to know over the course of this book. The fictitious systems make it easier for me to think about judgment and choice, and will make it easier for you to understand what I say.

SPEAKING OF SYSTEM 1 AND SYSTEM 2

"He had an impression, but some of his impressions are illusions."

"This was a pure System 1 response. She reacted to the threat before she recognized it."

"This is your System 1 talking. Slow down and let your System 2 take control."

2

ATTENTION AND EFFORT

In the unlikely event of this book being made into a film, System 2 would be a supporting character who believes herself to be the hero. The defining feature of System 2, in this story, is that its operations are effortful, and one of its main characteristics is laziness, a reluctance to invest more effort than is strictly necessary. As a consequence, the thoughts and actions that System 2 believes it has chosen are often guided by the figure at the center of the story, System 1. However, there are vital tasks that only System 2 can perform because they require effort and acts of self-control in which the intuitions and impulses of System 1 are overcome.

MENTAL EFFORT

If you wish to experience your System 2 working at full tilt, the following exercise will do; it should bring you to the limits of your cognitive abilities within 5 seconds. To start, make up several strings of 4 digits, all different, and write each string on an index card. Place a blank card on top of the deck. The task that you will perform is called Add-1. Here is how it goes:

> Start beating a steady rhythm (or better yet, set a metronome at 1/sec). Remove the blank card and read the four digits aloud. Wait for two beats, then report a string in which each of the original digits is incremented by 1. If the digits on the card are 5294, the correct response is 6305. Keeping the rhythm is important.

Few people can cope with more than four digits in the Add-1 task, but if you want a harder challenge, please try Add-3.

If you would like to know what your body is doing while your mind is hard at work, set up two piles of books on a sturdy table, place a video camera on one and lean your chin on the other, get the video going, and stare at the camera lens while you work on Add-1 or Add-3 exercises. Later, you will find in the changing size of your pupils a faithful record of how hard you worked.

I have a long personal history with the Add-1 task. Early in my career I spent a year at the University of Michigan, as a visitor in a laboratory that studied hypnosis. Casting about for a useful topic of research, I found an article in *Scientific American* in which the psychologist Eckhard Hess described the pupil of the eye as a window to the soul. I reread it recently and again found it inspiring. It begins with Hess reporting that his wife had noticed his pupils widening as he watched beautiful nature pictures, and it ends with two striking pictures of the same good-looking woman, who somehow appears much more attractive in one than in the other. There is only one difference: the pupils of the eyes appear dilated in the attractive picture and constricted in the other. Hess also wrote of belladonna, a pupil-dilating substance that was used as a cosmetic, and of bazaar shoppers who wear dark glasses in order to hide their level of interest from merchants.

One of Hess's findings especially captured my attention. He had noticed that the pupils are sensitive indicators of mental effort—they dilate substantially when people multiply two-digit numbers, and they dilate more if the problems are hard than if they are easy. His observations indicated that the response to mental effort is distinct from emotional arousal. Hess's work did not have much to do with hypnosis, but I concluded that the idea of a visible indication of mental effort had promise as a research topic. A graduate student in the lab, Jackson Beatty, shared my enthusiasm and we got to work.

Beatty and I developed a setup similar to an optician's examination room, in which the experimental participant leaned her head on a chin-and-forehead rest and stared at a camera while listening to prerecorded information and answering questions on the recorded beats of a metronome. The beats triggered an infrared flash every second, causing a picture to be taken. At the end of each experimental session, we would rush to have the film developed, project the images of the pupil on a screen, and go to work with a ruler. The method was a perfect fit for young and impatient researchers: we knew our results almost immediately, and they always told a clear story.

Beatty and I focused on paced tasks, such as Add-1, in which we knew precisely what was on the subject's mind at any time. We recorded strings of digits on beats of the metronome and instructed the subject to repeat or transform the digits one by one, maintaining the same rhythm. We soon discovered that the size of the pupil varied second by second, reflecting the changing demands of the task. The shape of the response was an inverted V. As you experienced it if you tried Add-1 or Add-3, effort builds up with every added digit that you hear, reaches an almost intolerable peak as you rush to produce a transformed string during and immediately after the pause, and relaxes gradually as you "unload" your short-term memory. The pupil data corresponded precisely to subjective experience: longer strings reliably caused larger dilations, the transformation task compounded the effort, and the peak of pupil size coincided with maximum effort. Add-1 with four digits caused a larger dilation than the task of holding seven digits for immediate recall. Add-3, which is much more difficult, is the most demanding that I ever observed. In the first 5 seconds, the pupil dilates by about 50% of its original area and heart rate increases by about 7 beats per minute. This is as hard as people can work—they give up if more is asked of them. When we exposed our subjects to more digits than they could remember, their pupils stopped dilating or actually shrank.

We worked for some months in a spacious basement suite in which we had set up a closed-circuit system that projected an image of the subject's pupil on a screen in the corridor; we also could hear what was happening in the laboratory. The diameter of the projected pupil was about a foot; watching it dilate and contract when the participant was at work was a fascinating sight, quite an attraction for visitors in our lab. We amused ourselves and impressed our guests by our ability to divine when the participant gave up on a task. During a mental multiplication, the pupil normally dilated to a large size within a few seconds and stayed large as long as the individual kept working on the problem; it contracted immediately when she found a solution or gave up. As we watched from the corridor, we would sometimes surprise both the owner of the pupil and our guests by asking, "Why did you stop working just now?" The answer from inside the lab was often, "How did you know?" to which we would reply, "We have a window to your soul."

The casual observations we made from the corridor were sometimes as informative as the formal experiments. I made a significant discovery as I was idly watching a woman's pupil during a break between two tasks. She had kept her position on the chin rest, so I could see the image of her eye while she engaged in routine conversation with the experimenter. I was surprised to see that the pupil remained small and did not noticeably dilate as she talked and listened. Unlike the tasks that we were studying, the mundane conversation apparently demanded little or no effort—no more than retaining two or three digits. This was a eureka moment: I realized that the tasks we had chosen for study were exceptionally effortful. An image came to mind: mental life—today I would speak of the life of System 2—is normally conducted at the pace of a comfortable walk, sometimes interrupted by episodes of jogging and on rare occasions by a frantic sprint. The Add-1 and Add-3 exercises are sprints, and casual chatting is a stroll.

We found that people, when engaged in a mental sprint, may become effectively blind. The authors of *The Invisible Gorilla* had made the gorilla "invisible" by keeping the observers intensely busy counting passes. We reported a rather less dramatic example of blindness during Add-1. Our subjects were exposed to a series of rapidly flashing letters while they worked. They were told to give the task complete priority, but they were also asked to report, at the end of the digit task, whether the letter *K* had appeared at any time during the trial. The main finding was that the ability to detect and report the target letter changed in the course of the 10 seconds of the exercise. The observers almost never missed a *K* that was shown at the beginning or near the end of the Add-1 task but they missed the target almost half the time when mental effort was at its peak, although we had pictures of their wide-open eye staring straight at it. Failures of detection followed the same inverted-V pattern as the dilating pupil. The similarity was reassuring: the pupil was a good measure of the physical arousal that accompanies mental effort, and we could go ahead and use it to understand how the mind works.

Much like the electricity meter outside your house or apartment, the pupils offer an index of the current rate at which mental energy is used. The analogy goes deep. Your use of electricity depends on what you choose to do, whether to light a room or toast a piece of bread. When you turn on a bulb or a toaster, it draws the energy it needs but no more. Similarly, we decide what to do, but we have limited control over the effort of doing it. Suppose you are shown four digits, say, 9462, and told that your life depends on holding them in memory for 10 seconds. However much you want to live, you cannot exert as much effort in this task as you would be forced to invest to complete an Add-3 transformation on the same digits.

System 2 and the electrical circuits in your home both have limited capacity, but they respond differently to threatened overload. A breaker trips when the demand for current is excessive, causing all devices on that circuit to lose power at once. In contrast, the response to mental overload is selective and precise: System 2 protects the most important activity, so it receives the attention it needs; "spare capacity" is allocated second by second to other tasks. In our version of the gorilla experiment, we instructed the participants to assign priority to the digit task. We know that they followed that instruction, because the timing of the visual target had no effect on the main task. If the critical letter was presented at a time of high demand, the subjects simply did not see it. When the transformation task was less demanding, detection performance was better.

The sophisticated allocation of attention has been honed by a long evolutionary history. Orienting and responding quickly to the gravest threats or most promising opportunities improved the chance of survival, and this capability is certainly not restricted to humans. Even in modern humans, System 1 takes over in emergencies and assigns total priority to self-protective actions. Imagine yourself at the wheel of a car that unexpectedly skids on a large oil slick. You will find that you have responded to the threat before you became fully conscious of it.

Beatty and I worked together for only a year, but our collaboration had a large effect on our subsequent careers. He eventually became the leading authority on "cognitive pupillometry," and I wrote a book titled *Attention and Effort*, which was based in large part on what we learned together and on follow-up research I did at Harvard the following year. We learned a great deal about the working mind—which I now think of as System 2— from measuring pupils in a wide variety of tasks.

As you become skilled in a task, its demand for energy diminishes. Studies of the brain have shown that the pattern of activity associated with an action changes as skill increases, with fewer brain regions involved. Talent has similar effects. Highly intelligent individuals need less effort to solve the same problems, as indicated by both pupil size and brain activity. A general "law of least effort" applies to cognitive as well as physical exertion. The law asserts that if there are several ways of achieving the same goal, people will eventually gravitate to the least demanding course of action. In the economy of action, effort is a cost, and the acquisition of skill is driven by the balance of benefits and costs. Laziness is built deep into our nature.

The tasks that we studied varied considerably in their effects on the pupil. At baseline, our subjects were awake, aware, and ready to engage in a task—probably at a higher level of arousal and cognitive readiness than usual. Holding one or two digits in memory or learning to associate a word with a digit (3 = door) produced reliable effects on momentary arousal above that baseline, but the effects were minuscule, only 5% of the increase in pupil diameter associated with Add-3. A task that required discriminating between the pitch of two tones yielded significantly larger dilations. Recent research has shown that inhibiting the tendency to read distracting words (as in figure 2 of the preceding chapter) also induces moderate effort. Tests of short-term memory for six or seven digits were more effortful. As you can experience, the request to retrieve and say aloud your phone number or your spouse's birthday also requires a brief but significant effort, because the entire string must be held in memory as a response is organized. Mental multiplication of two-digit numbers and the Add-3 task are near the limit of what most people can do.

What makes some cognitive operations more demanding and effortful than others? What outcomes must we purchase in the currency of attention? What can System 2 do that System 1 cannot? We now have tentative answers to these questions.

Effort is required to maintain simultaneously in memory several ideas that require separate actions, or that need to be combined according to a rule—rehearsing your shopping list as you enter the supermarket, choosing between the fish and the veal at a restaurant, or combining a surprising result from a survey with the information that the sample was small, for example. System 2 is the only one that can follow rules, compare objects on several attributes, and make deliberate choices between options. The automatic System 1 does not have these capabilities. System 1 detects simple relations ("they are all alike," "the son is much taller than the father") and excels at integrating information about one thing, but it does not deal with multiple distinct topics at once, nor is it adept at using purely statistical information. System 1 will detect that a person described as "a meek and tidy soul, with a need for order and structure, and a passion for detail" resembles a caricature librarian, but combining this intuition with knowledge about the small number of librarians is a task that only System 2 can perform—if System 2 knows how to do so, which is true of few people.

A crucial capability of System 2 is the adoption of "task sets": it can program memory to obey an instruction that overrides habitual responses. Consider the following: Count all occurrences of the letter f in this page. This is not a task you have ever performed before and it will not come naturally to you, but your System 2 can take it on. It will be effortful to set yourself up for this exercise, and effortful to carry it out, though you will surely improve with practice. Psychologists speak of "executive control" to describe the adoption and termination of task sets, and neuroscientists have identified the main regions of the brain that serve the executive function. One of these regions is involved whenever a conflict must be resolved. Another is the prefrontal area of the brain, a region that is substantially more developed in humans than in other primates, and is involved in operations that we associate with intelligence.

Now suppose that at the end of the page you get another instruction: count all the commas in the next page. This will be harder, because you will have to overcome the newly acquired tendency to focus attention on the letter *f*. One of the significant discoveries of cognitive psychologists in recent decades is that switching from one task to another is effortful, especially under time pressure. The need for rapid switching is one of the reasons that Add-3 and mental multiplication are so difficult. To perform the Add-3 task, you must hold several digits in your working memory at the same time, associating each with a particular operation: some digits are in the queue to be transformed, one is in the process of transformation, and others, already transformed, are retained for reporting. Modern tests of working memory require the individual to switch repeatedly between two demanding tasks, retaining the results of one operation while performing the other. People who do well on these tests tend to do well on tests of general intelligence. However, the ability to control attention is not simply a measure of intelligence; measures of efficiency in the control of attention predict performance of air traffic controllers and of Israeli Air Force pilots beyond the effects of intelligence.

Time pressure is another driver of effort. As you carried out the Add-3 exercise, the rush was imposed in part by the metronome and in part by the load on memory. Like a juggler with several balls in the air, you cannot afford to slow down; the rate at which material decays in memory forces the pace, driving you to refresh and rehearse information before it is lost. Any task that requires you to keep several ideas in mind at the same time has the same hurried character. Unless you have the good fortune of a capacious working memory, you may be forced to work uncomfortably hard. The most effortful forms of slow thinking are those that require you to think fast.

You surely observed as you performed Add-3 how unusual it is for your mind to work so hard. Even if you think for a living, few of the mental tasks in which you engage in the course of a working day are as demanding as

Add-3, or even as demanding as storing six digits for immediate recall. We normally avoid mental overload by dividing our tasks into multiple easy steps, committing intermediate results to long-term memory or to paper rather than to an easily overloaded working memory. We cover long distances by taking our time and conduct our mental lives by the law of least effort.

SPEAKING OF ATTENTION AND EFFORT

"I won't try to solve this while driving. This is a pupil-dilating task. It requires mental effort!"

"The law of least effort is operating here. He will think as little as possible."

"She did not forget about the meeting. She was completely focused on something else when the meeting was set and she just didn't hear you."

"What came quickly to my mind was an intuition from System 1. I'll have to start over and search my memory deliberately."

3

THE LAZY CONTROLLER

I spend a few months each year in Berkeley, and one of my great pleasures there is a daily four-mile walk on a marked path in the hills, with a fine view of San Francisco Bay. I usually keep track of my time and have learned a fair amount about effort from doing so. I have found a speed, about 17 minutes for a mile, which I experience as a stroll. I certainly exert physical effort and burn more calories at that speed than if I sat in a recliner, but I experience no strain, no conflict, and no need to push myself. I am also able to think and work while walking at that rate. Indeed, I suspect that the mild physical arousal of the walk may spill over into greater mental alertness.

System 2 also has a natural speed. You expend some mental energy in random thoughts and in monitoring what goes on around you even when your mind does nothing in particular, but there is little strain. Unless you are in a situation that makes you unusually wary or self-conscious, monitoring what happens in the environment or inside your head demands little effort. You make many small decisions as you drive your car, absorb some information as you read the newspaper, and conduct routine exchanges of pleasantries with a spouse or a colleague, all with little effort and no strain. Just like a stroll.

It is normally easy and actually quite pleasant to walk and think at the same time, but at the extremes these activities appear to compete for the limited resources of System 2. You can confirm this claim by a simple experiment. While walking comfortably with a friend, ask him to compute 23 × 78 in his head, and to do so immediately. He will almost certainly stop in his tracks. My experience is that I can think while strolling but cannot engage in mental work that imposes a heavy load on short-term memory. If I must construct an intricate argument under time pressure, I would rather be still, and I would prefer sitting to standing. Of course, not all slow thinking requires that form of intense concentration and effortful computation— I did the best thinking of my life on leisurely walks with Amos.

Accelerating beyond my strolling speed completely changes the experience of walking, because the transition to a faster walk brings about a sharp deterioration in my ability to think coherently. As I speed up, my attention is drawn with increasing frequency to the experience of walking and to the deliberate maintenance of the faster pace. My ability to bring a train of thought to a conclusion is impaired accordingly. At the highest speed I can sustain on the hills, about 14 minutes for a mile, I do not even try to think of anything else. In addition to the physical effort of moving my body rapidly along the path, a mental effort of self-control is needed to resist the urge to slow down. Self-control and deliberate thought apparently draw on the same limited budget of effort.

For most of us, most of the time, the maintenance of a coherent train of thought and the occasional engagement in effortful thinking also require self-control. Although I have not conducted a systematic survey, I suspect that frequent switching of tasks and speeded-up mental work are not intrinsically pleasurable, and that people avoid them when possible. This is how the law of least effort comes to be a law. Even in the absence of time pressure, maintaining a coherent train of thought requires discipline. An observer of the number of times I look at e-mail or investigate the refrigerator during an hour of writing could reasonably infer an urge to escape and conclude that keeping at it requires more self-control than I can readily muster.

Fortunately, cognitive work is not always aversive, and people sometimes expend considerable effort for long periods of time without having to exert willpower. The psychologist Mihaly Csikszentmihalyi (pronounced six-cent-mihaly) has done more than anyone else to study this state of effortless attending, and the name he proposed for it, *flow*, has become part of the language. People who experience flow describe it as "a state of effortless concentration so deep that they lose their sense of time, of themselves, of their problems," and their descriptions of the joy of that state are so compelling that Csikszentmihalyi has called it an "optimal experience." Many activities can induce a sense of flow, from painting to racing motorcycles— and for some fortunate authors I know, even writing a book is often an optimal experience. Flow neatly separates the two forms of effort: concentration on the task and the deliberate control of attention. Riding a motorcycle at 150 miles an hour and playing a competitive game of chess are certainly very effortful. In a state of flow, however, maintaining focused attention on these absorbing activities requires no exertion of self-control, thereby freeing resources to be directed to the task at hand.

THE BUSY AND DEPLETED SYSTEM 2

It is now a well-established proposition that both self-control and cognitive effort are forms of mental work. Several psychological studies have shown that people who are simultaneously challenged by a demanding cognitive task and by a temptation are more likely to yield to the temptation. Imagine that you are asked to retain a list of seven digits for a minute or two. You are told that remembering the digits is your top priority. While your attention is focused on the digits, you are offered a choice between two desserts: a sinful chocolate cake and a virtuous fruit salad. The evidence suggests that you would be more likely to select the tempting chocolate cake when your mind is loaded with digits. System 1 has more influence on behavior when System 2 is busy, and it has a sweet tooth.

People who are *cognitively busy* are also more likely to make selfish choices, use sexist language, and make superficial judgments in social situations. Memorizing and repeating digits loosens the hold of System 2 on behavior, but of course cognitive load is not the only cause of weakened self-control. A few drinks have the same effect, as does a sleepless night. The self-control of morning people is impaired at night; the reverse is true of night people. Too much concern about how well one is doing in a task sometimes disrupts performance by loading short-term memory with pointless anxious thoughts. The conclusion is straightforward: self-control requires attention and effort. Another way of saying this is that controlling thoughts and behaviors is one of the tasks that System 2 performs.

A series of surprising experiments by the psychologist Roy Baumeister and his colleagues has shown conclusively that all variants of voluntary effort—cognitive, emotional, or physical—draw at least partly on a shared pool of mental energy. Their experiments involve successive rather than simultaneous tasks.

Baumeister's group has repeatedly found that an effort of will or self-control is tiring; if you have had to force yourself to do something, you are less willing or less able to exert self-control when the next challenge comes around. The phenomenon has been named *ego depletion*. In a typical demonstration, participants who are instructed to stifle their emotional reaction to an emotionally charged film will later perform poorly on a test of physical stamina—how long they can maintain a strong grip on a dynamometer in spite of increasing discomfort. The emotional effort in the first phase of the experiment reduces the ability to withstand the pain of sustained muscle contraction, and ego-depleted people therefore succumb more quickly to the urge to quit. In another experiment, people are first depleted by a task in which they eat virtuous foods such as radishes and celery while resisting the temptation to indulge in chocolate and rich cookies. Later, these people will give up earlier than normal when faced with a difficult cognitive task.

The list of situations and tasks that are now known to deplete self-control is long and varied. All involve conflict and the need to suppress a natural tendency. They include:

avoiding the thought of white bears
inhibiting the emotional response to a stirring film
making a series of choices that involve conflict
trying to impress others
responding kindly to a partner's bad behavior
interacting with a person of a different race (for prejudiced individuals)

The list of indications of depletion is also highly diverse:

deviating from one's diet
overspending on impulsive purchases
reacting aggressively to provocation
persisting less time in a handgrip task
performing poorly in cognitive tasks and logical decision making

The evidence is persuasive: activities that impose high demands on System 2 require self-control, and the exertion of self-control is depleting and unpleasant. Unlike cognitive load, ego depletion is at least in part a loss of motivation. After exerting self-control in one task, you do not feel like making an effort in another, although you could do it if you really had to. In several experiments, people were able to resist the effects of ego depletion when given a strong incentive to do so. In contrast, increasing effort is not an option when you must keep six digits in short-term memory while performing a task. Ego depletion is not the same mental state as cognitive busyness.

The most surprising discovery made by Baumeister's group shows, as he puts it, that the idea of mental energy is more than a mere metaphor. The nervous system consumes more glucose than most other parts of the body, and effortful mental activity appears to be especially expensive in the currency of glucose. When you are actively involved in difficult cognitive reasoning or engaged in a task that requires self-control, your blood glucose level drops. The effect is analogous to a runner who draws down glucose stored in her muscles during a sprint. The bold implication of this idea is that the effects of ego depletion could be undone by ingesting glucose, and Baumeister and his colleagues have confirmed this hypothesis in several experiments.

Volunteers in one of their studies watched a short silent film of a woman being interviewed and were asked to interpret her body language. While they were performing the task, a series of words crossed the screen in slow succession. The participants were specifically instructed to ignore the words, and if they found their attention drawn away they had to refocus their concentration on the woman's behavior. This act of self-control was known to cause ego depletion. All the volunteers drank some lemonade before participating in a second task. The lemonade was sweetened with glucose for half of them and with Splenda for the others. Then all participants were given a task in which they needed to overcome an intuitive response to get the correct answer. Intuitive errors are normally much more frequent among ego-depleted people, and the drinkers of Splenda showed the expected depletion effect. On the other hand, the glucose drinkers were not depleted. Restoring the level of available sugar in the brain had prevented the deterioration of performance. It will take some time and much further research to establish whether the tasks that cause glucose-depletion also cause the momentary arousal that is reflected in increases of pupil size and heart rate.

A disturbing demonstration of depletion effects in judgment was recently reported in the *Proceedings of the National Academy of Sciences*. The unwitting participants in the study were eight parole judges in Israel. They spend entire days reviewing applications for parole. The cases are presented in random order, and the judges spend little time on each one, an average of 6 minutes. (The default decision is denial of parole; only 35% of requests are approved. The exact time of each decision is recorded, and the times of the judges' three food breaks—morning break, lunch, and afternoon break—during the day are recorded as well.) The authors of the study plotted the proportion of approved requests against the time since the last food break. The proportion spikes after each meal, when about 65% of requests are granted. During the two hours or so until the judges' next feeding, the approval rate drops steadily, to about zero just before the meal. As you might expect, this is an unwelcome result and the authors carefully checked many alternative explanations. The best possible account of the data provides bad news: tired and hungry judges tend to fall back on the easier default position of denying requests for parole. Both fatigue and hunger probably play a role.

THE LAZY SYSTEM 2

One of the main functions of System 2 is to monitor and control thoughts and actions "suggested" by System 1, allowing some to be expressed directly in behavior and suppressing or modifying others.

For an example, here is a simple puzzle. Do not try to solve it but listen to your intuition:

A bat and ball cost $1.10.
The bat costs one dollar more than the ball.
How much does the ball cost?

A number came to your mind. The number, of course, is 10: 10¢. The distinctive mark of this easy puzzle is that it evokes an answer that is intuitive, appealing, and wrong. Do the math, and you will see. If the ball costs 10¢, then the total cost will be $1.20 (10¢ for the ball and $1.10 for the bat), not $1.10. The correct answer is 5¢. It is safe to assume that the intuitive answer also came to the mind of those who ended up with the correct number—they somehow managed to resist the intuition.

Shane Frederick and I worked together on a theory of judgment based on two systems, and he used the bat-and-ball puzzle to study a central question: How closely does System 2 monitor the suggestions of System 1? His reasoning was that we know a significant fact about anyone who says that the ball costs 10¢: that person did not actively check whether the answer was correct, and her System 2 endorsed an intuitive answer that it could have rejected with a small investment of effort. Furthermore, we also know that the people who give the intuitive answer have missed an obvious social cue; they should have wondered why anyone would include in a questionnaire a puzzle with such an obvious answer. A failure to check is remarkable because the cost of checking is so low: a few seconds of mental work (the problem is moderately difficult), with slightly tensed muscles and dilated pupils, could avoid an embarrassing mistake. People who say 10¢ appear to be ardent followers of the law of least effort. People who avoid that answer appear to have more active minds.

Many thousands of university students have answered the bat-and-ball puzzle, and the results are shocking. More than 50% of students at Harvard, MIT, and Princeton gave the intuitive—incorrect—answer. At less selective universities, the rate of demonstrable failure to check was in excess of 80%. The bat-and-ball problem is our first encounter with an observation that will be a recurrent theme of this book: many people are overconfident, prone to place too much faith in their intuitions. They apparently find cognitive effort at least mildly unpleasant and avoid it as much as possible.

Now I will show you a logical argument—two premises and a conclusion. Try to determine, as quickly as you can, if the argument is logically valid. Does the conclusion follow from the premises?

All roses are flowers.
Some flowers fade quickly.
Therefore some roses fade quickly.

A large majority of college students endorse this syllogism as valid. In fact the argument is flawed, because it is possible that there are no roses among the flowers that fade quickly. Just as in the bat-and-ball problem, a plausible answer comes to mind immediately. Overriding it requires hard work—the insistent idea that "it's true, it's true!" makes it difficult to check the logic, and most people do not take the trouble to think through the problem.

This experiment has discouraging implications for reasoning in everyday life. It suggests that when people believe a conclusion is true, they are also very likely to believe arguments that appear to support it, even when these arguments are unsound. If System 1 is involved, the conclusion comes first and the arguments follow.

Next, consider the following question and answer it quickly before reading on:

How many murders occur in the state of Michigan in one year?

The question, which was also devised by Shane Frederick, is again a challenge to System 2. The "trick" is whether the respondent will remember that

Detroit, a high-crime city, is in Michigan. College students in the United States know this fact and will correctly identify Detroit as the largest city in Michigan. But knowledge of a fact is not all-or-none. Facts that we know do not always come to mind when we need them. People who remember that Detroit is in Michigan give higher estimates of the murder rate in the state than people who do not, but a majority of Frederick's respondents did not think of the city when questioned about the state. Indeed, the average guess by people who were asked about Michigan is *lower* than the guesses of a similar group who were asked about the murder rate in Detroit.

Blame for a failure to think of Detroit can be laid on both System 1 and System 2. Whether the city comes to mind when the state is mentioned depends in part on the automatic function of memory. People differ in this respect. The representation of the state of Michigan is very detailed in some people's minds: residents of the state are more likely to retrieve many facts about it than people who live elsewhere; geography buffs will retrieve more than others who specialize in baseball statistics; more intelligent individuals are more likely than others to have rich representations of most things. Intelligence is not only the ability to reason; it is also the ability to find relevant material in memory and to deploy attention when needed. Memory function is an attribute of System 1. However, everyone has the option of slowing down to conduct an active search of memory for all possibly relevant facts—just as they could slow down to check the intuitive answer in the bat-and-ball problem. The extent of deliberate checking and search is a characteristic of System 2, which varies among individuals.

The bat-and-ball problem, the flowers syllogism, and the Michigan/Detroit problem have something in common. Failing these minitests appears to be, at least to some extent, a matter of insufficient motivation, not trying hard enough. Anyone who can be admitted to a good university is certainly able to reason through the first two questions and to reflect about Michigan long enough to remember the major city in that state and its crime problem. These students can solve much more difficult problems when they are not tempted to accept a superficially plausible answer that comes readily to mind. The ease with which they are satisfied enough to stop thinking is rather troubling. "Lazy" is a harsh judgment about the self-monitoring of these young people and their System 2, but it does not seem to be unfair. Those who avoid the sin of intellectual sloth could be called "engaged." They are more alert, more intellectually active, less willing to be satisfied with superficially attractive answers, more skeptical about their intuitions. The psychologist Keith Stanovich would call them more rational.

INTELLIGENCE, CONTROL, RATIONALITY

Researchers have applied diverse methods to examine the connection between thinking and self-control. Some have addressed it by asking the correlation question: If people were ranked by their self-control and by their cognitive aptitude, would individuals have similar positions in the two rankings?

In one of the most famous experiments in the history of psychology, Walter Mischel and his students exposed four-year-old children to a cruel dilemma. They were given a choice between a small reward (one Oreo), which they could have at any time, or a larger reward (two cookies) for which they had to wait 15 minutes under difficult conditions. They were to remain alone in a room, facing a desk with two objects: a single cookie and a bell that the child could ring at any time to call in the experimenter and receive the one cookie. As the experiment was described: "There were no toys, books, pictures, or other potentially distracting items in the room. The experimenter left the room and did not return until 15 min had passed or the child had rung the bell, eaten the rewards, stood up, or shown any signs of distress."

The children were watched through a one-way mirror, and the film that shows their behavior during the waiting time always has the audience roaring in laughter. About half the children managed the feat of waiting for 15 minutes, mainly by keeping their attention away from the tempting reward. Ten or fifteen years later, a large gap had opened between those who had resisted temptation and those who had not. The resisters had higher measures of executive control in cognitive tasks, and especially the ability to reallocate their attention effectively. As young adults, they were less likely to take drugs. A significant difference in intellectual aptitude emerged: the children who had shown more self-control as four-year-olds had substantially higher scores on tests of intelligence.

A team of researchers at the University of Oregon explored the link between cognitive control and intelligence in several ways, including an attempt to raise intelligence by improving the control of attention. During five 40-minute sessions, they exposed children aged four to six to various computer games especially designed to demand attention and control. In one of the exercises, the children used a joystick to track a cartoon cat and move it to a grassy area while avoiding a muddy area. The grassy areas gradually shrank and the muddy area expanded, requiring progressively more precise control. The testers found that training attention not only improved executive control; scores on nonverbal tests of intelligence also improved and the improvement was maintained for several months. Other research by the same group identified specific genes that are involved in the control of attention, showed that parenting techniques also affected this ability, and demonstrated a close connection between the children's ability to control their attention and their ability to control their emotions.

Shane Frederick constructed a Cognitive Reflection Test, which consists of the bat-and-ball problem and two other questions, chosen because they also invite an intuitive answer that is both compelling and wrong (the questions are shown in chapter 5). He went on to study the characteristics of students who score very low on this test—the supervisory function of System 2 is weak in these people—and found that they are prone to answer questions with the first idea that comes to mind and unwilling to invest the effort needed to check their intuitions. Individuals who uncritically follow their intuitions about puzzles are also prone to accept other suggestions from System 1. In particular, they are impulsive, impatient, and keen to receive immediate gratification. For example, 63% of the intuitive respondents say they would prefer to get $3,400 this month rather than $3,800 next month. Only 37% of those who solve all three puzzles correctly have the same shortsighted preference for receiving a smaller amount immediately. When asked how much they will pay to get overnight delivery of a book they have ordered, the low scorers on the Cognitive Reflection Test are willing to pay twice as much as the high scorers. Frederick's findings suggest that the characters of our psychodrama have different "personalities." System 1 is impulsive and intuitive; System 2 is capable of reasoning, and it is cautious, but at least for some people it is also lazy. We recognize related differences among individuals: some people are more like their System 2; others are closer to their System 1. This simple test has emerged as one of the better predictors of lazy thinking.

Keith Stanovich and his longtime collaborator Richard West originally introduced the terms System 1 and System 2 (they now prefer to speak of Type 1 and Type 2 processes). Stanovich and his colleagues have spent decades studying differences among individuals in the kinds of problems with which this book is concerned. They have asked one basic question in many different ways: What makes some people more susceptible than others to biases of judgment? Stanovich published his conclusions in a book titled *Rationality and the Reflective Mind*, which offers a bold and distinctive approach to the topic of this chapter. He draws a sharp distinction between two parts of System 2—indeed, the distinction is so sharp that he calls them separate "minds." One of these minds (he calls it algorithmic) deals with slow thinking and demanding computation. Some people are better than others in these tasks of brain power—they are the individuals who excel in intelligence tests and are able to switch from one task to another quickly and efficiently. However, Stanovich argues that high intelligence does not make people immune to biases. Another ability is involved, which he labels rationality. Stanovich's concept of a rational person is similar to what I earlier labeled "engaged." The core of his argument is that *rationality* should be distinguished from *intelligence*. In his view, superficial or "lazy" thinking is a flaw in the reflective mind, a failure of rationality. This is an attractive and thought-provoking idea. In support of it, Stanovich and his colleagues have found that the bat-and-ball question and others like it are somewhat better indicators of our susceptibility to cognitive errors than are conventional measures of intelligence, such as IQ tests. Time will tell whether the distinction between intelligence and rationality can lead to new discoveries.

SPEAKING OF CONTROL

"She did not have to struggle to stay on task for hours. She was in a state of *flow.*"

"His ego was depleted after a long day of meetings. So he just turned to standard operating procedures instead of thinking through the problem."

"He didn't bother to check whether what he said made sense. Does he usually have a lazy System 2 or was he unusually tired?"

"Unfortunately, she tends to say the first thing that comes into her mind. She probably also has trouble delaying gratification. Weak System 2."

4

THE ASSOCIATIVE MACHINE

To begin your exploration of the surprising workings of System 1, look at the following words:

Bananas   Vomit

A lot happened to you during the last second or two. You experienced some unpleasant images and memories. Your face twisted slightly in an expression of disgust, and you may have pushed this book imperceptibly farther away. Your heart rate increased, the hair on your arms rose a little, and your sweat glands were activated. In short, you responded to the disgusting word with an attenuated version of how you would react to the actual event. All of this was completely automatic, beyond your control.

There was no particular reason to do so, but your mind automatically assumed a temporal sequence and a causal connection between the words *bananas* and *vomit*, forming a sketchy scenario in which bananas caused the sickness. As a result, you are experiencing a temporary aversion to bananas (don't worry, it will pass). The state of your memory has changed in other ways: you are now unusually ready to recognize and respond to objects and concepts associated with "vomit," such as sick, stink, or nausea, and words associated with "bananas," such as yellow and fruit, and perhaps apple and berries.

Vomiting normally occurs in specific contexts, such as hangovers and indigestion. You would also be unusually ready to recognize words associated with other causes of the same unfortunate outcome. Furthermore, your System 1 noticed the fact that the juxtaposition of the two words is uncommon; you probably never encountered it before. You experienced mild surprise.

This complex constellation of responses occurred quickly, automatically, and effortlessly. You did not will it and you could not stop it. It was an operation of System 1. The events that took place as a result of your seeing the words happened by a process called associative activation: ideas that have been evoked trigger many other ideas, in a spreading cascade of activity in your brain. The essential feature of this complex set of mental events is its coherence. Each element is connected, and each supports and strengthens the others. The word evokes memories, which evoke emotions, which in turn evoke facial expressions and other reactions, such as a general tensing up and an avoidance tendency. The facial expression and the avoidance motion intensify the feelings to which they are linked, and the feelings in turn reinforce compatible ideas. All this happens quickly and all at once, yielding a self-reinforcing pattern of cognitive, emotional, and physical responses that is both diverse and integrated—it has been called *associatively coherent*.

In a second or so you accomplished, automatically and unconsciously, a remarkable feat. Starting from a completely unexpected event, your System 1 made as much sense as possible of the situation—two simple words, oddly juxtaposed—by linking the words in a causal story; it evaluated the possible threat (mild to moderate) and created a context for future developments by preparing you for events that had just become more likely; it also created a context for the current event by evaluating how surprising it was. You ended up as informed about the past and as prepared for the future as you could be.

An odd feature of what happened is that your System 1 treated the mere conjunction of two words as representations of reality. Your body reacted in an attenuated replica of a reaction to the real thing, and the emotional response and physical recoil were part of the interpretation of the event. As cognitive scientists have emphasized in recent years, cognition is embodied; you think with your body, not only with your brain.

The mechanism that causes these mental events has been known for a long time: it is the association of ideas. We all understand from experience that ideas follow each other in our conscious mind in a fairly orderly way. The British philosophers of the seventeenth and eighteenth centuries searched for the rules that explain such sequences. In *An Enquiry Concerning Human Understanding*, published in 1748, the Scottish philosopher

David Hume reduced the principles of association to three: resemblance, contiguity in time and place, and causality. Our concept of association has changed radically since Hume's days, but his three principles still provide a good start.

I will adopt an expansive view of what an idea is. It can be concrete or abstract, and it can be expressed in many ways: as a verb, as a noun, as an adjective, or as a clenched fist. Psychologists think of ideas as nodes in a vast network, called associative memory, in which each idea is linked to many others. There are different types of links: causes are linked to their effects (virus → cold); things to their properties (lime → green); things to the categories to which they belong (banana → fruit). One way we have advanced beyond Hume is that we no longer think of the mind as going through a sequence of conscious ideas, one at a time. In the current view of how associative memory works, a great deal happens at once. An idea that has been activated does not merely evoke one other idea. It activates many ideas, which in turn activate others. Furthermore, only a few of the activated ideas will register in consciousness; most of the work of associative thinking is silent, hidden from our conscious selves. The notion that we have limited access to the workings of our minds is difficult to accept because, naturally, it is alien to our experience, but it is true: you know far less about yourself than you feel you do.

THE MARVELS OF PRIMING

As is common in science, the first big breakthrough in our understanding of the mechanism of association was an improvement in a method of measurement. Until a few decades ago, the only way to study associations was to ask many people questions such as, "What is the first word that comes to your mind when you hear the word DAY?" The researchers tallied the frequency of responses, such as "night," "sunny," or "long." In the 1980s, psychologists discovered that exposure to a word causes immediate and measurable changes in the ease with which many related words can be evoked. If you have recently seen or heard the word EAT, you are temporarily more likely to complete the word fragment SO_P as SOUP than as SOAP. The opposite would happen, of course, if you had just seen WASH. We call this a *priming effect* and say that the idea of EAT primes the idea of SOUP, and that WASH primes SOAP.

Priming effects take many forms. If the idea of EAT is currently on your mind (whether or not you are conscious of it), you will be quicker than

usual to recognize the word SOUP when it is spoken in a whisper or presented in a blurry font. And of course you are primed not only for the idea
of soup but also for a multitude of food-related ideas, including fork, hungry,
fat, diet, and cookie. If for your most recent meal you sat at a wobbly restaurant table, you will be primed for wobbly as well. Furthermore, the primed
ideas have some ability to prime other ideas, although more weakly. Like
ripples on a pond, activation spreads through a small part of the vast network of associated ideas. The mapping of these ripples is now one of the
most exciting pursuits in psychological research.

Another major advance in our understanding of memory was the discovery that priming is not restricted to concepts and words. You cannot
know this from conscious experience, of course, but you must accept the
alien idea that your actions and your emotions can be primed by events of
which you are not even aware. In an experiment that became an instant
classic, the psychologist John Bargh and his collaborators asked students
at New York University—most aged eighteen to twenty-two—to assemble
four-word sentences from a set of five words (for example, "finds he it yellow instantly"). For one group of students, half the scrambled sentences
contained words associated with the elderly, such as *Florida, forgetful, bald,
gray,* or *wrinkle.* When they had completed that task, the young participants were sent out to do another experiment in an office down the hall.
That short walk was what the experiment was about. The researchers unob-
trusively measured the time it took people to get from one end of the corridor to the other. As Bargh had predicted, the young people who had
fashioned a sentence from words with an elderly theme walked down the
hallway significantly more slowly than the others.

The "Florida effect" involves two stages of priming. First, the set of
words primes thoughts of old age, though the word *old* is never mentioned;
second, these thoughts prime a behavior, walking slowly, which is associated with old age. All this happens without any awareness. When they were
questioned afterward, none of the students reported noticing that the words
had had a common theme, and they all insisted that nothing they did after
the first experiment could have been influenced by the words they had
encountered. The idea of old age had not come to their conscious awareness, but their actions had changed nevertheless. This remarkable priming
phenomenon—the influencing of an action by the idea—is known as the
ideomotor effect. Although you surely were not aware of it, reading this
paragraph primed you as well. If you had needed to stand up to get a glass
of water, you would have been slightly slower than usual to rise from your

chair—unless you happen to dislike the elderly, in which case research suggests that you might have been slightly faster than usual!

The ideomotor link also works in reverse. A study conducted in a German university was the mirror image of the early experiment that Bargh and his colleagues had carried out in New York. Students were asked to walk around a room for 5 minutes at a rate of 30 steps per minute, which was about one-third their normal pace. After this brief experience, the participants were much quicker to recognize words related to old age, such as *forgetful*, *old*, and *lonely*. Reciprocal priming effects tend to produce a coherent reaction: if you were primed to think of old age, you would tend to act old, and acting old would reinforce the thought of old age.

Reciprocal links are common in the associative network. For example, being amused tends to make you smile, and smiling tends to make you feel amused. Go ahead and take a pencil, and hold it between your teeth for a few seconds with the eraser pointing to your right and the point to your left. Now hold the pencil so the point is aimed straight in front of you, by pursing your lips around the eraser end. You were probably unaware that one of these actions forced your face into a frown and the other into a smile. College students were asked to rate the humor of cartoons from Gary Larson's *The Far Side* while holding a pencil in their mouth. Those who were "smiling" (without any awareness of doing so) found the cartoons funnier than did those who were "frowning." In another experiment, people whose face was shaped into a frown (by squeezing their eyebrows together) reported an enhanced emotional response to upsetting pictures—starving children, people arguing, maimed accident victims.

Simple, common gestures can also unconsciously influence our thoughts and feelings. In one demonstration, people were asked to listen to messages through new headphones. They were told that the purpose of the experiment was to test the quality of the audio equipment and were instructed to move their heads repeatedly to check for any distortions of sound. Half the participants were told to nod their head up and down while others were told to shake it side to side. The messages they heard were radio editorials. Those who nodded (a yes gesture) tended to accept the message they heard, but those who shook their head tended to reject it. Again, there was no awareness, just a habitual connection between an attitude of rejection or acceptance and its common physical expression. You can see why the common admonition to "act calm and kind regardless of how you feel" is very good advice: you are likely to be rewarded by actually feeling calm and kind.

PRIMES THAT GUIDE US

Studies of priming effects have yielded discoveries that threaten our self-image as conscious and autonomous authors of our judgments and our choices. For instance, most of us think of voting as a deliberate act that reflects our values and our assessments of policies and is not influenced by irrelevancies. Our vote should not be affected by the location of the polling station, for example, but it is. A study of voting patterns in precincts of Arizona in 2000 showed that the support for propositions to increase the funding of schools was significantly greater when the polling station was in a school than when it was in a nearby location. A separate experiment showed that exposing people to images of classrooms and school lockers also increased the tendency of participants to support a school initiative. The effect of the images was larger than the difference between parents and other voters! The study of priming has come some way from the initial demonstrations that reminding people of old age makes them walk more slowly. We now know that the effects of priming can reach into every corner of our lives.

Reminders of money produce some troubling effects. Participants in one experiment were shown a list of five words from which they were required to construct a four-word phrase that had a money theme ("high a salary desk paying" became "a high-paying salary"). Other primes were much more subtle, including the presence of an irrelevant money-related object in the background, such as a stack of Monopoly money on a table, or a computer with a screen saver of dollar bills floating in water.

Money-primed people become more independent than they would be without the associative trigger. They persevered almost twice as long in trying to solve a very difficult problem before they asked the experimenter for help, a crisp demonstration of increased self-reliance. Money-primed people are also more selfish: they were much less willing to spend time helping another student who pretended to be confused about an experimental task. When an experimenter clumsily dropped a bunch of pencils on the floor, the participants with money (unconsciously) on their mind picked up fewer pencils. In another experiment in the series, participants were told that they would shortly have a get-acquainted conversation with another person and were asked to set up two chairs while the experimenter left to retrieve that person. Participants primed by money chose to stay much farther apart than their nonprimed peers (118 vs. 80 centimeters). Money-primed undergraduates also showed a greater preference for being alone.

The general theme of these findings is that the idea of money primes individualism: a reluctance to be involved with others, to depend on others, or to accept demands from others. The psychologist who has done this remarkable research, Kathleen Vohs, has been laudably restrained in discussing the implications of her findings, leaving the task to her readers. Her experiments are profound—her findings suggest that living in a culture that surrounds us with reminders of money may shape our behavior and our attitudes in ways that we do not know about and of which we may not be proud. Some cultures provide frequent reminders of respect, others constantly remind their members of God, and some societies prime obedience by large images of the Dear Leader. Can there be any doubt that the ubiquitous portraits of the national leader in dictatorial societies not only convey the feeling that "Big Brother Is Watching" but also lead to an actual reduction in spontaneous thought and independent action?

The evidence of priming studies suggests that reminding people of their mortality increases the appeal of authoritarian ideas, which may become reassuring in the context of the terror of death. Other experiments have confirmed Freudian insights about the role of symbols and metaphors in unconscious associations. For example, consider the ambiguous word fragments W_ _H and S_ _P. People who were recently asked to think of an action of which they are ashamed are more likely to complete those fragments as WASH and SOAP and less likely to see WISH and SOUP. Furthermore, merely thinking about stabbing a coworker in the back leaves people more inclined to buy soap, disinfectant, or detergent than batteries, juice, or candy bars. Feeling that one's soul is stained appears to trigger a desire to cleanse one's body, an impulse that has been dubbed the "Lady Macbeth effect."

The cleansing is highly specific to the body parts involved in a sin. Participants in an experiment were induced to "lie" to an imaginary person, either on the phone or in e-mail. In a subsequent test of the desirability of various products, people who had lied on the phone preferred mouthwash over soap, and those who had lied in e-mail preferred soap to mouthwash.

When I describe priming studies to audiences, the reaction is often disbelief. This is not a surprise: System 2 believes that it is in charge and that it knows the reasons for its choices. Questions are probably cropping up in your mind as well: How is it possible for such trivial manipulations of the context to have such large effects? Do these experiments demonstrate that we are completely at the mercy of whatever primes the environment provides at any moment? Of course not. The effects of the primes are robust but not necessarily large. Among a hundred voters, only a few whose initial preferences were uncertain will vote differently about a school issue if their precinct is located in a school rather than in a church—but a few percent could tip an election.

The idea you should focus on, however, is that disbelief is not an option. The results are not made up, nor are they statistical flukes. You have no choice but to accept that the major conclusions of these studies are true. More important, you must accept that they are true about *you*. If you had been exposed to a screen saver of floating dollar bills, you too would likely have picked up fewer pencils to help a clumsy stranger. You do not believe that these results apply to you because they correspond to nothing in your subjective experience. But your subjective experience consists largely of the story that your System 2 tells itself about what is going on. Priming phenomena arise in System 1, and you have no conscious access to them.

I conclude with a perfect demonstration of a priming effect, which was conducted in an office kitchen at a British university. For many years members of that office had paid for the tea or coffee to which they helped themselves during the day by dropping money into an "honesty box." A list of suggested prices was posted. One day a banner poster was displayed just above the price list, with no warning or explanation. For a period of ten weeks a new image was presented each week, either flowers or eyes that appeared to be looking directly at the observer. No one commented on the new decorations, but the contributions to the honesty box changed significantly. The posters and the amounts that people put into the cash box (relative to the amount they consumed) are shown in figure 4. They deserve a close look.

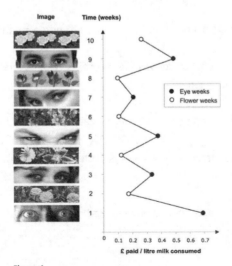

Figure 4

On the first week of the experiment (which you can see at the bottom of the figure), two wide-open eyes stare at the coffee or tea drinkers, whose average contribution was 70 pence per liter of milk. On week 2, the poster shows flowers and average contributions drop to about 15 pence. The trend continues. On average, the users of the kitchen contributed almost three times as much in "eye weeks" as they did in "flower weeks." Evidently, a purely symbolic reminder of being watched prodded people into improved behavior. As we expect at this point, the effect occurs without any awareness. Do you now believe that you would also fall into the same pattern?

Some years ago, the psychologist Timothy Wilson wrote a book with the evocative title *Strangers to Ourselves*. You have now been introduced to that stranger in you, which may be in control of much of what you do, although you rarely have a glimpse of it. System 1 provides the impressions that often turn into your beliefs, and is the source of the impulses that often become your choices and your actions. It offers a tacit interpretation of what happens to you and around you, linking the present with the recent past and with expectations about the near future. It contains the model of the world that instantly evaluates events as normal or surprising. It is the source of your rapid and often precise intuitive judgments. And it does most of this without your conscious awareness of its activities. System 1 is also, as we will see in the following chapters, the origin of many of the systematic errors in your intuitions.

SPEAKING OF PRIMING

"The sight of all these people in uniforms does not prime creativity."

"The world makes much less sense than you think. The coherence comes mostly from the way your mind works."

"They were primed to find flaws, and this is exactly what they found."

"His System 1 constructed a story, and his System 2 believed it. It happens to all of us."

"I made myself smile and I'm actually feeling better!"

5

COGNITIVE EASE

Whenever you are conscious, and perhaps even when you are not, multiple computations are going on in your brain, which maintain and update current answers to some key questions: Is anything new going on? Is there a threat? Are things going well? Should my attention be redirected? Is more effort needed for this task? You can think of a cockpit, with a set of dials that indicate the current values of each of these essential variables. The assessments are carried out automatically by System 1, and one of their functions is to determine whether extra effort is required from System 2.

One of the dials measures *cognitive ease*, and its range is between "Easy" and "Strained." Easy is a sign that things are going well—no threats, no major news, no need to redirect attention or mobilize effort. Strained indicates that a problem exists, which will require increased mobilization of System 2. Conversely, you experience *cognitive strain*. Cognitive strain is affected by both the current level of effort and the presence of unmet demands. The surprise is that a single dial of cognitive ease is connected to a large network of diverse inputs and outputs. Figure 5 on page 60 tells the story.

The figure suggests that a sentence that is printed in a clear font, or has been repeated, or has been primed, will be fluently processed with cognitive ease. Hearing a speaker when you are in a good mood, or even when you have a pencil stuck crosswise in your mouth to make you "smile," also induces cognitive ease. Conversely, you experience cognitive strain when you read instructions in a poor font, or in faint colors, or worded in complicated language, or when you are in a bad mood, and even when you frown.

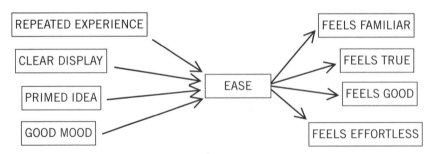

Figure 5. Causes and Consequences of Cognitive Ease

The various causes of ease or strain have interchangeable effects. When you are in a state of cognitive ease, you are probably in a good mood, like what you see, believe what you hear, trust your intuitions, and feel that the current situation is comfortably familiar. You are also likely to be relatively casual and superficial in your thinking. When you feel strained, you are more likely to be vigilant and suspicious, invest more effort in what you are doing, feel less comfortable, and make fewer errors, but you also are less intuitive and less creative than usual.

ILLUSIONS OF REMEMBERING

The word *illusion* brings visual illusions to mind, because we are all familiar with pictures that mislead. But vision is not the only domain of illusions; memory is also susceptible to them, as is thinking more generally.

David Stenbill, Monica Bigoutski, Shana Tirana. I just made up these names. If you encounter any of them within the next few minutes you are likely to remember where you saw them. You know, and will know for a while, that these are not the names of minor celebrities. But suppose that a few days from now you are shown a long list of names, including some minor celebrities and "new" names of people that you have never heard of; your task will be to check every name of a celebrity in the list. There is a substantial probability that you will identify David Stenbill as a well-known person, although you will not (of course) know whether you encountered his name in the context of movies, sports, or politics. Larry Jacoby, the psychologist who first demonstrated this memory illusion in the laboratory, titled his article "Becoming Famous Overnight." How does this happen? Start by asking yourself how you know whether or not someone is famous. In some cases of truly famous people (or of celebrities in an area you follow), you have a mental file with rich information about a person—think

Albert Einstein, Bono, Hillary Clinton. But you will have no file of information about David Stenbill if you encounter his name in a few days. All you will have is a sense of familiarity—you have seen this name somewhere.

Jacoby nicely stated the problem: "The experience of familiarity has a simple but powerful quality of 'pastness' that seems to indicate that it is a direct reflection of prior experience." This quality of pastness is an illusion. The truth is, as Jacoby and many followers have shown, that the name David Stenbill will look familiar when you see it *because you will see it more clearly*. Words that you have seen before become easier to see again—you can identify them better than other words when they are shown very briefly or masked by noise, and you will be quicker (by a few hundredths of a second) to read them than to read other words. In short, you experience greater cognitive ease in perceiving a word you have seen earlier, and it is this sense of ease that gives you the impression of familiarity.

Figure 5 suggests a way to test this. Choose a completely new word, make it easier to see, and it will be more likely to have the quality of pastness. Indeed, a new word is more likely to be recognized as familiar if it is unconsciously primed by showing it for a few milliseconds just before the test, or if it is shown in sharper contrast than some other words in the list. The link also operates in the other direction. Imagine you are shown a list of words that are more or less out of focus. Some of the words are severely blurred, others less so, and your task is to identify the words that are shown more clearly. A word that you have seen recently will appear to be clearer than unfamiliar words. As figure 5 indicates, the various ways of inducing cognitive ease or strain are interchangeable; you may not know precisely what it is that makes things cognitively easy or strained. This is how the illusion of familiarity comes about.

ILLUSIONS OF TRUTH

"New York is a large city in the United States." "The moon revolves around Earth." "A chicken has four legs." In all these cases, you quickly retrieved a great deal of related information, almost all pointing one way or another. You knew soon after reading them that the first two statements are true and the last one is false. Note, however, that the statement "A chicken has three legs" is more obviously false than "A chicken has four legs." Your associative machinery slows the judgment of the latter sentence by delivering the fact that many animals have four legs, and perhaps also that supermarkets often sell chicken legs in packages of four. System 2 was involved in sifting that information, perhaps raising the issue of whether the question about New York was too easy, or checking the meaning of *revolves*.

Think of the last time you took a driving test. Is it true that you need a special license to drive a vehicle that weighs more than three tons? Perhaps you studied seriously and can remember the side of the page on which the answer appeared, as well as the logic behind it. This is certainly not how I passed driving tests when I moved to a new state. My practice was to read the booklet of rules quickly once and hope for the best. I knew some of the answers from the experience of driving for a long time. But there were questions where no good answer came to mind, where all I had to go by was cognitive ease. If the answer felt familiar, I assumed that it was probably true. If it looked new (or improbably extreme), I rejected it. The impression of familiarity is produced by System 1, and System 2 relies on that impression for a true/false judgment.

The lesson of figure 5 is that predictable illusions inevitably occur if a judgment is based on an impression of cognitive ease or strain. Anything that makes it easier for the associative machine to run smoothly will also bias beliefs. A reliable way to make people believe in falsehoods is frequent repetition, because familiarity is not easily distinguished from truth. Authoritarian institutions and marketers have always known this fact. But it was psychologists who discovered that you do not have to repeat the entire statement of a fact or idea to make it appear true. People who were repeatedly exposed to the phrase "the body temperature of a chicken" were more likely to accept as true the statement that "the body temperature of a chicken is 144°" (or any other arbitrary number). The familiarity of one phrase in the statement sufficed to make the whole statement feel familiar, and therefore true. If you cannot remember the source of a statement, and have no way to relate it to other things you know, you have no option but to go with the sense of cognitive ease.

HOW TO WRITE A PERSUASIVE MESSAGE

Suppose you must write a message that you want the recipients to believe. Of course, your message will be true, but that is not necessarily enough for people to believe that it is true. It is entirely legitimate for you to enlist cognitive ease to work in your favor, and studies of *truth illusions* provide specific suggestions that may help you achieve this goal.

The general principle is that anything you can do to reduce cognitive strain will help, so you should first maximize legibility. Compare these two statements:

Adolf Hitler was born in 1892.
Adolf Hitler was born in 1887.

Both are false (Hitler was born in 1889), but experiments have shown that the first is more likely to be believed. More advice: if your message is to be printed, use high-quality paper to maximize the contrast between characters and their background. If you use color, you are more likely to be believed if your text is printed in bright blue or red than in middling shades of green, yellow, or pale blue.

If you care about being thought credible and intelligent, do not use complex language where simpler language will do. My Princeton colleague Danny Oppenheimer refuted a myth prevalent among undergraduates about the vocabulary that professors find most impressive. In an article titled "Consequences of Erudite Vernacular Utilized Irrespective of Necessity: Problems with Using Long Words Needlessly," he showed that couching familiar ideas in pretentious language is taken as a sign of poor intelligence and low credibility.

In addition to making your message simple, try to make it memorable. Put your ideas in verse if you can; they will be more likely to be taken as truth. Participants in a much cited experiment read dozens of unfamiliar aphorisms, such as:

Woes unite foes.
Little strokes will tumble great oaks.
A fault confessed is half redressed.

Other students read some of the same proverbs transformed into nonrhyming versions:

Woes unite enemies.
Little strokes will tumble great trees.
A fault admitted is half redressed.

The aphorisms were judged more insightful when they rhymed than when they did not.

Finally, if you quote a source, choose one with a name that is easy to pronounce. Participants in an experiment were asked to evaluate the prospects of fictitious Turkish companies on the basis of reports from two brokerage firms. For each stock, one of the reports came from an easily pronounced name (e.g., Artan) and the other report came from a firm with an unfortunate name (e.g., Taahhut). The reports sometimes disagreed. The best procedure for the observers would have been to average the two reports, but this is not what they did. They gave much more weight to the report from Artan than to the report from Taahhut. Remember that System 2 is lazy and that mental effort is aversive. If possible, the recipients of your message want to stay away from anything that reminds them of effort, including a source with a complicated name.

All this is very good advice, but we should not get carried away. High-quality paper, bright colors, and rhyming or simple language will not be much help if your message is obviously nonsensical, or if it contradicts facts that your audience knows to be true. The psychologists who do these experiments do not believe that people are stupid or infinitely gullible. What psychologists do believe is that all of us live much of our life guided by the impressions of System 1—and we often do not know the source of these impressions. How do you know that a statement is true? If it is strongly linked by logic or association to other beliefs or preferences you hold, or comes from a source you trust and like, you will feel a sense of cognitive ease. The trouble is that there may be other causes for your feeling of ease—including the quality of the font and the appealing rhythm of the prose—and you have no simple way of tracing your feelings to their source. This is the message of figure 5: the sense of ease or strain has multiple causes, and it is difficult to tease them apart. Difficult, but not impossible. People can overcome some of the superficial factors that produce illusions of truth when strongly motivated to do so. On most occasions, however, the lazy System 2 will adopt the suggestions of System 1 and march on.

STRAIN AND EFFORT

The symmetry of many associative connections was a dominant theme in the discussion of associative coherence. As we saw earlier, people who are made to "smile" or "frown" by sticking a pencil in their mouth or holding a ball between their furrowed brows are prone to experience the emotions that frowning and smiling normally express. The same self-reinforcing reciprocity is found in studies of cognitive ease. On the one hand, cognitive strain is experienced when the effortful operations of System 2 are engaged. On the other hand, the experience of cognitive strain, whatever its source, tends to mobilize System 2, shifting people's approach to problems from a casual intuitive mode to a more engaged and analytic mode.

The bat-and-ball problem was mentioned earlier as a test of people's tendency to answer questions with the first idea that comes to their mind, without checking it. Shane Frederick's Cognitive Reflection Test consists of the bat-and-ball problem and two others, all chosen because they evoke an immediate intuitive answer that is incorrect. The other two items in the CRT are:

> If it takes 5 machines 5 minutes to make 5 widgets, how long
> would it take 100 machines to make 100 widgets?
> 100 minutes   OR   5 minutes

> In a lake, there is a patch of lily pads. Every day, the patch doubles in size.
> If it takes 48 days for the patch to cover the entire lake, how long would
> it take for the patch to cover half of the lake?
> 24 days   OR   47 days

The correct answers to both problems are in a footnote at the bottom of the page.* The experimenters recruited 40 Princeton students to take the CRT. Half of them saw the puzzles in a small font in washed-out gray print. The puzzles were legible, but the font induced cognitive strain. The results tell a clear story: 90% of the students who saw the CRT in normal font made at least one mistake in the test, but the proportion dropped to 35% when the font was barely legible. You read this correctly: performance was better with the bad font. Cognitive strain, whatever its source, mobilizes System 2, which is more likely to reject the intuitive answer suggested by System 1.

THE PLEASURE OF COGNITIVE EASE

An article titled "Mind at Ease Puts a Smile on the Face" describes an experiment in which participants were briefly shown pictures of objects. Some of these pictures were made easier to recognize by showing the outline of the object just before the complete image was shown, so briefly that the con-

*5, 47.

tours were never noticed. Emotional reactions were measured by recording electrical impulses from facial muscles, registering changes of expression that are too slight and too brief to be detectable by observers. As expected, people showed a faint smile and relaxed brows when the pictures were easier to see. It appears to be a feature of System 1 that cognitive ease is associated with good feelings.

As expected, easily pronounced words evoke a favorable attitude. Companies with pronounceable names do better than others for the first week after the stock is issued, though the effect disappears over time. Stocks with pronounceable trading symbols (like KAR or LUNMOO) outperform those with tongue-twisting tickers like PXG or RDO—and they appear to retain a small advantage over some time. A study conducted in Switzerland found that investors believe that stocks with fluent names like Emmi, Swissfirst, and Comet will earn higher returns than those with clunky labels like Geberit and Ypsomed.

As we saw in figure 5, repetition induces cognitive ease and a comforting feeling of familiarity. The famed psychologist Robert Zajonc dedicated much of his career to the study of the link between the repetition of an arbitrary stimulus and the mild affection that people eventually have for it. Zajonc called it the *mere exposure effect*. A demonstration conducted in the student newspapers of the University of Michigan and of Michigan State University is one of my favorite experiments. For a period of some weeks, an ad-like box appeared on the front page of the paper, which contained one of the following Turkish (or Turkish-sounding) words: *kadirga, saricik, biwonjni, nansoma,* and *iktitaf.* The frequency with which the words were repeated varied: one of the words was shown only once, the others appeared on two, five, ten, or twenty-five separate occasions. (The words that were presented most often in one of the university papers were the least frequent in the other.) No explanation was offered, and readers' queries were answered by the statement that "the purchaser of the display wished for anonymity."

When the mysterious series of ads ended, the investigators sent questionnaires to the university communities, asking for impressions of whether each of the words "means something 'good' or something 'bad.'" The results were spectacular: the words that were presented more frequently were rated much more favorably than the words that had been shown only once or twice. The finding has been confirmed in many experiments, using Chinese ideographs, faces, and randomly shaped polygons.

The mere exposure effect does not depend on the conscious experience of familiarity. In fact, the effect does not depend on consciousness at all: it occurs even when the repeated words or pictures are shown so quickly that the observers never become aware of having seen them. They still end up liking the words or pictures that were presented more frequently. As should be clear by now, System 1 can respond to impressions of events of which System 2 is unaware. Indeed, the mere exposure effect is actually stronger for stimuli that the individual never consciously sees.

Zajonc argued that the effect of repetition on liking is a profoundly important biological fact, and that it extends to all animals. To survive in a frequently dangerous world, an organism should react cautiously to a novel stimulus, with withdrawal and fear. Survival prospects are poor for an animal that is not suspicious of novelty. However, it is also adaptive for the initial caution to fade if the stimulus is actually safe. The mere exposure effect occurs, Zajonc claimed, because the repeated exposure of a stimulus is followed by nothing bad. Such a stimulus will eventually become a safety signal, and safety is good. Obviously, this argument is not restricted to humans. To make that point, one of Zajonc's associates exposed two sets of fertile chicken eggs to different tones. After they hatched, the chicks consistently emitted fewer distress calls when exposed to the tone they had heard while inhabiting the shell.

Zajonc offered an eloquent summary of his program of research:

> The consequences of repeated exposures benefit the organism in its relations to the immediate animate and inanimate environment. They allow the organism to distinguish objects and habitats that are safe from those that are not, and they are the most primitive basis of social attachments. Therefore, they form the basis for social organization and cohesion—the basic sources of psychological and social stability.

The link between positive emotion and cognitive ease in System 1 has a long evolutionary history.

EASE, MOOD, AND INTUITION

Around 1960, a young psychologist named Sarnoff Mednick thought he had identified the essence of creativity. His idea was as simple as it was powerful: creativity is associative memory that works exceptionally well. He made up a test, called the Remote Association Test (RAT), which is still often used in studies of creativity.

For an easy example, consider the following three words:

cottage   Swiss   cake

Can you think of a word that is associated with all three? You probably worked out that the answer is *cheese*. Now try this:

dive   light   rocket

This problem is much harder, but it has a unique correct answer, which every speaker of English recognizes, although less than 20% of a sample of students found it within 15 seconds. The answer is *sky*. Of course, not every triad of words has a solution. For example, the words *dream, ball, book* do not have a shared association that everyone will recognize as valid.

Several teams of German psychologists that have studied the RAT in recent years have come up with remarkable discoveries about cognitive ease. One of the teams raised two questions: Can people feel that a triad of words has a solution before they know what the solution is? How does mood influence performance in this task? To find out, they first made some of their subjects happy and others sad, by asking them to think for several minutes about happy or sad episodes in their lives. Then they presented these subjects with a series of triads, half of them linked (such as *dive, light, rocket*) and half unlinked (such as *dream, ball, book*), and instructed them to press one of two keys very quickly to indicate their guess about whether the triad was linked. The time allowed for this guess, 2 seconds, was much too short for the actual solution to come to anyone's mind.

The first surprise is that people's guesses are much more accurate than they would be by chance. I find this astonishing. A sense of cognitive ease is apparently generated by a very faint signal from the associative machine, which "knows" that the three words are coherent (share an association) long before the association is retrieved. The role of cognitive ease in the judgment was confirmed experimentally by another German team: manipulations that increase cognitive ease (priming, a clear font, pre-exposing words) all increase the tendency to see the words as linked.

Another remarkable discovery is the powerful effect of mood on this intuitive performance. The experimenters computed an "intuition index" to measure accuracy. They found that putting the participants in a good

mood before the test by having them think happy thoughts more than doubled accuracy. An even more striking result is that unhappy subjects were
completely incapable of performing the intuitive task accurately; their
guesses were no better than random. Mood evidently affects the operation
of System 1: when we are uncomfortable and unhappy, we lose touch with
our intuition.

These findings add to the growing evidence that good mood, intuition,
creativity, gullibility, and increased reliance on System 1 form a cluster. At
the other pole, sadness, vigilance, suspicion, an analytic approach, and
increased effort also go together. A happy mood loosens the control of
System 2 over performance: when in a good mood, people become more
intuitive and more creative but also less vigilant and more prone to logical
errors. Here again, as in the mere exposure effect, the connection makes
biological sense. A good mood is a signal that things are generally going
well, the environment is safe, and it is all right to let one's guard down. A
bad mood indicates that things are not going very well, there may be a
threat, and vigilance is required. Cognitive ease is both a cause and a consequence of a pleasant feeling.

The Remote Association Test has more to tell us about the link between
cognitive ease and positive affect. Briefly consider two triads of words:

sleep mail switch
salt deep foam

You could not know it, of course, but measurements of electrical activity in
the muscles of your face would probably have shown a slight smile when
you read the second triad, which is coherent (*sea* is the solution). This smiling reaction to coherence appears in subjects who are told nothing about
common associates; they are merely shown a vertically arranged triad of
words and instructed to press the space bar after they have read it. The impression of cognitive ease that comes with the presentation of a coherent
triad appears to be mildly pleasurable in itself.

The evidence that we have about good feelings, cognitive ease, and the
intuition of coherence is, as scientists say, correlational but not necessarily
causal. Cognitive ease and smiling occur together, but do the good feelings
actually lead to intuitions of coherence? Yes, they do. The proof comes from
a clever experimental approach that has become increasingly popular. Some
participants were given a cover story that provided an alternative interpretation for their good feeling: they were told about music played in their

earphones that "previous research showed that this music influences the emotional reactions of individuals." This story completely eliminates the intuition of coherence. The finding shows that the brief emotional response that follows the presentation of a triad of words (pleasant if the triad is coherent, unpleasant otherwise) is actually the basis of judgments of coherence. There is nothing here that System 1 cannot do. Emotional changes are now expected, and because they are unsurprising they are not linked causally to the words.

This is as good as psychological research ever gets, in its combination of experimental techniques and in its results, which are both robust and extremely surprising. We have learned a great deal about the automatic workings of System 1 in the last decades. Much of what we now know would have sounded like science fiction thirty or forty years ago. It was beyond imagining that bad font influences judgments of truth and improves cognitive performance, or that an emotional response to the cognitive ease of a triad of words mediates impressions of coherence. Psychology has come a long way.

SPEAKING OF COGNITIVE EASE

"Let's not dismiss their business plan just because the font makes it hard to read."

"We must be inclined to believe it because it has been repeated so often, but let's think it through again."

"Familiarity breeds liking. This is a mere exposure effect."

"I'm in a very good mood today, and my System 2 is weaker than usual. I should be extra careful."

6

NORMS, SURPRISES, AND CAUSES

The central characteristics and functions of System 1 and System 2 have now been introduced, with a more detailed treatment of System 1. Freely mixing metaphors, we have in our head a remarkably powerful computer, not fast by conventional hardware standards, but able to represent the structure of our world by various types of associative links in a vast network of various types of ideas. The spreading of activation in the associative machine is automatic, but we (System 2) have some ability to control the search of memory, and also to program it so that the detection of an event in the environment can attract attention. We next go into more detail of the wonders and limitation of what System 1 can do.

ASSESSING NORMALITY

The main function of System 1 is to maintain and update a model of your personal world, which represents what is normal in it. The model is constructed by associations that link ideas of circumstances, events, actions, and outcomes that co-occur with some regularity, either at the same time or within a relatively short interval. As these links are formed and strengthened, the pattern of associated ideas comes to represent the structure of events in your life, and it determines your interpretation of the present as well as your expectations of the future.

A capacity for surprise is an essential aspect of our mental life, and surprise itself is the most sensitive indication of how we understand our world and what we expect from it. There are two main varieties of surprise. Some expectations are active and conscious—you know you are waiting for a particular event to happen. When the hour is near, you may be expecting the sound of the door as your child returns from school; when the door opens you expect the sound of a familiar voice. You will be surprised if an actively expected event does not occur. But there is a much larger category of events that you expect passively; you don't wait for them, but you are not surprised when they happen. These are events that are normal in a situation, though not sufficiently probable to be actively expected.

A single incident may make a recurrence less surprising. Some years ago, my wife and I were vacationing in a small island resort on the Great Barrier Reef. There are only forty guest rooms on the island. When we came to dinner, we were surprised to meet an acquaintance, a psychologist named Jon. We greeted each other warmly and commented on the coincidence. Jon left the resort the next day. About two weeks later, we were in a theater in London. A latecomer sat next to me after the lights went down. When the lights came up for the intermission, I saw that my neighbor was Jon. My wife and I commented later that we were simultaneously conscious of two facts: first, this was a more remarkable coincidence than the first meeting; second, we were distinctly *less* surprised to meet Jon on the second occasion than we had been on the first. Evidently, the first meeting had somehow changed the idea of Jon in our minds. He was now "the psychologist who shows up when we travel abroad." We (System 2) knew this was a ludicrous idea, but our System 1 had made it seem almost normal to meet Jon in strange places. We would have experienced much more surprise if we had met any acquaintance other than Jon in the next seat of a London theater. By any measure of probability, meeting Jon in the theater was much less likely than meeting any one of our hundreds of acquaintances— yet meeting Jon seemed more normal.

Under some conditions, passive expectations quickly turn active, as we found in another coincidence. On a Sunday evening some years ago, we were driving from New York City to Princeton, as we had been doing every week for a long time. We saw an unusual sight: a car on fire by the side of the road. When we reached the same stretch of road the following Sunday, another car was burning there. Here again, we found that we were distinctly less surprised on the second occasion than we had been on the first. This was now "the place where cars catch fire." Because the circumstances of the recurrence were the same, the second incident was sufficient to create an active expectation: for months, perhaps for years, after the event we were reminded of burning cars whenever we reached that spot of the road and were quite prepared to see another one (but of course we never did).

The psychologist Dale Miller and I wrote an essay in which we attempted to explain how events come to be perceived as normal or abnormal. I will use an example from our description of "norm theory," although my interpretation of it has changed slightly:

> An observer, casually watching the patrons at a neighboring table in a fashionable restaurant, notices that the first guest to taste the soup winces, as if in pain. The normality of a multitude of events will be altered by this incident. It is now unsurprising for the guest who first tasted the soup to startle violently when touched by a waiter; it is also unsurprising for another guest to stifle a cry when tasting soup from the same tureen. These events and many others appear more normal than they would have otherwise, but not necessarily because they confirm advance expectations. Rather, they appear normal because they recruit the original episode, retrieve it from memory, and are interpreted in conjunction with it.

Imagine yourself the observer at the restaurant. You were surprised by the first guest's unusual reaction to the soup, and surprised again by the startled response to the waiter's touch. However, the second abnormal event will retrieve the first from memory, and both make sense together. The two events fit into a pattern, in which the guest is an exceptionally tense person. On the other hand, if the next thing that happens after the first guest's grimace is that another customer rejects the soup, these two surprises will be linked and the soup will surely be blamed.

"How many animals of each kind did Moses take into the ark?" The number of people who detect what is wrong with this question is so small that it has been dubbed the "Moses illusion." Moses took no animals into the ark; Noah did. Like the incident of the wincing soup eater, the Moses illusion is readily explained by norm theory. The idea of animals going into the ark sets up a biblical context, and Moses is not abnormal in that context. You did not positively expect him, but the mention of his name is not surprising. It also helps that Moses and Noah have the same vowel sound and number of syllables. As with the triads that produce cognitive ease, you unconsciously detect associative coherence between "Moses" and "ark" and so quickly accept the question. Replace Moses with George W. Bush in this sentence and you will have a poor political joke but no illusion.

When something cement does not fit into the current context of activated ideas, the system detects an abnormality, as you just experienced. You had no particular idea of what was coming after *something*, but you knew when the word *cement* came that it was abnormal in that sentence. Studies of brain responses have shown that violations of normality are detected with astonishing speed and subtlety. In a recent experiment, people heard the sentence "Earth revolves around the trouble every year." A distinctive pattern was detected in brain activity, starting within two-tenths of a second of the onset of the odd word. Even more remarkable, the same brain response occurs at the same speed when a male voice says, "I believe I am pregnant because I feel sick every morning," or when an upper-class voice says, "I have a large tattoo on my back." A vast amount of world knowledge must instantly be brought to bear for the incongruity to be recognized: the voice must be identified as upper-class English and confronted with the generalization that large tattoos are uncommon in the upper class.

We are able to communicate with each other because our knowledge of the world and our use of words are largely shared. When I mention a table, without specifying further, you understand that I mean a normal table. You know with certainty that its surface is approximately level and that it has far fewer than 25 legs. We have *norms* for a vast number of categories, and these norms provide the background for the immediate detection of anomalies such as pregnant men and tattooed aristocrats.

To appreciate the role of norms in communication, consider the sentence "The large mouse climbed over the trunk of the very small elephant." I can count on your having norms for the size of mice and elephants that are not too far from mine. The norms specify a typical or average size for these animals, and they also contain information about the range or variability within the category. It is very unlikely that either of us got the image in our mind's eye of a mouse larger than an elephant striding over an elephant smaller than a mouse. Instead, we each separately but jointly visualized a mouse smaller than a shoe clambering over an elephant larger than a sofa. System 1, which understands language, has access to norms of categories, which specify the range of plausible values as well as the most typical cases.

SEEING CAUSES AND INTENTIONS

"Fred's parents arrived late. The caterers were expected soon. Fred was angry." You know why Fred was angry, and it is not because the caterers were expected soon. In your network of associations, anger and lack of punctuality are linked as an effect and its possible cause, but there is no such link between anger and the idea of expecting caterers. A coherent story was instantly constructed as you read; you immediately knew the cause of Fred's anger. Finding such causal connections is part of understanding a story and is an automatic operation of System 1. System 2, your conscious self, was offered the causal interpretation and accepted it.

A story in Nassim Taleb's *The Black Swan* illustrates this automatic search for causality. He reports that bond prices initially rose on the day of Saddam Hussein's capture in his hiding place in Iraq. Investors were apparently seeking safer assets that morning, and the Bloomberg News service flashed this headline: U.S. TREASURIES RISE; HUSSEIN CAPTURE MAY NOT CURB TERRORISM. Half an hour later, bond prices fell back and the revised headline read: U.S. TREASURIES FALL; HUSSEIN CAPTURE BOOSTS ALLURE OF RISKY ASSETS. Obviously, Hussein's capture was the major event of the day, and because of the way the automatic search for causes shapes our thinking, that event was destined to be the explanation of whatever happened in the market on that day. The two headlines look superficially like explanations of what happened in the market, but a statement that can explain two contradictory outcomes explains nothing at all. In fact, all the headlines do is satisfy our need for coherence: a large event is supposed to have consequences, and consequences need causes to explain them. We have limited information about what happened on a day, and System 1 is adept at finding a coherent causal story that links the fragments of knowledge at its disposal.

Read this sentence:

> After spending a day exploring beautiful sights in the crowded streets of New York, Jane discovered that her wallet was missing.

When people who had read this brief story (along with many others) were given a surprise recall test, the word *pickpocket* was more strongly associated with the story than the word *sights*, even though the latter was actually in the sentence while the former was not. The rules of associative coherence tell us what happened. The event of a lost wallet could evoke many different causes: the wallet slipped out of a pocket, was left in the restaurant, etc. However, when the ideas of lost wallet, New York, and crowds are juxtaposed, they jointly evoke the explanation that a pickpocket caused the loss. In the story of the startling soup, the outcome—whether another customer wincing at the taste of the soup or the first person's extreme reaction to the waiter's touch—brings about an associatively coherent interpretation of the initial surprise, completing a plausible story.

The aristocratic Belgian psychologist Albert Michotte published a book in 1945 (translated into English in 1963) that overturned centuries of thinking about causality, going back at least to Hume's examination of the association of ideas. The commonly accepted wisdom was that we infer physical causality from repeated observations of correlations among events. We have had myriad experiences in which we saw one object in motion touching another object, which immediately starts to move, often (but not always) in the same direction. This is what happens when a billiard ball hits another, and it is also what happens when you knock over a vase by brushing against it. Michotte had a different idea: he argued that we *see* causality, just as directly as we see color. To make his point, he created episodes in which a black square drawn on paper is seen in motion; it comes into contact with another square, which immediately begins to move. The observers know that there is no real physical contact, but they nevertheless have a powerful "illusion of causality." If the second object starts moving instantly, they describe it as having been "launched" by the first. Experiments have shown that six-month-old infants see the sequence of events as a cause-effect scenario, and they indicate surprise when the sequence is altered. We are evidently ready from birth to have *impressions* of causality, which do not depend on reasoning about patterns of causation. They are products of System 1.

In 1944, at about the same time as Michotte published his demonstrations of physical causality, the psychologists Fritz Heider and Mary-Ann Simmel used a method similar to Michotte's to demonstrate the perception of *intentional* causality. They made a film, which lasts all of one minute and forty seconds, in which you see a large triangle, a small triangle, and a circle moving around a shape that looks like a schematic view of a house with an open door. Viewers see an aggressive large triangle bullying a smaller triangle, a terrified circle, the circle and the small triangle joining forces to defeat the bully; they also observe much interaction around a door and then an explosive finale. The perception of intention and emotion is irresistible; only people afflicted by autism do not experience it. All this is entirely in your mind, of course. Your mind is ready and even eager to identify agents, assign them personality traits and specific intentions, and view their actions as expressing individual propensities. Here again, the evidence is that we are born prepared to make intentional attributions: infants under one year old identify bullies and victims, and expect a pursuer to follow the most direct path in attempting to catch whatever it is chasing.

The experience of freely willed action is quite separate from physical causality. Although it is your hand that picks up the salt, you do not think of the event in terms of a chain of physical causation. You experience it as caused by a decision that a disembodied *you* made, because you wanted to add salt to your food. Many people find it natural to describe their soul as the source and the cause of their actions. The psychologist Paul Bloom, writing in *The Atlantic* in 2005, presented the provocative claim that our inborn readiness to separate physical and intentional causality explains the near universality of religious beliefs. He observes that "we perceive the world of objects as essentially separate from the world of minds, making it possible for us to envision soulless bodies and bodiless souls." The two modes of causation that we are set to perceive make it natural for us to accept the two central beliefs of many religions: an immaterial divinity is the ultimate cause of the physical world, and immortal souls temporarily control our bodies while we live and leave them behind as we die. In Bloom's view, the two concepts of causality were shaped separately by evolutionary forces, building the origins of religion into the structure of System 1.

The prominence of causal intuitions is a recurrent theme in this book because people are prone to apply causal thinking inappropriately, to situations that require statistical reasoning. Statistical thinking derives conclusions about individual cases from properties of categories and ensembles. Unfortunately, System 1 does not have the capability for this mode of reasoning; System 2 can learn to think statistically, but few people receive the necessary training.

The psychology of causality was the basis of my decision to describe psychological processes by metaphors of agency, with little concern for consistency. I sometimes refer to System 1 as an agent with certain traits and preferences, and sometimes as an associative machine that represents reality by a complex pattern of links. The system and the machine are fictions; my reason for using them is that they fit the way we think about causes. Heider's triangles and circles are not really agents—it is just very easy and natural to think of them that way. It is a matter of mental economy. I assume that you (like me) find it easier to think about the mind if we describe what happens in terms of traits and intentions (the two systems) and sometimes in terms of mechanical regularities (the associative machine). I do not intend to convince you that the systems are real, any more than Heider intended you to believe that the large triangle is really a bully.

SPEAKING OF NORMS AND CAUSES

"When the second applicant also turned out to be an old friend of mine, I wasn't quite as surprised. Very little repetition is needed for a new experience to feel normal!"

"When we survey the reaction to these products, let's make sure we don't focus exclusively on the average. We should consider the entire range of normal reactions."

"She can't accept that she was just unlucky; she needs a causal story. She will end up thinking that someone intentionally sabotaged her work."

7

A MACHINE FOR JUMPING TO CONCLUSIONS

The great comedian Danny Kaye had a line that has stayed with me since my adolescence. Speaking of a woman he dislikes, he says, "Her favorite position is beside herself, and her favorite sport is jumping to conclusions." The line came up, I remember, in the initial conversation with Amos Tversky about the rationality of statistical intuitions, and now I believe it offers an apt description of how System 1 functions. Jumping to conclusions is efficient if the conclusions are likely to be correct and the costs of an occasional mistake acceptable, and if the jump saves much time and effort. Jumping to conclusions is risky when the situation is unfamiliar, the stakes are high, and there is no time to collect more information. These are the circumstances in which intuitive errors are probable, which may be prevented by a deliberate intervention of System 2.

NEGLECT OF AMBIGUITY AND SUPPRESSION OF DOUBT

Figure 6

What do the three exhibits in figure 6 have in common? The answer is that all are ambiguous. You almost certainly read the display on the left as A B C and the one on the right as 12 13 14, but the middle items in both displays are identical. You could just as well have read them as A 13 C or 12 B 14, but you did not. Why not? The same shape is read as a letter in a context of letters and as a number in a context of numbers. The entire context helps determine the interpretation of each element. The shape is ambiguous, but you jump to a conclusion about its identity and do not become aware of the ambiguity that was resolved.

As for Ann, you probably imagined a woman with money on her mind, walking toward a building with tellers and secure vaults. But this plausible interpretation is not the only possible one; the sentence is ambiguous. If an earlier sentence had been "They were floating gently down the river," you would have imagined an altogether different scene. When you have just been thinking of a river, the word *bank* is not associated with money. In the absence of an explicit context, System 1 generated a likely context on its own. We know that it is System 1 because you were not aware of the choice or of the possibility of another interpretation. Unless you have been canoeing recently, you probably spend more time going to banks than floating on rivers, and you resolved the ambiguity accordingly. When uncertain, System 1 bets on an answer, and the bets are guided by experience. The rules of the betting are intelligent: recent events and the current context have the most weight in determining an interpretation. When no recent event comes to mind, more distant memories govern. Among your earliest and most memorable experiences was singing your ABCs; you did not sing your A13Cs.

The most important aspect of both examples is that a definite choice was made, but you did not know it. Only one interpretation came to mind, and you were never aware of the ambiguity. System 1 does not keep track of alternatives that it rejects, or even of the fact that there were alternatives. Conscious doubt is not in the repertoire of System 1; it requires maintaining incompatible interpretations in mind at the same time, which demands mental effort. Uncertainty and doubt are the domain of System 2.

A BIAS TO BELIEVE AND CONFIRM

The psychologist Daniel Gilbert, widely known as the author of *Stumbling to Happiness*, once wrote an essay, titled "How Mental Systems Believe," in which he developed a theory of believing and unbelieving that he traced to the seventeenth-century philosopher Baruch Spinoza. Gilbert proposed that understanding a statement must begin with an attempt to believe it: you must first know what the idea would mean if it were true. Only then can you decide whether or not to *unbelieve* it. The initial attempt to believe is an automatic operation of System 1, which involves the construction of the best possible interpretation of the situation. Even a nonsensical statement, Gilbert argues, will evoke initial belief. Try his example: "whitefish eat candy." You probably were aware of vague impressions of fish and candy as an automatic process of associative memory searched for links between the two ideas that would make sense of the nonsense.

Gilbert sees unbelieving as an operation of System 2, and he reported an elegant experiment to make his point. The participants saw nonsensical assertions, such as "a dinca is a flame," followed after a few seconds by a single word, "true" or "false." They were later tested for their memory of which sentences had been labeled "true." In one condition of the experiment subjects were required to hold digits in memory during the task. The disruption of System 2 had a selective effect: it made it difficult for people to "unbelieve" false sentences. In a later test of memory, the depleted participants ended up thinking that many of the false sentences were true. The moral is significant: when System 2 is otherwise engaged, we will believe almost anything. System 1 is gullible and biased to believe, System 2 is in charge of doubting and unbelieving, but System 2 is sometimes busy, and often lazy. Indeed, there is evidence that people are more likely to be influenced by empty persuasive messages, such as commercials, when they are tired and depleted.

The operations of associative memory contribute to a general *confirmation bias*. When asked, "Is Sam friendly?" different instances of Sam's behavior will come to mind than would if you had been asked "Is Sam unfriendly?" A deliberate search for confirming evidence, known as *positive test strategy*, is also how System 2 tests a hypothesis. Contrary to the rules of philosophers of science, who advise testing hypotheses by trying to refute them, people (and scientists, quite often) seek data that are likely to be compatible with the beliefs they currently hold. The confirmatory bias of System 1 favors uncritical acceptance of suggestions and exaggeration of the likelihood of extreme and improbable events. If you are asked about the probability of a tsunami hitting California within the next thirty years, the images that come to your mind are likely to be images of tsunamis, in the manner Gilbert proposed for nonsense statements such as "whitefish eat candy." You will be prone to overestimate the probability of a disaster.

EXAGGERATED EMOTIONAL COHERENCE (HALO EFFECT)

If you like the president's politics, you probably like his voice and his appearance as well. The tendency to like (or dislike) everything about a person—including things you have not observed—is known as the halo effect. The term has been in use in psychology for a century, but it has not come into wide use in everyday language. This is a pity, because the halo effect is a good name for a common bias that plays a large role in shaping our view of people and situations. It is one of the ways the representation of the world that System 1 generates is simpler and more coherent than the real thing.

You meet a woman named Joan at a party and find her personable and easy to talk to. Now her name comes up as someone who could be asked to contribute to a charity. What do you know about Joan's generosity? The correct answer is that you know virtually nothing, because there is little reason to believe that people who are agreeable in social situations are also generous contributors to charities. But you like Joan and you will retrieve the feeling of liking her when you think of her. You also like generosity and generous people. By association, you are now predisposed to believe that Joan is generous. And now that you believe she is generous, you probably like Joan even better than you did earlier, because you have added generosity to her pleasant attributes.

Real evidence of generosity is missing in the story of Joan, and the gap is filled by a guess that fits one's emotional response to her. In other situations, evidence accumulates gradually and the interpretation is shaped by the emotion attached to the first impression. In an enduring classic of psychology, Solomon Asch presented descriptions of two people and asked for comments on their personality. What do you think of Alan and Ben?

Alan: intelligent—industrious—impulsive—critical—stubborn—envious
Ben: envious—stubborn—critical—impulsive—industrious—intelligent

If you are like most of us, you viewed Alan much more favorably than Ben. The initial traits in the list change the very meaning of the traits that appear later. The stubbornness of an intelligent person is seen as likely to be justified and may actually evoke respect, but intelligence in an envious and stubborn person makes him more dangerous. The halo effect is also an example of suppressed ambiguity: like the word *bank*, the adjective *stubborn* is ambiguous and will be interpreted in a way that makes it coherent with the context.

There have been many variations on this research theme. Participants in one study first considered the first three adjectives that describe Alan; then they considered the last three, which belonged, they were told, to another person. When they had imagined the two individuals, the participants were asked if it was plausible for all six adjectives to describe the same person, and most of them thought it was impossible!

The sequence in which we observe characteristics of a person is often determined by chance. Sequence matters, however, because the halo effect increases the weight of first impressions, sometimes to the point that subsequent information is mostly wasted. Early in my career as a professor, I graded students' essay exams in the conventional way. I would pick up one test booklet at a time and read all that student's essays in immediate succession, grading them as I went. I would then compute the total and go on to the next student. I eventually noticed that my evaluations of the essays in each booklet were strikingly homogeneous. I began to suspect that my grading exhibited a halo effect, and that the first question I scored had a disproportionate effect on the overall grade. The mechanism was simple: if I had given a high score to the first essay, I gave the student the benefit of the doubt whenever I encountered a vague or ambiguous statement later on. This seemed reasonable. Surely a student who had done so well on the first essay would not make a foolish mistake in the second one! But there was a serious problem with my way of doing things. If a student had written two essays, one strong and one weak, I would end up with different final grades depending on which essay I read first. I had told the students that the two essays had equal weight, but that was not true: the first one had a much greater impact on the final grade than the second. This was unacceptable.

I adopted a new procedure. Instead of reading the booklets in sequence, I read and scored all the students' answers to the first question, then went on to the next one. I made sure to write all the scores on the inside back page of the booklet so that I would not be biased (even unconsciously) when I read the second essay. Soon after switching to the new method, I made a disconcerting observation: my confidence in my grading was now much lower than it had been. The reason was that I frequently experienced a discomfort that was new to me. When I was disappointed with a student's second essay and went to the back page of the booklet to enter a poor grade, I occasionally discovered that I had given a top grade to the same student's first essay. I also noticed that I was tempted to reduce the discrepancy by changing the grade that I had not yet written down, and found it hard to follow the simple rule of never yielding to that temptation. My grades for the essays of a single student often varied over a considerable range. The lack of coherence left me uncertain and frustrated.

I was now less happy with and less confident in my grades than I had been earlier, but I recognized that this was a good sign, an indication that the new procedure was superior. The consistency I had enjoyed earlier was spurious; it produced a feeling of cognitive ease, and my System 2 was happy to lazily accept the final grade. By allowing myself to be strongly influenced by the first question in evaluating subsequent ones, I spared myself the dissonance of finding the same student doing very well on some questions and badly on others. The uncomfortable inconsistency that was revealed when I switched to the new procedure was real: it reflected both the inadequacy of any single question as a measure of what the student knew and the unreliability of my own grading.

The procedure I adopted to tame the halo effect conforms to a general principle: decorrelate error! To understand how this principle works, imagine that a large number of observers are shown glass jars containing pennies and are challenged to estimate the number of pennies in each jar. As James Surowiecki explained in his best-selling *The Wisdom of Crowds*, this is the kind of task in which individuals do very poorly, but pools of individual judgments do remarkably well. Some individuals greatly overestimate the true number, others underestimate it, but when many judgments are averaged, the average tends to be quite accurate. The mechanism is straightforward: all individuals look at the same jar, and all their judgments have a common basis. On the other hand, the errors that individuals make are independent of the errors made by others, and (in the absence of a systematic bias) they tend to average to zero. However, the magic of error reduction works well only when the observations are independent and their errors uncorrelated. If the observers share a bias, the aggregation of judgments will not reduce it. Allowing the observers to influence each other effectively reduces the size of the sample, and with it the precision of the group estimate.

To derive the most useful information from multiple sources of evidence, you should always try to make these sources independent of each other. This rule is part of good police procedure. When there are multiple witnesses to an event, they are not allowed to discuss it before giving their testimony. The goal is not only to prevent collusion by hostile witnesses, it is also to prevent unbiased witnesses from influencing each other. Witnesses who exchange their experiences will tend to make similar errors in their testimony, reducing the total value of the information they provide. Eliminating redundancy from your sources of information is always a good idea.

The principle of independent judgments (and decorrelated errors) has immediate applications for the conduct of meetings, an activity in which executives in organizations spend a great deal of their working days. A simple rule can help: before an issue is discussed, all members of the committee should be asked to write a very brief summary of their position. This procedure makes good use of the value of the diversity of knowledge and opinion in the group. The standard practice of open discussion gives too much weight to the opinions of those who speak early and assertively, causing others to line up behind them.

WHAT YOU SEE IS ALL THERE IS (WYSIATI)

One of my favorite memories of the early years of working with Amos is a comedy routine he enjoyed performing. In a perfect impersonation of one of the professors with whom he had studied philosophy as an undergraduate, Amos would growl in Hebrew marked by a thick German accent: "You must never forget the *Primat of the Is*." What exactly his teacher had meant by that phrase never became clear to me (or to Amos, I believe), but Amos's jokes always made a point. He was reminded of the old phrase (and eventually I was too) whenever we encountered the remarkable asymmetry between the ways our mind treats information that is currently available and information we do not have.

An essential design feature of the associative machine is that it represents only activated ideas. Information that is not retrieved (even unconsciously) from memory might as well not exist. System 1 excels at constructing the best possible story that incorporates ideas currently activated, but it does not (cannot) allow for information it does not have.

The measure of success for System 1 is the coherence of the story it manages to create. The amount and quality of the data on which the story is based are largely irrelevant. When information is scarce, which is a common occurrence, System 1 operates as a machine for jumping to conclusions. Consider the following: "Will Mindik be a good leader? She is intelligent and strong . . ." An answer quickly came to your mind, and it was yes. You picked the best answer based on the very limited information available, but you jumped the gun. What if the next two adjectives were *corrupt* and *cruel*?

Take note of what you did *not* do as you briefly thought of Mindik as a leader. You did not start by asking, "What would I need to know before I formed an opinion about the quality of someone's leadership?" System 1 got to work on its own from the first adjective: intelligent is good, intelligent and strong is very good. This is the best story that can be constructed from two adjectives, and System 1 delivered it with great cognitive ease. The story will be revised if new information comes in (such as Mindik is corrupt), but there is no waiting and no subjective discomfort. And there also remains a bias favoring the first impression.

The combination of a coherence-seeking System 1 with a lazy System 2 implies that System 2 will endorse many intuitive beliefs, which closely reflect the impressions generated by System 1. Of course, System 2 also is capable of a more systematic and careful approach to evidence, and of following a list of boxes that must be checked before making a decision—think of buying a home, when you deliberately seek information that you don't have. However, System 1 is expected to influence even the more careful decisions. Its input never ceases.

Jumping to conclusions on the basis of limited evidence is so important to an understanding of intuitive thinking, and comes up so often in this book, that I will use a cumbersome abbreviation for it: WYSIATI, which stands for what you see is all there is. System 1 is radically insensitive to both the quality and the quantity of the information that gives rise to impressions and intuitions.

Amos, with two of his graduate students at Stanford, reported a study that bears directly on WYSIATI, by observing the reaction of people who are given one-sided evidence and know it. The participants were exposed to legal scenarios such as the following:

> On September 3, plaintiff David Thornton, a forty-three-year-old union field representative, was present in Thrifty Drug Store #168, performing a routine union visit. Within ten minutes of his arrival, a store manager confronted him and told him he could no longer speak with the union employees on the floor of the store. Instead, he would have to see them in a back room while they were on break. Such a request is allowed by the union contract with Thrifty Drug but had never before been enforced. When Mr. Thornton objected, he was told that he had the choice of conforming to these requirements, leaving the store, or being arrested. At this point, Mr. Thornton indicated to the manager that he had always been allowed to speak to employees on the floor for as much as ten minutes, as long as no

business was disrupted, and that he would rather be arrested than change the procedure of his routine visit. The manager then called the police and had Mr. Thornton handcuffed in the store for trespassing. After he was booked and put into a holding cell for a brief time, all charges were dropped. Mr. Thornton is suing Thrifty Drug for false arrest.

In addition to this background material, which all participants read, different ent groups were exposed to presentations by the lawyers for the two parties. Naturally, the lawyer for the union organizer described the arrest as an intimidation attempt, while the lawyer for the store argued that having the talk in the store was disruptive and that the manager was acting properly. Some participants, like a jury, heard both sides. The lawyers added no useful information that you could not infer from the background story.

The participants were fully aware of the setup, and those who heard only one side could easily have generated the argument for the other side. Nevertheless, the presentation of one-sided evidence had a very pronounced effect on judgments. Furthermore, participants who saw one-sided evidence were more confident of their judgments than those who saw both sides. This is just what you would expect if the confidence that people experience is determined by the coherence of the story they manage to construct from available information. It is the consistency of the information that matters for a good story, not its completeness. Indeed, you will often find that knowing little makes it easier to fit everything you know into a coherent pattern.

WYSIATI facilitates the achievement of coherence and of the cognitive ease that causes us to accept a statement as true. It explains why we can think fast, and how we are able to make sense of partial information in a complex world. Much of the time, the coherent story we put together is close enough to reality to support reasonable action. However, I will also invoke WYSIATI to help explain a long and diverse list of biases of judgment and choice, including the following among many others:

- Overconfidence: As the WYSIATI rule implies, neither the quantity nor the quality of the evidence counts for much in subjective confidence. The confidence that individuals have in their beliefs depends mostly on the quality of the story they can tell about what they see, even if they see little. We often fail to allow for the possibility that evidence that should be critical to our judgment is missing—what we see is all there is. Furthermore, our associative system tends to settle on a coherent pattern of activation and suppresses doubt and ambiguity.

- Framing effects: Different ways of presenting the same information often evoke different emotions. The statement that "the odds of survival one month after surgery are 90%" is more reassuring than the equivalent statement that "mortality within one month of surgery is 10%." Similarly, cold cuts described as "90% fat-free" are more attractive than when they are described as "10% fat." The equivalence of the alternative formulations is transparent, but an individual normally sees only one formulation, and what she sees is all there is.

- Base-rate neglect: Recall Steve, the meek and tidy soul who is often believed to be a librarian. The personality description is salient and vivid, and although you surely know that there are more male farmers than male librarians, that statistical fact almost certainly did not come to your mind when you first considered the question. What you saw was all there was.

SPEAKING OF JUMPING TO CONCLUSIONS

"She knows nothing about this person's management skills. All she is going by is the halo effect from a good presentation."

"Let's decorrelate errors by obtaining separate judgments on the issue before any discussion. We will get more information from independent assessments."

"They made that big decision on the basis of a good report from one consultant. WYSIATI—what you see is all there is. They did not seem to realize how little information they had."

"They didn't want more information that might spoil their story. WYSIATI."

8

HOW JUDGMENTS HAPPEN

There is no limit to the number of questions you can answer, whether they are questions someone else asks or questions you ask yourself. Nor is there a limit to the number of attributes you can evaluate. You are capable of counting the number of capital letters on this page, comparing the height of the windows of your house to the one across the street, and assessing the political prospects of your senator on a scale from excellent to disastrous. The questions are addressed to System 2, which will direct attention and search memory to find the answers. System 2 receives questions or generates them: in either case it directs attention and searches memory to find the answers. System 1 operates differently. It continuously monitors what is going on outside and inside the mind, and continuously generates assessments of various aspects of the situation without specific intention and with little or no effort. These *basic assessments* play an important role in intuitive judgment, because they are easily substituted for more difficult questions—this is the essential idea of the heuristics and biases approach. Two other features of System 1 also support the substitution of one judgment for another. One is the ability to translate values across dimensions, which you do in answering a question that most people find easy: "If Sam were as tall as he is intelligent, how tall would he be?" Finally, there is the mental shotgun. An intention of System 2 to answer a specific question or evaluate a particular attribute of the situation automatically triggers other computations, including basic assessments.

BASIC ASSESSMENTS

System 1 has been shaped by evolution to provide a continuous assessment of the main problems that an organism must solve to survive: How are things going? Is there a threat or a major opportunity? Is everything normal? Should I approach or avoid? The questions are perhaps less urgent for a human in a city environment than for a gazelle on the savannah, but we have inherited the neural mechanisms that evolved to provide ongoing assessments of threat level, and they have not been turned off. Situations are constantly evaluated as good or bad, requiring escape or permitting approach. Good mood and cognitive ease are the human equivalents of assessments of safety and familiarity.

For a specific example of a *basic assessment*, consider the ability to discriminate friend from foe at a glance. This contributes to one's chances of survival in a dangerous world, and such a specialized capability has indeed evolved. Alex Todorov, my colleague at Princeton, has explored the biological roots of the rapid judgments of how safe it is to interact with a stranger. He showed that we are endowed with an ability to evaluate, in a single glance at a stranger's face, two potentially crucial facts about that person: how dominant (and therefore potentially threatening) he is, and how trustworthy he is, whether his intentions are more likely to be friendly or hostile. The shape of the face provides the cues for assessing dominance: a "strong" square chin is one such cue. Facial expression (smile or frown) provides the cues for assessing the stranger's intentions. The combination of a square chin with a turned-down mouth may spell trouble. The accuracy of face reading is far from perfect: round chins are not a reliable indicator of meekness, and smiles can (to some extent) be faked. Still, even an imperfect ability to assess strangers confers a survival advantage.

This ancient mechanism is put to a novel use in the modern world: it has some influence on how people vote. Todorov showed his students pictures of men's faces, sometimes for as little as one-tenth of a second, and asked them to rate the faces on various attributes, including likability and competence. Observers agreed quite well on those ratings. The faces that Todorov showed were not a random set: they were the campaign portraits of politicians competing for elective office. Todorov then compared the results of the electoral races to the ratings of competence that Princeton students had made, based on brief exposure to photographs and without any political context. In about 70% of the races for senator, congressman, and governor, the election winner was the candidate whose face had earned a higher rating of competence. This striking result was quickly confirmed in national elections in Finland, in zoning board elections in England, and in various electoral contests in Australia, Germany, and Mexico. Surprisingly (at least to me), ratings of competence were far more predictive of voting outcomes in Todorov's study than ratings of likability.

Todorov has found that people judge competence by combining the two dimensions of strength and trustworthiness. The faces that exude competence combine a strong chin with a slight confident-appearing smile. There is no evidence that these facial features actually predict how well politicians will perform in office. But studies of the brain's response to winning and losing candidates show that we are biologically predisposed to reject candidates who lack the attributes we value—in this research, losers evoked stronger indications of (negative) emotional response. This is an example of what I will call a *judgment heuristic* in the following chapters. Voters are attempting to form an impression of how good a candidate will be in office, and they fall back on a simpler assessment that is made quickly and automatically and is available when System 2 must make its decision.

Political scientists followed up on Todorov's initial research by identifying a category of voters for whom the automatic preferences of System 1 are particularly likely to play a large role. They found what they were looking for among politically uninformed voters who watch a great deal of television. As expected, the effect of facial competence on voting is about three times larger for information-poor and TV-prone voters than for others who are better informed and watch less television. Evidently, the relative importance of System 1 in determining voting choices is not the same for all people. We will encounter other examples of such individual differences.

System 1 understands language, of course, and understanding depends on the basic assessments that are routinely carried out as part of the perception of events and the comprehension of messages. These assessments include computations of similarity and representativeness, attributions of causality, and evaluations of the availability of associations and exemplars. They are performed even in the absence of a specific task set, although the results are used to meet task demands as they arise.

The list of basic assessments is long, but not every possible attribute is assessed. For an example, look briefly at figure 7 on page 92.

A glance provides an immediate impression of many features of the display. You know that the two towers are equally tall and that they are more similar to each other than the tower on the left is to the array of blocks in

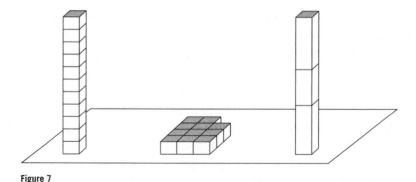

Figure 7

the middle. However, you do not immediately know that the number of blocks in the left-hand tower is the same as the number of blocks arrayed on the floor, and you have no impression of the height of the tower that you could build from them. To confirm that the numbers are the same, you would need to count the two sets of blocks and compare the results, an activity that only System 2 can carry out.

SETS AND PROTOTYPES

For another example, consider the question: What is the average length of the lines in figure 8?

Figure 8

This question is easy and System 1 answers it without prompting. Experiments have shown that a fraction of a second is sufficient for people to register the average length of an array of lines with considerable precision. Furthermore, the accuracy of these judgments is not impaired when the observer is cognitively busy with a memory task. They do not necessarily know how to describe the average in inches or centimeters, but they will be very accurate in adjusting the length of another line to match the average. System 2 is not needed to form an impression of the norm of length for an array. System 1 does it, automatically and effortlessly, just as it registers the color of the lines and the fact that they are not parallel. We also can form an immediate impression of the number of objects in an array—precisely if there are four or fewer objects, crudely if there are more.

Now to another question: What is the total length of the lines in figure 8? This is a different experience, because System 1 has no suggestions to offer. The only way you can answer this question is by activating System 2, which will laboriously estimate the average, estimate or count the lines, and multiply average length by the number of lines.

The failure of System 1 to compute the total length of a set of lines at a glance may look obvious to you; you never thought you could do it. It is in fact an instance of an important limitation of that system. Because System 1 represents categories by a prototype or a set of typical exemplars, it deals well with averages but poorly with sums. The size of the category, the number of instances it contains, tends to be ignored in judgments of what I will call *sum-like variables*.

Participants in one of the numerous experiments that were prompted by the litigation following the disastrous *Exxon Valdez* oil spill were asked their willingness to pay for nets to cover oil ponds in which migratory birds often drown. Different groups of participants stated their willingness to pay to save 2,000, 20,000, or 200,000 birds. If saving birds is an economic good it should be a sum-like variable: saving 200,000 birds should be worth much more than saving 2,000 birds. In fact, the average contributions of the three groups were $80, $78, and $88 respectively. The number of birds made very little difference. What the participants reacted to, in all three groups, was a prototype—the awful image of a helpless bird drowning, its feathers soaked in thick oil. The almost complete neglect of quantity in such emotional contexts has been confirmed many times.

INTENSITY MATCHING

Questions about your happiness, the president's popularity, the proper punishment of financial evildoers, and the future prospects of a politician share an important characteristic: they all refer to an underlying dimension of intensity or amount, which permits the use of the word *more*: more happy, more popular, more severe, or more powerful (for a politician). For example, a candidate's political future can range from the low of "She will be defeated in the primary" to a high of "She will someday be president of the United States."

Here we encounter a new aptitude of System 1. An underlying scale of intensity allows *matching* across diverse dimensions. If crimes were colors, murder would be a deeper shade of red than theft. If crimes were expressed as music, mass murder would be played fortissimo while accumulating unpaid parking tickets would be a faint pianissimo. And of course you have similar feelings about the intensity of punishments. In classic experiments, people adjusted the loudness of a sound to the severity of crimes; other people adjusted loudness to the severity of legal punishments. If you heard two notes, one for the crime and one for the punishment, you would feel a sense of injustice if one tone was much louder than the other.

Consider an example that we will encounter again later:

Julie read fluently when she was four years old.

Now match Julie's reading prowess as a child to the following intensity scales:

How tall is a man who is as tall as Julie was precocious?

What do you think of 6 feet? Obviously too little. What about 7 feet? Probably too much. You are looking for a height that is as remarkable as the achievement of reading at age four. Fairly remarkable, but not extraordinary. Reading at fifteen months would be extraordinary, perhaps like a man who is 7'8".

What level of income in your profession matches Julie's reading achievement?
Which crime is as severe as Julie was precocious?
Which graduating GPA in an Ivy League college matches Julie's reading?

Not very hard, was it? Furthermore, you can be assured that your matches will be quite close to those of other people in your cultural milieu. We will see that when people are asked to predict Julie's GPA from the information about the age at which she learned to read, they answer by translating from one scale to another and pick the matching GPA. And we will also see why this mode of prediction by matching is statistically wrong—although it is perfectly natural to System 1, and for most people except statisticians it is also acceptable to System 2.

THE MENTAL SHOTGUN

System 1 carries out many computations at any one time. Some of these are routine assessments that go on continuously. Whenever your eyes are open, your brain computes a three-dimensional representation of what is in your field of vision, complete with the shape of objects, their position in space, and their identity. No intention is needed to trigger this operation or the continuous monitoring for violated expectations. In contrast to these routine assessments, other computations are undertaken only when needed: you do not maintain a continuous evaluation of how happy or wealthy you are, and even if you are a political addict you do not continuously assess the president's prospects. The occasional judgments are voluntary. They occur only when you intend them to do so.

You do not automatically count the number of syllables of every word you read, but you can do it if you so choose. However, the control over intended computations is far from precise: we often compute much more than we want or need. I call this excess computation the *mental shotgun*. It is impossible to aim at a single point with a shotgun because it shoots pellets that scatter, and it seems almost equally difficult for System 1 not to do more than System 2 charges it to do. Two experiments that I read long ago suggested this image.

Participants in one experiment listened to pairs of words, with the instruction to press a key as quickly as possible whenever they detected that the words rhymed. The words rhyme in both these pairs:

VOTE—NOTE

VOTE—GOAT

The difference is obvious to you because you see the two pairs. VOTE and GOAT rhyme, but they are spelled differently. The participants only heard the words, but they were also influenced by the spelling. They were distinctly slower to recognize the words as rhyming if their spelling was discrepant. Although the instructions required only a comparison of sounds, the participants also compared their spelling, and the mismatch on the irrelevant dimension slowed them down. An intention to answer one question evoked another, which was not only superfluous but actually detrimental to the main task.

In another study, people listened to a series of sentences, with the instruction to press one key as quickly as possible to indicate if the sentence was literally true, and another key if the sentence was not literally true. What are the correct responses for the following sentences?

> Some roads are snakes.
> Some jobs are snakes.
> Some jobs are jails.

All three sentences are literally false. However, you probably noticed that the second sentence is more obviously false than the other two—the reaction times collected in the experiment confirmed a substantial difference. The reason for the difference is that the two difficult sentences can be metaphorically true. Here again, the intention to perform one computation evoked another. And here again, the correct answer prevailed in the conflict, but the conflict with the irrelevant answer disrupted performance. In the next chapter we will see that the combination of a mental shotgun with intensity matching explains why we have intuitive judgments about many things that we know little about.

SPEAKING OF JUDGMENT

"Evaluating people as attractive or not is a basic assessment. You do that automatically whether or not you want to, and it influences you."

"There are circuits in the brain that evaluate dominance from the shape of the face. He looks the part for a leadership role."

"The punishment won't feel just unless its intensity matches the crime. Just like you can match the loudness of a sound to the brightness of a light."

"This was a clear instance of a mental shotgun. He was asked whether he thought the company was financially sound, but he couldn't forget that he likes their product."

9

ANSWERING AN EASIER QUESTION

A remarkable aspect of your mental life is that you are rarely stumped. True, you occasionally face a question such as 17 × 24 = ? to which no answer comes immediately to mind, but these dumbfounded moments are rare. The normal state of your mind is that you have intuitive feelings and opinions about almost everything that comes your way. You like or dislike people long before you know much about them; you trust or distrust strangers without knowing why; you feel that an enterprise is bound to succeed without analyzing it. Whether you state them or not, you often have answers to questions that you do not completely understand, relying on evidence that you can neither explain nor defend.

SUBSTITUTING QUESTIONS

I propose a simple account of how we generate intuitive opinions on complex matters. If a satisfactory answer to a hard question is not found quickly, System 1 will find a related question that is easier and will answer it. I call the operation of answering one question in place of another *substitution*. I also adopt the following terms:

The target question is the assessment you intend to produce.
The heuristic question is the simpler question that you answer instead.

The technical definition of *heuristic* is a simple procedure that helps find adequate, though often imperfect, answers to difficult questions. The word comes from the same root as *eureka*.

The idea of substitution came up early in my work with Amos, and it was the core of what became the heuristics and biases approach. We asked ourselves how people manage to make judgments of probability without knowing precisely what probability is. We concluded that people must somehow simplify that impossible task, and we set out to find how they do it. Our answer was that when called upon to judge probability, people actually judge something else and believe they have judged probability. System 1 often makes this move when faced with difficult target questions, if the answer to a related and easier heuristic question comes readily to mind.

Substituting one question for another can be a good strategy for solving difficult problems, and George Pólya included substitution in his classic *How to Solve It*: "If you can't solve a problem, then there is an easier problem you can solve: find it." Pólya's heuristics are strategic procedures that are deliberately implemented by System 2. But the heuristics that I discuss in this chapter are not chosen; they are a consequence of the mental shotgun, the imprecise control we have over targeting our responses to questions.

Consider the questions listed in the left-hand column of table 1. These are difficult questions, and before you can produce a reasoned answer to any of them you must deal with other difficult issues. What is the meaning of happiness? What are the likely political developments in the next six months? What are the standard sentences for other financial crimes? How strong is the competition that the candidate faces? What other environmental or other causes should be considered? Dealing with these questions seriously is completely impractical. But you are not limited to perfectly reasoned answers to questions. There is a heuristic alternative to careful reasoning, which sometimes works fairly well and sometimes leads to serious errors.

Target Question	*Heuristic Question*
How much would you contribute to save an endangered species?	How much emotion do I feel when I think of dying dolphins?
How happy are you with your life these days?	What is my mood right now?
How popular will the president be six months from now?	How popular is the president right now?

| How should financial advisers who prey on the elderly be punished? | How much anger do I feel when I think of financial predators? |
| This woman is running for the primary. How far will she go in politics? | Does this woman look like a political winner? |

Table 1

The mental shotgun makes it easy to generate quick answers to difficult questions without imposing much hard work on your lazy System 2. The right-hand counterpart of each of the left-hand questions is very likely to be evoked and very easily answered. Your feelings about dolphins and financial crooks, your current mood, your impressions of the political skill of the primary candidate, or the current standing of the president will readily come to mind. The heuristic questions provide an off-the-shelf answer to each of the difficult target questions.

Something is still missing from this story: the answers need to be fitted to the original questions. For example, my feelings about dying dolphins must be expressed in dollars. Another capability of System 1, intensity matching, is available to solve that problem. Recall that both feelings and contribution dollars are intensity scales. I can feel more or less strongly about dolphins and there is a contribution that matches the intensity of my feelings. The dollar amount that will come to my mind is the matching amount. Similar intensity matches are possible for all the questions. For example, the political skills of a candidate can range from pathetic to extraordinarily impressive, and the scale of political success can range from the low of "She will be defeated in the primary" to a high of "She will someday be president of the United States."

The automatic processes of the mental shotgun and intensity matching often make available one or more answers to easy questions that could be mapped onto the target question. On some occasions, substitution will occur and a heuristic answer will be endorsed by System 2. Of course, System 2 has the opportunity to reject this intuitive answer, or to modify it by incorporating other information. However, a lazy System 2 often follows the path of least effort and endorses a heuristic answer without much scrutiny of whether it is truly appropriate. You will not be stumped, you will not have to work very hard, and you may not even notice that you did not answer the question you were asked. Furthermore, you may not realize that the target question was difficult, because an intuitive answer to it came readily to mind.

THE 3-D HEURISTIC

Have a look at the picture of the three men and answer the question that follows.

Figure 9

> As printed on the page, is the figure on the right larger than the figure on the left?

The obvious answer comes quickly to mind: the figure on the right is larger. If you take a ruler to the two figures, however, you will discover that in fact the figures are exactly the same size. Your impression of their relative size is dominated by a powerful illusion, which neatly illustrates the process of substitution.

The corridor in which the figures are seen is drawn in perspective and appears to go into the depth plane. Your perceptual system automatically interprets the picture as a three-dimensional scene, not as an image printed on a flat paper surface. In the 3-D interpretation, the person on the right is both much farther away and much larger than the person on the left. For most of us, this impression of 3-D size is overwhelming. Only visual artists and experienced photographers have developed the skill of seeing the drawing as an object on the page. For the rest of us, substitution occurs: the dominant impression of 3-D size dictates the judgment of 2-D size. The illusion is due to a 3-D heuristic.

What happens here is a true illusion, not a misunderstanding of the question. You knew that the question was about the size of the figures in the picture, as printed on the page. If you had been asked to estimate the size of the figures, we know from experiments that your answer would have been in inches, not feet. You were not confused about the question, but you were influenced by the answer to a question that you were not asked: "How tall are the three people?"

The essential step in the heuristic—the substitution of three-dimensional for two-dimensional size—occurred automatically. The picture contains cues that suggest a 3-D interpretation. These cues are irrelevant to the task at hand—the judgment of size of the figure on the page—and you should have ignored them, but you could not. The bias associated with the heuristic is that objects that appear to be more distant also appear to be larger on the page. As this example illustrates, a judgment that is based on substitution will inevitably be biased in predictable ways. In this case, it happens so deep in the perceptual system that you simply cannot help it.

THE MOOD HEURISTIC FOR HAPPINESS

A survey of German students is one of the best examples of substitution. The survey that the young participants completed included the following two questions:

How happy are you these days?
How many dates did you have last month?

The experimenters were interested in the correlation between the two answers. Would the students who reported many dates say that they were happier than those with fewer dates? Surprisingly, no: the correlation between the answers was about zero. Evidently, dating was not what came first to the students' minds when they were asked to assess their happiness. Another group of students saw the same two questions, but in reverse order:

How many dates did you have last month?
How happy are you these days?

The results this time were completely different. In this sequence, the correlation between the number of dates and reported happiness was about as high as correlations between psychological measures can get. What happened?

The explanation is straightforward, and it is a good example of substitution. Dating was apparently not the center of these students' life (in the first survey, happiness and dating were uncorrelated), but when they were asked to think about their romantic life, they certainly had an emotional reaction. The students who had many dates were reminded of a happy aspect of their life, while those who had none were reminded of loneliness and rejection. The emotion aroused by the dating question was still on everyone's mind when the query about general happiness came up.

The psychology of what happened is precisely analogous to the psychology of the size illusion in figure 9. "Happiness these days" is not a natural or an easy assessment. A good answer requires a fair amount of thinking. However, the students who had just been asked about their dating did not need to think hard because they already had in their mind an answer to a related question: how happy they were with their love life. They substituted the question to which they had a ready-made answer for the question they were asked.

Here again, as we did for the illusion, we can ask: Are the students confused? Do they really think that the two questions—the one they were asked and the one they answer—are synonymous? Of course not. The students do not temporarily lose their ability to distinguish romantic life from life as a whole. If asked about the two concepts, they would say they are different. But they were not asked whether the concepts are different. They were asked how happy they were, and System 1 has a ready answer.

Dating is not unique. The same pattern is found if a question about the students' relations with their parents or about their finances immediately precedes the question about general happiness. In both cases, satisfaction in the particular domain dominates happiness reports. Any emotionally significant question that alters a person's mood will have the same effect. WYSIATI. The present state of mind looms very large when people evaluate their happiness.

THE AFFECT HEURISTIC

The dominance of conclusions over arguments is most pronounced where emotions are involved. The psychologist Paul Slovic has proposed an *affect heuristic* in which people let their likes and dislikes determine their beliefs about the world. Your political preference determines the arguments that you find compelling. If you like the current health policy, you believe its benefits are substantial and its costs more manageable than the costs of alternatives. If you are a hawk in your attitude toward other nations, you probably think they are relatively weak and likely to submit to your country's will. If you are a dove, you probably think they are strong and will not be easily coerced. Your emotional attitude to such things as irradiated food, red meat, nuclear power, tattoos, or motorcycles drives your beliefs about their benefits and their risks. If you dislike any of these things, you probably believe that its risks are high and its benefits negligible.

The primacy of conclusions does not mean that your mind is completely closed and that your opinions are wholly immune to information and sensible reasoning. Your beliefs, and even your emotional attitude, may change (at least a little) when you learn that the risk of an activity you disliked is smaller than you thought. However, the information about lower risks will also change your view of the benefits (for the better) even if nothing was said about benefits in the information you received.

We see here a new side of the "personality" of System 2. Until now I have mostly described it as a more or less acquiescent monitor, which allows considerable leeway to System 1. I have also presented System 2 as active in deliberate memory search, complex computations, comparisons, planning, and choice. In the bat-and-ball problem and in many other examples of the interplay between the two systems, it appeared that System 2 is ultimately in charge, with the ability to resist the suggestions of System 1, slow things down, and impose logical analysis. Self-criticism is one of the functions of System 2. In the context of attitudes, however, System 2 is more of an apologist for the emotions of System 1 than a critic of those emotions—an endorser rather than an enforcer. Its search for information and arguments is mostly constrained to information that is consistent with existing beliefs, not with an intention to examine them. An active, coherence-seeking System 1 suggests solutions to an undemanding System 2.

SPEAKING OF SUBSTITUTION AND HEURISTICS

"Do we still remember the question we are trying to answer? Or have we substituted an easier one?"

"The question we face is whether this candidate can succeed. The question we seem to answer is whether she interviews well. Let's not substitute."

"He likes the project, so he thinks its costs are low and its benefits are high. Nice example of the affect heuristic."

"We are using last year's performance as a heuristic to predict the value of the firm several years from now. Is this heuristic good enough? What other information do we need?"

The table below contains a list of features and activities that have been attributed to System 1. Each of the active sentences replaces a statement, technically more accurate but harder to understand, to the effect that a mental event occurs automatically and fast. My hope is that the list of traits will help you develop an intuitive sense of the "personality" of the fictitious System 1. As happens with other characters you know, you will have hunches about what System 1 would do under different circumstances, and most of your hunches will be correct.

Characteristics of System 1

- generates impressions, feelings, and inclinations; when endorsed by System 2 these become beliefs, attitudes, and intentions
- operates automatically and quickly, with little or no effort, and no sense of voluntary control
- can be programmed by System 2 to mobilize attention when a particular pattern is detected (search)
- executes skilled responses and generates skilled intuitions, after adequate training
- creates a coherent pattern of activated ideas in associative memory
- links a sense of cognitive ease to illusions of truth, pleasant feelings, and reduced vigilance
- distinguishes the surprising from the normal
- infers and invents causes and intentions
- neglects ambiguity and suppresses doubt
- is biased to believe and confirm
- exaggerates emotional consistency (halo effect)
- focuses on existing evidence and ignores absent evidence (WYSIATI)
- generates a limited set of basic assessments
- represents sets by norms and prototypes, does not integrate
- matches intensities across scales (e.g., size to loudness)
- computes more than intended (mental shotgun)
- sometimes substitutes an easier question for a difficult one (heuristics)
- is more sensitive to changes than to states (prospect theory)*
- overweights low probabilities*
- shows diminishing sensitivity to quantity (psychophysics)*
- responds more strongly to losses than to gains (loss aversion)*
- frames decision problems narrowly, in isolation from one another*

*Feature introduced in detail in part 4.

PART 2

HEURISTICS AND

BIASES

10

THE LAW OF SMALL NUMBERS

A study of the incidence of kidney cancer in the 3,141 counties of the United States reveals a remarkable pattern. The counties in which the incidence of kidney cancer is lowest are mostly rural, sparsely populated, and located in traditionally Republican states in the Midwest, the South, and the West. What do you make of this?

Your mind has been very active in the last few seconds, and it was mainly a System 2 operation. You deliberately searched memory and formulated hypotheses. Some effort was involved; your pupils dilated, and your heart rate increased measurably. But System 1 was not idle: the operation of System 2 depended on the facts and suggestions retrieved from associative memory. You probably rejected the idea that Republican politics provide protection against kidney cancer. Very likely, you ended up focusing on the fact that the counties with low incidence of cancer are mostly rural. The witty statisticians Howard Wainer and Harris Zwerling, from whom I learned this example, commented, "It is both easy and tempting to infer that their low cancer rates are directly due to the clean living of the rural lifestyle—no air pollution, no water pollution, access to fresh food without additives." This makes perfect sense.

Now consider the counties in which the incidence of kidney cancer is highest. These ailing counties tend to be mostly rural, sparsely populated, and located in traditionally Republican states in the Midwest, the South, and the West. Tongue-in-cheek, Wainer and Zwerling comment: "It is easy to infer that their high cancer rates might be directly due to the poverty of the rural lifestyle—no access to good medical care, a high-fat diet, and too much alcohol, too much tobacco." Something is wrong, of course. The rural lifestyle cannot explain both very high and very low incidence of kidney cancer.

The key factor is not that the counties were rural or predominantly Republican. It is that rural counties have small populations. And the main lesson to be learned is not about epidemiology, it is about the difficult relationship between our mind and statistics. System 1 is highly adept in one form of thinking—it automatically and effortlessly identifies causal connections between events, sometimes even when the connection is spurious. When told about the high-incidence counties, you immediately assumed that these counties are different from other counties for a reason, that there must be a cause that explains this difference. As we shall see, however, System 1 is inept when faced with "merely statistical" facts, which change the probability of outcomes but do not cause them to happen.

A random event, by definition, does not lend itself to explanation, but collections of random events do behave in a highly regular fashion. Imagine a large urn filled with marbles. Half the marbles are red, half are white. Next, imagine a very patient person (or a robot) who blindly draws 4 marbles from the urn, records the number of red balls in the sample, throws the balls back into the urn, and then does it all again, many times. If you summarize the results, you will find that the outcome "2 red, 2 white" occurs (almost exactly) 6 times as often as the outcome "4 red" or "4 white." This relationship is a mathematical fact. You can predict the outcome of repeated sampling from an urn just as confidently as you can predict what will happen if you hit an egg with a hammer. You cannot predict every detail of how the shell will shatter, but you can be sure of the general idea. There is a difference: the satisfying sense of causation that you experience when thinking of a hammer hitting an egg is altogether absent when you think about sampling.

A related statistical fact is relevant to the cancer example. From the same urn, two very patient marble counters take turns. Jack draws 4 marbles on each trial, Jill draws 7. They both record each time they observe a homogeneous sample—all white or all red. If they go on long enough, Jack will observe such extreme outcomes more often than Jill—by a factor of 8 (the expected percentages are 12.5% and 1.56%). Again, no hammer, no causation, but a mathematical fact: samples of 4 marbles yield extreme results more often than samples of 7 marbles do.

Now imagine the population of the United States as marbles in a giant urn. Some marbles are marked KC, for kidney cancer. You draw samples of marbles and populate each county in turn. Rural samples are smaller than other samples. Just as in the game of Jack and Jill, extreme outcomes (very high and/or very low cancer rates) are most likely to be found in sparsely populated counties. This is all there is to the story.

We started from a fact that calls for a cause: the incidence of kidney cancer varies widely across counties and the differences are systematic. The explanation I offered is statistical: extreme outcomes (both high and low) are more likely to be found in small than in large samples. This explanation is not causal. The small population of a county neither causes nor prevents cancer; it merely allows the incidence of cancer to be much higher (or much lower) than it is in the larger population. The deeper truth is that there is nothing to explain. The incidence of cancer is not truly lower or higher than normal in a county with a small population, it just appears to be so in a particular year because of an accident of sampling. If we repeat the analysis next year, we will observe the same general pattern of extreme results in the small samples, but the counties where cancer was common last year will not necessarily have a high incidence this year. If this is the case, the differences between dense and rural counties do not really count as facts: they are what scientists call artifacts, observations that are produced entirely by some aspect of the method of research—in this case, by differences in sample size.

The story I have told may have surprised you, but it was not a revelation. You have long known that the results of large samples deserve more trust than smaller samples, and even people who are innocent of statistical knowledge have heard about this law of large numbers. But "knowing" is not a yes-no affair and you may find that the following statements apply to you:

- The feature "sparsely populated" did not immediately stand out as relevant when you read the epidemiological story.
- You were at least mildly surprised by the size of the difference between samples of 4 and samples of 7.
- Even now, you must exert some mental effort to see that the following two statements mean exactly the same thing:
  - Large samples are more precise than small samples.
  - Small samples yield extreme results more often than large samples do.

The first statement has a clear ring of truth, but until the second version makes intuitive sense, you have not truly understood the first.

The bottom line: yes, you did know that the results of large samples are more precise, but you may now realize that you did not know it very well.

You are not alone. The first study that Amos and I did together showed that even sophisticated researchers have poor intuitions and a wobbly understanding of sampling effects.

THE LAW OF SMALL NUMBERS

My collaboration with Amos in the early 1970s began with a discussion of the claim that people who have had no training in statistics are good "intuitive statisticians." He told my seminar and me of researchers at the University of Michigan who were generally optimistic about intuitive statistics. I had strong feelings about that claim, which I took personally: I had recently discovered that I was not a good intuitive statistician, and I did not believe that I was worse than others.

For a research psychologist, sampling variation is not a curiosity; it is a nuisance and a costly obstacle, which turns the undertaking of every research project into a gamble. Suppose that you wish to confirm the hypothesis that the vocabulary of the average six-year-old girl is larger than the vocabulary of an average boy of the same age. The hypothesis is true in the population; the average vocabulary of girls is indeed larger. Girls and boys vary a great deal, however, and by the luck of the draw you could select a sample in which the difference is inconclusive, or even one in which boys actually score higher. If you are the researcher, this outcome is costly to you because you have wasted time and effort, and failed to confirm a hypothesis that was in fact true. Using a sufficiently large sample is the only way to reduce the risk. Researchers who pick too small a sample leave themselves at the mercy of sampling luck.

The risk of error can be estimated for any given sample size by a fairly simple procedure. Traditionally, however, psychologists do not use calculations to decide on a sample size. They use their judgment, which is commonly flawed. An article I had read shortly before the debate with Amos demonstrated the mistake that researchers made (they still do) by a dramatic observation. The author pointed out that psychologists commonly chose samples so small that they exposed themselves to a 50% risk of failing to confirm their true hypotheses! No researcher in his right mind would accept such a risk. A plausible explanation was that psychologists' decisions about sample size reflected prevalent intuitive misconceptions of the extent of sampling variation.

The article shocked me, because it explained some troubles I had had in my own research. Like most research psychologists, I had routinely chosen samples that were too small and had often obtained results that made no sense. Now I knew why: the odd results were actually artifacts of my research method. My mistake was particularly embarrassing because I taught statistics and knew how to compute the sample size that would reduce the risk of failure to an acceptable level. But I had never chosen a sample size by computation. Like my colleagues, I had trusted tradition and my intuition in planning my experiments and had never thought seriously about the issue. When Amos visited the seminar, I had already reached the conclusion that my intuitions were deficient, and in the course of the seminar we quickly agreed that the Michigan optimists were wrong.

Amos and I set out to examine whether I was the only fool or a member of a majority of fools, by testing whether researchers selected for mathematical expertise would make similar mistakes. We developed a questionnaire that described realistic research situations, including replications of successful experiments. It asked the researchers to choose sample sizes, to assess the risks of failure to which their decisions exposed them, and to provide advice to hypothetical graduate students planning their research. Amos collected the responses of a group of sophisticated participants (including authors of two statistical textbooks) at a meeting of the Society of Mathematical Psychology. The results were straightforward: I was not the only fool. Every one of the mistakes I had made was shared by a large majority of our respondents. It was evident that even the experts paid insufficient attention to sample size.

Amos and I called our first joint article "Belief in the Law of Small Numbers." We explained, tongue-in-cheek, that "intuitions about random sampling appear to satisfy the law of small numbers, which asserts that the law of large numbers applies to small numbers as well." We also included a strongly worded recommendation that researchers regard their "statistical intuitions with proper suspicion and replace impression formation by computation whenever possible."

A BIAS OF CONFIDENCE OVER DOUBT

In a telephone poll of 300 seniors, 60% support the president.

If you had to summarize the message of this sentence in exactly three words, what would they be? Almost certainly you would choose "elderly support president." These words provide the gist of the story. The omitted details of the poll, that it was done on the phone with a sample of 300, are of no interest in themselves; they provide background information that attracts little attention. Your summary would be the same if the sample size had been different. Of course, a completely absurd number would draw your attention ("a telephone poll of 6 [or 60 million] elderly voters . . ."). Unless you are a professional, however, you may not react very differently to a sample of 150 and to a sample of 3,000. That is the meaning of the statement that "people are not adequately sensitive to sample size."

The message about the poll contains information of two kinds: the story and the source of the story. Naturally, you focus on the story rather than on the reliability of the results. When the reliability is obviously low, however, the message will be discredited. If you are told that "a partisan group has conducted a flawed and biased poll to show that the elderly support the president . . ." you will of course reject the findings of the poll, and they will not become part of what you believe. Instead, the partisan poll and its false results will become a new story about political lies. You can choose to disbelieve a message in such clear-cut cases. But do you discriminate sufficiently between "I read in *The New York Times* . . ." and "I heard at the watercooler . . ."? Can your System 1 distinguish degrees of belief? The principle of WYSIATI suggests that it cannot.

As I described earlier, System 1 is not prone to doubt. It suppresses ambiguity and spontaneously constructs stories that are as coherent as possible. Unless the message is immediately negated, the associations that it evokes will spread as if the message were true. System 2 is capable of doubt, because it can maintain incompatible possibilities at the same time. However, sustaining doubt is harder work than sliding into certainty. The law of small numbers is a manifestation of a general bias that favors certainty over doubt, which will turn up in many guises in following chapters.

The strong bias toward believing that small samples closely resemble the population from which they are drawn is also part of a larger story: we are prone to exaggerate the consistency and coherence of what we see. The exaggerated faith of researchers in what can be learned from a few observations is closely related to the halo effect, the sense we often get that we know and understand a person about whom we actually know very little. System 1 runs ahead of the facts in constructing a rich image on the basis of scraps of evidence. A machine for jumping to conclusions will act as if it believed in the law of small numbers. More generally, it will produce a representation of reality that makes too much sense.

CAUSE AND CHANCE

The associative machinery seeks causes. The difficulty we have with statistical regularities is that they call for a different approach. Instead of focusing on how the event at hand came to be, the statistical view relates it to what could have happened instead. Nothing in particular caused it to be what it is—chance selected it from among its alternatives.

Our predilection for causal thinking exposes us to serious mistakes in evaluating the randomness of truly random events. For an example, take the sex of six babies born in sequence at a hospital. The sequence of boys and girls is obviously random; the events are independent of each other, and the number of boys and girls who were born in the hospital in the last few hours has no effect whatsoever on the sex of the next baby. Now consider three possible sequences:

BBBGGG

GGGGGG

BGBBGB

Are the sequences equally likely? The intuitive answer—"of course not!"—is false. Because the events are independent and because the outcomes B and G are (approximately) equally likely, then any possible sequence of six births is as likely as any other. Even now that you know this conclusion is true, it remains counterintuitive, because only the third sequence appears random. As expected, BGBBGB is judged much more likely than the other two sequences. We are pattern seekers, believers in a coherent world, in which regularities (such as a sequence of six girls) appear not by accident but as a result of mechanical causality or of someone's intention. We do not expect to see regularity produced by a random process, and when we detect what appears to be a rule, we quickly reject the idea that the process is truly random. Random processes produce many sequences that convince people that the process is not random after all. You can see why assuming causality could have had evolutionary advantages. It is part of the general vigilance that we have inherited from ancestors. We are automatically on the lookout for the possibility that the environment has changed. Lions may appear on the plain at random times, but it would be safer to notice and respond to an apparent increase in the rate of appearance of prides of lions, even if it is actually due to the fluctuations of a random process.

The widespread misunderstanding of randomness sometimes has significant consequences. In our article on representativeness, Amos and I cited the statistician William Feller, who illustrated the ease with which people see patterns where none exists. During the intensive rocket bombing of London in World War II, it was generally believed that the bombing could not be random because a map of the hits revealed conspicuous gaps. Some suspected that German spies were located in the unharmed areas. A careful statistical analysis revealed that the distribution of hits was typical of a random process—and typical as well in evoking a strong impression that it was not random. "To the untrained eye," Feller remarks, "randomness appears as regularity or tendency to cluster."

I soon had an occasion to apply what I had learned from Feller. The Yom Kippur War broke out in 1973, and my only significant contribution to the war effort was to advise high officers in the Israeli Air Force to stop an investigation. The air war initially went quite badly for Israel, because of the unexpectedly good performance of Egyptian ground-to-air missiles. Losses were high, and they appeared to be unevenly distributed. I was told of two squadrons flying from the same base, one of which had lost four planes while the other had lost none. An inquiry was initiated in the hope of learning what it was that the unfortunate squadron was doing wrong. There was no prior reason to believe that one of the squadrons was more effective than the other, and no operational differences were found, but of course the lives of the pilots differed in many random ways, including, as I recall, how often they went home between missions and something about the conduct of debriefings. My advice was that the command should accept that the different outcomes were due to blind luck, and that the interviewing of the pilots should stop. I reasoned that luck was the most likely answer, that a random search for a nonobvious cause was hopeless, and that in the meantime the pilots in the squadron that had sustained losses did not need the extra burden of being made to feel that they and their dead friends were at fault.

Some years later, Amos and his students Tom Gilovich and Robert Vallone caused a stir with their study of misperceptions of randomness in basketball. The "fact" that players occasionally acquire a hot hand is generally accepted by players, coaches, and fans. The inference is irresistible: a player sinks three or four baskets in a row and you cannot help forming the causal judgment that this player is now hot, with a temporarily increased propensity to score. Players on both teams adapt to this judgment—teammates are more likely to pass to the hot scorer and the defense is more likely to double-team. Analysis of thousands of sequences of shots led to a disappointing conclusion: there is no such thing as a hot hand in professional basketball, either in shooting from the field or scoring from the foul line. Of course, some players are more accurate than others, but the sequence of successes and missed shots satisfies all tests of randomness. The hot hand is entirely in the eye of the beholders, who are consistently too quick to perceive order and causality in randomness. The hot hand is a massive and widespread cognitive illusion.

The public reaction to this research is part of the story. The finding was picked up by the press because of its surprising conclusion, and the general response was disbelief. When the celebrated coach of the Boston Celtics, Red Auerbach, heard of Gilovich and his study, he responded, "Who is this guy? So he makes a study. I couldn't care less." The tendency to see patterns in randomness is overwhelming—certainly more impressive than a guy making a study.

The illusion of pattern affects our lives in many ways off the basketball court. How many good years should you wait before concluding that an investment adviser is unusually skilled? How many successful acquisitions should be needed for a board of directors to believe that the CEO has extraordinary flair for such deals? The simple answer to these questions is that if you follow your intuition, you will more often than not err by misclassifying a random event as systematic. We are far too willing to reject the belief that much of what we see in life is random.

I began this chapter with the example of cancer incidence across the United States. The example appears in a book intended for statistics teachers, but I learned about it from an amusing article by the two statisticians I quoted earlier, Howard Wainer and Harris Zwerling. Their essay focused on a large investment, some $1.7 billion, which the Gates Foundation made to follow up intriguing findings on the characteristics of the most successful schools. Many researchers have sought the secret of successful education by identifying the most successful schools in the hope of discovering what distinguishes them from others. One of the conclusions of this research is that the most successful schools, on average, are small. In a survey of 1,662 schools in Pennsylvania, for instance, 6 of the top 50 were small, which is an overrepresentation by a factor of 4. These data encouraged the Gates Foundation to make a substantial investment in the creation of small schools, sometimes by splitting large schools into smaller units. At least half a dozen other prominent institutions, such as the Annenberg Foundation and the Pew Charitable Trust, joined the effort, as did the U.S. Department of Education's Smaller Learning Communities Program.

This probably makes intuitive sense to you. It is easy to construct a causal story that explains how small schools are able to provide superior education and thus produce high-achieving scholars by giving them more personal attention and encouragement than they could get in larger schools.

Unfortunately, the causal analysis is pointless because the facts are wrong. If the statisticians who reported to the Gates Foundation had asked about the characteristics of the worst schools, they would have found that bad schools also tend to be smaller than average. The truth is that small schools are not better on average; they are simply more variable. If anything, say Wainer and Zwerling, large schools tend to produce better results, especially in higher grades where a variety of curricular options is valuable.

Thanks to recent advances in cognitive psychology, we can now see clearly what Amos and I could only glimpse: the law of small numbers is part of two larger stories about the workings of the mind.

- The exaggerated faith in small samples is only one example of a more general illusion—we pay more attention to the content of messages than to information about their reliability, and as a result end up with a view of the world around us that is simpler and more coherent than the data justify. Jumping to conclusions is a safer sport in the world of our imagination than it is in reality.
- Statistics produce many observations that appear to beg for causal explanations but do not lend themselves to such explanations. Many facts of the world are due to chance, including accidents of sampling. Causal explanations of chance events are inevitably wrong.

SPEAKING OF THE LAW OF SMALL NUMBERS

"Yes, the studio has had three successful films since the new CEO took over. But it is too early to declare he has a hot hand."

"I won't believe that the new trader is a genius before consulting a statistician who could estimate the likelihood of his streak being a chance event."

"The sample of observations is too small to make any inferences. Let's not follow the law of small numbers."

"I plan to keep the results of the experiment secret until we have a sufficiently large sample. Otherwise we will face pressure to reach a conclusion prematurely."

11

ANCHORS

Amos and I once rigged a wheel of fortune. It was marked from 0 to 100, but we had it built so that it would stop only at 10 or 65. We recruited students of the University of Oregon as participants in our experiment. One of us would stand in front of a small group, spin the wheel, and ask them to write down the number on which the wheel stopped, which of course was either 10 or 65. We then asked them two questions:

Is the percentage of African nations among UN members larger or smaller than the number you just wrote?

What is your best guess of the percentage of African nations in the UN?

The spin of a wheel of fortune—even one that is not rigged—cannot possibly yield useful information about anything, and the participants in our experiment should simply have ignored it. But they did not ignore it. The average estimates of those who saw 10 and 65 were 25% and 45%, respectively.

The phenomenon we were studying is so common and so important in the everyday world that you should know its name: it is an *anchoring effect*. It occurs when people consider a particular value for an unknown quantity before estimating that quantity. What happens is one of the most reliable and robust results of experimental psychology: the estimates stay close to the number that people considered—hence the image of an anchor. If you are asked whether Gandhi was more than 114 years old when he died you will end up with a much higher estimate of his age at death than you would if the anchoring question referred to death at 35. If you consider how much you should pay for a house, you will be influenced by the asking price. The same house will appear more valuable if its listing price is high than if it is low, even if you are determined to resist the influence of this number; and so on—the list of anchoring effects is endless. Any number that you are asked to consider as a possible solution to an estimation problem will induce an anchoring effect.

We were not the first to observe the effects of anchors, but our experiment was the first demonstration of its absurdity: people's judgments were influenced by an obviously uninformative number. There was no way to describe the anchoring effect of a wheel of fortune as reasonable. Amos and I published the experiment in our *Science* paper, and it is one of the best known of the findings we reported there.

There was only one trouble: Amos and I did not fully agree on the psychology of the anchoring effect. He supported one interpretation, I liked another, and we never found a way to settle the argument. The problem was finally solved decades later by the efforts of numerous investigators. It is now clear that Amos and I were both right. Two different mechanisms produce anchoring effects—one for each system. There is a form of anchoring that occurs in a deliberate process of adjustment, an operation of System 2. And there is anchoring that occurs by a priming effect, an automatic manifestation of System 1.

ANCHORING AS ADJUSTMENT

Amos liked the idea of an adjust-and-anchor heuristic as a strategy for estimating uncertain quantities: start from an anchoring number, assess whether it is too high or too low, and gradually adjust your estimate by mentally "moving" from the anchor. The adjustment typically ends prematurely, because people stop when they are no longer certain that they should move farther. Decades after our disagreement, and years after Amos's death, convincing evidence of such a process was offered independently by two psychologists who had worked closely with Amos early in their careers: Eldar Shafir and Tom Gilovich together with their own students—Amos's intellectual grandchildren!

To get the idea, take a sheet of paper and draw a 2½-inch line going up, starting at the bottom of the page—without a ruler. Now take another sheet, and start at the top and draw a line going down until it is 2½ inches from the bottom. Compare the lines. There is a good chance that your first estimate of 2½ inches was shorter than the second. The reason is that you do not know exactly what such a line looks like; there is a range of uncertainty. You stop near the bottom of the region of uncertainty when you start from the bottom of the page and near the top of the region when you start from the top. Robyn LeBoeuf and Shafir found many examples of that mechanism in daily experience. Insufficient adjustment neatly explains why you are likely to drive too fast when you come off the highway onto city streets—especially if you are talking with someone as you drive. Insufficient adjustment is also a source of tension between exasperated parents and teenagers who enjoy loud music in their room. LeBoeuf and Shafir note that a "well-intentioned child who turns down exceptionally loud music to meet a parent's demand that it be played at a 'reasonable' volume may fail to adjust sufficiently from a high anchor, and may feel that genuine attempts at compromise are being overlooked." The driver and the child both deliberately adjust down, and both fail to adjust enough.

Now consider these questions:

When did George Washington become president?
What is the boiling temperature of water at the top of Mount Everest?

The first thing that happens when you consider each of these questions is that an anchor comes to your mind, and you know both that it is wrong and the direction of the correct answer. You know immediately that George Washington became president after 1776, and you also know that the boiling temperature of water at the top of Mount Everest is lower than 100°C. You have to adjust in the appropriate direction by finding arguments to move away from the anchor. As in the case of the lines, you are likely to stop when you are no longer sure you should go farther—at the near edge of the region of uncertainty.

Nick Epley and Tom Gilovich found evidence that adjustment is a deliberate attempt to find reasons to move away from the anchor: people who are instructed to shake their head when they hear the anchor, as if they rejected it, move farther from the anchor, and people who nod their head show enhanced anchoring. Epley and Gilovich also confirmed that adjustment is an effortful operation. People adjust less (stay closer to the anchor) when their mental resources are depleted, either because their memory is loaded with digits or because they are slightly drunk. Insufficient adjustment is a failure of a weak or lazy System 2.

So we now know that Amos was right for at least some cases of anchoring, which involve a deliberate System 2 adjustment in a specified direction from an anchor.

ANCHORING AS PRIMING EFFECT

When Amos and I debated anchoring, I agreed that adjustment sometimes occurs, but I was uneasy. Adjustment is a deliberate and conscious activity, but in most cases of anchoring there is no corresponding subjective experience. Consider these two questions:

Was Gandhi more or less than 144 years old when he died?
How old was Gandhi when he died?

Did you produce your estimate by adjusting down from 144? Probably not, but the absurdly high number still affected your estimate. My hunch was that anchoring is a case of suggestion. This is the word we use when someone causes us to see, hear, or feel something by merely bringing it to mind. For example, the question "Do you now feel a slight numbness in your left leg?" always prompts quite a few people to report that their left leg does indeed feel a little strange.

Amos was more conservative than I was about hunches, and he correctly pointed out that appealing to suggestion did not help us understand anchoring, because we did not know how to explain suggestion. I had to agree that he was right, but I never became enthusiastic about the idea of insufficient adjustment as the sole cause of anchoring effects. We conducted many inconclusive experiments in an effort to understand anchoring, but we failed and eventually gave up the idea of writing more about it.

The puzzle that defeated us is now solved, because the concept of suggestion is no longer obscure: suggestion is a priming effect, which selectively evokes compatible evidence. You did not believe for a moment that Gandhi lived for 144 years, but your associative machinery surely generated an impression of a very ancient person. System 1 understands sentences by trying to make them true, and the selective activation of compatible thoughts produces a family of systematic errors that make us gullible and prone to believe too strongly whatever we believe. We can now see why Amos and I did not realize that there were two types of anchoring: the research techniques and theoretical ideas we needed did not yet exist. They were developed, much later, by other people. A process that resembles suggestion is indeed at work in many situations: System 1 tries its best to construct a world in which the anchor is the true number. This is one of the manifestations of associative coherence that I described in the first part of the book.

The German psychologists Thomas Mussweiler and Fritz Strack offered the most compelling demonstrations of the role of associative coherence in anchoring. In one experiment, they asked an anchoring question about temperature: "Is the annual mean temperature in Germany higher or lower than 20°C (68°F)?" or "Is the annual mean temperature in Germany higher or lower than 5°C (40°F)?"

All participants were then briefly shown words that they were asked to identify. The researchers found that 68°F made it easier to recognize summer words (like *sun* and *beach*), and 40°F facilitated winter words (like *frost* and *ski*). The selective activation of compatible memories explains anchoring: the high and the low numbers activate different sets of ideas in memory. The estimates of annual temperature draw on these biased samples of ideas and are therefore biased as well. In another elegant study in the same vein, participants were asked about the average price of German cars. A high anchor selectively primed the names of luxury brands (Mercedes, Audi), whereas the low anchor primed brands associated with mass-market cars (Volkswagen). We saw earlier that any prime will tend to evoke information that is compatible with it. Suggestion and anchoring are both explained by the same automatic operation of System 1. Although I did not know how to prove it at the time, my hunch about the link between anchoring and suggestion turned out to be correct.

THE ANCHORING INDEX

Many psychological phenomena can be demonstrated experimentally, but few can actually be measured. The effect of anchors is an exception. Anchoring can be measured, and it is an impressively large effect. Some visitors at the San Francisco Exploratorium were asked the following two questions:

Is the height of the tallest redwood more or less than 1,200 feet?
What is your best guess about the height of the tallest redwood?

The "high anchor" in this experiment was 1,200 feet. For other participants, the first question referred to a "low anchor" of 180 feet. The difference between the two anchors was 1,020 feet.

As expected, the two groups produced very different mean estimates: 844 and 282 feet. The difference between them was 562 feet. The anchoring index is simply the ratio of the two differences (562/1,020) expressed as a percentage: 55%. The anchoring measure would be 100% for people who slavishly adopt the anchor as an estimate, and zero for people who are able to ignore the anchor altogether. The value of 55% that was observed in this example is typical. Similar values have been observed in numerous other problems.

The anchoring effect is not a laboratory curiosity; it can be just as strong in the real world. In an experiment conducted some years ago, real-estate agents were given an opportunity to assess the value of a house that was actually on the market. They visited the house and studied a comprehensive booklet of information that included an asking price. Half the agents saw an asking price that was substantially higher than the listed price of the house; the other half saw an asking price that was substantially lower. Each agent gave her opinion about a reasonable buying price for the house and the lowest price at which she would agree to sell the house if she owned it. The agents were then asked about the factors that had affected their judgment. Remarkably, the asking price was not one of these factors; the agents took pride in their ability to ignore it. They insisted that the listing price had no effect on their responses, but they were wrong: the anchoring effect was 41%. Indeed, the professionals were almost as susceptible to anchoring effects as business school students with no real-estate experience, whose anchoring index was 48%. The only difference between the two groups was that the students conceded that they were influenced by the anchor, while the professionals denied that influence.

Powerful anchoring effects are found in decisions that people make about money, such as when they choose how much to contribute to a cause. To demonstrate this effect, we told participants in the Exploratorium study about the environmental damage caused by oil tankers in the Pacific Ocean and asked about their willingness to make an annual contribution "to save 50,000 offshore Pacific Coast seabirds from small offshore oil spills, until ways are found to prevent spills or require tanker owners to pay for the operation." This question requires intensity matching: the respondents are asked, in effect, to find the dollar amount of a contribution that matches the intensity of their feelings about the plight of the seabirds. Some of the visitors were first asked an anchoring question, such as, "Would you be willing to pay $5 . . . ," before the point-blank question of how much they would contribute.

When no anchor was mentioned, the visitors at the Exploratorium—generally an environmentally sensitive crowd—said they were willing to pay $64, on average. When the anchoring amount was only $5, contributions averaged $20. When the anchor was a rather extravagant $400, the willingness to pay rose to an average of $143.

The difference between the high-anchor and low-anchor groups was $123. The anchoring effect was above 30%, indicating that increasing the initial request by $100 brought a return of $30 in average willingness to pay.

Similar or even larger anchoring effects have been obtained in numerous studies of estimates and of willingness to pay. For example, French residents of the heavily polluted Marseilles region were asked what increase in living costs they would accept if they could live in a less polluted region. The anchoring effect was over 50% in that study. Anchoring effects are easily observed in online trading, where the same item is often offered at different "buy now" prices. The "estimate" in fine-art auctions is also an anchor that influences the first bid.

There are situations in which anchoring appears reasonable. After all, it is not surprising that people who are asked difficult questions clutch at straws, and the anchor is a plausible straw. If you know next to nothing about the trees of California and are asked whether a redwood can be taller than 1,200 feet, you might infer that this number is not too far from the truth. Somebody who knows the true height thought up that question, so the anchor may be a valuable hint. However, a key finding of anchoring research is that anchors that are obviously random can be just as effective as potentially informative anchors. When we used a wheel of fortune to anchor estimates of the proportion of African nations in the UN, the anchoring index was 44%, well within the range of effects observed with anchors that could plausibly be taken as hints. Anchoring effects of similar size have been observed in experiments in which the last few digits of the respondent's Social Security number was used as the anchor (e.g., for estimating the number of physicians in their city). The conclusion is clear: anchors do not have their effects because people believe they are informative.

The power of random anchors has been demonstrated in some unsettling ways. German judges with an average of more than fifteen years of experience on the bench first read a description of a woman who had been caught shoplifting, then rolled a pair of dice that were loaded so every roll resulted in either a 3 or a 9. As soon as the dice came to a stop, the judges were asked whether they would sentence the woman to a term in prison greater or lesser, in months, than the number showing on the dice. Finally, the judges were instructed to specify the exact prison sentence they would give to the shoplifter. On average, those who had rolled a 9 said they would sentence her to 8 months; those who rolled a 3 said they would sentence her to 5 months; the anchoring effect was 50%.

USES AND ABUSES OF ANCHORS

By now you should be convinced that anchoring effects—sometimes due to priming, sometimes to insufficient adjustment—are everywhere. The psychological mechanisms that produce anchoring make us far more suggestible than most of us would want to be. And of course there are quite a few people who are willing and able to exploit our gullibility.

Anchoring effects explain why, for example, arbitrary rationing is an effective marketing ploy. A few years ago, supermarket shoppers in Sioux City, Iowa, encountered a sales promotion for Campbell's soup at about 10% off the regular price. On some days, a sign on the shelf said LIMIT OF 12 PER PERSON. On other days, the sign said NO LIMIT PER PERSON. Shoppers purchased an average of 7 cans when the limit was in force, twice as many as they bought when the limit was removed. Anchoring is not the sole explanation. Rationing also implies that the goods are flying off the shelves, and shoppers should feel some urgency about stocking up. But we also know that the mention of 12 cans as a possible purchase would produce anchoring even if the number were produced by a roulette wheel.

We see the same strategy at work in the negotiation over the price of a home, when the seller makes the first move by setting the list price. As in many other games, moving first is an advantage in single-issue negotiations—for example, when price is the only issue to be settled between a buyer and a seller. As you may have experienced when negotiating for the first time in a bazaar, the initial anchor has a powerful effect. My advice to students when I taught negotiations was that if you think the other side has made an outrageous proposal, you should not come back with an equally outrageous counteroffer, creating a gap that will be difficult to bridge in further negotiations. Instead you should make a scene, storm out or threaten to do so, and make it clear—to yourself as well as to the other side—that you will not continue the negotiation with that number on the table.

The psychologists Adam Galinsky and Thomas Mussweiler proposed more subtle ways to resist the anchoring effect in negotiations. They instructed negotiators to focus their attention and search their memory for arguments against the anchor. The instruction to activate System 2 was successful. For example, the anchoring effect is reduced or eliminated when the second mover focuses his attention on the minimal offer that the opponent would accept, or on the costs to the opponent of failing to reach an agreement. In general, a strategy of deliberately "thinking the opposite" may be a good defense against anchoring effects, because it negates the biased recruitment of thoughts that produces these effects.

Finally, try your hand at working out the effect of anchoring on a problem of public policy: the size of damages in personal injury cases. These awards are sometimes very large. Businesses that are frequent targets of such lawsuits, such as hospitals and chemical companies, have lobbied to set a cap on the awards. Before you read this chapter you might have thought that capping awards is certainly good for potential defendants, but now you should not be so sure. Consider the effect of capping awards at $1 million. This rule would eliminate all larger awards, but the anchor would also pull up the size of many awards that would otherwise be much smaller. It would almost certainly benefit serious offenders and large firms much more than small ones.

ANCHORING AND THE TWO SYSTEMS

The effects of random anchors have much to tell us about the relationship between System 1 and System 2. Anchoring effects have always been studied in tasks of judgment and choice that are ultimately completed by System 2. However, System 2 works on data that is retrieved from memory, in an automatic and involuntary operation of System 1. System 2 is therefore susceptible to the biasing influence of anchors that make some information easier to retrieve. Furthermore, System 2 has no control over the effect and no knowledge of it. The participants who have been exposed to random or absurd anchors (such as Gandhi's death at age 144) confidently deny that this obviously useless information could have influenced their estimate, and they are wrong.

We saw in the discussion of the law of small numbers that a message, unless it is immediately rejected as a lie, will have the same effect on the associative system regardless of its reliability. The gist of the message is the story, which is based on whatever information is available, even if the quantity of the information is slight and its quality is poor: WYSIATI. When you read a story about the heroic rescue of a wounded mountain climber, its effect on your associative memory is much the same if it is a news report or the synopsis of a film. Anchoring results from this associative activation. Whether the story is true, or believable, matters little, if at all. The powerful effect of random anchors is an extreme case of this phenomenon, because a random anchor obviously provides no information at all.

Earlier I discussed the bewildering variety of priming effects, in which your thoughts and behavior may be influenced by stimuli to which you pay no attention at all, and even by stimuli of which you are completely unaware. The main moral of priming research is that our thoughts and our behavior are influenced, much more than we know or want, by the environment of the moment. Many people find the priming results unbelievable, because they do not correspond to subjective experience. Many others find the results upsetting, because they threaten the subjective sense of agency and autonomy. If the content of a screen saver on an irrelevant computer can affect your willingness to help strangers without your being aware of it, how free are you? Anchoring effects are threatening in a similar way. You are always aware of the anchor and even pay attention to it, but you do not know how it guides and constrains your thinking, because you cannot imagine how you would have thought if the anchor had been different (or absent). However, you should assume that any number that is on the table has had an anchoring effect on you, and if the stakes are high you should mobilize yourself (your System 2) to combat the effect.

SPEAKING OF ANCHORS

"The firm we want to acquire sent us their business plan, with the revenue they expect. We shouldn't let that number influence our thinking. Set it aside."

"Plans are best-case scenarios. Let's avoid anchoring on plans when we forecast actual outcomes. Thinking about ways the plan could go wrong is one way to do it."

"Our aim in the negotiation is to get them anchored on this number."

"Let's make it clear that if that is their proposal, the negotiations are over. We do not want to start there."

"The defendant's lawyers put in a frivolous reference in which they mentioned a ridiculously low amount of damages, and they got the judge anchored on it!"

12

THE SCIENCE OF AVAILABILITY

Amos and I had our most productive year in 1971–72, which we spent in Eugene, Oregon. We were the guests of the Oregon Research Institute, which housed several future stars of all the fields in which we worked—judgment, decision making, and intuitive prediction. Our main host was Paul Slovic, who had been Amos's classmate at Ann Arbor and remained a lifelong friend. Paul was on his way to becoming the leading psychologist among scholars of risk, a position he has held for decades, collecting many honors along the way. Paul and his wife, Roz, introduced us to life in Eugene, and soon we were doing what people in Eugene do—jogging, barbecuing, and taking children to basketball games. We also worked very hard, running dozens of experiments and writing our articles on judgment heuristics. At night I wrote *Attention and Effort*. It was a busy year.

One of our projects was the study of what we called the *availability heuristic*. We thought of that heuristic when we asked ourselves what people actually do when they wish to estimate the frequency of a category, such as "people who divorce after the age of 60" or "dangerous plants." The answer was straightforward: instances of the class will be retrieved from memory, and if retrieval is easy and fluent, the category will be judged to be large. We defined the availability heuristic as the process of judging frequency by "the ease with which instances come to mind." The statement seemed clear when we formulated it, but the concept of availability has been refined since then. The two-system approach had not yet been developed when we studied availability, and we did not attempt to determine whether this heuristic is a deliberate problem-solving strategy or an automatic operation. We now know that both systems are involved.

A question we considered early was how many instances must be retrieved to get an impression of the ease with which they come to mind. We now know the answer: none. For an example, think of the number of words that can be constructed from the two sets of letters below.

XUZONLCJM

TAPCERHOB

You knew almost immediately, without generating any instances, that one set offers far more possibilities than the other, probably by a factor of 10 or more. Similarly, you do not need to retrieve specific news stories to have a good idea of the relative frequency with which different countries have appeared in the news during the past year (Belgium, China, France, Congo, Nicaragua, Romania . . .).

The availability heuristic, like other heuristics of judgment, substitutes one question for another: you wish to estimate the size of a category or the frequency of an event, but you report an impression of the ease with which instances come to mind. Substitution of questions inevitably produces systematic errors. You can discover how the heuristic leads to biases by following a simple procedure: list factors other than frequency that make it easy to come up with instances. Each factor in your list will be a potential source of bias. Here are some examples:

- A salient event that attracts your attention will be easily retrieved from memory. Divorces among Hollywood celebrities and sex scandals among politicians attract much attention, and instances will come easily to mind. You are therefore likely to exaggerate the frequency of both Hollywood divorces and political sex scandals.
- A dramatic event temporarily increases the availability of its category. A plane crash that attracts media coverage will temporarily alter your feelings about the safety of flying. Accidents are on your mind, for a while, after you see a car burning at the side of the road, and the world is for a while a more dangerous place.
- Personal experiences, pictures, and vivid examples are more available than incidents that happened to others, or mere words, or statistics. A judicial error that affects you will undermine your faith in the justice system more than a similar incident you read about in a newspaper.

Resisting this large collection of potential availability biases is possible, but tiresome. You must make the effort to reconsider your impressions and intuitions by asking such questions as, "Is our belief that thefts by teenagers are a major problem due to a few recent instances in our neighborhood?" or "Could it be that I feel no need to get a flu shot because none of my acquaintances got the flu last year?" Maintaining one's vigilance against biases is a chore—but the chance to avoid a costly mistake is sometimes worth the effort.

One of the best-known studies of availability suggests that awareness of your own biases can contribute to peace in marriages, and probably in other joint projects. In a famous study, spouses were asked, "How large was your personal contribution to keeping the place tidy, in percentages?" They also answered similar questions about "taking out the garbage," "initiating social engagements," etc. Would the self-estimated contributions add up to 100%, or more, or less? As expected, the self-assessed contributions added up to more than 100%. The explanation is a simple *availability bias*: both spouses remember their own individual efforts and contributions much more clearly than those of the other, and the difference in availability leads to a difference in judged frequency. The bias is not necessarily self-serving: spouses also overestimated their contribution to causing quarrels, although to a smaller extent than their contributions to more desirable outcomes. The same bias contributes to the common observation that many members of a collaborative team feel they have done more than their share and also feel that the others are not adequately grateful for their individual contributions.

I am generally not optimistic about the potential for personal control of biases, but this is an exception. The opportunity for successful debiasing exists because the circumstances in which issues of credit allocation come up are easy to identify, the more so because tensions often arise when several people at once feel that their efforts are not adequately recognized. The mere observation that there is usually more than 100% credit to go around is sometimes sufficient to defuse the situation. In any event, it is a good thing for every individual to remember. You will occasionally do more than your share, but it is useful to know that you are likely to have that feeling even when each member of the team feels the same way.

THE PSYCHOLOGY OF AVAILABILITY

A major advance in the understanding of the availability heuristic occurred in the early 1990s, when a group of German psychologists led by Norbert

Schwarz raised an intriguing question: How will people's impressions of the frequency of a category be affected by a requirement to list a specified number of instances? Imagine yourself a subject in that experiment:

First, list six instances in which you behaved assertively.
Next, evaluate how assertive you are.

Imagine that you had been asked for twelve instances of assertive behavior (a number most people find difficult). Would your view of your own assertiveness be different?

Schwarz and his colleagues observed that the task of listing instances may enhance the judgments of the trait by two different routes:

- the number of instances retrieved
- the ease with which they come to mind

The request to list twelve instances pits the two determinants against each other. On the one hand, you have just retrieved an impressive number of cases in which you were assertive. On the other hand, while the first three or four instances of your own assertiveness probably came easily to you, you almost certainly struggled to come up with the last few to complete a set of twelve; fluency was low. Which will count more—the amount retrieved or the ease and fluency of the retrieval?

The contest yielded a clear-cut winner: people who had just listed twelve instances rated themselves as less assertive than people who had listed only six. Furthermore, participants who had been asked to list twelve cases in which they had *not* behaved assertively ended up thinking of themselves as quite assertive! If you cannot easily come up with instances of meek behavior, you are likely to conclude that you are not meek at all. Self-ratings were dominated by the ease with which examples had come to mind. The experience of fluent retrieval of instances trumped the number retrieved.

An even more direct demonstration of the role of fluency was offered by other psychologists in the same group. All the participants in their experiment listed six instances of assertive (or nonassertive) behavior, while maintaining a specified facial expression. "Smilers" were instructed to contract the zygomaticus muscle, which produces a light smile; "frowners" were required to furrow their brow. As you already know, frowning normally accompanies cognitive strain and the effect is symmetric: when people are instructed to frown while doing a task, they actually try harder and experience greater cognitive strain. The researchers anticipated that the frowners would have more difficulty retrieving examples of assertive behavior and would therefore rate themselves as relatively lacking in assertiveness. And so it was.

Psychologists enjoy experiments that yield paradoxical results, and they have applied Schwarz's discovery with gusto. For example, people:

- believe that they use their bicycles less often after recalling many rather than few instances
- are less confident in a choice when they are asked to produce more arguments to support it
- are less confident that an event was avoidable after listing more ways it could have been avoided
- are less impressed by a car after listing many of its advantages

A professor at UCLA found an ingenious way to exploit the availability bias. He asked different groups of students to list ways to improve the course, and he varied the required number of improvements. As expected, the students who listed more ways to improve the class rated it higher!

Perhaps the most interesting finding of this paradoxical research is that the paradox is not always found: people sometimes go by content rather than by ease of retrieval. The proof that you truly understand a pattern of behavior is that you know how to reverse it. Schwarz and his colleagues took on this challenge of discovering the conditions under which this reversal would take place.

The ease with which instances of assertiveness come to the subject's mind changes during the task. The first few instances are easy, but retrieval soon becomes much harder. Of course, the subject also expects fluency to drop gradually, but the drop of fluency between six and twelve instances appears to be steeper than the participant expected. The results suggest that the participants make an inference: if I am having so much more trouble than expected coming up with instances of my assertiveness, then I can't be very assertive. Note that this inference rests on a surprise—fluency being worse than expected. The availability heuristic that the subjects apply is better described as an "unexplained unavailability" heuristic.

Schwarz and his colleagues reasoned that they could disrupt the heuristic by providing the subjects with an explanation for the fluency of retrieval that they experienced. They told the participants they would hear background music while recalling instances and that the music would affect performance in the memory task. Some subjects were told that the music would help, others were told to expect diminished fluency. As predicted, participants whose experience of fluency was "explained" did not use it as a heuristic; the subjects who were told that music would make retrieval more difficult rated themselves as equally assertive when they retrieved twelve instances as when they retrieved six. Other cover stories have been used with the same result: judgments are no longer influenced by ease of retrieval when the experience of fluency is given a spurious explanation by the presence of curved or straight text boxes, by the background color of the screen, or by other irrelevant factors that the experimenters dreamed up.

As I have described it, the process that leads to judgment by availability appears to involve a complex chain of reasoning. The subjects have an experience of diminishing fluency as they produce instances. They evidently have expectations about the rate at which fluency decreases, and those expectations are wrong: the difficulty of coming up with new instances increases more rapidly than they expect. It is the unexpectedly low fluency that causes people who were asked for twelve instances to describe themselves as unassertive. When the surprise is eliminated, low fluency no longer influences the judgment. The process appears to consist of a sophisticated set of inferences. Is the automatic System 1 capable of it?

The answer is that in fact no complex reasoning is needed. Among the basic features of System 1 is its ability to set expectations and to be surprised when these expectations are violated. The system also retrieves possible causes of a surprise, usually by finding a possible cause among recent surprises. Furthermore, System 2 can reset the expectations of System 1 on the fly, so that an event that would normally be surprising is now almost normal. Suppose you are told that the three-year-old boy who lives next door frequently wears a top hat in his stroller. You will be far less surprised when you actually see him with his top hat than you would have been without the warning. In Schwarz's experiment, the background music has been mentioned as a possible cause of retrieval problems. The difficulty of retrieving twelve instances is no longer a surprise and therefore is less likely to be evoked by the task of judging assertiveness.

Schwarz and his colleagues discovered that people who are personally involved in the judgment are more likely to consider the number of instances they retrieve from memory and less likely to go by fluency. They recruited two groups of students for a study of risks to cardiac health. Half the students had a family history of cardiac disease and were expected to take the task more seriously than the others, who had no such history. All were asked to recall either three or eight behaviors in their routine that could affect their cardiac health (some were asked for risky behaviors, others for protective behaviors). Students with no family history of heart disease were casual about the task and followed the availability heuristic. Students who found it difficult to find eight instances of risky behavior felt themselves relatively safe, and those who struggled to retrieve examples of safe behaviors felt themselves at risk. The students with a family history of heart disease showed the opposite pattern—they felt safer when they retrieved many instances of safe behavior and felt greater danger when they retrieved many instances of risky behavior. They were also more likely to feel that their future behavior would be affected by the experience of evaluating their risk.

The conclusion is that the ease with which instances come to mind is a System 1 heuristic, which is replaced by a focus on content when System 2 is more engaged. Multiple lines of evidence converge on the conclusion that people who let themselves be guided by System 1 are more strongly susceptible to availability biases than others who are in a state of higher vigilance. The following are some conditions in which people "go with the flow" and are affected more strongly by ease of retrieval than by the content they retrieved:

- when they are engaged in another effortful task at the same time
- when they are in a good mood because they just thought of a happy episode in their life
- if they score low on a depression scale
- if they are knowledgeable novices on the topic of the task, in contrast to true experts
- when they score high on a scale of faith in intuition
- if they are (or are made to feel) powerful

I find the last finding particularly intriguing. The authors introduce their article with a famous quote: "I don't spend a lot of time taking polls around the world to tell me what I think is the right way to act. I've just got to know how I feel" (George W. Bush, November 2002). They go on to show that reliance on intuition is only in part a personality trait. Merely reminding people of a time when they had power increases their apparent trust in their own intuition.

SPEAKING OF AVAILABILITY

"Because of the coincidence of two planes crashing last month, she now prefers to take the train. That's silly. The risk hasn't really changed; it is an availability bias."

"He underestimates the risks of indoor pollution because there are few media stories on them. That's an availability effect. He should look at the statistics."

"She has been watching too many spy movies recently, so she's seeing conspiracies everywhere."

"The CEO has had several successes in a row, so failure doesn't come easily to her mind. The availability bias is making her overconfident."

13

AVAILABILITY, EMOTION, AND RISK

Students of risk were quick to see that the idea of availability was relevant to their concerns. Even before our work was published, the economist Howard Kunreuther, who was then in the early stages of a career that he has devoted to the study of risk and insurance, noticed that availability effects help explain the pattern of insurance purchase and protective action after disasters. Victims and near victims are very concerned after a disaster. After each significant earthquake, Californians are for a while diligent in purchasing insurance and adopting measures of protection and mitigation. They tie down their boiler to reduce quake damage, seal their basement doors against floods, and maintain emergency supplies in good order. However, the memories of the disaster dim over time, and so do worry and diligence. The dynamics of memory help explain the recurrent cycles of disaster, concern, and growing complacency that are familiar to students of large-scale emergencies.

Kunreuther also observed that protective actions, whether by individuals or governments, are usually designed to be adequate to the worst disaster actually experienced. As long ago as pharaonic Egypt, societies have tracked the high-water mark of rivers that periodically flood—and have always prepared accordingly, apparently assuming that floods will not rise higher than the existing high-water mark. Images of a worse disaster do not come easily to mind.

AVAILABILITY AND AFFECT

The most influential studies of availability biases were carried out by our friends in Eugene, where Paul Slovic and his longtime collaborator Sarah Lichtenstein were joined by our former student Baruch Fischhoff. They carried out groundbreaking research on public perceptions of risks, including a survey that has become the standard example of an availability bias. They asked participants in their survey to consider pairs of causes of death: diabetes and asthma, or stroke and accidents. For each pair, the subjects indicated the more frequent cause and estimated the ratio of the two frequencies. The judgments were compared to health statistics of the time. Here's a sample of their findings:

- Strokes cause almost twice as many deaths as all accidents combined, but 80% of respondents judged accidental death to be more likely.
- Tornadoes were seen as more frequent killers than asthma, although the latter cause 20 times more deaths.
- Death by lightning was judged less likely than death from botulism even though it is 52 times more frequent.
- Death by disease is 18 times as likely as accidental death, but the two were judged about equally likely.
- Death by accidents was judged to be more than 300 times more likely than death by diabetes, but the true ratio is 1:4.

The lesson is clear: estimates of causes of death are warped by media coverage. The coverage is itself biased toward novelty and poignancy. The media do not just shape what the public is interested in, but also are shaped by it. Editors cannot ignore the public's demands that certain topics and viewpoints receive extensive coverage. Unusual events (such as botulism) attract disproportionate attention and are consequently perceived as less unusual than they really are. The world in our heads is not a precise replica of reality; our expectations about the frequency of events are distorted by the prevalence and emotional intensity of the messages to which we are exposed.

The estimates of causes of death are an almost direct representation of the activation of ideas in associative memory, and are a good example of substitution. But Slovic and his colleagues were led to a deeper insight: they saw that the ease with which ideas of various risks come to mind and the emotional reactions to these risks are inextricably linked. Frightening thoughts and images occur to us with particular ease, and thoughts of danger that are fluent and vivid exacerbate fear.

As mentioned earlier, Slovic eventually developed the notion of an affect heuristic, in which people make judgments and decisions by consulting their emotions: Do I like it? Do I hate it? How strongly do I feel about it? In many domains of life, Slovic said, people form opinions and make choices that directly express their feelings and their basic tendency to approach or avoid, often without knowing that they are doing so. The affect heuristic is an instance of substitution, in which the answer to an easy question (How do I feel about it?) serves as an answer to a much harder question (What do I think about it?). Slovic and his colleagues related their views to the work of the neuroscientist Antonio Damasio, who had proposed that people's emotional evaluations of outcomes, and the bodily states and the approach and avoidance tendencies associated with them, all play a central role in guiding decision making. Damasio and his colleagues have observed that people who do not display the appropriate emotions before they decide, sometimes because of brain damage, also have an impaired ability to make good decisions. An inability to be guided by a "healthy fear" of bad consequences is a disastrous flaw.

In a compelling demonstration of the workings of the affect heuristic, Slovic's research team surveyed opinions about various technologies, including water fluoridation, chemical plants, food preservatives, and cars, and asked their respondents to list both the benefits and the risks of each technology. They observed an implausibly high negative correlation between two estimates that their respondents made: the level of benefit and the level of risk that they attributed to the technologies. When people were favorably disposed toward a technology, they rated it as offering large benefits and imposing little risk; when they disliked a technology, they could think only of its disadvantages, and few advantages came to mind. Because the technologies lined up neatly from good to bad, no painful tradeoffs needed to be faced. Estimates of risk and benefit corresponded even more closely when people rated risks and benefits under time pressure. Remarkably, members of the British Toxicology Society responded similarly: they found little benefit in substances or technologies that they thought risky, and vice versa. Consistent affect is a central element of what I have called associative coherence.

The best part of the experiment came next. After completing the initial survey, the respondents read brief passages with arguments in favor of various technologies. Some were given arguments that focused on the numerous benefits of a technology; others, arguments that stressed the low risks. These messages were effective in changing the emotional appeal of the technologies. The striking finding was that people who had received a message extolling the benefits of a technology also changed their beliefs about its risks. Although they had received no relevant evidence, the technology they now liked more than before was also perceived as less risky. Similarly, respondents who were told only that the risks of a technology were mild developed a more favorable view of its benefits. The implication is clear: as the psychologist Jonathan Haidt said in another context, "The emotional tail wags the rational dog." The affect heuristic simplifies our lives by creating a world that is much tidier than reality. Good technologies have few costs in the imaginary world we inhabit, bad technologies have no benefits, and all decisions are easy. In the real world, of course, we often face painful tradeoffs between benefits and costs.

THE PUBLIC AND THE EXPERTS

Paul Slovic probably knows more about the peculiarities of human judgment of risk than any other individual. His work offers a picture of Mr. and Ms. Citizen that is far from flattering: guided by emotion rather than by reason, easily swayed by trivial details, and inadequately sensitive to differences between low and negligibly low probabilities. Slovic has also studied experts, who are clearly superior in dealing with numbers and amounts. Experts show many of the same biases as the rest of us in attenuated form, but often their judgments and preferences about risks diverge from those of other people.

Differences between experts and the public are explained in part by biases in lay judgments, but Slovic draws attention to situations in which the differences reflect a genuine conflict of values. He points out that experts often measure risks by the number of lives (or life-years) lost, while the public draws finer distinctions, for example between "good deaths" and "bad deaths," or between random accidental fatalities and deaths that occur in the course of voluntary activities such as skiing. These legitimate distinctions are often ignored in statistics that merely count cases. Slovic argues from such observations that the public has a richer conception of risks than the experts do. Consequently, he strongly resists the view that the experts should rule, and that their opinions should be accepted without question when they conflict with the opinions and wishes of other citizens. When experts and the public disagree on their priorities, he says, "Each side must respect the insights and intelligence of the other."

In his desire to wrest sole control of risk policy from experts, Slovic has challenged the foundation of their expertise: the idea that risk is objective.

> "Risk" does not exist "out there," independent of our minds and culture, waiting to be measured. Human beings have invented the concept of "risk" to help them understand and cope with the dangers and uncertainties of life. Although these dangers are real, there is no such thing as "real risk" or "objective risk."

To illustrate his claim, Slovic lists nine ways of defining the mortality risk associated with the release of a toxic material into the air, ranging from "death per million people" to "death per million dollars of product produced." His point is that the evaluation of the risk depends on the choice of a measure—with the obvious possibility that the choice may have been guided by a preference for one outcome or another. He goes on to conclude that "defining risk is thus an exercise in power." You might not have guessed that one can get to such thorny policy issues from experimental studies of the psychology of judgment! However, policy is ultimately about people, what they want and what is best for them. Every policy question involves assumptions about human nature, in particular about the choices that people may make and the consequences of their choices for themselves and for society.

Another scholar and friend whom I greatly admire, Cass Sunstein, disagrees sharply with Slovic's stance on the different views of experts and citizens, and defends the role of experts as a bulwark against "populist" excesses. Sunstein is one of the foremost legal scholars in the United States, and shares with other leaders of his profession the attribute of intellectual fearlessness. He knows he can master any body of knowledge quickly and thoroughly, and he has mastered many, including both the psychology of judgment and choice and issues of regulation and risk policy. His view is that the existing system of regulation in the United States displays a very poor setting of priorities, which reflects reaction to public pressures more than careful objective analysis. He starts from the position that risk regulation and government intervention to reduce risks should be guided by rational weighting of costs and benefits, and that the natural units for this analysis are the number of lives saved (or perhaps the number of life-years saved, which gives more weight to saving the young) and the dollar cost to the economy. Poor regulation is wasteful of lives and money, both of which can be measured objectively. Sunstein has not been persuaded by Slovic's argument that risk and its measurement is subjective. Many aspects of risk assessment are debatable, but he has faith in the objectivity that may be achieved by science, expertise, and careful deliberation.

Sunstein came to believe that biased reactions to risks are an important source of erratic and misplaced priorities in public policy. Lawmakers and regulators may be overly responsive to the irrational concerns of citizens, both because of political sensitivity and because they are prone to the same cognitive biases as other citizens.

Sunstein and a collaborator, the jurist Timur Kuran, invented a name for the mechanism through which biases flow into policy: the *availability cascade*. They comment that in the social context, "all heuristics are equal, but availability is more equal than the others." They have in mind an expanded notion of the heuristic, in which availability provides a heuristic for judgments other than frequency. In particular, the importance of an idea is often judged by the fluency (and emotional charge) with which that idea comes to mind.

An availability cascade is a self-sustaining chain of events, which may start from media reports of a relatively minor event and lead up to public panic and large-scale government action. On some occasions, a media story about a risk catches the attention of a segment of the public, which becomes aroused and worried. This emotional reaction becomes a story in itself, prompting additional coverage in the media, which in turn produces greater concern and involvement. The cycle is sometimes sped along deliberately by "availability entrepreneurs," individuals or organizations who work to ensure a continuous flow of worrying news. The danger is increasingly exaggerated as the media compete for attention-grabbing headlines. Scientists and others who try to dampen the increasing fear and revulsion attract little attention, most of it hostile: anyone who claims that the danger is overstated is suspected of association with a "heinous cover-up." The issue becomes politically important because it is on everyone's mind, and the response of the political system is guided by the intensity of public sentiment. The availability cascade has now reset priorities. Other risks, and other ways that resources could be applied for the public good, all have faded into the background.

Kuran and Sunstein focused on two examples that are still controversial: the Love Canal affair and the so-called Alar scare. In Love Canal, buried toxic waste was exposed during a rainy season in 1979, causing contamination of the water well beyond standard limits, as well as a foul smell. The residents of the community were angry and frightened, and one of them,

Lois Gibbs, was particularly active in an attempt to sustain interest in the problem. The availability cascade unfolded according to the standard script. At its peak there were daily stories about Love Canal, scientists attempting to claim that the dangers were overstated were ignored or shouted down, ABC News aired a program titled *The Killing Ground*, and empty baby-size coffins were paraded in front of the legislature. A large number of residents were relocated at government expense, and the control of toxic waste became the major environmental issue of the 1980s. The legislation that mandated the cleanup of toxic sites, called CERCLA, established a Superfund and is considered a significant achievement of environmental legislation. It was also expensive, and some have claimed that the same amount of money could have saved many more lives if it had been directed to other priorities. Opinions about what actually happened at Love Canal are still sharply divided, and claims of actual damage to health appear not to have been substantiated. Kuran and Sunstein wrote up the Love Canal story almost as a pseudo-event, while on the other side of the debate, environmentalists still speak of the "Love Canal disaster."

Opinions are also divided on the second example Kuran and Sunstein used to illustrate their concept of an availability cascade, the Alar incident, known to detractors of environmental concerns as the "Alar scare" of 1989. Alar is a chemical that was sprayed on apples to regulate their growth and improve their appearance. The scare began with press stories that the chemical, when consumed in gigantic doses, caused cancerous tumors in rats and mice. The stories understandably frightened the public, and those fears encouraged more media coverage, the basic mechanism of an availability cascade. The topic dominated the news and produced dramatic media events such as the testimony of the actress Meryl Streep before Congress. The apple industry sustained large losses as apples and apple products became objects of fear. Kuran and Sunstein quote a citizen who called in to ask "whether it was safer to pour apple juice down the drain or to take it to a toxic waste dump." The manufacturer withdrew the product and the FDA banned it. Subsequent research confirmed that the substance might pose a very small risk as a possible carcinogen, but the Alar incident was certainly an enormous overreaction to a minor problem. The net effect of the incident on public health was probably detrimental because fewer good apples were consumed.

The Alar tale illustrates a basic limitation in the ability of our mind to deal with small risks: we either ignore them altogether or give them far too much weight—nothing in between. Every parent who has stayed up waiting for a teenage daughter who is late from a party will recognize the feeling. You may know that there is really (almost) nothing to worry about, but you cannot help images of disaster from coming to mind. As Slovic has argued, the amount of concern is not adequately sensitive to the probability of harm; you are imagining the numerator—the tragic story you saw on the news—and not thinking about the denominator. Sunstein has coined the phrase "probability neglect" to describe the pattern. The combination of probability neglect with the social mechanisms of availability cascades inevitably leads to gross exaggeration of minor threats, sometimes with important consequences.

In today's world, terrorists are the most significant practitioners of the art of inducing availability cascades. With a few horrible exceptions such as 9/11, the number of casualties from terror attacks is very small relative to other causes of death. Even in countries that have been targets of intensive terror campaigns, such as Israel, the weekly number of casualties almost never came close to the number of traffic deaths. The difference is in the availability of the two risks, the ease and the frequency with which they come to mind. Gruesome images, endlessly repeated in the media, cause everyone to be on edge. As I know from experience, it is difficult to reason oneself into a state of complete calm. Terrorism speaks directly to System 1.

Where do I come down in the debate between my friends? Availability cascades are real and they undoubtedly distort priorities in the allocation of public resources. Cass Sunstein would seek mechanisms that insulate decision makers from public pressures, letting the allocation of resources be determined by impartial experts who have a broad view of all risks and of the resources available to reduce them. Paul Slovic trusts the experts much less and the public somewhat more than Sunstein does, and he points out that insulating the experts from the emotions of the public produces policies that the public will reject—an impossible situation in a democracy. Both are eminently sensible, and I agree with both.

I share Sunstein's discomfort with the influence of irrational fears and availability cascades on public policy in the domain of risk. However, I also share Slovic's belief that widespread fears, even if they are unreasonable, should not be ignored by policy makers. Rational or not, fear is painful and debilitating, and policy makers must endeavor to protect the public from fear, not only from real dangers.

Slovic rightly stresses the resistance of the public to the idea of decisions being made by unelected and unaccountable experts. Furthermore, availability cascades may have a long-term benefit by calling attention to classes of risks and by increasing the overall size of the risk-reduction budget. The Love Canal incident may have caused excessive resources to be allocated to the management of toxic waste, but it also had a more general effect in raising the priority level of environmental concerns. Democracy is inevitably messy, in part because the availability and affect heuristics that guide citizens' beliefs and attitudes are inevitably biased, even if they generally point in the right direction. Psychology should inform the design of risk policies that combine the experts' knowledge with the public's emotions and intuitions.

SPEAKING OF AVAILABILITY CASCADES

"She's raving about an innovation that has large benefits and no costs. I suspect the affect heuristic."

"This is an availability cascade: a nonevent that is inflated by the media and the public until it fills our TV screens and becomes all anyone is talking about."

14

TOM W'S SPECIALTY

Have a look at a simple puzzle:

> Tom W is a graduate student at the main university in your state. Please rank the following nine fields of graduate specialization in order of the likelihood that Tom W is now a student in each of these fields. Use 1 for the most likely, 9 for the least likely.
>
>   business administration
>   computer science
>   engineering
>   humanities and education
>   law
>   medicine
>   library science
>   physical and life sciences
>   social science and social work

This question is easy, and you knew immediately that the relative size of enrollment in the different fields is the key to a solution. So far as you know, Tom W was picked at random from the graduate students at the university, like a single marble drawn from an urn. To decide whether a marble is more likely to be red or green, you need to know how many marbles of each color there are in the urn. The proportion of marbles of a particular kind is called a *base rate*. Similarly, the base rate of humanities and education in this problem is the proportion of students of that field among all the graduate students. In the absence of specific information about Tom W, you will go by the base rates and guess that he is more likely to be enrolled in humanities and education than in computer science or library science, because there are more students overall in the humanities and education than in the other two fields. Using base-rate information is the obvious move when no other information is provided.

Next comes a task that has nothing to do with base rates.

> The following is a personality sketch of Tom W written during Tom's senior year in high school by a psychologist, on the basis of psychological tests of uncertain validity:
>
>> Tom W is of high intelligence, although lacking in true creativity. He has a need for order and clarity, and for neat and tidy systems in which every detail finds its appropriate place. His writing is rather dull and mechanical, occasionally enlivened by somewhat corny puns and flashes of imagination of the sci-fi type. He has a strong drive for competence. He seems to have little feel and little sympathy for other people, and does not enjoy interacting with others. Self-centered, he nonetheless has a deep moral sense.
>
> Now please take a sheet of paper and rank the nine fields of specialization listed below by how similar the description of Tom W is to the typical graduate student in each of the following fields. Use 1 for the most likely and 9 for the least likely.

You will get more out of the chapter if you give the task a quick try; reading the report on Tom W is necessary to make your judgments about the various graduate specialties.

This question too is straightforward. It requires you to retrieve, or perhaps to construct, a stereotype of graduate students in the different fields. When the experiment was first conducted, in the early 1970s, the average ordering was as follows. Yours is probably not very different:

1. computer science
2. engineering
3. business administration
4. physical and life sciences
5. library science
6. law
7. medicine
8. humanities and education
9. social science and social work

You probably ranked computer science among the best fitting because of hints of nerdiness ("corny puns"). In fact, the description of Tom W was written to fit that stereotype. Another specialty that most people ranked high is engineering ("neat and tidy systems"). You probably thought that Tom W is not a good fit with your idea of social science and social work ("little feel and little sympathy for other people"). Professional stereotypes appear to have changed little in the nearly forty years since I designed the description of Tom W.

The task of ranking the nine careers is complex and certainly requires the discipline and sequential organization of which only System 2 is capable. However, the hints planted in the description (corny puns and others) were intended to activate an association with a stereotype, an automatic activity of System 1.

The instructions for this similarity task required a comparison of the description of Tom W to the stereotypes of the various fields of specialization. For the purposes of that task, the accuracy of the description—whether or not it is a true portrait of Tom W—is irrelevant. So is your knowledge of the base rates of the various fields. The similarity of an individual to the stereotype of a group is unaffected by the size of the group. Indeed, you could compare the description of Tom to an image of graduate students in library science even if there is no such department at the university.

If you examine Tom W again, you will see that he is a good fit to stereotypes of some small groups of students (computer scientists, librarians, engineers) and a much poorer fit to the largest groups (humanities and education, social science and social work). Indeed, the participants almost always ranked the two largest fields very low. Tom W was intentionally designed as an "anti-base-rate" character, a good fit to small fields and a poor fit to the most populated specialties.

PREDICTING BY REPRESENTATIVENESS

The third task in the sequence was administered to graduate students in psychology, and it is the critical one: rank the fields of specialization in order of the likelihood that Tom W is now a graduate student in each of these fields. The members of this prediction group knew the relevant statistical facts: they were familiar with the base rates of the different fields, and they knew that the source of Tom W's description was not highly trustworthy. However, we expected them to focus exclusively on the similarity of the description to the stereotypes—we called it *representativeness*—ignoring both the base rates and the doubts about the veracity of the description. They would then rank the small specialty—computer science—as highly probable, because that outcome gets the highest representativeness score.

Amos and I worked hard during the year we spent in Eugene, and I sometimes stayed in the office through the night. One of my tasks for such a night was to make up a description that would pit representativeness and base rates against each other. Tom W was the result of my efforts, and I completed the description in the early morning hours. The first person who showed up to work that morning was our colleague and friend Robyn Dawes, who was both a sophisticated statistician and a skeptic about the validity of intuitive judgment. If anyone would see the relevance of the base rate, it would have to be Robyn. I called Robyn over, gave him the question I had just typed, and asked him to guess Tom W's profession. I still remember his sly smile as he said tentatively, "computer scientist?" That was a happy moment—even the mighty had fallen. Of course, Robyn immediately recognized his mistake as soon as I mentioned "base rate," but he had not spontaneously thought of it. Although he knew as much as anyone about the role of base rates in prediction, he neglected them when presented with the description of an individual's personality. As expected, he substituted a judgment of representativeness for the probability he was asked to assess.

Amos and I then collected answers to the same question from 114 graduate students in psychology at three major universities, all of whom had taken several courses in statistics. They did not disappoint us. Their rankings of the nine fields by probability did not differ from ratings by similarity to the stereotype. Substitution was perfect in this case: there was no indication that the participants did anything else but judge representativeness. The question about probability (likelihood) was difficult, but the question about similarity was easier, and it was answered instead. This is a serious mistake, because judgments of similarity and probability are not constrained by the same logical rules. It is entirely acceptable for judgments of similarity to be unaffected by base rates and also by the possibility that the description was inaccurate, but anyone who ignores base rates and the quality of evidence in probability assessments will certainly make mistakes.

The concept "the probability that Tom W studies computer science" is not a simple one. Logicians and statisticians disagree about its meaning, and some would say it has no meaning at all. For many experts it is a measure of subjective degree of belief. There are some events you are sure of, for example, that the sun rose this morning, and others you consider impossible, such as the Pacific Ocean freezing all at once. Then there are many events, such as your next-door neighbor being a computer scientist, to which you assign an intermediate degree of belief—which is your probability of that event.

Logicians and statisticians have developed competing definitions of probability, all very precise. For laypeople, however, probability (a synonym of *likelihood* in everyday language) is a vague notion, related to uncertainty, propensity, plausibility, and surprise. The vagueness is not particular to this concept, nor is it especially troublesome. We know, more or less, what we mean when we use a word such as *democracy* or *beauty* and the people we are talking to understand, more or less, what we intended to say. In all the years I spent asking questions about the probability of events, no one ever raised a hand to ask me, "Sir, what do you mean by probability?" as they would have done if I had asked them to assess a strange concept such as globability. Everyone acted as if they knew how to answer my questions, although we all understood that it would be unfair to ask them for an explanation of what the word means.

People who are asked to assess probability are not stumped, because they do not try to judge probability as statisticians and philosophers use the word. A question about probability or likelihood activates a mental shotgun, evoking answers to easier questions. One of the easy answers is an automatic assessment of representativeness—routine in understanding language. The (false) statement that "Elvis Presley's parents wanted him to be a dentist" is mildly funny because the discrepancy between the images of Presley and a dentist is detected automatically. System 1 generates an impression of similarity without intending to do so. The representativeness heuristic is involved when someone says "She will win the election; you can see she is a winner" or "He won't go far as an academic; too many tattoos." We rely on representativeness when we judge the potential leadership of a candidate for office by the shape of his chin or the forcefulness of his speeches.

Although it is common, prediction by representativeness is not statistically optimal. Michael Lewis's bestselling *Moneyball* is a story about the inefficiency of this mode of prediction. Professional baseball scouts traditionally forecast the success of possible players in part by their build and look. The hero of Lewis's book is Billy Beane, the manager of the Oakland A's, who made the unpopular decision to overrule his scouts and to select players by the statistics of past performance. The players the A's picked were inexpensive, because other teams had rejected them for not looking the part. The team soon achieved excellent results at low cost.

THE SINS OF REPRESENTATIVENESS

Judging probability by representativeness has important virtues: the intuitive impressions that it produces are often—indeed, usually—more accurate than chance guesses would be.

- On most occasions, people who act friendly are in fact friendly.
- A professional athlete who is very tall and thin is much more likely to play basketball than football.
- People with a PhD are more likely to subscribe to *The New York Times* than people who ended their education after high school.
- Young men are more likely than elderly women to drive aggressively.

In all these cases and in many others, there is some truth to the stereotypes that govern judgments of representativeness, and predictions that follow this heuristic may be accurate. In other situations, the stereotypes are false and the representativeness heuristic will mislead, especially if it causes people to neglect base-rate information that points in another direction. Even when the heuristic has some validity, exclusive reliance on it is associated with grave sins against statistical logic.

One sin of representativeness is an excessive willingness to predict the occurrence of unlikely (low base-rate) events. Here is an example: you see a person reading *The New York Times* on the New York subway. Which of the following is a better bet about the reading stranger?

She has a PhD.
She does not have a college degree.

Representativeness would tell you to bet on the PhD, but this is not necessarily wise. You should seriously consider the second alternative, because many more nongraduates than PhDs ride in New York subways. And if you must guess whether a woman who is described as "a shy poetry lover" studies Chinese literature or business administration, you should opt for the latter option. Even if every female student of Chinese literature is shy and loves poetry, it is almost certain that there are more bashful poetry lovers in the much larger population of business students.

People without training in statistics are quite capable of using base rates in predictions under some conditions. In the first version of the Tom W problem, which provides no details about him, it is obvious to everyone that the probability of Tom W's being in a particular field is simply the base-rate frequency of enrollment in that field. However, concern for base rates evidently disappears as soon as Tom W's personality is described.

Amos and I originally believed, on the basis of our early evidence, that base-rate information will *always* be neglected when information about the specific instance is available, but that conclusion was too strong. Psychologists have conducted many experiments in which base-rate information is explicitly provided as part of the problem, and many of the participants are influenced by those base rates, although the information about the individual case is almost always weighted more than mere statistics. Norbert Schwarz and his colleagues showed that instructing people to "think like a statistician" enhanced the use of base-rate information, while the instruction to "think like a clinician" had the opposite effect.

An experiment that was conducted a few years ago with Harvard undergraduates yielded a finding that surprised me: enhanced activation of System 2 caused a significant improvement of predictive accuracy in the Tom W problem. The experiment combined the old problem with a modern variation of cognitive fluency. Half the students were told to puff out their cheeks during the task, while the others were told to frown. Frowning, as we have seen, generally increases the vigilance of System 2 and reduces both overconfidence and the reliance on intuition. The students who puffed out their cheeks (an emotionally neutral expression) replicated the original results: they relied exclusively on representativeness and ignored the base rates. As the authors had predicted, however, the frowners did show some sensitivity to the base rates. This is an instructive finding.

When an incorrect intuitive judgment is made, System 1 and System 2 should both be indicted. System 1 suggested the incorrect intuition, and

System 2 endorsed it and expressed it in a judgment. However, there are two possible reasons for the failure of System 2—ignorance or laziness. Some people ignore base rates because they believe them to be irrelevant in the presence of individual information. Others make the same mistake because they are not focused on the task. If frowning makes a difference, laziness seems to be the proper explanation of base-rate neglect, at least among Harvard undergrads. Their System 2 "knows" that base rates are relevant even when they are not explicitly mentioned, but applies that knowledge only when it invests special effort in the task.

The second sin of representativeness is insensitivity to the quality of evidence. Recall the rule of System 1: WYSIATI. In the Tom W example, what activates your associative machinery is a description of Tom, which may or may not be an accurate portrayal. The statement that Tom W "has little feel and little sympathy for people" was probably enough to convince you (and most other readers) that he is very unlikely to be a student of social science or social work. But you were explicitly told that the description should not be trusted!

You surely understand in principle that worthless information should not be treated differently from a complete lack of information, but WYSIATI makes it very difficult to apply that principle. Unless you decide immediately to reject evidence (for example, by determining that you received it from a liar), your System 1 will automatically process the information available as if it were true. There is one thing you can do when you have doubts about the quality of the evidence: let your judgments of probability stay close to the base rate. Don't expect this exercise of discipline to be easy—it requires a significant effort of self-monitoring and self-control.

The correct answer to the Tom W puzzle is that you should stay very close to your prior beliefs, slightly reducing the initially high probabilities of well-populated fields (humanities and education; social science and social work) and slightly raising the low probabilities of rare specialties (library science, computer science). You are not exactly where you would be if you had known nothing at all about Tom W, but the little evidence you have is not trustworthy, so the base rates should dominate your estimates.

HOW TO DISCIPLINE INTUITION

Your probability that it will rain tomorrow is your subjective degree of belief, but you should not let yourself believe whatever comes to your mind.

To be useful, your beliefs should be constrained by the logic of probability. So if you believe that there is a 40% chance that it will rain sometime tomorrow, you must also believe that there is a 60% chance it will not rain tomorrow, and you must not believe that there is a 50% chance that it will rain tomorrow morning. And if you believe that there is a 30% chance that candidate X will be elected president, and an 80% chance that he will be reelected if he wins the first time, then you must believe that the chances that he will be elected twice in a row are 24%.

The relevant "rules" for cases such as the Tom W problem are provided by Bayesian statistics. This influential modern approach to statistics is named after an English minister of the eighteenth century, the Reverend Thomas Bayes, who is credited with the first major contribution to a large problem: the logic of how people should change their mind in the light of evidence. Bayes's rule specifies how prior beliefs (in the examples of this chapter, base rates) should be combined with the diagnosticity of the evidence, the degree to which it favors the hypothesis over the alternative. For example, if you believe that 3% of graduate students are enrolled in computer science (the base rate), and you also believe that the description of Tom W is 4 times more likely for a graduate student in that field than in other fields, then Bayes's rule says you must believe that the probability that Tom W is a computer scientist is now 11%. If the base rate had been 80%, the new degree of belief would be 94.1%. And so on.

The mathematical details are not relevant in this book. There are two ideas to keep in mind about Bayesian reasoning and how we tend to mess it up. The first is that base rates matter, even in the presence of evidence about the case at hand. This is often not intuitively obvious. The second is that intuitive impressions of the diagnosticity of evidence are often exaggerated. The combination of WYSIATI and associative coherence tends to make us believe in the stories we spin for ourselves. The essential keys to disciplined Bayesian reasoning can be simply summarized:

- Anchor your judgment of the probability of an outcome on a plausible base rate.
- Question the diagnosticity of your evidence.

Both ideas are straightforward. It came as a shock to me when I realized that I was never taught how to implement them, and that even now I find it unnatural to do so.

SPEAKING OF REPRESENTATIVENESS

"The lawn is well trimmed, the receptionist looks competent, and the furniture is attractive, but this doesn't mean it is a well-managed company. I hope the board does not go by representativeness."

"This start-up looks as if it could not fail, but the base rate of success in the industry is extremely low. How do we know this case is different?"

"They keep making the same mistake: predicting rare events from weak evidence. When the evidence is weak, one should stick with the base rates."

"I know this report is absolutely damning, and it may be based on solid evidence, but how sure are we? We must allow for that uncertainty in our thinking."

15

LINDA: LESS IS MORE

The best-known and most controversial of our experiments involved a fictitious lady called Linda. Amos and I made up the Linda problem to provide conclusive evidence of the role of heuristics in judgment and of their incompatibility with logic. This is how we described Linda:

> Linda is thirty-one years old, single, outspoken, and very bright. She majored in philosophy. As a student, she was deeply concerned with issues of discrimination and social justice, and also participated in antinuclear demonstrations.

The audiences who heard this description in the 1980s always laughed because they immediately knew that Linda had attended the University of California at Berkeley, which was famous at the time for its radical, politically engaged students. In one of our experiments we presented participants with a list of eight possible scenarios for Linda. As in the Tom W problem, some ranked the scenarios by representativeness, others by probability. The Linda problem is similar, but with a twist.

> Linda is a teacher in elementary school.
> Linda works in a bookstore and takes yoga classes.
> Linda is active in the feminist movement.
> Linda is a psychiatric social worker.
> Linda is a member of the League of Women Voters.

Linda is a bank teller.

Linda is an insurance salesperson.

Linda is a bank teller and is active in the feminist movement.

The problem shows its age in several ways. The League of Women Voters is no longer as prominent as it was, and the idea of a feminist "movement" sounds quaint, a testimonial to the change in the status of women over the last thirty years. Even in the Facebook era, however, it is still easy to guess the almost perfect consensus of judgments: Linda is a very good fit for an active feminist, a fairly good fit for someone who works in a bookstore and takes yoga classes—and a very poor fit for a bank teller or an insurance salesperson.

Now focus on the critical items in the list: Does Linda look more like a bank teller, or more like a bank teller who is active in the feminist movement? Everyone agrees that Linda fits the idea of a "feminist bank teller" better than she fits the stereotype of bank tellers. The stereotypical bank teller is not a feminist activist, and adding that detail to the description makes for a more coherent story.

The twist comes in the judgments of likelihood, because there is a logical relation between the two scenarios. Think in terms of Venn diagrams. The set of feminist bank tellers is wholly included in the set of bank tellers, as every feminist bank teller is a bank teller. Therefore the probability that Linda is a feminist bank teller *must* be lower than the probability of her being a bank teller. When you specify a possible event in greater detail you can only lower its probability. The problem therefore sets up a conflict between the intuition of representativeness and the logic of probability.

Our initial experiment was between-subjects. Each participant saw a set of seven outcomes that included only one of the critical items ("bank teller" or "feminist bank teller"). Some ranked the outcomes by resemblance, others by likelihood. As in the case of Tom W, the average rankings by resemblance and by likelihood were identical; "feminist bank teller" ranked higher than "bank teller" in both.

Then we took the experiment further, using a within-subject design. We made up the questionnaire as you saw it, with "bank teller" in the sixth position in the list and "feminist bank teller" as the last item. We were convinced that subjects would notice the relation between the two outcomes, and that their rankings would be consistent with logic. Indeed, we were so certain of this that we did not think it worthwhile to conduct a special experiment. My assistant was running another experiment in the lab, and she asked the subjects to complete the new Linda questionnaire while signing out, just before they got paid.

About ten questionnaires had accumulated in a tray on my assistant's desk before I casually glanced at them and found that all the subjects had ranked "feminist bank teller" as more probable than "bank teller." I was so surprised that I still retain a "flashbulb memory" of the gray color of the metal desk and of where everyone was when I made that discovery. I quickly called Amos in great excitement to tell him what we had found: we had pitted logic against representativeness, and representativeness had won!

In the language of this book, we had observed a failure of System 2: our participants had a fair opportunity to detect the relevance of the logical rule, since both outcomes were included in the same ranking. They did not take advantage of that opportunity. When we extended the experiment, we found that 89% of the undergraduates in our sample violated the logic of probability. We were convinced that statistically sophisticated respondents would do better, so we administered the same questionnaire to doctoral students in the decision-science program of the Stanford Graduate School of Business, all of whom had taken several advanced courses in probability, statistics, and decision theory. We were surprised again: 85% of these respondents also ranked "feminist bank teller" as more likely than "bank teller."

In what we later described as "increasingly desperate" attempts to eliminate the error, we introduced large groups of people to Linda and asked them this simple question:

> Which alternative is more probable?
> Linda is a bank teller.
> Linda is a bank teller and is active in the feminist movement.

This stark version of the problem made Linda famous in some circles, and it earned us years of controversy. About 85% to 90% of undergraduates at several major universities chose the second option, contrary to logic. Remarkably, the sinners seemed to have no shame. When I asked my large undergraduate class in some indignation, "Do you realize that you have violated an elementary logical rule?" someone in the back row shouted, "So what?" and a graduate student who made the same error explained herself by saying, "I thought you just asked for my opinion."

The word *fallacy* is used, in general, when people fail to apply a logical rule that is obviously relevant. Amos and I introduced the idea of a *conjunction fallacy*, which people commit when they judge a conjunction of two events (here, bank teller and feminist) to be more probable than one of the events (bank teller) in a direct comparison.

As in the Muller-Lyer illusion, the fallacy remains attractive even when you recognize it for what it is. The naturalist Stephen Jay Gould described his own struggle with the Linda problem. He knew the correct answer, of course, and yet, he wrote, "a little homunculus in my head continues to jump up and down, shouting at me—'but she can't just be a bank teller; read the description.'" The little homunculus is of course Gould's System 1 speaking to him in insistent tones. (The two-system terminology had not yet been introduced when he wrote.)

The correct answer to the short version of the Linda problem was the majority response in only one of our studies: 64% of a group of graduate students in the social sciences at Stanford and at Berkeley correctly judged "feminist bank teller" to be less probable than "bank teller." In the original version with eight outcomes (shown above), only 15% of a similar group of graduate students had made that choice. The difference is instructive. The longer version separated the two critical outcomes by an intervening item (insurance salesperson), and the readers judged each outcome independently, without comparing them. The shorter version, in contrast, required an explicit comparison that mobilized System 2 and allowed most of the statistically sophisticated students to avoid the fallacy. Unfortunately, we did not explore the reasoning of the substantial minority (36%) of this knowledgeable group who chose incorrectly.

The judgments of probability that our respondents offered, in both the Tom W and Linda problems, corresponded precisely to judgments of representativeness (similarity to stereotypes). Representativeness belongs to a cluster of closely related basic assessments that are likely to be generated together. The most representative outcomes combine with the personality description to produce the most coherent stories. The most coherent stories are not necessarily the most probable, but they are *plausible*, and the notions of coherence, plausibility, and probability are easily confused by the unwary.

The uncritical substitution of plausibility for probability has pernicious effects on judgments when scenarios are used as tools of forecasting. Consider these two scenarios, which were presented to different groups, with a request to evaluate their probability:

A massive flood somewhere in North America next year, in which more than 1,000 people drown

An earthquake in California sometime next year, causing a flood in which more than 1,000 people drown

The California earthquake scenario is more plausible than the North America scenario, although its probability is certainly smaller. As expected, probability judgments were higher for the richer and more detailed scenario, contrary to logic. This is a trap for forecasters and their clients: adding detail to scenarios makes them more persuasive, but less likely to come true.

To appreciate the role of plausibility, consider the following questions:

> Which alternative is more probable?
> Mark has hair.
> Mark has blond hair.

and

> Which alternative is more probable?
> Jane is a teacher.
> Jane is a teacher and walks to work.

The two questions have the same logical structure as the Linda problem, but they cause no fallacy, because the more detailed outcome is only more detailed—it is not more plausible, or more coherent, or a better story. The evaluation of plausibility and coherence does not suggest and answer to the probability question. In the absence of a competing intuition, logic prevails.

LESS IS MORE, SOMETIMES EVEN IN JOINT EVALUATION

Christopher Hsee, of the University of Chicago, asked people to price sets of dinnerware offered in a clearance sale in a local store, where dinnerware regularly runs between $30 and $60. There were three groups in his experiment. The display below was shown to one group; Hsee labels that *joint evaluation*, because it allows a comparison of the two sets. The other two groups were shown only one of the two sets; this is *single evaluation*. Joint evaluation is a within-subject experiment, and single evaluation is between-subjects.

	Set A: 40 pieces	Set B: 24 pieces
Dinner plates	8, all in good condition	8, all in good condition
Soup/salad bowls	8, all in good condition	8, all in good condition

Dessert plates	8, all in good condition	8, all in good condition
Cups	8, 2 of them broken	
Saucers	8, 7 of them broken	

Assuming that the dishes in the two sets are of equal quality, which is worth more? This question is easy. You can see that Set A contains all the dishes of Set B, and seven additional intact dishes, and it *must* be valued more. Indeed, the participants in Hsee's joint evaluation experiment were willing to pay a little more for Set A than for Set B: $32 versus $30.

The results reversed in single evaluation, where Set B was priced much higher than Set A: $33 versus $23. We know why this happened. Sets (including dinnerware sets!) are represented by norms and prototypes. You can sense immediately that the average value of the dishes is much lower for Set A than for Set B, because no one wants to pay for broken dishes. If the average dominates the evaluation, it is not surprising that Set B is valued more. Hsee called the resulting pattern *less is more*. By removing 16 items from Set A (7 of them intact), its value is improved.

Hsee's finding was replicated by the experimental economist John List in a real market for baseball cards. He auctioned sets of ten high-value cards, and identical sets to which three cards of modest value were added. As in the dinnerware experiment, the larger sets were valued more than the smaller ones in joint evaluation, but less in single evaluation. From the perspective of economic theory, this result is troubling: the economic value of a dinnerware set or of a collection of baseball cards is a sum-like variable. Adding a positively valued item to the set can only increase its value.

The Linda problem and the dinnerware problem have exactly the same structure. Probability, like economic value, is a sum-like variable, as illustrated by this example:

probability (Linda is a teller) = probability (Linda is feminist teller) +
probability (Linda is non-feminist teller)

This is also why, as in Hsee's dinnerware study, single evaluations of the Linda problem produce a less-is-more pattern. System 1 averages instead of adding, so when the non-feminist bank tellers are removed from the set, subjective probability increases. However, the sum-like nature of the variable is less obvious for probability than for money. As a result, joint evaluation eliminates the error only in Hsee's experiment, not in the Linda experiment.

Linda was not the only conjunction error that survived joint evaluation.

We found similar violations of logic in many other judgments. Participants in one of these studies were asked to rank four possible outcomes of the next Wimbledon tournament from most to least probable. Björn Borg was the dominant tennis player of the day when the study was conducted. These were the outcomes:

A. Borg will win the match.
B. Borg will lose the first set.
C. Borg will lose the first set but win the match.
D. Borg will win the first set but lose the match.

The critical items are B and C. B is the more inclusive event and its probability *must* be higher than that of an event it includes. Contrary to logic, but not to representativeness or plausibility, 72% assigned B a lower probability than C—another instance of less is more in a direct comparison. Here again, the scenario that was judged more probable was unquestionably more plausible, a more coherent fit with all that was known about the best tennis player in the world.

To head off the possible objection that the conjunction fallacy is due to a misinterpretation of probability, we constructed a problem that required probability judgments, but in which the events were not described in words, and the term *probability* did not appear at all. We told participants about a regular six-sided die with four green faces and two red faces, which would be rolled 20 times. They were shown three sequences of greens (G) and reds (R), and were asked to choose one. They would (hypothetically) win $25 if their chosen sequence showed up. The sequences were:

1. RGRRR
2. GRGRRR
3. GRRRRR

Because the die has twice as many green as red faces, the first sequence is quite unrepresentative—like Linda being a bank teller. The second sequence, which contains six tosses, is a better fit to what we would expect from this die, because it includes two G's. However, this sequence was constructed by adding a G to the beginning of the first sequence, so it can only be less likely than the first. This is the nonverbal equivalent to Linda being a feminist bank teller. As in the Linda study, representativeness dominated. Almost two-thirds of respondents preferred to bet on sequence 2 rather than on sequence 1. When presented with arguments for the two choices, however, a large majority found the correct argument (favoring sequence 1) more convincing.

The next problem was a breakthrough, because we finally found a condition in which the incidence of the conjunction fallacy was much reduced. Two groups of subjects saw slightly different variants of the same problem:

A health survey was conducted in a sample of adult males in British Columbia, of all ages and occupations. Please give your best estimate of the following values:	A health survey was conducted in a sample of 100 adult males in British Columbia, of all ages and occupations. Please give your best estimate of the following values:
What percentage of the men surveyed have had one or more heart attacks?	How many of the 100 participants have had one or more heart attacks?
What percentage of the men surveyed are both over 55 years old and have had one or more heart attacks?	How many of the 100 participants both are over 55 years old and have had one or more heart attacks?

The incidence of errors was 65% in the group that saw the problem on the left, and only 25% in the group that saw the problem on the right.

Why is the question "How many of the 100 participants . . ." so much easier than "What percentage . . ."? A likely explanation is that the reference to 100 individuals brings a spatial representation to mind. Imagine that a large number of people are instructed to sort themselves into groups in a room: "Those whose names begin with the letters A to L are told to gather in the front left corner." They are then instructed to sort themselves further. The relation of inclusion is now obvious, and you can see that individuals whose name begins with C will be a subset of the crowd in the front left corner. In the medical survey question, heart attack victims end up in a corner of the room, and some of them are less than 55 years old. Not everyone will share this particular vivid imagery, but many subsequent experiments have shown that the frequency representation, as it is known, makes it easy to appreciate that one group is wholly included in the other. The solution to the puzzle appears to be that a question phrased as "how many?" makes you think of individuals, but the same question phrased as "what percentage?" does not.

What have we learned from these studies about the workings of System 2? One conclusion, which is not new, is that System 2 is not impressively alert. The undergraduates and graduate students who participated in our studies of the conjunction fallacy certainly "knew" the logic of Venn diagrams, but they did not apply it reliably even when all the relevant information was laid out in front of them. The absurdity of the less-is-more pattern was obvious in Hsee's dinnerware study and was easily recognized in the "how many?" representation, but it was not apparent to the thousands of people who have committed the conjunction fallacy in the original Linda problem and in others like it. In all these cases, the conjunction appeared plausible, and that sufficed for an endorsement of System 2.

The laziness of System 2 is part of the story. If their next vacation had depended on it, and if they had been given indefinite time and told to follow logic and not to answer until they were sure of their answer, I believe that most of our subjects would have avoided the conjunction fallacy. However, their vacation did not depend on a correct answer; they spent very little time on it, and were content to answer as if they had only been "asked for their opinion." The laziness of System 2 is an important fact of life, and the observation that representativeness can block the application of an obvious logical rule is also of some interest.

The remarkable aspect of the Linda story is the contrast to the broken-dishes study. The two problems have the same structure, but yield different results. People who see the dinnerware set that includes broken dishes put a very low price on it; their behavior reflects a rule of intuition. Others who see both sets at once apply the logical rule that more dishes can only add value. Intuition governs judgments in the between-subjects condition; logic rules in joint evaluation. In the Linda problem, in contrast, intuition often overcame logic even in joint evaluation, although we identified some conditions in which logic prevails.

Amos and I believed that the blatant violations of the logic of probability that we had observed in transparent problems were interesting and worth reporting to our colleagues. We also believed that the results strengthened our argument about the power of judgment heuristics, and that they would persuade doubters. And in this we were quite wrong. Instead, the Linda problem became a case study in the norms of controversy.

The Linda problem attracted a great deal of attention, but it also became a magnet for critics of our approach to judgment. As we had already done, researchers found combinations of instructions and hints that reduced the incidence of the fallacy; some argued that, in the context of the Linda problem, it is reasonable for subjects to understand the word "probability" as if it means "plausibility." These arguments were sometimes extended to suggest that our entire enterprise was misguided: if one salient cognitive illusion could be weakened or explained away, others could be as well. This reasoning neglects the unique feature of the conjunction fallacy as a case of conflict between intuition and logic. The evidence that we had built up for heuristics from between-subjects experiment (including studies of Linda) was not challenged—it was simply not addressed, and its salience was diminished by the exclusive focus on the conjunction fallacy. The net effect of the Linda problem was an increase in the visibility of our work to the general public, and a small dent in the credibility of our approach among scholars in the field. This was not at all what we had expected.

If you visit a courtroom you will observe that lawyers apply two styles of criticism: to demolish a case they raise doubts about the strongest arguments that favor it; to discredit a witness, they focus on the weakest part of the testimony. The focus on weaknesses is also normal in political debates. I do not believe it is appropriate in scientific controversies, but I have come to accept as a fact of life that the norms of debate in the social sciences do not prohibit the political style of argument, especially when large issues are at stake—and the prevalence of bias in human judgment is a large issue.

Some years ago I had a friendly conversation with Ralph Hertwig, a persistent critic of the Linda problem, with whom I had collaborated in a vain attempt to settle our differences. I asked him why he and others had chosen to focus exclusively on the conjunction fallacy, rather than on other findings that provided stronger support for our position. He smiled as he answered, "It was more interesting," adding that the Linda problem had attracted so much attention that we had no reason to complain.

SPEAKING OF LESS IS MORE

"They constructed a very complicated scenario and insisted on calling it highly probable. It is not—it is only a plausible story."

"They added a cheap gift to the expensive product, and made the whole deal less attractive. Less is more in this case."

"In most situations, a direct comparison makes people more careful and more logical. But not always. Sometimes intuition beats logic even when the correct answer stares you in the face."

16

CAUSES TRUMP STATISTICS

Consider the following scenario and note your intuitive answer to the question.

> A cab was involved in a hit-and-run accident at night.
> Two cab companies, the Green and the Blue, operate in the city.
> You are given the following data:
>
> - 85% of the cabs in the city are Green and 15% are Blue.
> - A witness identified the cab as Blue. The court tested the reliability of the witness under the circumstances that existed on the night of the accident and concluded that the witness correctly identified each one of the two colors 80% of the time and failed 20% of the time.
>
> What is the probability that the cab involved in the accident was Blue rather than Green?

This is a standard problem of Bayesian inference. There are two items of information: a base rate and the imperfectly reliable testimony of a witness. In the absence of a witness, the probability of the guilty cab being Blue is 15%, which is the base rate of that outcome. If the two cab companies had been equally large, the base rate would be uninformative and you would consider only the reliability of the witness, concluding that the probability is 80%. The two sources of information can be combined by Bayes's rule.

The correct answer is 41%. However, you can probably guess what people do when faced with this problem: they ignore the base rate and go with the witness. The most common answer is 80%.

CAUSAL STEREOTYPES

Now consider a variation of the same story, in which only the presentation of the base rate has been altered.

You are given the following data:

- The two companies operate the same number of cabs, but Green cabs are involved in 85% of accidents.
- The information about the witness is as in the previous version.

The two versions of the problem are mathematically indistinguishable, but they are psychologically quite different. People who read the first version do not know how to use the base rate and often ignore it. In contrast, people who see the second version give considerable weight to the base rate, and their average judgment is not too far from the Bayesian solution. Why?

In the first version, the base rate of Blue cabs is a statistical fact about the cabs in the city. A mind that is hungry for causal stories finds nothing to chew on: How does the number of Green and Blue cabs in the city cause this cab driver to hit and run?

In the second version, in contrast, the drivers of Green cabs cause more than 5 times as many accidents as the Blue cabs do. The conclusion is immediate: the Green drivers must be a collection of reckless madmen! You have now formed a stereotype of Green recklessness, which you apply to unknown individual drivers in the company. The stereotype is easily fitted into a causal story, because recklessness is a causally relevant fact about individual cabdrivers. In this version, there are two causal stories that need to be combined or reconciled. The first is the hit and run, which naturally evokes the idea that a reckless Green driver was responsible. The second is the witness's testimony, which strongly suggests the cab was Blue. The inferences from the two stories about the color of the car are contradictory and approximately cancel each other. The chances for the two colors are about equal (the Bayesian estimate is 41%, reflecting the fact that the base rate of Green cabs is a little more extreme than the reliability of the witness who reported a Blue cab).

The cab example illustrates two types of base rates. *Statistical base rates* are facts about a population to which a case belongs, but they are not relevant to the individual case. *Causal base rates* change your view of how the individual case came to be. The two types of base-rate information are treated differently:

- Statistical base rates are generally underweighted, and sometimes neglected altogether, when specific information about the case at hand is available.
- Causal base rates are treated as information about the individual case and are easily combined with other case-specific information.

The causal version of the cab problem had the form of a stereotype: Green drivers are dangerous. Stereotypes are statements about the group that are (at least tentatively) accepted as facts about every member. Here are two examples:

Most of the graduates of this inner-city school go to college.
Interest in cycling is widespread in France.

These statements are readily interpreted as setting up a propensity in individual members of the group, and they fit in a causal story. Many graduates of this particular inner-city school are eager and able to go to college, presumably because of some beneficial features of life in that school. There are forces in French culture and social life that cause many Frenchmen to take an interest in cycling. You will be reminded of these facts when you think about the likelihood that a particular graduate of the school will attend college, or when you wonder whether to bring up the Tour de France in a conversation with a Frenchman you just met.

Stereotyping is a bad word in our culture, but in my usage it is neutral. One of the basic characteristics of System 1 is that it represents categories as norms and prototypical exemplars. This is how we think of horses, refrigerators, and New York police officers; we hold in memory a representation of one or more "normal" members of each of these categories. When the categories are social, these representations are called stereotypes. Some stereotypes are perniciously wrong, and hostile stereotyping can have dreadful consequences, but the psychological facts cannot be avoided: stereotypes, both correct and false, are how we think of categories.

You may note the irony. In the context of the cab problem, the neglect of base-rate information is a cognitive flaw, a failure of Bayesian reasoning, and the reliance on causal base rates is desirable. Stereotyping the Green drivers improves the accuracy of judgment. In other contexts, however, such as hiring or profiling, there is a strong social norm against stereotyping, which is also embedded in the law. This is as it should be. In sensitive social contexts, we do not want to draw possibly erroneous conclusions about the individual from the statistics of the group. We consider it morally desirable for base rates to be treated as statistical facts about the group rather than as presumptive facts about individuals. In other words, we reject causal base rates.

The social norm against stereotyping, including the opposition to profiling, has been highly beneficial in creating a more civilized and more equal society. It is useful to remember, however, that neglecting valid stereotypes inevitably results in suboptimal judgments. Resistance to stereotyping is a laudable moral position, but the simplistic idea that the resistance is costless is wrong. The costs are worth paying to achieve a better society, but denying that the costs exist, while satisfying to the soul and politically correct, is not scientifically defensible. Reliance on the affect heuristic is common in politically charged arguments. The positions we favor have no cost and those we oppose have no benefits. We should be able to do better.

CAUSAL SITUATIONS

Amos and I constructed the variants of the cab problem, but we did not invent the powerful notion of causal base rates; we borrowed it from the psychologist Icek Ajzen. In his experiment, Ajzen showed his participants brief vignettes describing some students who had taken an exam at Yale and asked the participants to judge the probability that each student had passed the test. The manipulation of causal base rates was straightforward: Ajzen told one group that the students they saw had been drawn from a class in which 75% passed the exam, and told another group that the same students had been in a class in which only 25% passed. This is a powerful manipulation, because the base rate of passing suggests the immediate inference that the test that only 25% passed must have been brutally difficult. The difficulty of a test is, of course, one of the causal factors that determine every student's outcome. As expected, Ajzen's subjects were highly sensitive to the causal base rates, and every student was judged more likely to pass in the high-success condition than in the high-failure rate.

Ajzen used an ingenious method to suggest a noncausal base rate. He told his subjects that the students they saw had been drawn from a sample, which itself was constructed by selecting students who had passed or failed the exam. For example, the information for the high-failure group read as follows:

> The investigator was mainly interested in the causes of failure and constructed a sample in which 75% had failed the examination.

Note the difference. This base rate is a purely statistical fact about the ensemble from which cases have been drawn. It has no bearing on the question asked, which is whether the individual student passed or failed the test. As expected, the explicitly stated base rates had some effects on judgment, but they had much less impact than the statistically equivalent causal base rates. System 1 can deal with stories in which the elements are causally linked, but it is weak in statistical reasoning. For a Bayesian thinker, of course, the versions are equivalent. It is tempting to conclude that we have reached a satisfactory conclusion: causal base rates are used; merely statistical facts are (more or less) neglected. The next study, one of my all-time favorites, shows that the situation is rather more complex.

CAN PSYCHOLOGY BE TAUGHT?

The reckless cabdrivers and the impossibly difficult exam illustrate two inferences that people can draw from causal base rates: a stereotypical trait that is attributed to an individual, and a significant feature of the situation that affects an individual's outcome. The participants in the experiments made the correct inferences and their judgments improved. Unfortunately, things do not always work out so well. The classic experiment I describe next shows that people will not draw from base-rate information an inference that conflicts with other beliefs. It also supports the uncomfortable conclusion that teaching psychology is mostly a waste of time.

The experiment was conducted a long time ago by the social psychologist Richard Nisbett and his student Eugene Borgida, at the University of Michigan. They told students about the renowned "helping experiment" that had been conducted a few years earlier at New York University. Participants in that experiment were led to individual booths and invited to speak over the intercom about their personal lives and problems. They were to talk in turn for about two minutes. Only one microphone was active at any one time. There were six participants in each group, one of whom was a stooge. The stooge spoke first, following a script prepared by the experimenters. He described his problems adjusting to New York and admitted with obvious embarrassment that he was prone to seizures, especially when stressed. All the participants then had a turn. When the microphone was again turned over to the stooge, he became agitated and incoherent, said he felt a seizure coming on, and asked for someone to help him. The last words heard from him were, "C-could somebody-er-er-help-er-uh-uh-uh [choking sounds]. I . . . I'm gonna die-er-er-er I'm . . . gonna die-er-er-I seizure I-er [chokes, then quiet]." At this point the microphone of the next participant automatically became active, and nothing more was heard from the possibly dying individual.

What do you think the participants in the experiment did? So far as the participants knew, one of them was having a seizure and had asked for help. However, there were several other people who could possibly respond, so perhaps one could stay safely in one's booth. These were the results: only four of the fifteen participants responded immediately to the appeal for help. Six never got out of their booth, and five others came out only well after the "seizure victim" apparently choked. The experiment shows that individuals feel relieved of responsibility when they know that others have heard the same request for help.

Did the results surprise you? Very probably. Most of us think of ourselves as decent people who would rush to help in such a situation, and we expect other decent people to do the same. The point of the experiment, of course, was to show that this expectation is wrong. Even normal, decent people do not rush to help when they expect others to take on the unpleasantness of dealing with a seizure. And that means you, too.

Are you willing to endorse the following statement? "When I read the procedure of the helping experiment I thought I would come to the stranger's help immediately, as I probably would if I found myself alone with a seizure victim. I was probably wrong. If I find myself in a situation in which other people have an opportunity to help, I might not step forward. The presence of others would reduce my sense of personal responsibility more than I initially thought." This is what a teacher of psychology would hope you would learn. Would you have made the same inferences by yourself?

The psychology professor who describes the helping experiment wants the students to view the low base rate as causal, just as in the case of the fictitious Yale exam. He wants them to infer, in both cases, that a surprisingly high rate of failure implies a very difficult test. The lesson students are meant to take away is that some potent feature of the situation, such as the diffusion of responsibility, induces normal and decent people such as them to behave in a surprisingly unhelpful way.

Changing one's mind about human nature is hard work, and changing one's mind for the worse about oneself is even harder. Nisbett and Borgida suspected that students would resist the work and the unpleasantness. Of course, the students would be able and willing to recite the details of the helping experiment on a test, and would even repeat the "official" interpretation in terms of diffusion of responsibility. But did their beliefs about human nature really change? To find out, Nisbett and Borgida showed them videos of brief interviews allegedly conducted with two people who had participated in the New York study. The interviews were short and bland. The interviewees appeared to be nice, normal, decent people. They described their hobbies, their spare-time activities, and their plans for the future, which were entirely conventional. After watching the video of an interview, the students guessed how quickly that particular person had come to the aid of the stricken stranger.

To apply Bayesian reasoning to the task the students were assigned, you should first ask yourself what you would have guessed about the two individuals if you had not seen their interviews. This question is answered by consulting the base rate. We have been told that only 4 of the 15 participants in the experiment rushed to help after the first request. The probability that an unidentified participant had been immediately helpful is therefore 27%. Thus your prior belief about any unspecified participant should be that he did not rush to help. Next, Bayesian logic requires you to adjust your judgment in light of any relevant information about the individual. However, the videos were carefully designed to be uninformative; they provided no reason to suspect that the individuals would be either more or less helpful than a randomly chosen student. In the absence of useful new information, the Bayesian solution is to stay with the base rates.

Nisbett and Borgida asked two groups of students to watch the videos and predict the behavior of the two individuals. The students in the first group were told only about the procedure of the helping experiment, not about its results. Their predictions reflected their views of human nature and their understanding of the situation. As you might expect, they predicted that both individuals would immediately rush to the victim's aid. The second group of students knew both the procedure of the experiment and its results. The comparison of the predictions of the two groups provides an answer to a significant question: Did students learn from the results of the helping experiment anything that significantly changed their way of thinking? The answer is straightforward: they learned nothing at all. Their predictions about the two individuals were indistinguishable from the predictions made by students who had not been exposed to the statistical results of the experiment. They knew the base rate in the group from which the individuals had been drawn, but they remained convinced that the people they saw on the video had been quick to help the stricken stranger.

For teachers of psychology, the implications of this study are disheartening. When we teach our students about the behavior of people in the helping experiment, we expect them to learn something they had not known before; we wish to change how they think about people's behavior in a particular situation. This goal was not accomplished in the Nisbett-Borgida study, and there is no reason to believe that the results would have been different if they had chosen another surprising psychological experiment. Indeed, Nisbett and Borgida reported similar findings in teaching another study, in which mild social pressure caused people to accept much more painful electric shocks than most of us (and them) would have expected. Students who do not develop a new appreciation for the power of social setting have learned nothing of value from the experiment. The predictions they make about random strangers, or about their own behavior, indicate that they have not changed their view of how they would have behaved. In the words of Nisbett and Borgida, students "quietly exempt themselves" (and their friends and acquaintances) from the conclusions of experiments that surprise them. Teachers of psychology should not despair, however, because Nisbett and Borgida report a way to make their students appreciate the point of the helping experiment. They took a new group of students and taught them the procedure of the experiment but did not tell them the group results. They showed the two videos and simply told their students that the two individuals they had just seen had not helped the stranger, then asked them to guess the global results. The outcome was dramatic: the students' guesses were extremely accurate.

To teach students any psychology they did not know before, you must surprise them. But which surprise will do? Nisbett and Borgida found that when they presented their students with a surprising statistical fact, the students managed to learn nothing at all. But when the students were surprised by individual cases—two nice people who had not helped—they immediately made the generalization and inferred that helping is more difficult than they had thought. Nisbett and Borgida summarize the results in a memorable sentence:

> Subjects' unwillingness to deduce the particular from the general was matched only by their willingness to infer the general from the particular.

This is a profoundly important conclusion. People who are taught surprising statistical facts about human behavior may be impressed to the point of telling their friends about what they have heard, but this does not mean that their understanding of the world has really changed. The test of learning psychology is whether your understanding of situations you encounter has changed, not whether you have learned a new fact. There is a deep gap between our thinking about statistics and our thinking about individual cases. Statistical results with a causal interpretation have a stronger effect on our thinking than noncausal information. But even compelling causal statistics will not change long-held beliefs or beliefs rooted in personal experience. On the other hand, surprising individual cases have a powerful impact and are a more effective tool for teaching psychology because the incongruity must be resolved and embedded in a causal story. That is why this book contains questions that are addressed personally to the reader. You are more likely to learn something by finding surprises in your own behavior than by hearing surprising facts about people in general.

SPEAKING OF CAUSES AND STATISTICS

"We can't assume that they will really learn anything from mere statistics. Let's show them one or two representative individual cases to influence their System 1."

"No need to worry about this statistical information being ignored. On the contrary, it will immediately be used to feed a stereotype."

17

REGRESSION TO THE MEAN

I had one of the most satisfying eureka experiences of my career while teaching flight instructors in the Israeli Air Force about the psychology of effective training. I was telling them about an important principle of skill training: rewards for improved performance work better than punishment of mistakes. This proposition is supported by much evidence from research on pigeons, rats, humans, and other animals.

When I finished my enthusiastic speech, one of the most seasoned instructors in the group raised his hand and made a short speech of his own. He began by conceding that rewarding improved performance might be good for the birds, but he denied that it was optimal for flight cadets. This is what he said: "On many occasions I have praised flight cadets for clean execution of some aerobatic maneuver. The next time they try the same maneuver they usually do worse. On the other hand, I have often screamed into a cadet's earphone for bad execution, and in general he does better on his next try. So please don't tell us that reward works and punishment does not, because the opposite is the case."

This was a joyous moment of insight, when I saw in a new light a principle of statistics that I had been teaching for years. The instructor was right—but he was also completely wrong! His observation was astute and correct: occasions on which he praised a performance were likely to be followed by a disappointing performance, and punishments were typically followed by an improvement. But the inference he had drawn about the efficacy of reward and punishment was completely off the mark. What he had observed is known as *regression to the mean*, which in that case was due to random fluctuations in the quality of performance. Naturally, he praised only a cadet whose performance was far better than average. But the cadet was probably just lucky on that particular attempt and therefore likely to deteriorate regardless of whether or not he was praised. Similarly, the instructor would shout into a cadet's earphones only when the cadet's performance was unusually bad and therefore likely to improve regardless of what the instructor did. The instructor had attached a causal interpretation to the inevitable fluctuations of a random process.

The challenge called for a response, but a lesson in the algebra of prediction would not be enthusiastically received. Instead, I used chalk to mark a target on the floor. I asked every officer in the room to turn his back to the target and throw two coins at it in immediate succession, without looking. We measured the distances from the target and wrote the two results of each contestant on the blackboard. Then we rewrote the results in order, from the best to the worst performance on the first try. It was apparent that most (but not all) of those who had done best the first time deteriorated on their second try, and those who had done poorly on the first attempt generally improved. I pointed out to the instructors that what they saw on the board coincided with what we had heard about the performance of aerobatic maneuvers on successive attempts: poor performance was typically followed by improvement and good performance by deterioration, without any help from either praise or punishment.

The discovery I made on that day was that the flight instructors were trapped in an unfortunate contingency: because they punished cadets when performance was poor, they were mostly rewarded by a subsequent improvement, even if punishment was actually ineffective. Furthermore, the instructors were not alone in that predicament. I had stumbled onto a significant fact of the human condition: the feedback to which life exposes us is perverse. Because we tend to be nice to other people when they please us and nasty when they do not, we are statistically punished for being nice and rewarded for being nasty.

TALENT AND LUCK

A few years ago, John Brockman, who edits the online magazine *Edge*, asked a number of scientists to report their "favorite equation." These were my offerings:

success = talent + luck

great success = a little more talent + a lot of luck

The unsurprising idea that luck often contributes to success has surprising consequences when we apply it to the first two days of a high-level golf tournament. To keep things simple, assume that on both days the average score of the competitors was at par 72. We focus on a player who did very well on the first day, closing with a score of 66. What can we learn from that excellent score? An immediate inference is that the golfer is more talented than the average participant in the tournament. The formula for success suggests that another inference is equally justified: the golfer who did so well on day 1 probably enjoyed better-than-average luck on that day. If you accept that talent and luck both contribute to success, the conclusion that the successful golfer was lucky is as warranted as the conclusion that he is talented.

By the same token, if you focus on a player who scored 5 over par on that day, you have reason to infer both that he is rather weak *and* had a bad day. Of course, you know that neither of these inferences is certain. It is entirely possible that the player who scored 77 is actually very talented but had an exceptionally dreadful day. Uncertain though they are, the following inferences from the score on day 1 are plausible and will be correct more often than they are wrong.

above-average score on day 1 = above-average talent +
lucky on day 1

and

below-average score on day 1 = below-average talent +
unlucky on day 1

Now, suppose you know a golfer's score on day 1 and are asked to predict his score on day 2. You expect the golfer to retain the same level of talent on the second day, so your best guesses will be "above average" for the first player and "below average" for the second player. Luck, of course, is a different matter. Since you have no way of predicting the golfers' luck on the second (or any) day, your best guess must be that it will be average, neither good nor bad. This means that in the absence of any other information, your best guess about the players' score on day 2 should not be a repeat of their performance on day 1. This is the most you can say:

- The golfer who did well on day 1 is likely to be successful on day 2 as well, but less than on the first, because the unusual luck he probably enjoyed on day 1 is unlikely to hold.
- The golfer who did poorly on day 1 will probably be below average on day 2, but will improve, because his probable streak of bad luck is not likely to continue.

We also expect the difference between the two golfers to shrink on the second day, although our best guess is that the first player will still do better than the second.

My students were always surprised to hear that the best predicted performance on day 2 is more moderate, closer to the average than the evidence on which it is based (the score on day 1). This is why the pattern is called regression to the mean. The more extreme the original score, the more regression we expect, because an extremely good score suggests a very lucky day. The regressive prediction is reasonable, but its accuracy is not guaranteed. A few of the golfers who scored 66 on day 1 will do even better on the second day, if their luck improves. Most will do worse, because their luck will no longer be above average.

Now let us go against the time arrow. Arrange the players by their performance on day 2 and look at their performance on day 1. You will find precisely the same pattern of regression to the mean. The golfers who did best on day 2 were probably lucky on that day, and the best guess is that they had been less lucky and had done less well on day 1. The fact that you observe regression when you predict an early event from a later event should help convince you that regression does not have a causal explanation.

Regression effects are ubiquitous, and so are misguided causal stories to explain them. A well-known example is the "*Sports Illustrated* jinx," the claim that an athlete whose picture appears on the cover of the magazine is doomed to perform poorly the following season. Overconfidence and the pressure of meeting high expectations are often offered as explanations. But there is a simpler account of the jinx: an athlete who gets to be on the cover of *Sports Illustrated* must have performed exceptionally well in the preceding season, probably with the assistance of a nudge from luck—and luck is fickle.

I happened to watch the men's ski jump event in the Winter Olympics while Amos and I were writing an article about intuitive prediction. Each athlete has two jumps in the event, and the results are combined for the final score. I was startled to hear the sportscaster's comments while athletes were preparing for their second jump: "Norway had a great first jump; he will be tense, hoping to protect his lead and will probably do worse" or "Sweden had a bad first jump and now he knows he has nothing to lose and will be relaxed, which should help him do better." The commentator had obviously detected regression to the mean and had invented a causal story for which there was no evidence. The story itself could even be true. Perhaps if we measured the athletes' pulse before each jump we might find that they are indeed more relaxed after a bad first jump. And perhaps not. The point to remember is that the change from the first to the second jump does not need a causal explanation. It is a mathematically inevitable consequence of the fact that luck played a role in the outcome of the first jump. Not a very satisfactory story—we would all prefer a causal account—but that is all there is.

UNDERSTANDING REGRESSION

Whether undetected or wrongly explained, the phenomenon of regression is strange to the human mind. So strange, indeed, that it was first identified and understood two hundred years after the theory of gravitation and differential calculus. Furthermore, it took one of the best minds of nineteenth-century Britain to make sense of it, and that with great difficulty.

Regression to the mean was discovered and named late in the nineteenth century by Sir Francis Galton, a half cousin of Charles Darwin and a renowned polymath. You can sense the thrill of discovery in an article he published in 1886 under the title "Regression towards Mediocrity in Hereditary Stature," which reports measurements of size in successive generations of seeds and in comparisons of the height of children to the height of their parents. He writes about his studies of seeds:

> They yielded results that seemed very noteworthy, and I used them as the basis of a lecture before the Royal Institution on February 9th, 1877. It appeared from these experiments that the offspring did *not* tend to resemble their parent seeds in size, but to be always more mediocre than they—to be smaller than the parents, if the parents were large; to be larger than the parents, if the parents were very small . . . The experiments showed further that the mean filial regression towards mediocrity was directly proportional to the parental deviation from it.

Galton obviously expected his learned audience at the Royal Institution—
the oldest independent research society in the world—to be as surprised by
his "noteworthy observation" as he had been. What is truly noteworthy is
that he was surprised by a statistical regularity that is as common as the air
we breathe. Regression effects can be found wherever we look, but we do
not recognize them for what they are. They hide in plain sight. It took Galton several years to work his way from his discovery of filial regression in
size to the broader notion that regression inevitably occurs when the correlation between two measures is less than perfect, and he needed the help of
the most brilliant statisticians of his time to reach that conclusion.

One of the hurdles Galton had to overcome was the problem of measuring regression between variables that are measured on different scales,
such as weight and piano playing. This is done by using the population as a
standard of reference. Imagine that weight and piano playing have been
measured for 100 children in all grades of an elementary school, and that
they have been ranked from high to low on each measure. If Jane ranks
third in piano playing and twenty-seventh in weight, it is appropriate to
say that she is a better pianist than she is tall. Let us make some assumptions
that will simplify things:

At any age,

- Piano-playing success depends only on weekly hours of practice.
- Weight depends only on consumption of ice cream.
- Ice cream consumption and weekly hours of practice are unrelated.

Now, using ranks (or the *standard scores* that statisticians prefer), we can
write some equations:

weight = age + ice cream consumption
piano playing = age + weekly hours of practice

You can see that there will be regression to the mean when we predict piano
playing from weight, or vice versa. If all you know about Tom is that he
ranks twelfth in weight (well above average), you can infer (statistically)
that he is probably older than average and also that he probably consumes
more ice cream than other children. If all you know about Barbara is that
she is eighty-fifth in piano (far below the average of the group), you can
infer that she is likely to be young and that she is likely to practice less than
most other children.

The *correlation coefficient* between two measures, which varies between 0 and 1, is a measure of the relative weight of the factors they share. For example, we all share half our genes with each of our parents, and for traits in which environmental factors have relatively little influence, such as height, the correlation between parent and child is not far from .50. To appreciate the meaning of the correlation measure, the following are some examples of coefficients:

- The correlation between the size of objects measured with precision in English or in metric units is 1. Any factor that influences one measure also influences the other; 100% of determinants are shared.
- The correlation between self-reported height and weight among adult American males is .41. If you included women and children, the correlation would be much higher, because individuals' gender and age influence both their height and their weight, boosting the relative weight of shared factors.
- The correlation between SAT scores and college GPA is approximately .60. However, the correlation between aptitude tests and success in graduate school is much lower, largely because measured aptitude varies little in this selected group. If everyone has similar aptitude, differences in this measure are unlikely to play a large role in measures of success.
- The correlation between income and education level in the United States is approximately .40.
- The correlation between family income and the last four digits of their phone number is 0.

It took Francis Galton several years to figure out that correlation and regression are not two concepts—they are different perspectives on the same concept. The general rule is straightforward but has surprising consequences: whenever the correlation between two scores is imperfect, there will be regression to the mean. To illustrate Galton's insight, take a proposition that most people find quite interesting:

Highly intelligent women tend to marry men who are less intelligent than they are.

You can get a good conversation started at a party by asking for an explanation, and your friends will readily oblige. Even people who have had some exposure to statistics will spontaneously interpret the statement in causal terms. Some may think of highly intelligent women wanting to avoid the competition of equally intelligent men, or being forced to compromise in their choice of spouse because intelligent men do not want to compete with intelligent women. More far-fetched explanations will come up at a good party. Now consider this statement:

The correlation between the intelligence scores of spouses is less than perfect.

This statement is obviously true and not interesting at all. Who would expect the correlation to be perfect? There is nothing to explain. But the statement you found interesting and the statement you found trivial are algebraically equivalent. If the correlation between the intelligence of spouses is less than perfect (and if men and women on average do not differ in intelligence), then it is a mathematical inevitability that highly intelligent women will be married to husbands who are on average less intelligent than they are (and vice versa, of course). The observed regression to the mean cannot be more interesting or more explainable than the imperfect correlation.

You probably sympathize with Galton's struggle with the concept of regression. Indeed, the statistician David Freedman used to say that if the topic of regression comes up in a criminal or civil trial, the side that must explain regression to the jury will lose the case. Why is it so hard? The main reason for the difficulty is a recurrent theme of this book: our mind is strongly biased toward causal explanations and does not deal well with "mere statistics." When our attention is called to an event, associative memory will look for its cause—more precisely, activation will automatically spread to any cause that is already stored in memory. Causal explanations will be evoked when regression is detected, but they will be wrong because the truth is that regression to the mean has an explanation but does not have a cause. The event that attracts our attention in the golfing tournament is the frequent deterioration of the performance of the golfers who were successful on day 1. The best explanation of it is that those golfers were unusually lucky that day, but this explanation lacks the causal force that our minds prefer. Indeed, we pay people quite well to provide interesting explanations of regression effects. A business commentator who correctly announces that "the business did better this year because it had done poorly last year" is likely to have a short tenure on the air.

Our difficulties with the concept of regression originate with both System 1 and System 2. Without special instruction, and in quite a few cases even after some statistical instruction, the relationship between correlation and regression remains obscure. System 2 finds it difficult to understand and learn. This is due in part to the insistent demand for causal interpretations, which is a feature of System 1.

> Depressed children treated with an energy drink improve significantly over a three-month period.

I made up this newspaper headline, but the fact it reports is true: if you treated a group of depressed children for some time with an energy drink, they would show a clinically significant improvement. It is also the case that depressed children who spend some time standing on their head or hug a cat for twenty minutes a day will also show improvement. Most readers of such headlines will automatically infer that the energy drink or the cat hugging caused an improvement, but this conclusion is completely unjustified. Depressed children are an extreme group, they are more depressed than most other children—and extreme groups regress to the mean over time. The correlation between depression scores on successive occasions of testing is less than perfect, so there will be regression to the mean: depressed children will get somewhat better over time even if they hug no cats and drink no Red Bull. In order to conclude that an energy drink—or any other treatment—is effective, you must compare a group of patients who receive this treatment to a "control group" that receives no treatment (or, better, receives a placebo). The control group is expected to improve by regression alone, and the aim of the experiment is to determine whether the treated patients improve more than regression can explain.

Incorrect causal interpretations of regression effects are not restricted to readers of the popular press. The statistician Howard Wainer has drawn up a long list of eminent researchers who have made the same mistake—confusing mere correlation with causation. Regression effects are a common source of trouble in research, and experienced scientists develop a healthy fear of the trap of unwarranted causal inference.

One of my favorite examples of the errors of intuitive prediction is adapted from Max Bazerman's excellent text *Judgment in Managerial Decision Making*:

You are the sales forecaster for a department store chain. All stores are similar in size and merchandise selection, but their sales differ because of location, competition, and random factors. You are given the results for 2011 and asked to forecast sales for 2012. You have been instructed to accept the overall forecast of economists that sales will increase overall by 10%. How would you complete the following table?

Store	2011	2012
1	$11,000,000	_____
2	$23,000,000	_____
3	$18,000,000	_____
4	$29,000,000	_____
Total	$61,000,000	$67,100,000

Having read this chapter, you know that the obvious solution of adding 10% to the sales of each store is wrong. You want your forecasts to be regressive, which requires adding more than 10% to the low-performing branches and adding less (or even subtracting) to others. But if you ask other people, you are likely to encounter puzzlement: Why do you bother them with an obvious question? As Galton painfully discovered, the concept of regression is far from obvious.

SPEAKING OF REGRESSION TO MEDIOCRITY

"She says experience has taught her that criticism is more effective than praise. What she doesn't understand is that it's all due to regression to the mean."

"Perhaps his second interview was less impressive than the first because he was afraid of disappointing us, but more likely it was his first that was unusually good."

"Our screening procedure is good but not perfect, so we should anticipate regression. We shouldn't be surprised that the very best candidates often fail to meet our expectations."

18

TAMING INTUITIVE PREDICTIONS

Life presents us with many occasions to forecast. Economists forecast inflation and unemployment, financial analysts forecast earnings, military experts predict casualties, venture capitalists assess profitability, publishers and producers predict audiences, contractors estimate the time required to complete projects, chefs anticipate the demand for the dishes on their menu, engineers estimate the amount of concrete needed for a building, fireground commanders assess the number of trucks that will be needed to put out a fire. In our private lives, we forecast our spouse's reaction to a proposed move or our own future adjustment to a new job.

Some predictive judgments, such as those made by engineers, rely largely on look-up tables, precise calculations, and explicit analyses of outcomes observed on similar occasions. Others involve intuition and System 1, in two main varieties. Some intuitions draw primarily on skill and expertise acquired by repeated experience. The rapid and automatic judgments and choices of chess masters, fireground commanders, and physicians that Gary Klein has described in *Sources of Power* and elsewhere illustrate these skilled intuitions, in which a solution to the current problem comes to mind quickly because familiar cues are recognized.

Other intuitions, which are sometimes subjectively indistinguishable from the first, arise from the operation of heuristics that often substitute an easy question for the harder one that was asked. Intuitive judgments can be made with high confidence even when they are based on nonregressive assessments of weak evidence. Of course, many judgments, especially in the professional domain, are influenced by a combination of analysis and intuition.

NONREGRESSIVE INTUITIONS

Let us return to a person we have already met:

> Julie is currently a senior in a state university. She read fluently when she was four years old. What is her grade point average (GPA)?

People who are familiar with the American educational scene quickly come up with a number, which is often in the vicinity of 3.7 or 3.8. How does this occur? Several operations of System 1 are involved.

- A causal link between the evidence (Julie's reading) and the target of the prediction (her GPA) is sought. The link can be indirect. In this instance, early reading and a high GDP are both indications of academic talent. Some connection is necessary. You (your System 2) would probably reject as irrelevant a report of Julie winning a fly-fishing competition or excelling at weight lifting in high school. The process is effectively dichotomous. We are capable of rejecting information as irrelevant or false, but adjusting for smaller weaknesses in the evidence is not something that System 1 can do. As a result, intu-itive predictions are almost completely insensitive to the actual pre-dictive quality of the evidence. When a link is found, as in the case of Julie's early reading, WYSIATI applies: your associative memory quickly and automatically constructs the best possible story from the information available.
- Next, the evidence is evaluated in relation to a relevant norm. How precocious is a child who reads fluently at age four? What relative rank or percentile score corresponds to this achievement? The group to which the child is compared (we call it a reference group) is not fully specified, but this is also the rule in normal speech: if someone graduating from college is described as "quite clever" you rarely need to ask, "When you say 'quite clever,' which reference group do you have in mind?"
- The next step involves substitution and intensity matching. The eval-uation of the flimsy evidence of cognitive ability in childhood is sub-stituted as an answer to the question about her college GPA. Julie will

be assigned the same percentile score for her GPA and for her achievements as an early reader.

- The question specified that the answer must be on the GPA scale, which requires another intensity-matching operation, from a general impression of Julie's academic achievements to the GPA that matches the evidence for her talent. The final step is a translation, from an impression of Julie's relative academic standing to the GPA that corresponds to it.

Intensity matching yields predictions that are as extreme as the evidence on which they are based, leading people to give the same answer to two quite different questions:

What is Julie's percentile score on reading precocity?
What is Julie's percentile score on GPA?

By now you should easily recognize that all these operations are features of System 1. I listed them here as an orderly sequence of steps, but of course the spread of activation in associative memory does not work this way. You should imagine a process of spreading activation that is initially prompted by the evidence and the question, feeds back upon itself, and eventually settles on the most coherent solution possible.

Amos and I once asked participants in an experiment to judge descriptions of eight college freshmen, allegedly written by a counselor on the basis of interviews of the entering class. Each description consisted of five adjectives, as in the following example:

intelligent, self-confident, well-read, hardworking, inquisitive

We asked some participants to answer two questions:

How much does this description impress you with respect to academic ability?

What percentage of descriptions of freshmen do you believe would impress you more?

The questions require you to evaluate the evidence by comparing the description to your norm for descriptions of students by counselors. The very existence of such a norm is remarkable. Although you surely do not know how you acquired it, you have a fairly clear sense of how much enthusiasm the description conveys: the counselor believes that this student is good, but not spectacularly good. There is room for stronger adjectives than *intelligent* (*brilliant, creative*), *well-read* (*scholarly, erudite, impressively knowledgeable*), and *hardworking* (*passionate, perfectionist*). The verdict: very likely to be in the top 15% but unlikely to be in the top 3%. There is impressive consensus in such judgments, at least within a culture.

The other participants in our experiment were asked different questions:

What is your estimate of the grade point average that the student will obtain?
What is the percentage of freshmen who obtain a higher GPA?

You need another look to detect the subtle difference between the two sets of questions. The difference should be obvious, but it is not. Unlike the first questions, which required you only to evaluate the evidence, the second set involves a great deal of uncertainty. The question refers to actual performance at the end of the freshman year. What happened during the year since the interview was performed? How accurately can you predict the student's actual achievements in the first year at college from five adjectives? Would the counselor herself be perfectly accurate if she predicted GPA from an interview?

The objective of this study was to compare the percentile judgments that the participants made when evaluating the evidence in one case, and when predicting the ultimate outcome in another. The results are easy to summarize: the judgments were identical. Although the two sets of questions differ (one is about the description, the other about the student's future academic performance), the participants treated them as if they were the same. As was the case with Julie, the prediction of the future is not distinguished from an evaluation of current evidence—prediction matches evaluation. This is perhaps the best evidence we have for the role of substitution. People are asked for a prediction but they substitute an evaluation of the evidence, without noticing that the question they answer is not the one they were asked. This process is guaranteed to generate predictions that are systematically biased; they completely ignore regression to the mean.

During my military service in the Israeli Defense Forces, I spent some time attached to a unit that selected candidates for officer training on the basis of a series of interviews and field tests. The designated criterion for successful prediction was a cadet's final grade in officer school. The validity of the ratings was known to be rather poor (I will tell more about it in a later chapter). The unit still existed years later, when I was a professor and collaborating with Amos in the study of intuitive judgment. I had good contacts with the people at the unit and asked them for a favor. In addition to the usual grading system they used to evaluate the candidates, I asked for their best guess of the grade that each of the future cadets would obtain in officer school. They collected a few hundred such forecasts. The officers who had produced the predictions were all familiar with the letter grading system that the school applied to its cadets and the approximate proportions of A's, B's, etc., among them. The results were striking: the relative frequency of A's and B's in the predictions was almost identical to the frequencies in the final grades of the school.

These findings provide a compelling example of both substitution and intensity matching. The officers who provided the predictions completely failed to discriminate between two tasks:

- their usual mission, which was to evaluate the performance of candidates during their stay at the unit
- the task I had asked them to perform, which was an actual prediction of a future grade

They had simply translated their own grades onto the scale used in officer school, applying intensity matching. Once again, the failure to address the (considerable) uncertainty of their predictions had led them to predictions that were completely nonregressive.

A CORRECTION FOR INTUITIVE PREDICTIONS

Back to Julie, our precocious reader. The correct way to predict her GPA was introduced in the preceding chapter. As I did there for golf on successive days and for weight and piano playing, I write a schematic formula for the factors that determine reading age and college grades:

reading age = shared factors + factors specific to reading age = 100%
GPA = shared factors + factors specific to GPA = 100%

The shared factors involve genetically determined aptitude, the degree to which the family supports academic interests, and anything else that would cause the same people to be precocious readers as children and academically successful as young adults. Of course there are many factors that would affect one of these outcomes and not the other. Julie could have been pushed to read early by overly ambitious parents, she may have had an unhappy love affair that depressed her college grades, she could have had a skiing accident during adolescence that left her slightly impaired, and so on.

Recall that the correlation between two measures—in the present case reading age and GPA—is equal to the proportion of shared factors among their determinants. What is your best guess about that proportion? My most optimistic guess is about 30%. Assuming this estimate, we have all we need to produce an unbiased prediction. Here are the directions for how to get there in four simple steps:

1. Start with an estimate of average GPA.
2. Determine the GPA that matches your impression of the evidence.
3. Estimate the correlation between your evidence and GPA.
4. If the correlation is .30, move 30% of the distance from the average to the matching GPA.

Step 1 gets you the baseline, the GPA you would have predicted if you were told nothing about Julie beyond the fact that she is a graduating senior. In the absence of information, you would have predicted the average. (This is similar to assigning the base-rate probability of business administration graduates when you are told nothing about Tom W.) Step 2 is your intuitive prediction, which matches your evaluation of the evidence. Step 3 moves you from the baseline toward your intuition, but the distance you are allowed to move depends on your estimate of the correlation. You end up, at step 4, with a prediction that is influenced by your intuition but is far more moderate.

This approach to prediction is general. You can apply it whenever you need to predict a quantitative variable, such as GPA, profit from an investment, or the growth of a company. The approach builds on your intuition, but it moderates it, regresses it toward the mean. When you have good reasons to trust the accuracy of your intuitive prediction—a strong correlation between the evidence and the prediction—the adjustment will be small.

Intuitive predictions need to be corrected because they are not regressive and therefore are biased. Suppose that I predict for each golfer in a tournament that his score on day 2 will be the same as his score on day 1. This prediction does not allow for regression to the mean: the golfers who fared well on day 1 will on average do less well on day 2, and those who did poorly will mostly improve. When they are eventually compared to actual outcomes, nonregressive predictions will be found to be biased. They are on average overly optimistic for those who did best on the first day and overly pessimistic for those who had a bad start. The predictions are as extreme as the evidence. Similarly, if you use childhood achievements to predict grades in college without regressing your predictions toward the mean, you will more often than not be disappointed by the academic outcomes of early readers and happily surprised by the grades of those who learned to read relatively late. The corrected intuitive predictions eliminate these biases, so that predictions (both high and low) are about equally likely to over-estimate and to underestimate the true value. You still make errors when your predictions are unbiased, but the errors are smaller and do not favor either high or low outcomes.

A DEFENSE OF EXTREME PREDICTIONS?

I introduced Tom W earlier to illustrate predictions of discrete outcomes such as field of specialization or success in an examination, which are ex-pressed by assigning a probability to a specified event (or in that case by ranking outcomes from the most to the least probable). I also described a procedure that counters the common biases of discrete prediction: neglect of base rates and insensitivity to the quality of information.

The biases we find in predictions that are expressed on a scale, such as GPA or the revenue of a firm, are similar to the biases observed in judging the probabilities of outcomes.

The corrective procedures are also similar:

- Both contain a baseline prediction, which you would make if you knew nothing about the case at hand. In the categorical case, it was the base rate. In the numerical case, it is the average outcome in the relevant category.
- Both contain an intuitive prediction, which expresses the number that comes to your mind, whether it is a probability or a GPA.
- In both cases, you aim for a prediction that is intermediate between the baseline and your intuitive response.
- In the default case of no useful evidence, you stay with the baseline.
- At the other extreme, you also stay with your initial prediction. This will happen, of course, only if you remain completely confident in

your initial prediction after a critical review of the evidence that supports it.

- In most cases you will find some reason to doubt that the correlation between your intuitive judgment and the truth is perfect, and you will end up somewhere between the two poles.

This procedure is an approximation of the likely results of an appropriate statistical analysis. If successful, it will move you toward unbiased predictions, reasonable assessments of probability, and moderate predictions of numerical outcomes. The two procedures are intended to address the same bias: intuitive predictions tend to be overconfident and overly extreme.

Correcting your intuitive predictions is a task for System 2. Significant effort is required to find the relevant reference category, estimate the baseline prediction, and evaluate the quality of the evidence. The effort is justified only when the stakes are high and when you are particularly keen not to make mistakes. Furthermore, you should know that correcting your intuitions may complicate your life. A characteristic of unbiased predictions is that they permit the prediction of rare or extreme events only when the information is very good. If you expect your predictions to be of modest validity, you will never guess an outcome that is either rare or far from the mean. If your predictions are unbiased, you will never have the satisfying experience of correctly calling an extreme case. You will never be able to say, "I thought so!" when your best student in law school becomes a Supreme Court justice, or when a start-up that you thought very promising eventually becomes a major commercial success. Given the limitations of the evidence, you will never predict that an outstanding high school student will be a straight-A student at Princeton. For the same reason, a venture capitalist will never be told that the probability of success for a start-up in its early stages is "very high."

The objections to the principle of moderating intuitive predictions must be taken seriously, because absence of bias is not always what matters most. A preference for unbiased predictions is justified if all errors of prediction are treated alike, regardless of their direction. But there are situations in which one type of error is much worse than another. When a venture capitalist looks for "the next big thing," the risk of missing the next Google or Facebook is far more important than the risk of making a modest investment in a start-up that ultimately fails. The goal of venture capitalists is to call the extreme cases correctly, even at the cost of overestimating the prospects of many other ventures. For a conservative banker making large loans, the risk of a single borrower going bankrupt may outweigh the risk of turning down several would-be clients who would fulfill their obligations. In such cases, the use of extreme language ("very good prospect," "serious risk of default") may have some justification for the comfort it provides, even if the information on which these judgments are based is of only modest validity.

For a rational person, predictions that are unbiased and moderate should not present a problem. After all, the rational venture capitalist knows that even the most promising start-ups have only a moderate chance of success. She views her job as picking the most promising bets from the bets that are available and does not feel the need to delude herself about the prospects of a start-up in which she plans to invest. Similarly, rational individuals predicting the revenue of a firm will not be bound to a single number—they should consider the range of uncertainty around the most likely outcome. A rational person will invest a large sum in an enterprise that is most likely to fail if the rewards of success are large enough, without deluding herself about the chances of success. However, we are not all rational, and some of us may need the security of distorted estimates to avoid paralysis. If you choose to delude yourself by accepting extreme predictions, however, you will do well to remain aware of your self-indulgence.

Perhaps the most valuable contribution of the corrective procedures I propose is that they will require you to think about how much you know. I will use an example that is familiar in the academic world, but the analogies to other spheres of life are immediate. A department is about to hire a young professor and wants to choose the one whose prospects for scientific productivity are the best. The search committee has narrowed down the choice to two candidates:

Kim recently completed her graduate work. Her recommendations are spectacular and she gave a brilliant talk and impressed everyone in her interviews. She has no substantial track record of scientific productivity.

Jane has held a postdoctoral position for the last three years. She has been very productive and her research record is excellent, but her talk and interviews were less sparkling than Kim's.

The intuitive choice favors Kim, because she left a stronger impression, and WYSIATI. But it is also the case that there is much less information about Kim than about Jane. We are back to the law of small numbers. In effect, you have a smaller sample of information from Kim than from Jane, and extreme outcomes are much more likely to be observed in small samples. There is more luck in the outcomes of small samples, and you should therefore regress your prediction more deeply toward the mean in your prediction of Kim's future performance. When you allow for the fact that Kim is likely to regress more than Jane, you might end up selecting Jane although you were less impressed by her. In the context of academic choices, I would vote for Jane, but it would be a struggle to overcome my intuitive impression that Kim is more promising. Following our intuitions is more natural, and somehow more pleasant, than acting against them.

You can readily imagine similar problems in different contexts, such as a venture capitalist choosing between investments in two start-ups that operate in different markets. One start-up has a product for which demand can be estimated with fair precision. The other candidate is more exciting and intuitively promising, but its prospects are less certain. Whether the best guess about the prospects of the second start-up is still superior when the uncertainty is factored in is a question that deserves careful consideration.

A TWO-SYSTEMS VIEW OF REGRESSION

Extreme predictions and a willingness to predict rare events from weak evidence are both manifestations of System 1. It is natural for the associative machinery to match the extremeness of predictions to the perceived extremeness of evidence on which it is based—this is how substitution works. And it is natural for System 1 to generate overconfident judgments, because confidence, as we have seen, is determined by the coherence of the best story you can tell from the evidence at hand. Be warned: your intuitions will deliver predictions that are too extreme and you will be inclined to put far too much faith in them.

Regression is also a problem for System 2. The very idea of regression to the mean is alien and difficult to communicate and comprehend. Galton had a hard time before he understood it. Many statistics teachers dread the class in which the topic comes up, and their students often end up with only a vague understanding of this crucial concept. This is a case where System 2 requires special training. Matching predictions to the evidence is not only something we do intuitively; it also seems a reasonable thing to do. We will not learn to understand regression from experience. Even when a regression is identified, as we saw in the story of the flight instructors, it will be given a causal interpretation that is almost always wrong.

SPEAKING OF INTUITIVE PREDICTIONS

"That start-up achieved an outstanding proof of concept, but we shouldn't expect them to do as well in the future. They are still a long way from the market and there is a lot of room for regression."

"Our intuitive prediction is very favorable, but it is probably too high. Let's take into account the strength of our evidence and regress the prediction toward the mean."

"The investment may be a good idea, even if the best guess is that it will fail. Let's not say we really believe it is the next Google."

"I read one review of that brand and it was excellent. Still, that could have been a fluke. Let's consider only the brands that have a large number of reviews and pick the one that looks best."

PART 3

OVERCONFIDENCE

19

THE ILLUSION OF UNDERSTANDING

The trader-philosopher-statistician Nassim Taleb could also be considered a psychologist. In *The Black Swan*, Taleb introduced the notion of a *narrative fallacy* to describe how flawed stories of the past shape our views of the world and our expectations for the future. Narrative fallacies arise inevitably from our continuous attempt to make sense of the world. The explanatory stories that people find compelling are simple; are concrete rather than abstract; assign a larger role to talent, stupidity, and intentions than to luck; and focus on a few striking events that happened rather than on the countless events that failed to happen. Any recent salient event is a candidate to become the kernel of a causal narrative. Taleb suggests that we humans constantly fool ourselves by constructing flimsy accounts of the past and believing they are true.

Good stories provide a simple and coherent account of people's actions and intentions. You are always ready to interpret behavior as a manifestation of general propensities and personality traits—causes that you can readily match to effects. The halo effect discussed earlier contributes to coherence, because it inclines us to match our view of all the qualities of a person to our judgment of one attribute that is particularly significant. If we think a baseball pitcher is handsome and athletic, for example, we are likely to rate him better at throwing the ball, too. Halos can also be negative: if we think a player is ugly, we will probably underrate his athletic ability. The halo effect helps keep explanatory narratives simple and coherent by exaggerating the consistency of evaluations: good people do only good things and bad people are all bad. The statement "Hitler loved dogs and little children" is shocking no matter how many times you hear it, because any trace of kindness in someone so evil violates the expectations set up by the halo effect. Inconsistencies reduce the ease of our thoughts and the clarity of our feelings.

A compelling narrative fosters an illusion of inevitability. Consider the story of how Google turned into a giant of the technology industry. Two creative graduate students in the computer science department at Stanford University come up with a superior way of searching information on the Internet. They seek and obtain funding to start a company and make a series of decisions that work out well. Within a few years, the company they started is one of the most valuable stocks in America, and the two former graduate students are among the richest people on the planet. On one memorable occasion, they were lucky, which makes the story even more compelling: a year after founding Google, they were willing to sell their company for less than $1 million, but the buyer said the price was too high. Mentioning the single lucky incident actually makes it easier to underestimate the multitude of ways in which luck affected the outcome.

A detailed history would specify the decisions of Google's founders, but for our purposes it suffices to say that almost every choice they made had a good outcome. A more complete narrative would describe the actions of the firms that Google defeated. The hapless competitors would appear to be blind, slow, and altogether inadequate in dealing with the threat that eventually overwhelmed them.

I intentionally told this tale blandly, but you get the idea: there is a very good story here. Fleshed out in more detail, the story could give you the sense that you understand what made Google succeed; it would also make you feel that you have learned a valuable general lesson about what makes businesses succeed. Unfortunately, there is good reason to believe that your sense of understanding and learning from the Google story is largely illusory. The ultimate test of an explanation is whether it would have made the event predictable in advance. No story of Google's unlikely success will meet that test, because no story can include the myriad of events that would have caused a different outcome. The human mind does not deal well with nonevents. The fact that many of the important events that did occur involve choices further tempts you to exaggerate the role of skill and underestimate the part that luck played in the outcome. Because every critical decision turned out well, the record suggests almost flawless prescience—but bad luck could have disrupted any one of the successful steps. The halo effect adds the final touches, lending an aura of invincibility to the heroes of the story.

Like watching a skilled rafter avoiding one potential calamity after another as he goes down the rapids, the unfolding of the Google story is thrilling because of the constant risk of disaster. However, there is an instructive difference between the two cases. The skilled rafter has gone down rapids hundreds of times. He has learned to read the roiling water in front of him and to anticipate obstacles. He has learned to make the tiny adjustments of posture that keep him upright. There are fewer opportunities for young men to learn how to create a giant company, and fewer chances to avoid hidden rocks—such as a brilliant innovation by a competing firm. Of course there was a great deal of skill in the Google story, but luck played a more important role in the actual event than it does in the telling of it. And the more luck was involved, the less there is to be learned.

At work here is that powerful WYSIATI rule. You cannot help dealing with the limited information you have as if it were all there is to know. You build the best possible story from the information available to you, and if it is a good story, you believe it. Paradoxically, it is easier to construct a coherent story when you know little, when there are fewer pieces to fit into the puzzle. Our comforting conviction that the world makes sense rests on a secure foundation: our almost unlimited ability to ignore our ignorance.

I have heard of too many people who "knew well before it happened that the 2008 financial crisis was inevitable." This sentence contains a highly objectionable word, which should be removed from our vocabulary in discussions of major events. The word is, of course, *knew*. Some people thought well in advance that there would be a crisis, but they did not know it. They now say they knew it because the crisis did in fact happen. This is a misuse of an important concept. In everyday language, we apply the word *know* only when what was known is true and can be shown to be true. We can know something only if it is both true and knowable. But the people who thought there would be a crisis (and there are fewer of them than now remember thinking it) could not conclusively show it at the time. Many intelligent and well-informed people were keenly interested in the future of the economy and did not believe a catastrophe was imminent; I infer from this fact that the crisis was not knowable. What is perverse about the use of *know* in this context is not that some individuals get credit for prescience that they do not deserve. It is that the language implies that the world is more knowable than it is. It helps perpetuate a pernicious illusion.

The core of the illusion is that we believe we understand the past, which implies that the future also should be knowable, but in fact we understand the past less than we believe we do. *Know* is not the only word that fosters this illusion. In common usage, the words *intuition* and *premonition* also are reserved for past thoughts that turned out to be true. The statement "I had a premonition that the marriage would not last, but I was wrong" sounds odd, as does any sentence about an intuition that turned out to be false. To think clearly about the future, we need to clean up the language that we use in labeling the beliefs we had in the past.

THE SOCIAL COSTS OF HINDSIGHT

The mind that makes up narratives about the past is a sense-making organ. When an unpredicted event occurs, we immediately adjust our view of the world to accommodate the surprise. Imagine yourself before a football game between two teams that have the same record of wins and losses. Now the game is over, and one team trashed the other. In your revised model of the world, the winning team is much stronger than the loser, and your view of the past as well as of the future has been altered by that new perception. Learning from surprises is a reasonable thing to do, but it can have some dangerous consequences.

A general limitation of the human mind is its imperfect ability to reconstruct past states of knowledge, or beliefs that have changed. Once you adopt a new view of the world (or of any part of it), you immediately lose much of your ability to recall what you used to believe before your mind changed.

Many psychologists have studied what happens when people change their minds. Choosing a topic on which minds are not completely made up—say, the death penalty—the experimenter carefully measures people's attitudes. Next, the participants see or hear a persuasive pro or con message. Then the experimenter measures people's attitudes again; they usually are closer to the persuasive message they were exposed to. Finally, the participants report the opinion they held beforehand. This task turns out to be surprisingly difficult. Asked to reconstruct their former beliefs, people retrieve their current ones instead—an instance of substitution—and many cannot believe that they ever felt differently.

Your inability to reconstruct past beliefs will inevitably cause you to underestimate the extent to which you were surprised by past events. Baruch Fischhoff first demonstrated this "I-knew-it-all-along" effect, or *hindsight bias*, when he was a student in Jerusalem. Together with Ruth Beyth (another of our students), Fischhoff conducted a survey before President Richard Nixon visited China and Russia in 1972. The respondents assigned probabilities to fifteen possible outcomes of Nixon's diplomatic initiatives. Would Mao Zedong agree to meet with Nixon? Might the United States grant diplomatic recognition to China? After decades of enmity, could the United States and the Soviet Union agree on anything significant?

After Nixon's return from his travels, Fischhoff and Beyth asked the same people to recall the probability that they had originally assigned to each of the fifteen possible outcomes. The results were clear. If an event had actually occurred, people exaggerated the probability that they had assigned to it earlier. If the possible event had not come to pass, the participants erroneously recalled that they had always considered it unlikely. Further experiments showed that people were driven to overstate the accuracy not only of their original predictions but also of those made by others. Similar results have been found for other events that gripped public attention, such as the O. J. Simpson murder trial and the impeachment of President Bill Clinton. The tendency to revise the history of one's beliefs in light of what actually happened produces a robust cognitive illusion.

Hindsight bias has pernicious effects on the evaluations of decision makers. It leads observers to assess the quality of a decision not by whether the process was sound but by whether its outcome was good or bad. Consider a low-risk surgical intervention in which an unpredictable accident occurred that caused the patient's death. The jury will be prone to believe, after the fact, that the operation was actually risky and that the doctor who ordered it should have known better. This outcome bias makes it almost impossible to evaluate a decision properly—in terms of the beliefs that were reasonable when the decision was made.

Hindsight is especially unkind to decision makers who act as agents for others—physicians, financial advisers, third-base coaches, CEOs, social workers, diplomats, politicians. We are prone to blame decision makers for good decisions that worked out badly and to give them too little credit for successful moves that appear obvious only after the fact. There is a clear *outcome bias*. When the outcomes are bad, the clients often blame their agents for not seeing the handwriting on the wall—forgetting that it was written in invisible ink that became legible only afterward. Actions that seemed prudent in foresight can look irresponsibly negligent in hindsight. Based on an actual legal case, students in California were asked whether the city of Duluth, Minnesota, should have shouldered the considerable cost of hiring a full-time bridge monitor to protect against the risk that debris might get caught and block the free flow of water. One group was shown only the evidence available at the time of the city's decision; 24% of these people felt that Duluth should take on the expense of hiring a flood monitor. The second group was informed that debris had blocked the river, causing major flood damage; 56% of these people said the city should have hired the monitor, although they had been explicitly instructed not to let hindsight distort their judgment.

The worse the consequence, the greater the hindsight bias. In the case of a catastrophe, such as 9/11, we are especially ready to believe that the officials who failed to anticipate it were negligent or blind. On July 10, 2001, the Central Intelligence Agency obtained information that al-Qaeda might be planning a major attack against the United States. George Tenet, director of the CIA, brought the information not to President George W. Bush but to National Security Adviser Condoleezza Rice. When the facts later emerged, Ben Bradlee, the legendary executive editor of *The Washington Post*, declared, "It seems to me elementary that if you've got the story that's going to dominate history you might as well go right to the president." But on July 10, no one knew—or could have known—that this tidbit of intelligence would turn out to dominate history.

Because adherence to standard operating procedures is difficult to second-guess, decision makers who expect to have their decisions scrutinized with hindsight are driven to bureaucratic solutions—and to an extreme reluctance to take risks. As malpractice litigation became more common, physicians changed their procedures in multiple ways: ordered more tests, referred more cases to specialists, applied conventional treatments even when they were unlikely to help. These actions protected the physicians more than they benefited the patients, creating the potential for conflicts of interest. Increased accountability is a mixed blessing.

Although hindsight and the outcome bias generally foster risk aversion, they also bring undeserved rewards to irresponsible risk seekers, such as a general or an entrepreneur who took a crazy gamble and won. Leaders who have been lucky are never punished for having taken too much risk. Instead, they are believed to have had the flair and foresight to anticipate success, and the sensible people who doubted them are seen in hindsight as mediocre, timid, and weak. A few lucky gambles can crown a reckless leader with a halo of prescience and boldness.

RECIPES FOR SUCCESS

The sense-making machinery of System 1 makes us see the world as more tidy, simple, predictable, and coherent than it really is. The illusion that one has understood the past feeds the further illusion that one can predict and control the future. These illusions are comforting. They reduce the anxiety that we would experience if we allowed ourselves to fully acknowledge the uncertainties of existence. We all have a need for the reassuring message that actions have appropriate consequences, and that success will reward wisdom and courage. Many business books are tailor-made to satisfy this need.

Do leaders and management practices influence the outcomes of firms in the market? Of course they do, and the effects have been confirmed by systematic research that objectively assessed the characteristics of CEOs and their decisions, and related them to subsequent outcomes of the firm. In one study, the CEOs were characterized by the strategy of the companies they had led before their current appointment, as well as by management rules and procedures adopted after their appointment. CEOs do influence performance, but the effects are much smaller than a reading of the business press suggests.

Researchers measure the strength of relationships by a correlation coefficient, which varies between 0 and 1. The coefficient was defined earlier (in relation to regression to the mean) by the extent to which two measures are determined by shared factors. A very generous estimate of the correlation between the success of the firm and the quality of its CEO might be as high as .30, indicating 30% overlap. To appreciate the significance of this number, consider the following question:

Suppose you consider many pairs of firms. The two firms in each pair are generally similar, but the CEO of one of them is better than the other. How often will you find that the firm with the stronger CEO is the more successful of the two?

In a well-ordered and predictable world, the correlation would be perfect (1), and the stronger CEO would be found to lead the more successful firm in 100% of the pairs. If the relative success of similar firms was determined entirely by factors that the CEO does not control (call them luck, if you wish), you would find the more successful firm led by the weaker CEO 50% of the time. A correlation of .30 implies that you would find the stronger CEO leading the stronger firm in about 60% of the pairs—an improvement of a mere 10 percentage points over random guessing, hardly grist for the hero worship of CEOs we so often witness.

If you expected this value to be higher—and most of us do—then you should take that as an indication that you are prone to overestimate the predictability of the world you live in. Make no mistake: improving the odds of success from 1:1 to 3:2 is a very significant advantage, both at the racetrack and in business. From the perspective of most business writers, however, a CEO who has so little control over performance would not be particularly impressive even if her firm did well. It is difficult to imagine people lining up at airport bookstores to buy a book that enthusiastically describes the practices of business leaders who, on average, do somewhat better than chance. Consumers have a hunger for a clear message about the determinants of success and failure in business, and they need stories that offer a sense of understanding, however illusory.

In his penetrating book *The Halo Effect*, Philip Rosenzweig, a business school professor based in Switzerland, shows how the demand for illusory certainty is met in two popular genres of business writing: histories of the rise (usually) and fall (occasionally) of particular individuals and companies, and analyses of differences between successful and less successful firms. He concludes that stories of success and failure consistently exaggerate the impact of leadership style and management practices on firm outcomes, and thus their message is rarely useful.

To appreciate what is going on, imagine that business experts, such as other CEOs, are asked to comment on the reputation of the chief executive of a company. They are keenly aware of whether the company has recently been thriving or failing. As we saw earlier in the case of Google, this knowledge generates a halo. The CEO of a successful company is likely to be called flexible, methodical, and decisive. Imagine that a year has passed and things have gone sour. The same executive is now described as confused, rigid, and authoritarian. Both descriptions sound right at the time: it seems almost absurd to call a successful leader rigid and confused, or a struggling leader flexible and methodical.

Indeed, the halo effect is so powerful that you probably find yourself resisting the idea that the same person and the same behaviors appear methodical when things are going well and rigid when things are going poorly. Because of the halo effect, we get the causal relationship backward: we are prone to believe that the firm fails because its CEO is rigid, when the truth is that the CEO appears to be rigid because the firm is failing. This is how illusions of understanding are born.

The halo effect and outcome bias combine to explain the extraordinary appeal of books that seek to draw operational morals from systematic examination of successful businesses. One of the best-known examples of this genre is Jim Collins and Jerry I. Porras's *Built to Last*. The book contains a thorough analysis of eighteen pairs of competing companies, in which one was more successful than the other. The data for these comparisons are ratings of various aspects of corporate culture, strategy, and management practices. "We believe every CEO, manager, and entrepreneur in the world should read this book," the authors proclaim. "You can build a visionary company."

The basic message of *Built to Last* and other similar books is that good managerial practices can be identified and that good practices will be rewarded by good results. Both messages are overstated. The comparison of firms that have been more or less successful is to a significant extent a comparison between firms that have been more or less lucky. Knowing the importance of luck, you should be particularly suspicious when highly consistent patterns emerge from the comparison of successful and less successful firms. In the presence of randomness, regular patterns can only be mirages.

Because luck plays a large role, the quality of leadership and management practices cannot be inferred reliably from observations of success. And even if you had perfect foreknowledge that a CEO has brilliant vision and extraordinary competence, you still would be unable to predict how the company will perform with much better accuracy than the flip of a coin. On average, the gap in corporate profitability and stock returns between the outstanding firms and the less successful firms studied in *Built to Last* shrank to almost nothing in the period following the study. The average profitability of the companies identified in the famous *In Search of Excellence* dropped sharply as well within a short time. A study of *Fortune*'s "Most Admired Companies" finds that over a twenty-year period, the firms with the worst ratings went on to earn much higher stock returns than the most admired firms.

You are probably tempted to think of causal explanations for these observations: perhaps the successful firms became complacent, the less successful firms tried harder. But this is the wrong way to think about what happened. The average gap must shrink, because the original gap was due in good part to luck, which contributed both to the success of the top firms and to the lagging performance of the rest. We have already encountered this statistical fact of life: regression to the mean.

Stories of how businesses rise and fall strike a chord with readers by offering what the human mind needs: a simple message of triumph and failure that identifies clear causes and ignores the determinative power of luck and the inevitability of regression. These stories induce and maintain an illusion of understanding, imparting lessons of little enduring value to readers who are all too eager to believe them.

SPEAKING OF HINDSIGHT

"The mistake appears obvious, but it is just hindsight. You could not have known in advance."

"He's learning too much from this success story, which is too tidy. He has fallen for a narrative fallacy."

"She has no evidence for saying that the firm is badly managed. All she knows is that its stock has gone down. This is an outcome bias, part hindsight and part halo effect."

"Let's not fall for the outcome bias. This was a stupid decision even though it worked out well."

20

THE ILLUSION OF VALIDITY

System 1 is designed to jump to conclusions from little evidence—and it is not designed to know the size of its jumps. Because of WYSIATI, only the evidence at hand counts. Because of confidence by coherence, the subjective confidence we have in our opinions reflects the coherence of the story that System 1 and System 2 have constructed. The amount of evidence and its quality do not count for much, because poor evidence can make a very good story. For some of our most important beliefs we have no evidence at all, except that people we love and trust hold these beliefs. Considering how little we know, the confidence we have in our beliefs is preposterous—and it is also essential.

THE ILLUSION OF VALIDITY

Many decades ago I spent what seemed like a great deal of time under a scorching sun, watching groups of sweaty soldiers as they solved a problem. I was doing my national service in the Israeli Army at the time. I had completed an undergraduate degree in psychology, and after a year as an infantry officer was assigned to the army's Psychology Branch, where one of my occasional duties was to help evaluate candidates for officer training. We used methods that had been developed by the British Army in World War II.

One test, called the "leaderless group challenge," was conducted on an obstacle field. Eight candidates, strangers to each other, with all insignia of rank removed and only numbered tags to identify them, were instructed to lift a long log from the ground and haul it to a wall about six feet high. The entire group had to get to the other side of the wall without the log touching either the ground or the wall, and without anyone touching the wall. If any of these things happened, they had to declare it and start again.

There was more than one way to solve the problem. A common solution was for the team to send several men to the other side by crawling over the pole as it was held at an angle, like a giant fishing rod, by other members of the group. Or else some soldiers would climb onto someone's shoulders and jump across. The last man would then have to jump up at the pole, held up at an angle by the rest of the group, shinny his way along its length as the others kept him and the pole suspended in the air, and leap safely to the other side. Failure was common at this point, which required them to start all over again.

As a colleague and I monitored the exercise, we made note of who took charge, who tried to lead but was rebuffed, how cooperative each soldier was in contributing to the group effort. We saw who seemed to be stubborn, submissive, arrogant, patient, hot-tempered, persistent, or a quitter. We sometimes saw competitive spite when someone whose idea had been rejected by the group no longer worked very hard. And we saw reactions to crisis: who berated a comrade whose mistake had caused the whole group to fail, who stepped forward to lead when the exhausted team had to start over. Under the stress of the event, we felt, each man's true nature revealed itself. Our impression of each candidate's character was as direct and compelling as the color of the sky.

After watching the candidates make several attempts, we had to summarize our impressions of soldiers' leadership abilities and determine, with a numerical score, who should be eligible for officer training. We spent some time discussing each case and reviewing our impressions. The task was not difficult, because we felt we had already seen each soldier's leadership skills. Some of the men had looked like strong leaders, others had seemed like wimps or arrogant fools, others mediocre but not hopeless. Quite a few looked so weak that we ruled them out as candidates for officer rank. When our multiple observations of each candidate converged on a coherent story, we were completely confident in our evaluations and felt that what we had seen pointed directly to the future. The soldier who took over when the group was in trouble and led the team over the wall was a leader at that moment. The obvious best guess about how he would do in training, or in combat, was that he would be as effective then as he had been at the wall. Any other prediction seemed inconsistent with the evidence before our eyes.

Because our impressions of how well each soldier had performed were generally coherent and clear, our formal predictions were just as definite. A single score usually came to mind and we rarely experienced doubts or formed conflicting impressions. We were quite willing to declare, "This one will never make it," "That fellow is mediocre, but he should do okay," or "He will be a star." We felt no need to question our forecasts, moderate them, or equivocate. If challenged, however, we were prepared to admit, "But of course anything could happen." We were willing to make that admission because, despite our definite impressions about individual candidates, we knew with certainty that our forecasts were largely useless.

The evidence that we could not forecast success accurately was overwhelming. Every few months we had a feedback session in which we learned how the cadets were doing at the officer-training school and could compare our assessments against the opinions of commanders who had been monitoring them for some time. The story was always the same: our ability to predict performance at the school was negligible. Our forecasts were better than blind guesses, but not by much.

We were downcast for a while after receiving the discouraging news. But this was the army. Useful or not, there was a routine to be followed and orders to be obeyed. Another batch of candidates arrived the next day. We took them to the obstacle field, we faced them with the wall, they lifted the log, and within a few minutes we saw their true natures revealed, as clearly as before. The dismal truth about the quality of our predictions had no effect whatsoever on how we evaluated candidates and very little effect on the confidence we felt in our judgments and predictions about individuals.

What happened was remarkable. The global evidence of our previous failure should have shaken our confidence in our judgments of the candidates, but it did not. It should also have caused us to moderate our predictions, but it did not. We knew as a general fact that our predictions were little better than random guesses, but we continued to feel and act as if each of our specific predictions was valid. I was reminded of the Müller-Lyer illusion, in which we know the lines are of equal length yet still see them as being different. I was so struck by the analogy that I coined a term for our experience: the *illusion of validity*.

I had discovered my first cognitive illusion.

Decades later, I can see many of the central themes of my thinking—and of this book—in that old story. Our expectations for the soldiers' future performance were a clear instance of substitution, and of the representativeness heuristic in particular. Having observed one hour of a soldier's behavior in an artificial situation, we felt we knew how well he would face the challenges of officer training and of leadership in combat. Our predictions were completely nonregressive—we had no reservations about predicting failure or outstanding success from weak evidence. This was a clear instance of WYSIATI. We had compelling impressions of the behavior we observed and no good way to represent our ignorance of the factors that would eventually determine how well the candidate would perform as an officer.

Looking back, the most striking part of the story is that our knowledge of the general rule—that we could not predict—had no effect on our confidence in individual cases. I can see now that our reaction was similar to that of Nisbett and Borgida's students when they were told that most people did not help a stranger suffering a seizure. They certainly believed the statistics they were shown, but the base rates did not influence their judgment of whether an individual they saw on the video would or would not help a stranger. Just as Nisbett and Borgida showed, people are often reluctant to infer the particular from the general.

Subjective confidence in a judgment is not a reasoned evaluation of the probability that this judgment is correct. Confidence is a feeling, which reflects the coherence of the information and the cognitive ease of processing it. It is wise to take admissions of uncertainty seriously, but declarations of high confidence mainly tell you that an individual has constructed a coherent story in his mind, not necessarily that the story is true.

THE ILLUSION OF STOCK-PICKING SKILL

In 1984, Amos and I and our friend Richard Thaler visited a Wall Street firm. Our host, a senior investment manager, had invited us to discuss the role of judgment biases in investing. I knew so little about finance that I did not even know what to ask him, but I remember one exchange. "When you sell a stock," I asked, "who buys it?" He answered with a wave in the vague direction of the window, indicating that he expected the buyer to be someone else very much like him. That was odd: What made one person buy and the other sell? What did the sellers think they knew that the buyers did not?

Since then, my questions about the stock market have hardened into a larger puzzle: a major industry appears to be built largely on an *illusion of skill*. Billions of shares are traded every day, with many people buying each stock and others selling it to them. It is not unusual for more than 100 million shares of a single stock to change hands in one day. Most of the buyers and sellers know that they have the same information; they exchange the stocks primarily because they have different opinions. The buyers think the price is too low and likely to rise, while the sellers think the price is high and likely to drop. The puzzle is why buyers and sellers alike think that the current price is wrong. What makes them believe they know more about what the price should be than the market does? For most of them, that belief is an illusion.

In its broad outlines, the standard theory of how the stock market works is accepted by all the participants in the industry. Everybody in the investment business has read Burton Malkiel's wonderful book *A Random Walk Down Wall Street*. Malkiel's central idea is that a stock's price incorporates all the available knowledge about the value of the company and the best predictions about the future of the stock. If some people believe that the price of a stock will be higher tomorrow, they will buy more of it today. This, in turn, will cause its price to rise. If all assets in a market are correctly priced, no one can expect either to gain or to lose by trading. Perfect prices leave no scope for cleverness, but they also protect fools from their own folly. We now know, however, that the theory is not quite right. Many individual investors lose consistently by trading, an achievement that a dart-throwing chimp could not match. The first demonstration of this startling conclusion was collected by Terry Odean, a finance professor at UC Berkeley who was once my student.

Odean began by studying the trading records of 10,000 brokerage accounts of individual investors spanning a seven-year period. He was able to analyze every transaction the investors executed through that firm, nearly 163,000 trades. This rich set of data allowed Odean to identify all instances in which an investor sold some of his holdings in one stock and soon afterward bought another stock. By these actions the investor revealed that he (most of the investors were men) had a definite idea about the future of the two stocks: he expected the stock that he chose to buy to do better than the stock he chose to sell.

To determine whether those ideas were well founded, Odean compared the returns of the stock the investor had sold and the stock he had bought in its place, over the course of one year after the transaction. The results were unequivocally bad. On average, the shares that individual traders sold did better than those they bought, by a very substantial margin: 3.2 percentage points per year, above and beyond the significant costs of executing the two trades.

It is important to remember that this is a statement about averages: some individuals did much better, others did much worse. However, it is clear that for the large majority of individual investors, taking a shower and doing nothing would have been a better policy than implementing the ideas that came to their minds. Later research by Odean and his colleague Brad Barber supported this conclusion. In a paper titled "Trading Is Hazardous to Your Wealth," they showed that, on average, the most active traders had the poorest results, while the investors who traded the least earned the highest returns. In another paper, titled "Boys Will Be Boys," they showed that men acted on their useless ideas significantly more often than women, and that as a result women achieved better investment results than men.

Of course, there is always someone on the other side of each transaction; in general, these are financial institutions and professional investors, who are ready to take advantage of the mistakes that individual traders make in choosing a stock to sell and another stock to buy. Further research by Barber and Odean has shed light on these mistakes. Individual investors like to lock in their gains by selling "winners," stocks that have appreciated since they were purchased, and they hang on to their losers. Unfortunately for them, recent winners tend to do better than recent losers in the short run, so individuals sell the wrong stocks. They also buy the wrong stocks. Individual investors predictably flock to companies that draw their attention because they are in the news. Professional investors are more selective in responding to news. These findings provide some justification for the label of "smart money" that finance professionals apply to themselves.

Although professionals are able to extract a considerable amount of wealth from amateurs, few stock pickers, if any, have the skill needed to beat the market consistently, year after year. Professional investors, including fund managers, fail a basic test of skill: persistent achievement. The diagnostic for the existence of any skill is the consistency of individual differences in achievement. The logic is simple: if individual differences in any one year are due entirely to luck, the ranking of investors and funds will vary erratically and the year-to-year correlation will be zero. Where there is skill, however, the rankings will be more stable. The persistence of individual differences is the measure by which we confirm the existence of skill among golfers, car salespeople, orthodontists, or speedy toll collectors on the turnpike.

Mutual funds are run by highly experienced and hardworking professionals who buy and sell stocks to achieve the best possible results for their clients. Nevertheless, the evidence from more than fifty years of research is conclusive: for a large majority of fund managers, the selection of stocks is more like rolling dice than like playing poker. Typically at least two out of every three mutual funds underperform the overall market in any given year.

More important, the year-to-year correlation between the outcomes of mutual funds is very small, barely higher than zero. The successful funds in any given year are mostly lucky; they have a good roll of the dice. There is general agreement among researchers that nearly all stock pickers, whether they know it or not—and few of them do—are playing a game of chance. The subjective experience of traders is that they are making sensible educated guesses in a situation of great uncertainty. In highly efficient markets, however, educated guesses are no more accurate than blind guesses.

Some years ago I had an unusual opportunity to examine the illusion of financial skill up close. I had been invited to speak to a group of investment advisers in a firm that provided financial advice and other services to very wealthy clients. I asked for some data to prepare my presentation and was granted a small treasure: a spreadsheet summarizing the investment outcomes of some twenty-five anonymous wealth advisers, for each of eight consecutive years. Each adviser's score for each year was his (most of them were men) main determinant of his year-end bonus. It was a simple matter to rank the advisers by their performance in each year and to determine whether there were persistent differences in skill among them and whether the same advisers consistently achieved better returns for their clients year after year.

To answer the question, I computed correlation coefficients between the rankings in each pair of years: year 1 with year 2, year 1 with year 3, and so on up through year 7 with year 8. That yielded 28 correlation coefficients, one for each pair of years. I knew the theory and was prepared to find weak evidence of persistence of skill. Still, I was surprised to find that the average of the 28 correlations was .01. In other words, zero. The consistent correlations that would indicate differences in skill were not to be found. The results resembled what you would expect from a dice-rolling contest, not a game of skill.

No one in the firm seemed to be aware of the nature of the game that its stock pickers were playing. The advisers themselves felt they were competent professionals doing a serious job, and their superiors agreed. On the evening before the seminar, Richard Thaler and I had dinner with some of the top executives of the firm, the people who decide on the size of bonuses. We asked them to guess the year-to-year correlation in the rankings of individual advisers. They thought they knew what was coming and smiled as they said "not very high" or "performance certainly fluctuates." It quickly became clear, however, that no one expected the average correlation to be zero.

Our message to the executives was that, at least when it came to building portfolios, the firm was rewarding luck as if it were skill. This should have been shocking news to them, but it was not. There was no sign that they disbelieved us. How could they? After all, we had analyzed their own results, and they were sophisticated enough to see the implications, which we politely refrained from spelling out. We all went on calmly with our dinner, and I have no doubt that both our findings and their implications were quickly swept under the rug and that life in the firm went on just as before. The illusion of skill is not only an individual aberration; it is deeply ingrained in the culture of the industry. Facts that challenge such basic assumptions—and thereby threaten people's livelihood and self-esteem—are simply not absorbed. The mind does not digest them. This is particularly true of statistical studies of performance, which provide base-rate information that people generally ignore when it clashes with their personal impressions from experience.

The next morning, we reported the findings to the advisers, and their response was equally bland. Their own experience of exercising careful judgment on complex problems was far more compelling to them than an obscure statistical fact. When we were done, one of the executives I had dined with the previous evening drove me to the airport. He told me, with a trace of defensiveness, "I have done very well for the firm and no one can take that away from me." I smiled and said nothing. But I thought, "Well, I took it away from you this morning. If your success was due mostly to chance, how much credit are you entitled to take for it?"

WHAT SUPPORTS THE ILLUSIONS OF SKILL AND VALIDITY?

Cognitive illusions can be more stubborn than visual illusions. What you learned about the Müller-Lyer illusion did not change the way you see the lines, but it changed your behavior. You now know that you cannot trust your impression of the length of lines that have fins appended to them, and you also know that in the standard Müller-Lyer display you cannot trust what you see. When asked about the length of the lines, you will report your informed belief, not the illusion that you continue to see. In contrast, when my colleagues and I in the army learned that our leadership assessment tests had low validity, we accepted that fact intellectually, but it had no impact on either our feelings or our subsequent actions. The response we encountered in the financial firm was even more extreme. I am convinced that the message that Thaler and I delivered to both the executives and the portfolio managers was instantly put away in a dark corner of memory where it would cause no damage.

Why do investors, both amateur and professional, stubbornly believe that they can do better than the market, contrary to an economic theory that most of them accept, and contrary to what they could learn from a dispassionate evaluation of their personal experience? Many of the themes of previous chapters come up again in the explanation of the prevalence and persistence of an illusion of skill in the financial world.

The most potent psychological cause of the illusion is certainly that the people who pick stocks are exercising high-level skills. They consult economic data and forecasts, they examine income statements and balance sheets, they evaluate the quality of top management, and they assess the competition. All this is serious work that requires extensive training, and the people who do it have the immediate (and valid) experience of using these skills. Unfortunately, skill in evaluating the business prospects of a firm is not sufficient for successful stock trading, where the key question is whether the information about the firm is already incorporated in the price of its stock. Traders apparently lack the skill to answer this crucial question, but they appear to be ignorant of their ignorance. As I had discovered from watching cadets on the obstacle field, subjective confidence of traders is a feeling, not a judgment. Our understanding of cognitive ease and associative coherence locates subjective confidence firmly in System 1.

Finally, the illusions of validity and skill are supported by a powerful professional culture. We know that people can maintain an unshakable faith in any proposition, however absurd, when they are sustained by a community of like-minded believers. Given the professional culture of the financial community, it is not surprising that large numbers of individuals in that world believe themselves to be among the chosen few who can do what they believe others cannot.

THE ILLUSIONS OF PUNDITS

The idea that the future is unpredictable is undermined every day by the ease with which the past is explained. As Nassim Taleb pointed out in *The Black Swan*, our tendency to construct and believe coherent narratives of the past makes it difficult for us to accept the limits of our forecasting ability. Everything makes sense in hindsight, a fact that financial pundits exploit every evening as they offer convincing accounts of the day's events. And we cannot suppress the powerful intuition that what makes sense in hindsight today was predictable yesterday. The illusion that we understand the past fosters overconfidence in our ability to predict the future.

The often-used image of the "march of history" implies order and direction. Marches, unlike strolls or walks, are not random. We think that we should be able to explain the past by focusing on either large social movements and cultural and technological developments or the intentions and abilities of a few great men. The idea that large historical events are determined by luck is profoundly shocking, although it is demonstrably true. It is hard to think of the history of the twentieth century, including its large social movements, without bringing in the role of Hitler, Stalin, and Mao Zedong. But there was a moment in time, just before an egg was fertilized, when there was a fifty-fifty chance that the embryo that became Hitler could have been a female. Compounding the three events, there was a probability of one-eighth of a twentieth century without any of the three great villains and it is impossible to argue that history would have been roughly the same in their absence. The fertilization of these three eggs had momentous consequences, and it makes a joke of the idea that long-term developments are predictable.

Yet the illusion of valid prediction remains intact, a fact that is exploited by people whose business is prediction—not only financial experts but pundits in business and politics, too. Television and radio stations and newspapers have their panels of experts whose job it is to comment on the recent past and foretell the future. Viewers and readers have the impression that they are receiving information that is somehow privileged, or at least extremely insightful. And there is no doubt that the pundits and their promoters genuinely believe they are offering such information. Philip Tetlock, a psychologist at the University of Pennsylvania, explained these so-called expert predictions in a landmark twenty-year study, which he published in his 2005 book *Expert Political Judgment: How Good Is It? How Can We Know?* Tetlock has set the terms for any future discussion of this topic.

Tetlock interviewed 284 people who made their living "commenting or offering advice on political and economic trends." He asked them to assess the probabilities that certain events would occur in the not too distant future, both in areas of the world in which they specialized and in regions about which they had less knowledge. Would Gorbachev be ousted in a coup? Would the United States go to war in the Persian Gulf? Which country would become the next big emerging market? In all, Tetlock gathered more than 80,000 predictions. He also asked the experts how they reached their conclusions, how they reacted when proved wrong, and how they evaluated evidence that did not support their positions. Respondents were asked to rate the probabilities of three alternative outcomes in every case: the persistence of the status quo, more of something such as political freedom or economic growth, or less of that thing.

The results were devastating. The experts performed worse than they would have if they had simply assigned equal probabilities to each of the three potential outcomes. In other words, people who spend their time, and earn their living, studying a particular topic produce poorer predictions than dart-throwing monkeys who would have distributed their choices evenly over the options. Even in the region they knew best, experts were not significantly better than nonspecialists.

Those who know more forecast very slightly better than those who know less. But those with the most knowledge are often less reliable. The reason is that the person who acquires more knowledge develops an enhanced illusion of her skill and becomes unrealistically overconfident. "We reach the point of diminishing marginal predictive returns for knowledge disconcertingly quickly," Tetlock writes. "In this age of academic hyperspecialization, there is no reason for supposing that contributors to top journals—distinguished political scientists, area study specialists, economists, and so on—are any better than journalists or attentive readers of *The New York Times* in 'reading' emerging situations." The more famous the forecaster, Tetlock discovered, the more flamboyant the forecasts. "Experts in demand," he writes, "were more overconfident than their colleagues who eked out existences far from the limelight."

Tetlock also found that experts resisted admitting that they had been wrong, and when they were compelled to admit error, they had a large collection of excuses: they had been wrong only in their timing, an unforeseeable event had intervened, or they had been wrong but for the right reasons. Experts are just human in the end. They are dazzled by their own brilliance and hate to be wrong. Experts are led astray not by what they believe, but by how they think, says Tetlock. He uses the terminology from Isaiah Berlin's essay on Tolstoy, "The Hedgehog and the Fox." Hedgehogs "know one big thing" and have a theory about the world; they account for particular events within a coherent framework, bristle with impatience toward those who don't see things their way, and are confident in their forecasts. They are also especially reluctant to admit error. For hedgehogs, a failed prediction is almost always "off only on timing" or "very nearly right." They are opinionated and clear, which is exactly what television producers love to see on programs. Two hedgehogs on different sides of an issue, each attacking the idiotic ideas of the adversary, make for a good show.

Foxes, by contrast, are complex thinkers. They don't believe that one big thing drives the march of history (for example, they are unlikely to accept the view that Ronald Reagan single-handedly ended the cold war by standing tall against the Soviet Union). Instead the foxes recognize that reality emerges from the interactions of many different agents and forces, including blind luck, often producing large and unpredictable outcomes. It was the foxes who scored best in Tetlock's study, although their performance was still very poor. They are less likely than hedgehogs to be invited to participate in television debates.

IT IS NOT THE EXPERTS' FAULT—THE WORLD IS DIFFICULT

The main point of this chapter is not that people who attempt to predict the future make many errors; that goes without saying. The first lesson is that errors of prediction are inevitable because the world is unpredictable. The second is that high subjective confidence is not to be trusted as an indicator of accuracy (low confidence could be more informative).

Short-term trends can be forecast, and behavior and achievements can be predicted with fair accuracy from previous behaviors and achievements. But we should not expect performance in officer training and in combat to be predictable from behavior on an obstacle field—behavior both on the test and in the real world is determined by many factors that are specific to the particular situation. Remove one highly assertive member from a group of eight candidates and everyone else's personalities will appear to change. Let a sniper's bullet move by a few centimeters and the performance of an officer will be transformed. I do not deny the validity of all tests—if a test predicts an important outcome with a validity of .20 or .30, the test should be used. But you should not expect more. You should expect little or nothing from Wall Street stock pickers who hope to be more accurate than the market in predicting the future of prices. And you should not expect much from pundits making long-term forecasts—although they may have valuable insights into the near future. The line that separates the possibly predictable future from the unpredictable distant future is yet to be drawn.

SPEAKING OF ILLUSORY SKILL

"He knows that the record indicates that the development of this illness is mostly unpredictable. How can he be so confident in this case? Sounds like an illusion of validity."

"She has a coherent story that explains all she knows, and the coherence makes her feel good."

"What makes him believe that he is smarter than the market? Is this an illusion of skill?"

"She is a hedgehog. She has a theory that explains everything, and it gives her the illusion that she understands the world."

"The question is not whether these experts are well trained. It is whether their world is predictable."

21

INTUITIONS VS. FORMULAS

Paul Meehl was a strange and wonderful character, and one of the most versatile psychologists of the twentieth century. Among the departments in which he had faculty appointments at the University of Minnesota were psychology, law, psychiatry, neurology, and philosophy. He also wrote on religion, political science, and learning in rats. A statistically sophisticated researcher and a fierce critic of empty claims in clinical psychology, Meehl was also a practicing psychoanalyst. He wrote thoughtful essays on the philosophical foundations of psychological research that I almost memorized while I was a graduate student. I never met Meehl, but he was one of my heroes from the time I read his *Clinical vs. Statistical Prediction: A Theoretical Analysis and a Review of the Evidence*.

In the slim volume that he later called "my disturbing little book," Meehl reviewed the results of 20 studies that had analyzed whether *clinical predictions* based on the subjective impressions of trained professionals were more accurate than *statistical* predictions made by combining a few scores or ratings according to a rule. In a typical study, trained counselors predicted the grades of freshmen at the end of the school year. The counselors interviewed each student for forty-five minutes. They also had access to high school grades, several aptitude tests, and a four-page personal statement. The statistical algorithm used only a fraction of this information: high school grades and one aptitude test. Nevertheless, the formula was more accurate than 11 of the 14 counselors. Meehl reported generally similar results across a variety of other forecast outcomes, including violations of parole, success in pilot training, and criminal recidivism.

Not surprisingly, Meehl's book provoked shock and disbelief among clinical psychologists, and the controversy it started has engendered a stream of research that is still flowing today, more than fifty years after its publication. The number of studies reporting comparisons of clinical and statistical predictions has increased to roughly two hundred, but the score in the contest between algorithms and humans has not changed. About 60% of the studies have shown significantly better accuracy for the algorithms. The other comparisons scored a draw in accuracy, but a tie is tantamount to a win for the statistical rules, which are normally much less expensive to use than expert judgment. No exception has been convincingly documented.

The range of predicted outcomes has expanded to cover medical variables such as the longevity of cancer patients, the length of hospital stays, the diagnosis of cardiac disease, and the susceptibility of babies to sudden infant death syndrome; economic measures such as the prospects of success for new businesses, the evaluation of credit risks by banks, and the future career satisfaction of workers; questions of interest to government agencies, including assessments of the suitability of foster parents, the odds of recidivism among juvenile offenders, and the likelihood of other forms of violent behavior; and miscellaneous outcomes such as the evaluation of scientific presentations, the winners of football games, and the future prices of Bordeaux wine. Each of these domains entails a significant degree of uncertainty and unpredictability. We describe them as "low-validity environments." In every case, the accuracy of experts was matched or exceeded by a simple algorithm.

As Meehl pointed out with justified pride thirty years after the publication of his book, "There is no controversy in social science which shows such a large body of qualitatively diverse studies coming out so uniformly in the same direction as this one."

The Princeton economist and wine lover Orley Ashenfelter has offered a compelling demonstration of the power of simple statistics to outdo world-renowned experts. Ashenfelter wanted to predict the future value of fine Bordeaux wines from information available in the year they are made. The question is important because fine wines take years to reach their peak quality, and the prices of mature wines from the same vineyard vary dramatically across different vintages; bottles filled only twelve months apart can differ in value by a factor of 10 or more. An ability to forecast future prices is of substantial value, because investors buy wine, like art, in the anticipation that its value will appreciate.

It is generally agreed that the effect of vintage can be due only to variations in the weather during the grape-growing season. The best wines are produced when the summer is warm and dry, which makes the Bordeaux wine industry a likely beneficiary of global warming. The industry is also helped by wet springs, which increase quantity without much effect on quality. Ashenfelter converted that conventional knowledge into a statistical formula that predicts the price of a wine—for a particular property and at a particular age—by three features of the weather: the average temperature over the summer growing season, the amount of rain at harvest-time, and the total rainfall during the previous winter. His formula provides accurate price forecasts years and even decades into the future. Indeed, his formula forecasts future prices much more accurately than the current prices of young wines do. This new example of a "Meehl pattern" challenges the abilities of the experts whose opinions help shape the early price. It also challenges economic theory, according to which prices should reflect all the available information, including the weather. Ashenfelter's formula is extremely accurate—the correlation between his predictions and actual prices is above .90.

Why are experts inferior to algorithms? One reason, which Meehl suspected, is that experts try to be clever, think outside the box, and consider complex combinations of features in making their predictions. Complexity may work in the odd case, but more often than not it reduces validity. Simple combinations of features are better. Several studies have shown that human decision makers are inferior to a prediction formula even when they are given the score suggested by the formula! They feel that they can overrule the formula because they have additional information about the case, but they are wrong more often than not. According to Meehl, there are few circumstances under which it is a good idea to substitute judgment for a formula. In a famous thought experiment, he described a formula that predicts whether a particular person will go to the movies tonight and noted that it is proper to disregard the formula if information is received that the individual broke a leg today. The name "broken-leg rule" has stuck. The point, of course, is that broken legs are very rare—as well as decisive.

Another reason for the inferiority of expert judgment is that humans are incorrigibly inconsistent in making summary judgments of complex information. When asked to evaluate the same information twice, they frequently give different answers. The extent of the inconsistency is often a matter of real concern. Experienced radiologists who evaluate chest X-rays as "normal" or "abnormal" contradict themselves 20% of the time when they see the same picture on separate occasions. A study of 101 independent auditors who were asked to evaluate the reliability of internal corporate audits revealed a similar degree of inconsistency. A review of 41 separate studies of the reliability of judgments made by auditors, pathologists, psychologists, organizational managers, and other professionals suggests that this level of inconsistency is typical, even when a case is reevaluated within a few minutes. Unreliable judgments cannot be valid predictors of anything.

The widespread inconsistency is probably due to the extreme context dependency of System 1. We know from studies of priming that unnoticed stimuli in our environment have a substantial influence on our thoughts and actions. These influences fluctuate from moment to moment. The brief pleasure of a cool breeze on a hot day may make you slightly more positive and optimistic about whatever you are evaluating at the time. The prospects of a convict being granted parole may change significantly during the time that elapses between successive food breaks in the parole judges' schedule. Because you have little direct knowledge of what goes on in your mind, you will never know that you might have made a different judgment or reached a different decision under very slightly different circumstances. Formulas do not suffer from such problems. Given the same input, they always return the same answer. When predictability is poor—which it is in most of the studies reviewed by Meehl and his followers—inconsistency is destructive of any predictive validity.

The research suggests a surprising conclusion: to maximize predictive accuracy, final decisions should be left to formulas, especially in low-validity environments. In admission decisions for medical schools, for example, the final determination is often made by the faculty members who interview the candidate. The evidence is fragmentary, but there are solid grounds for a conjecture: conducting an interview is likely to diminish the accuracy of a selection procedure, if the interviewers also make the final admission decisions. Because interviewers are overconfident in their intuitions, they will assign too much weight to their personal impressions and too little weight to other sources of information, lowering validity. Similarly, the experts who evaluate the quality of immature wine to predict its future have a source of information that almost certainly makes things worse rather than better: they can taste the wine. In addition, of course, even if they have a good understanding of the effects of the weather on wine quality, they will not be able to maintain the consistency of a formula.

The most important development in the field since Meehl's original work is Robyn Dawes's famous article "The Robust Beauty of Improper Linear Models in Decision Making." The dominant statistical practice in the social sciences is to assign weights to the different predictors by following an algorithm, called multiple regression, that is now built into conventional software. The logic of multiple regression is unassailable: it finds the optimal formula for putting together a weighted combination of the predictors. However, Dawes observed that the complex statistical algorithm adds little or no value. One can do just as well by selecting a set of scores that have some validity for predicting the outcome and adjusting the values to make them comparable (by using standard scores or ranks). A formula that combines these predictors with equal weights is likely to be just as accurate in predicting new cases as the multiple-regression formula that was optimal in the original sample. More recent research went further: formulas that assign equal weights to all the predictors are often superior, because they are not affected by accidents of sampling.

The surprising success of equal-weighting schemes has an important practical implication: it is possible to develop useful algorithms without any prior statistical research. Simple equally weighted formulas based on existing statistics or on common sense are often very good predictors of significant outcomes. In a memorable example, Dawes showed that marital stability is well predicted by a formula:

frequency of lovemaking minus frequency of quarrels

You don't want your result to be a negative number.

The important conclusion from this research is that an algorithm that is constructed on the back of an envelope is often good enough to compete with an optimally weighted formula, and certainly good enough to outdo expert judgment. This logic can be applied in many domains, ranging from the selection of stocks by portfolio managers to the choices of medical treatments by doctors or patients.

A classic application of this approach is a simple algorithm that has saved the lives of hundreds of thousands of infants. Obstetricians had always known that an infant who is not breathing normally within a few minutes of birth is at high risk of brain damage or death. Until the anesthesiologist Virginia Apgar intervened in 1953, physicians and midwives used their clinical judgment to determine whether a baby was in distress. Different practitioners focused on different cues. Some watched for breathing problems while others monitored how soon the baby cried. Without a standardized procedure, danger signs were often missed, and many newborn infants died.

One day over breakfast, a medical resident asked how Dr. Apgar would make a systematic assessment of a newborn. "That's easy," she replied. "You would do it like this." Apgar jotted down five variables (heart rate, respiration, reflex, muscle tone, and color) and three scores (0, 1, or 2, depending on the robustness of each sign). Realizing that she might have made a breakthrough that any delivery room could implement, Apgar began rating infants by this rule one minute after they were born. A baby with a total score of 8 or above was likely to be pink, squirming, crying, grimacing, with a pulse of 100 or more—in good shape. A baby with a score of 4 or below was probably bluish, flaccid, passive, with a slow or weak pulse—in need of immediate intervention. Applying Apgar's score, the staff in delivery rooms finally had consistent standards for determining which babies were in trouble, and the formula is credited for an important contribution to reducing infant mortality. The Apgar test is still used every day in every delivery room. Atul Gawande's recent *A Checklist Manifesto* provides many other examples of the virtues of checklists and simple rules.

THE HOSTILITY TO ALGORITHMS

From the very outset, clinical psychologists responded to Meehl's ideas with hostility and disbelief. Clearly, they were in the grip of an illusion of skill in terms of their ability to make long-term predictions. On reflection, it is easy to see how the illusion came about and easy to sympathize with the clinicians' rejection of Meehl's research.

The statistical evidence of clinical inferiority contradicts clinicians' everyday experience of the quality of their judgments. Psychologists who work with patients have many hunches during each therapy session, anticipating how the patient will respond to an intervention, guessing what will happen next. Many of these hunches are confirmed, illustrating the reality of clinical skill.

The problem is that the correct judgments involve short-term predictions in the context of the therapeutic interview, a skill in which therapists may have years of practice. The tasks at which they fail typically require long-term predictions about the patient's future. These are much more difficult, even the best formulas do only modestly well, and they are also tasks that the clinicians have never had the opportunity to learn properly—they would have to wait years for feedback, instead of receiving the instantaneous feedback of the clinical session. However, the line between what clinicians can do well and what they cannot do at all well is not obvious, and certainly not obvious to them. They know they are skilled, but they don't necessarily know the boundaries of their skill. Not surprisingly, then, the idea that a mechanical combination of a few variables could outperform the subtle complexity of human judgment strikes experienced clinicians as obviously wrong.

The debate about the virtues of clinical and statistical prediction has always had a moral dimension. The statistical method, Meehl wrote, was criticized by experienced clinicians as "mechanical, atomistic, additive, cut and dried, artificial, unreal, arbitrary, incomplete, dead, pedantic, fractionated, trivial, forced, static, superficial, rigid, sterile, academic, pseudoscientific and blind." The clinical method, on the other hand, was lauded by its proponents as "dynamic, global, meaningful, holistic, subtle, sympathetic, configural, patterned, organized, rich, deep, genuine, sensitive, sophisticated, real, living, concrete, natural, true to life, and understanding."

This is an attitude we can all recognize. When a human competes with a machine, whether it is John Henry a-hammerin' on the mountain or the chess genius Garry Kasparov facing off against the computer Deep Blue, our sympathies lie with our fellow human. The aversion to algorithms making decisions that affect humans is rooted in the strong preference that many people have for the natural over the synthetic or artificial. Asked whether they would rather eat an organic or a commercially grown apple, most people prefer the "all natural" one. Even after being informed that the two apples taste the same, have identical nutritional value, and are equally healthful, a majority still prefer the organic fruit. Even the producers of beer have found that they can increase sales by putting "All Natural" or "No Preservatives" on the label.

The deep resistance to the demystification of expertise is illustrated by the reaction of the European wine community to Ashenfelter's formula for predicting the price of Bordeaux wines. Ashenfelter's formula answered a prayer: one might thus have expected that wine lovers everywhere would be grateful to him for demonstrably improving their ability to identify the wines that later would be good. Not so. The response in French wine circles, wrote *The New York Times*, ranged "somewhere between violent and hysterical." Ashenfelter reports that one oenophile called his findings "ludicrous and absurd." Another scoffed, "It is like judging movies without actually seeing them."

The prejudice against algorithms is magnified when the decisions are consequential. Meehl remarked, "I do not quite know how to alleviate the horror some clinicians seem to experience when they envisage a treatable case being denied treatment because a 'blind, mechanical' equation misclassifies him." In contrast, Meehl and other proponents of algorithms have argued strongly that it is unethical to rely on intuitive judgments for important decisions if an algorithm is available that will make fewer mistakes. Their rational argument is compelling, but it runs against a stubborn psychological reality: for most people, the cause of a mistake matters. The story of a child dying because an algorithm made a mistake is more poignant than the story of the same tragedy occurring as a result of human error, and the difference in emotional intensity is readily translated into a moral preference.

Fortunately, the hostility to algorithms will probably soften as their role in everyday life continues to expand. Looking for books or music we might enjoy, we appreciate recommendations generated by software. We take it for granted that decisions about credit limits are made without the direct intervention of any human judgment. We are increasingly exposed to guidelines that have the form of simple algorithms, such as the ratio of good and bad cholesterol levels we should strive to attain. The public is now well aware that formulas may do better than humans in some critical decisions in the world of sports: how much a professional team should pay for particular rookie players, or when to punt on fourth down. The expanding list of tasks that are assigned to algorithms should eventually reduce the discomfort that most people feel when they first encounter the pattern of results that Meehl described in his disturbing little book.

LEARNING FROM MEEHL

In 1955, as a twenty-one-year-old lieutenant in the Israeli Defense Forces, I was assigned to set up an interview system for the entire army. If you wonder why such a responsibility would be forced upon someone so young, bear in mind that the state of Israel itself was only seven years old at the time; all its institutions were under construction, and someone had to build them. Odd as it sounds today, my bachelor's degree in psychology probably qualified me as the best-trained psychologist in the army. My direct supervisor, a brilliant researcher, had a degree in chemistry.

An interview routine was already in place when I was given my mission. Every soldier drafted into the army completed a battery of psychometric tests, and each man considered for combat duty was interviewed for an assessment of personality. The goal was to assign the recruit a score of general fitness for combat and to find the best match of his personality among various branches: infantry, artillery, armor, and so on. The interviewers were themselves young draftees, selected for this assignment by virtue of their high intelligence and interest in dealing with people. Most were women, who were at the time exempt from combat duty. Trained for a few weeks in how to conduct a fifteen- to twenty-minute interview, they were encouraged to cover a range of topics and to form a general impression of how well the recruit would do in the army.

Unfortunately, follow-up evaluations had already indicated that this interview procedure was almost useless for predicting the future success of recruits. I was instructed to design an interview that would be more useful but would not take more time. I was also told to try out the new interview and to evaluate its accuracy. From the perspective of a serious professional, I was no more qualified for the task than I was to build a bridge across the Amazon.

Fortunately, I had read Paul Meehl's "little book," which had appeared just a year earlier. I was convinced by his argument that simple, statistical rules are superior to intuitive "clinical" judgments. I concluded that the then current interview had failed at least in part because it allowed the interviewers to do what they found most interesting, which was to learn about the dynamics of the interviewee's mental life. Instead, we should use the limited time at our disposal to obtain as much specific information as possible about the interviewee's life in his normal environment. Another lesson I learned from Meehl was that we should abandon the procedure in which the interviewers' global evaluations of the recruit determined the final decision. Meehl's book suggested that such evaluations should not be trusted and that statistical summaries of separately evaluated attributes would achieve higher validity.

I decided on a procedure in which the interviewers would evaluate several relevant personality traits and score each separately. The final score of fitness for combat duty would be computed according to a standard formula, with no further input from the interviewers. I made up a list of six characteristics that appeared relevant to performance in a combat unit, including "responsibility," "sociability," and "masculine pride." I then composed, for each trait, a series of factual questions about the individual's life before his enlistment, including the number of different jobs he had held, how regular and punctual he had been in his work or studies, the frequency of his interactions with friends, and his interest and participation in sports, among others. The idea was to evaluate as objectively as possible how well the recruit had done on each dimension.

By focusing on standardized, factual questions, I hoped to combat the halo effect, where favorable first impressions influence later judgments. As a further precaution against halos, I instructed the interviewers to go through the six traits in a fixed sequence, rating each trait on a five-point scale before going on to the next. And that was that. I informed the interviewers that they need not concern themselves with the recruit's future adjustment to the military. Their only task was to elicit relevant facts about his past and to use that information to score each personality dimension. "Your function is to provide reliable measurements," I told them. "Leave the predictive validity to me," by which I meant the formula that I was going to devise to combine their specific ratings.

The interviewers came close to mutiny. These bright young people were displeased to be ordered, by someone hardly older than themselves, to switch off their intuition and focus entirely on boring factual questions. One of them complained, "You are turning us into robots!" So I compromised. "Carry out the interview exactly as instructed," I told them, "and when you are done, have your wish: close your eyes, try to imagine the recruit as a soldier, and assign him a score on a scale of 1 to 5."

Several hundred interviews were conducted by this new method, and a few months later we collected evaluations of the soldiers' performance from the commanding officers of the units to which they had been assigned. The results made us happy. As Meehl's book had suggested, the new interview procedure was a substantial improvement over the old one. The sum of our six ratings predicted soldiers' performance much more accurately than the global evaluations of the previous interviewing method, although far from perfectly. We had progressed from "completely useless" to "moderately useful."

The big surprise to me was that the intuitive judgment that the interviewers summoned up in the "close your eyes" exercise also did very well, indeed just as well as the sum of the six specific ratings. I learned from this finding a lesson that I have never forgotten: intuition adds value even in the justly derided selection interview, but only after a disciplined collection of objective information and disciplined scoring of separate traits. I set a formula that gave the "close your eyes" evaluation the same weight as the sum of the six trait ratings. A more general lesson that I learned from this episode was do not simply trust intuitive judgment—your own or that of others—but do not dismiss it, either.

Some forty-five years later, after I won a Nobel Prize in economics, I was for a short time a minor celebrity in Israel. On one of my visits, someone had the idea of escorting me around my old army base, which still housed the unit that interviews new recruits. I was introduced to the commanding officer of the Psychological Unit, and she described their current interviewing practices, which had not changed much from the system I had designed; there was, it turned out, a considerable amount of research indicating that the interviews still worked well. As she came to the end of her description of how the interviews are conducted, the officer added, "And then we tell them, 'Close your eyes.'"

DO IT YOURSELF

The message of this chapter is readily applicable to tasks other than making manpower decisions for an army. Implementing interview procedures in the spirit of Meehl and Dawes requires relatively little effort but substantial discipline. Suppose that you need to hire a sales representative for your firm. If you are serious about hiring the best possible person for the job, this is what you should do. First, select a few traits that are prerequisites for success in this position (technical proficiency, engaging personality, reliability, and so on). Don't overdo it—six dimensions is a good number. The traits you choose should be as independent as possible from each other, and you should feel that you can assess them reliably by asking a few factual questions. Next, make a list of those questions for each trait and think about how you will score it, say on a 1–5 scale. You should have an idea of what you will call "very weak" or "very strong."

These preparations should take you half an hour or so, a small investment that can make a significant difference in the quality of the people you hire. To avoid halo effects, you must collect the information on one trait at a time, scoring each before you move on to the next one. Do not skip around. To evaluate each candidate, add up the six scores. Because you are in charge of the final decision, you should not do a "close your eyes." Firmly resolve that you will hire the candidate whose final score is the highest, even if there is another one whom you like better—try to resist your wish to invent broken legs to change the ranking. A vast amount of research offers a promise: you are much more likely to find the best candidate if you use this procedure than if you do what people normally do in such situations, which is to go into the interview unprepared and to make choices by an overall intuitive judgment such as "I looked into his eyes and liked what I saw."

SPEAKING OF JUDGES VS. FORMULAS

"Whenever we can replace human judgment by a formula, we should at least consider it."

"He thinks his judgments are complex and subtle, but a simple combination of scores could probably do better."

"Let's decide in advance what weight to give to the data we have on the candidates' past performance. Otherwise we will give too much weight to our impression from the interviews."

22

EXPERT INTUITION: WHEN CAN WE TRUST IT?

Professional controversies bring out the worst in academics. Scientific journals occasionally publish exchanges, often beginning with someone's critique of another's research, followed by a reply and a rejoinder. I have always thought that these exchanges are a waste of time. Especially when the original critique is sharply worded, the reply and the rejoinder are often exercises in what I have called sarcasm for beginners and advanced sarcasm. The replies rarely concede anything to a biting critique, and it is almost unheard of for a rejoinder to admit that the original critique was misguided or erroneous in any way. On a few occasions I have responded to criticisms that I thought were grossly misleading, because a failure to respond can be interpreted as conceding error, but I have never found the hostile exchanges instructive. In search of another way to deal with disagreements, I have engaged in a few "adversarial collaborations," in which scholars who disagree on the science agree to write a jointly authored paper on their differences, and sometimes conduct research together. In especially tense situations, the research is moderated by an arbiter.

My most satisfying and productive adversarial collaboration was with Gary Klein, the intellectual leader of an association of scholars and practitioners who do not like the kind of work I do. They call themselves students of Naturalistic Decision Making, or NDM, and mostly work in organizations where they often study how experts work. The NDMers adamantly reject the focus on biases in the heuristics and biases approach. They criticize this model as overly concerned with failures and driven by artificial experiments rather than by the study of real people doing things that matter. They are deeply skeptical about the value of using rigid algorithms to replace human judgment, and Paul Meehl is not among their heroes. Gary Klein has eloquently articulated this position over many years.

This is hardly the basis for a beautiful friendship, but there is more to the story. I had never believed that intuition is always misguided. I had also been a fan of Klein's studies of expertise in firefighters since I first saw a draft of a paper he wrote in the 1970s, and was impressed by his book *Sources of Power*, much of which analyzes how experienced professionals develop intuitive skills. I invited him to join in an effort to map the boundary that separates the marvels of intuition from its flaws. He was intrigued by the idea and we went ahead with the project—with no certainty that it would succeed. We set out to answer a specific question: When can you trust an experienced professional who claims to have an intuition? It was obvious that Klein would be more disposed to be trusting, and I would be more skeptical. But could we agree on principles for answering the general question?

Over seven or eight years we had many discussions, resolved many disagreements, almost blew up more than once, wrote many drafts, became friends, and eventually published a joint article with a title that tells the story: "Conditions for Intuitive Expertise: A Failure to Disagree." Indeed, we did not encounter real issues on which we disagreed—but we did not really agree.

MARVELS AND FLAWS

Malcolm Gladwell's bestseller *Blink* appeared while Klein and I were working on the project, and it was reassuring to find ourselves in agreement about it. Gladwell's book opens with the memorable story of art experts faced with an object that is described as a magnificent example of a kouros, a sculpture of a striding boy. Several of the experts had strong visceral reactions: they felt in their gut that the statue was a fake but were not able to articulate what it was about it that made them uneasy. Everyone who read the book—millions did—remembers that story as a triumph of intuition. The experts agreed that they knew the sculpture was a fake without knowing how they knew—the very definition of intuition. The story appears to imply that a systematic search for the cue that guided the experts would have failed, but Klein and I both rejected that conclusion. From our point of view, such an inquiry was needed, and if it had been conducted properly (which Klein knows how to do), it would probably have succeeded.

Although many readers of the kouros example were surely drawn to an almost magical view of expert intuition, Gladwell himself does not hold that position. In a later chapter he describes a massive failure of intuition: Americans elected President Harding, whose only qualification for the position was that he perfectly looked the part. Square jawed and tall, he was the perfect image of a strong and decisive leader. People voted for someone who looked strong and decisive without any other reason to believe that he was. An intuitive prediction of how Harding would perform as president arose from substituting one question for another. A reader of this book should expect such an intuition to be held with confidence.

INTUITION AS RECOGNITION

The early experiences that shaped Klein's views of intuition were starkly different from mine. My thinking was formed by observing the illusion of validity in myself and by reading Paul Meehl's demonstrations of the inferiority of clinical prediction. In contrast, Klein's views were shaped by his early studies of fireground commanders (the leaders of firefighting teams). He followed them as they fought fires and later interviewed the leader about his thoughts as he made decisions. As Klein described it in our joint article, he and his collaborators

> investigated how the commanders could make good decisions without comparing options. The initial hypothesis was that commanders would restrict their analysis to only a pair of options, but that hypothesis proved to be incorrect. In fact, the commanders usually generated only a single option, and that was all they needed. They could draw on the repertoire of patterns that they had compiled during more than a decade of both real and virtual experience to identify a plausible option, which they considered first. They evaluated this option by mentally simulating it to see if it would work in the situation they were facing. . . . If the course of action they were considering seemed appropriate, they would implement it. If it had shortcomings, they would modify it. If they could not easily modify it, they would turn to the next most plausible option and run through the same procedure until an acceptable course of action was found.

Klein elaborated this description into a theory of decision making that he called the recognition-primed decision (RPD) model, which applies to firefighters but also describes expertise in other domains, including chess. The process involves both System 1 and System 2. In the first phase, a tentative plan comes to mind by an automatic function of associative memory—System 1. The next phase is a deliberate process in which the plan is mentally simulated to check if it will work—an operation of System 2. The model of intuitive decision making as pattern recognition develops ideas presented some time ago by Herbert Simon, perhaps the only scholar who is recognized and admired as a hero and founding figure by all the competing clans and tribes in the study of decision making. I quoted Herbert Simon's definition of intuition in the introduction, but it will make more sense when I repeat it now: "The situation has provided a cue; this cue has given the expert access to information stored in memory, and the information provides the answer. Intuition is nothing more and nothing less than recognition."

This strong statement reduces the apparent magic of intuition to the everyday experience of memory. We marvel at the story of the firefighter who has a sudden urge to escape a burning house just before it collapses, because the firefighter knows the danger intuitively, "without knowing how he knows." However, we also do not know how we immediately know that a person we see as we enter a room is our friend Peter. The moral of Simon's remark is that the mystery of knowing without knowing is not a distinctive feature of intuition; it is the norm of mental life.

ACQUIRING SKILL

How does the information that supports intuition get "stored in memory"? Certain types of intuitions are acquired very quickly. We have inherited from our ancestors a great facility to learn when to be afraid. Indeed, one experience is often sufficient to establish a long-term aversion and fear. Many of us have the visceral memory of a single dubious dish that still leaves us vaguely reluctant to return to a restaurant. All of us tense up when we approach a spot in which an unpleasant event occurred, even when there is no reason to expect it to happen again. For me, one such place is the ramp leading to the San Francisco airport, where years ago a driver in the throes of road rage followed me from the freeway, rolled down his window, and hurled obscenities at me. I never knew what caused his hatred, but I remember his voice whenever I reach that point on my way to the airport.

My memory of the airport incident is conscious and it fully explains the emotion that comes with it. On many occasions, however, you may feel uneasy in a particular place or when someone uses a particular turn of phrase without having a conscious memory of the triggering event. In hindsight, you will label that unease an intuition if it is followed by a bad experience. This mode of emotional learning is closely related to what happened in Pavlov's famous conditioning experiments, in which the dogs learned to recognize the sound of the bell as a signal that food was coming. What Pavlov's dogs learned can be described as a learned hope. Learned fears are even more easily acquired.

Fear can also be learned—quite easily, in fact—by words rather than by experience. The fireman who had the "sixth sense" of danger had certainly had many occasions to discuss and think about types of fires he was not involved in, and to rehearse in his mind what the cues might be and how he should react. As I remember from experience, a young platoon commander with no experience of combat will tense up while leading troops through a narrowing ravine, because he was taught to identify the terrain as favoring an ambush. Little repetition is needed for learning.

Emotional learning may be quick, but what we consider as "expertise" usually takes a long time to develop. The acquisition of expertise in complex tasks such as high-level chess, professional basketball, or firefighting is intricate and slow because expertise in a domain is not a single skill but rather a large collection of miniskills. Chess is a good example. An expert player can understand a complex position at a glance, but it takes years to develop that level of ability. Studies of chess masters have shown that at least 10,000 hours of dedicated practice (about 6 years of playing chess 5 hours a day) are required to attain the highest levels of performance. During those hours of intense concentration, a serious chess player becomes familiar with thousands of configurations, each consisting of an arrangement of related pieces that can threaten or defend each other.

Learning high-level chess can be compared to learning to read. A first grader works hard at recognizing individual letters and assembling them into syllables and words, but a good adult reader perceives entire clauses. An expert reader has also acquired the ability to assemble familiar elements in a new pattern and can quickly "recognize" and correctly pronounce a word that she has never seen before. In chess, recurrent patterns of interacting pieces play the role of letters, and a chess position is a long word or a sentence.

A skilled reader who sees it for the first time will be able to read the opening stanza of Lewis Carroll's "Jabberwocky" with perfect rhythm and intonation, as well as pleasure:

'Twas brillig, and the slithy toves
Did gyre and gimble in the wabe:

> All mimsy were the borogoves,
> And the mome raths outgrabe.

Acquiring expertise in chess is harder and slower than learning to read because there are many more letters in the "alphabet" of chess and because the "words" consist of many letters. After thousands of hours of practice, however, chess masters are able to read a chess situation at a glance. The few moves that come to their mind are almost always strong and sometimes creative. They can deal with a "word" they have never encountered, and they can find a new way to interpret a familiar one.

THE ENVIRONMENT OF SKILL

Klein and I quickly found that we agreed both on the nature of intuitive skill and on how it is acquired. We still needed to agree on our key question: When can you trust a self-confident professional who claims to have an intuition?

We eventually concluded that our disagreement was due in part to the fact that we had different experts in mind. Klein had spent much time with fireground commanders, clinical nurses, and other professionals who have real expertise. I had spent more time thinking about clinicians, stock pickers, and political scientists trying to make unsupportable long-term forecasts. Not surprisingly, his default attitude was trust and respect; mine was skepticism. He was more willing to trust experts who claim an intuition because, as he told me, true experts know the limits of their knowledge. I argued that there are many pseudo-experts who have no idea that they do not know what they are doing (the illusion of validity), and that as a general proposition subjective confidence is commonly too high and often uninformative.

Earlier I traced people's confidence in a belief to two related impressions: cognitive ease and coherence. We are confident when the story we tell ourselves comes easily to mind, with no contradiction and no competing scenario. But ease and coherence do not guarantee that a belief held with confidence is true. The associative machine is set to suppress doubt and to evoke ideas and information that are compatible with the currently dominant story. A mind that follows WYSIATI will achieve high confidence much too easily by ignoring what it does not know. It is therefore not surprising that many of us are prone to have high confidence in unfounded intuitions. Klein and I eventually agreed on an important principle: the confidence that people have in their intuitions is not a reliable guide to their validity. In other words, do not trust anyone—including yourself—to tell you how much you should trust their judgment.

If subjective confidence is not to be trusted, how can we evaluate the probable validity of an intuitive judgment? When do judgments reflect true expertise? When do they display an illusion of validity? The answer comes from the two basic conditions for acquiring a skill:

- an environment that is sufficiently regular to be predictable
- an opportunity to learn these regularities through prolonged practice

When both these conditions are satisfied, intuitions are likely to be skilled. Chess is an extreme example of a regular environment, but bridge and poker also provide robust statistical regularities that can support skill. Physicians, nurses, athletes, and firefighters also face complex but fundamentally orderly situations. The accurate intuitions that Gary Klein has described are due to highly valid cues that the expert's System 1 has learned to use, even if System 2 has not learned to name them. In contrast, stock pickers and political scientists who make long-term forecasts operate in a zero-validity environment. Their failures reflect the basic unpredictability of the events that they try to forecast.

Some environments are worse than irregular. Robin Hogarth described "wicked" environments, in which professionals are likely to learn the wrong lessons from experience. He borrows from Lewis Thomas the example of a physician in the early twentieth century who often had intuitions about patients who were about to develop typhoid. Unfortunately, he tested his hunch by palpating the patient's tongue, without washing his hands between patients. When patient after patient became ill, the physician developed a sense of clinical infallibility. His predictions were accurate—but not because he was exercising professional intuition!

Meehl's clinicians were not inept and their failure was not due to lack of talent. They performed poorly because they were assigned tasks that did not have a simple solution. The clinicians' predicament was less extreme than the zero-validity environment of long-term political forecasting, but they operated in low-validity situations that did not allow high accuracy. We know this to be the case because the best statistical algorithms, although more accurate than human judges, were never very accurate. Indeed, the studies by Meehl and his followers never produced a "smoking gun" demonstration, a case in which clinicians completely missed a highly valid cue that the algorithm detected. An extreme failure of this kind is unlikely because human learning is normally efficient. If a strong predictive cue exists, human observers will find it, given a decent opportunity to do so. Statistical algorithms greatly outdo humans in noisy environments for two reasons: they are more likely than human judges to detect weakly valid cues and much more likely to maintain a modest level of accuracy by using such cues consistently.

It is wrong to blame anyone for failing to forecast accurately in an unpredictable world. However, it seems fair to blame professionals for believing they can succeed in an impossible task. Claims for correct intuitions in an unpredictable situation are self-delusional at best, sometimes worse. In the absence of valid cues, intuitive "hits" are due either to luck or to lies. If you find this conclusion surprising, you still have a lingering belief that intuition is magic. Remember this rule: intuition cannot be trusted in the absence of stable regularities in the environment.

FEEDBACK AND PRACTICE

Some regularities in the environment are easier to discover and apply than others. Think of how you developed your style of using the brakes on your car. As you were mastering the skill of taking curves, you gradually learned when to let go of the accelerator and when and how hard to use the brakes. Curves differ, and the variability you experienced while learning ensures that you are now ready to brake at the right time and strength for any curve you encounter. The conditions for learning this skill are ideal, because you receive immediate and unambiguous feedback every time you go around a bend: the mild reward of a comfortable turn or the mild punishment of some difficulty in handling the car if you brake either too hard or not quite hard enough. The situations that face a harbor pilot maneuvering large ships are no less regular, but skill is much more difficult to acquire by sheer experience because of the long delay between actions and their noticeable outcomes. Whether professionals have a chance to develop intuitive expertise depends essentially on the quality and speed of feedback, as well as on sufficient opportunity to practice.

Expertise is not a single skill; it is a collection of skills, and the same professional may be highly expert in some of the tasks in her domain while remaining a novice in others. By the time chess players become experts, they have "seen everything" (or almost everything), but chess is an exception in this regard. Surgeons can be much more proficient in some operations than in others. Furthermore, some aspects of any professional's tasks are much easier to learn than others. Psychotherapists have many opportunities to observe the immediate reactions of patients to what they say. The feedback enables them to develop the intuitive skill to find the words and the tone that will calm anger, forge confidence, or focus the patient's attention. On the other hand, therapists do not have a chance to identify which general treatment approach is most suitable for different patients. The feedback they receive from their patients' long-term outcomes is sparse, delayed, or (usually) nonexistent, and in any case too ambiguous to support learning from experience.

Among medical specialties, anesthesiologists benefit from good feedback, because the effects of their actions are likely to be quickly evident. In contrast, radiologists obtain little information about the accuracy of the diagnoses they make and about the pathologies they fail to detect. Anesthesiologists are therefore in a better position to develop useful intuitive skills. If an anesthesiologist says, "I have a feeling something is wrong," everyone in the operating room should be prepared for an emergency.

Here again, as in the case of subjective confidence, the experts may not know the limits of their expertise. An experienced psychotherapist knows that she is skilled in working out what is going on in her patient's mind and that she has good intuitions about what the patient will say next. It is tempting for her to conclude that she can also anticipate how well the patient will do next year, but this conclusion is not equally justified. Short-term anticipation and long-term forecasting are different tasks, and the therapist has had adequate opportunity to learn one but not the other. Similarly, a financial expert may have skills in many aspects of his trade but not in picking stocks, and an expert in the Middle East knows many things but not the future. The clinical psychologist, the stock picker, and the pundit do have intuitive skills in some of their tasks, but they have not learned to identify the situations and the tasks in which intuition will betray them. The unrecognized limits of professional skill help explain why experts are often overconfident.

EVALUATING VALIDITY

At the end of our journey, Gary Klein and I agreed on a general answer to our initial question: When can you trust an experienced professional who claims to have an intuition? Our conclusion was that for the most part it is possible to distinguish intuitions that are likely to be valid from those that are likely to be bogus. As in the judgment of whether a work of art is genuine or a fake, you will usually do better by focusing on its provenance than by looking at the piece itself. If the environment is sufficiently regular and if the judge has had a chance to learn its regularities, the associative machinery will recognize situations and generate quick and accurate predictions and decisions. You can trust someone's intuitions if these conditions are met.

Unfortunately, associative memory also generates subjectively compelling intuitions that are false. Anyone who has watched the chess progress of a talented youngster knows well that skill does not become perfect all at once, and that on the way to near perfection some mistakes are made with great confidence. When evaluating expert intuition you should always consider whether there was an adequate opportunity to learn the cues, even in a regular environment.

In a less regular, or low-validity, environment, the heuristics of judgment are invoked. System 1 is often able to produce quick answers to difficult questions by substitution, creating coherence where there is none. The question that is answered is not the one that was intended, but the answer is produced quickly and may be sufficiently plausible to pass the lax and lenient review of System 2. You may want to forecast the commercial future of a company, for example, and believe that this is what you are judging, while in fact your evaluation is dominated by your impressions of the energy and competence of its current executives. Because substitution occurs automatically, you often do not know the origin of a judgment that you (your System 2) endorse and adopt. If it is the only one that comes to mind, it may be subjectively undistinguishable from valid judgments that you make with expert confidence. This is why subjective confidence is not a good diagnostic of accuracy: judgments that answer the wrong question can also be made with high confidence.

You may be asking, Why didn't Gary Klein and I come up immediately with the idea of evaluating an expert's intuition by assessing the regularity of the environment and the expert's learning history—mostly setting aside the expert's confidence? And what did we think the answer could be? These are good questions because the contours of the solution were apparent from the beginning. We knew at the outset that fireground commanders and pediatric nurses would end up on one side of the boundary of valid intuitions and that the specialties studied by Meehl would be on the other, along with stock pickers and pundits.

It is difficult to reconstruct what it was that took us years, long hours of discussion, endless exchanges of drafts and hundreds of e-mails negotiating over words, and more than once almost giving up. But this is what always happens when a project ends reasonably well: once you understand the main conclusion, it seems it was always obvious.

As the title of our article suggests, Klein and I disagreed less than we had expected and accepted joint solutions of almost all the substantive issues that were raised. However, we also found that our early differences were more than an intellectual disagreement. We had different attitudes, emotions, and tastes, and those changed remarkably little over the years. This is most obvious in the facts that we find amusing and interesting. Klein still winces when the word *bias* is mentioned, and he still enjoys stories in which algorithms or formal procedures lead to obviously absurd decisions. I tend to view the occasional failures of algorithms as opportunities to improve them. On the other hand, I find more pleasure than Klein does in the comeuppance of arrogant experts who claim intuitive powers in zero-validity situations. In the long run, however, finding as much intellectual agreement as we did is surely more important than the persistent emotional differences that remained.

SPEAKING OF EXPERT INTUITION

"How much expertise does she have in this particular task? How much practice has she had?"

"Does he really believe that the environment of start-ups is sufficiently regular to justify an intuition that goes against the base rates?"

"She is very confident in her decision, but subjective confidence is a poor index of the accuracy of a judgment."

"Did he really have an opportunity to learn? How quick and how clear was the feedback he received on his judgments?"

23

THE OUTSIDE VIEW

A few years after my collaboration with Amos began, I convinced some officials in the Israeli Ministry of Education of the need for a curriculum to teach judgment and decision making in high schools. The team that I assembled to design the curriculum and write a textbook for it included several experienced teachers, some of my psychology students, and Seymour Fox, then dean of the Hebrew University's School of Education, who was an expert in curriculum development.

After meeting every Friday afternoon for about a year, we had constructed a detailed outline of the syllabus, had written a couple of chapters, and had run a few sample lessons in the classroom. We all felt that we had made good progress. One day, as we were discussing procedures for estimating uncertain quantities, the idea of conducting an exercise occurred to me. I asked everyone to write down an estimate of how long it would take us to submit a finished draft of the textbook to the Ministry of Education. I was following a procedure that we already planned to incorporate into our curriculum: the proper way to elicit information from a group is not by starting with a public discussion but by confidentially collecting each person's judgment. This procedure makes better use of the knowledge available to members of the group than the common practice of open discussion. I collected the estimates and jotted the results on the blackboard. They were narrowly centered around two years; the low end was one and a half, the high end two and a half years.

Then I had another idea. I turned to Seymour, our curriculum expert, and asked whether he could think of other teams similar to ours that had developed a curriculum from scratch. This was a time when several pedagogical innovations like "new math" had been introduced, and Seymour said he could think of quite a few. I then asked whether he knew the history of these teams in some detail, and it turned out that he was familiar with several. I asked him to think of these teams when they had made as much progress as we had. How long, from that point, did it take them to finish their textbook projects?

He fell silent. When he finally spoke, it seemed to me that he was blushing, embarrassed by his own answer: "You know, I never realized this before, but in fact not all the teams at a stage comparable to ours ever did complete their task. A substantial fraction of the teams ended up failing to finish the job."

This was worrisome; we had never considered the possibility that we might fail. My anxiety rising, I asked how large he estimated that fraction was. "About 40%," he answered. By now, a pall of gloom was falling over the room. The next question was obvious: "Those who finished," I asked. "How long did it take them?" "I cannot think of any group that finished in less than seven years," he replied, "nor any that took more than ten."

I grasped at a straw: "When you compare our skills and resources to those of the other groups, how good are we? How would you rank us in comparison with these teams?" Seymour did not hesitate long this time. "We're below average," he said, "but not by much." This came as a complete surprise to all of us—including Seymour, whose prior estimate had been well within the optimistic consensus of the group. Until I prompted him, there was no connection in his mind between his knowledge of the history of other teams and his forecast of our future.

Our state of mind when we heard Seymour is not well described by stating what we "knew." Surely all of us "knew" that a minimum of seven years and a 40% chance of failure was a more plausible forecast of the fate of our project than the numbers we had written on our slips of paper a few minutes earlier. But we did not acknowledge what we knew. The new forecast still seemed unreal, because we could not imagine how it could take so long to finish a project that looked so manageable. No crystal ball was available to tell us the strange sequence of unlikely events that were in our future. All we could see was a reasonable plan that should produce a book in about two years, conflicting with statistics indicating that other teams had failed or had taken an absurdly long time to complete their mission. What we had heard was base-rate information, from which we should have inferred a causal story: if so many teams failed, and if those that succeeded took so long, writing a curriculum was surely much harder than we had thought. But such an inference would have conflicted with our direct experience of the good progress we had been making. The statistics that Seymour provided were treated as base rates normally are—noted and promptly set aside.

We should have quit that day. None of us was willing to invest six more years of work in a project with a 40% chance of failure. Although we must have sensed that persevering was not reasonable, the warning did not provide an immediately compelling reason to quit. After a few minutes of desultory debate, we gathered ourselves together and carried on as if nothing had happened. The book was eventually completed eight(!) years later. By that time I was no longer living in Israel and had long since ceased to be part of the team, which completed the task after many unpredictable vicissitudes. The initial enthusiasm for the idea in the Ministry of Education had waned by the time the text was delivered and it was never used.

This embarrassing episode remains one of the most instructive experiences of my professional life. I eventually learned three lessons from it. The first was immediately apparent: I had stumbled onto a distinction between two profoundly different approaches to forecasting, which Amos and I later labeled the inside view and the outside view. The second lesson was that our initial forecasts of about two years for the completion of the project exhibited a planning fallacy. Our estimates were closer to a best-case scenario than to a realistic assessment. I was slower to accept the third lesson, which I call irrational perseverance: the folly we displayed that day in failing to abandon the project. Facing a choice, we gave up rationality rather than give up the enterprise.

DRAWN TO THE INSIDE VIEW

On that long-ago Friday, our curriculum expert made two judgments about the same problem and arrived at very different answers. The *inside view* is the one that all of us, including Seymour, spontaneously adopted to assess the future of our project. We focused on our specific circumstances and searched for evidence in our own experiences. We had a sketchy plan: we knew how many chapters we were going to write, and we had an idea of how long it had taken us to write the two that we had already done. The more cautious among us probably added a few months to their estimate as a margin of error.

Extrapolating was a mistake. We were forecasting based on the information in front of us—WYSIATI—but the chapters we wrote first were probably easier than others, and our commitment to the project was probably then at its peak. But the main problem was that we failed to allow for what Donald Rumsfeld famously called the "unknown unknowns." There was no way for us to foresee, that day, the succession of events that would cause the project to drag out for so long. The divorces, the illnesses, the crises of coordination with bureaucracies that delayed the work could not be anticipated. Such events not only cause the writing of chapters to slow down, they also produce long periods during which little or no progress is made at all. The same must have been true, of course, for the other teams that Seymour knew about. The members of those teams were also unable to imagine the events that would cause them to spend seven years to finish, or ultimately fail to finish, a project that they evidently had thought was very feasible. Like us, they did not know the odds they were facing. There are many ways for any plan to fail, and although most of them are too improbable to be anticipated, the likelihood that *something* will go wrong in a big project is high.

The second question I asked Seymour directed his attention away from us and toward a class of similar cases. Seymour estimated the base rate of success in that reference class: 40% failure and seven to ten years for completion. His informal survey was surely not up to scientific standards of evidence, but it provided a reasonable basis for a baseline prediction: the prediction you make about a case if you know nothing except the category to which it belongs. As we saw earlier, the *baseline prediction* should be the anchor for further adjustments. If you are asked to guess the height of a woman about whom you know only that she lives in New York City, your baseline prediction is your best guess of the average height of women in the city. If you are now given case-specific information, for example that the woman's son is the starting center of his high school basketball team, you will adjust your estimate away from the mean in the appropriate direction. Seymour's comparison of our team to others suggested that the forecast of our outcome was slightly worse than the baseline prediction, which was already grim.

The spectacular accuracy of the outside-view forecast in our problem was surely a fluke and should not count as evidence for the validity of the *outside view*. The argument for the outside view should be made on general grounds: if the reference class is properly chosen, the outside view will give an indication of where the ballpark is, and it may suggest, as it did in our case, that the inside-view forecasts are not even close to it.

For a psychologist, the discrepancy between Seymour's two judgments is striking. He had in his head all the knowledge required to estimate the statistics of an appropriate reference class, but he reached his initial estimate without ever using that knowledge. Seymour's forecast from his inside view was not an adjustment from the baseline prediction, which had not come to his mind. It was based on the particular circumstances of our efforts. Like the participants in the Tom W experiment, Seymour knew the relevant base rate but did not think of applying it.

Unlike Seymour, the rest of us did not have access to the outside view and could not have produced a reasonable baseline prediction. It is noteworthy, however, that we did not feel we needed information about other teams to make our guesses. My request for the outside view surprised all of us, including me! This is a common pattern: people who have information about an individual case rarely feel the need to know the statistics of the class to which the case belongs.

When we were eventually exposed to the outside view, we collectively ignored it. We can recognize what happened to us; it is similar to the experiment that suggested the futility of teaching psychology. When they made predictions about individual cases about which they had a little information (a brief and bland interview), Nisbett and Borgida's students completely neglected the global results they had just learned. "Pallid" statistical information is routinely discarded when it is incompatible with one's personal impressions of a case. In the competition with the inside view, the outside view doesn't stand a chance.

The preference for the inside view sometimes carries moral overtones. I once asked my cousin, a distinguished lawyer, a question about a reference class: "What is the probability of the defendant winning in cases like this one?" His sharp answer that "every case is unique" was accompanied by a look that made it clear he found my question inappropriate and superficial. A proud emphasis on the uniqueness of cases is also common in medicine, in spite of recent advances in evidence-based medicine that point the other way. Medical statistics and baseline predictions come up with increasing frequency in conversations between patients and physicians. However, the remaining ambivalence about the outside view in the medical profession is expressed in concerns about the impersonality of procedures that are guided by statistics and checklists.

THE PLANNING FALLACY

In light of both the outside-view forecast and the eventual outcome, the original estimates we made that Friday afternoon appear almost delusional.

This should not come as a surprise: overly optimistic forecasts of the outcome of projects are found everywhere. Amos and I coined the term *planning fallacy* to describe plans and forecasts that

- are unrealistically close to best-case scenarios
- could be improved by consulting the statistics of similar cases

Examples of the planning fallacy abound in the experiences of individuals, governments, and businesses. The list of horror stories is endless.

- In July 1997, the proposed new Scottish Parliament building in Edinburgh was estimated to cost up to £40 million. By June 1999, the budget for the building was £109 million. In April 2000, legislators imposed a £195 million "cap on costs." By November 2001, they demanded an estimate of "final cost," which was set at £241 million. That estimated final cost rose twice in 2002, ending the year at £294.6 million. It rose three times more in 2003, reaching £375.8 million by June. The building was finally completed in 2004 at an ultimate cost of roughly £431 million.
- A 2005 study examined rail projects undertaken worldwide between 1969 and 1998. In more than 90% of the cases, the number of passengers projected to use the system was overestimated. Even though these passenger shortfalls were widely publicized, forecasts did not improve over those thirty years; on average, planners overestimated how many people would use the new rail projects by 106%, and the average cost overrun was 45%. As more evidence accumulated, the experts did not become more reliant on it.
- In 2002, a survey of American homeowners who had remodeled their kitchens found that, on average, they had expected the job to cost $18,658; in fact, they ended up paying an average of $38,769.

The optimism of planners and decision makers is not the only cause of overruns. Contractors of kitchen renovations and of weapon systems readily admit (though not to their clients) that they routinely make most of their profit on additions to the original plan. The failures of forecasting in these cases reflect the customers' inability to imagine how much their wishes will escalate over time. They end up paying much more than they would if they had made a realistic plan and stuck to it.

Errors in the initial budget are not always innocent. The authors of unrealistic plans are often driven by the desire to get the plan approved—

whether by their superiors or by a client—supported by the knowledge that projects are rarely abandoned unfinished merely because of overruns in costs or completion times. In such cases, the greatest responsibility for avoiding the planning fallacy lies with the decision makers who approve the plan. If they do not recognize the need for an outside view, they commit a planning fallacy.

MITIGATING THE PLANNING FALLACY

The diagnosis of and the remedy for the planning fallacy have not changed since that Friday afternoon, but the implementation of the idea has come a long way. The renowned Danish planning expert Bent Flyvbjerg, now at Oxford University, offered a forceful summary:

> The prevalent tendency to underweight or ignore distributional information is perhaps the major source of error in forecasting. Planners should therefore make every effort to frame the forecasting problem so as to facilitate utilizing all the distributional information that is available.

This may be considered the single most important piece of advice regarding how to increase accuracy in forecasting through improved methods. Using such distributional information from other ventures similar to that being forecasted is called taking an "outside view" and is the cure to the planning fallacy.

The treatment for the planning fallacy has now acquired a technical name, *reference class forecasting*, and Flyvbjerg has applied it to transportation projects in several countries. The outside view is implemented by using a large database, which provides information on both plans and outcomes for hundreds of projects all over the world, and can be used to provide statistical information about the likely overruns of cost and time, and about the likely underperformance of projects of different types.

The forecasting method that Flyvbjerg applies is similar to the practices recommended for overcoming base-rate neglect:

1. Identify an appropriate reference class (kitchen renovations, large railway projects, etc.).
2. Obtain the statistics of the reference class (in terms of cost per mile of railway, or of the percentage by which expenditures exceeded budget). Use the statistics to generate a baseline prediction.

3. Use specific information about the case to adjust the baseline prediction, if there are particular reasons to expect the optimistic bias to be more or less pronounced in this project than in others of the same type.

Flyvbjerg's analyses are intended to guide the authorities that commission public projects, by providing the statistics of overruns in similar projects. Decision makers need a realistic assessment of the costs and benefits of a proposal before making the final decision to approve it. They may also wish to estimate the budget reserve that they need in anticipation of overruns, although such precautions often become self-fulfilling prophecies. As one official told Flyvbjerg, "A budget reserve is to contractors as red meat is to lions, and they will devour it."

Organizations face the challenge of controlling the tendency of executives competing for resources to present overly optimistic plans. A well-run organization will reward planners for precise execution and penalize them for failing to anticipate difficulties, and for failing to allow for difficulties that they could not have anticipated—the unknown unknowns.

DECISIONS AND ERRORS

That Friday afternoon occurred more than thirty years ago. I often thought about it and mentioned it in lectures several times each year. Some of my friends got bored with the story, but I kept drawing new lessons from it. Almost fifteen years after I first reported on the planning fallacy with Amos, I returned to the topic with Dan Lovallo. Together we sketched a theory of decision making in which the optimistic bias is a significant source of risk taking. In the standard rational model of economics, people take risks because the odds are favorable—they accept some probability of a costly failure because the probability of success is sufficient. We proposed an alternative idea.

When forecasting the outcomes of risky projects, executives too easily fall victim to the planning fallacy. In its grip, they make decisions based on delusional optimism rather than on a rational weighting of gains, losses, and probabilities. They overestimate benefits and underestimate costs. They spin scenarios of success while overlooking the potential for mistakes and miscalculations. As a result, they pursue initiatives that are unlikely to come in on budget or on time or to deliver the expected returns—or even to be completed.

In this view, people often (but not always) take on risky projects because they are overly optimistic about the odds they face. I will return to this idea several times in this book—it probably contributes to an explanation of why people litigate, why they start wars, and why they open small businesses.

FAILING A TEST

For many years, I thought that the main point of the curriculum story was what I had learned about my friend Seymour: that his best guess about the future of our project was not informed by what he knew about similar projects. I came off quite well in my telling of the story, in which I had the role of clever questioner and astute psychologist. I only recently realized that I had actually played the roles of chief dunce and inept leader.

The project was my initiative, and it was therefore my responsibility to ensure that it made sense and that major problems were properly discussed by the team, but I failed that test. My problem was no longer the planning fallacy. I was cured of that fallacy as soon as I heard Seymour's statistical summary. If pressed, I would have said that our earlier estimates had been absurdly optimistic. If pressed further, I would have admitted that we had started the project on faulty premises and that we should at least consider seriously the option of declaring defeat and going home. But nobody pressed me and there was no discussion; we tacitly agreed to go on without an explicit forecast of how long the effort would last. This was easy to do because we had not made such a forecast to begin with. If we had had a reasonable baseline prediction when we started, we would not have gone into it, but we had already invested a great deal of effort—an instance of the sunk-cost fallacy, which we will look at more closely in the next part of the book. It would have been embarrassing for us—especially for me—to give up at that point, and there seemed to be no immediate reason to do so. It is easier to change directions in a crisis, but this was not a crisis, only some new facts about people we did not know. The outside view was much easier to ignore than bad news in our own effort. I can best describe our state as a form of lethargy—an unwillingness to think about what had happened. So we carried on. There was no further attempt at rational planning for the rest of the time I spent as a member of the team—a particularly troubling omission for a team dedicated to teaching rationality. I hope I am wiser today, and I have acquired a habit of looking for the outside view. But it will never be the natural thing to do.

SPEAKING OF THE OUTSIDE VIEW

"He's taking an inside view. He should forget about his own case and look for what happened in other cases."

"She is the victim of a planning fallacy. She's assuming a best-case scenario, but there are too many different ways for the plan to fail, and she cannot foresee them all."

"Suppose you did not know a thing about this particular legal case, only that it involves a malpractice claim by an individual against a surgeon. What would be your baseline prediction? How many of these cases succeed in court? How many settle? What are the amounts? Is the case we are discussing stronger or weaker than similar claims?"

"We are making an additional investment because we do not want to admit failure. This is an instance of the sunk-cost fallacy."

24

THE ENGINE OF CAPITALISM

The planning fallacy is only one of the manifestations of a pervasive optimistic bias. Most of us view the world as more benign than it really is, our own attributes as more favorable than they truly are, and the goals we adopt as more achievable than they are likely to be. We also tend to exaggerate our ability to forecast the future, which fosters optimistic overconfidence. In terms of its consequences for decisions, the optimistic bias may well be the most significant of the cognitive biases. Because optimistic bias can be both a blessing and a risk, you should be both happy and wary if you are temperamentally optimistic.

OPTIMISTS

Optimism is normal, but some fortunate people are more optimistic than the rest of us. If you are genetically endowed with an optimistic bias, you hardly need to be told that you are a lucky person—you already feel fortunate. An optimistic attitude is largely inherited, and it is part of a general disposition for well-being, which may also include a preference for seeing the bright side of everything. If you were allowed one wish for your child, seriously consider wishing him or her optimism. Optimists are normally cheerful and happy, and therefore popular; they are resilient in adapting to failures and hardships, their chances of clinical depression are reduced, their immune system is stronger, they take better care of their health, they feel healthier than others and are in fact likely to live longer. A study of people who exaggerate their expected life span beyond actuarial predictions showed that they work longer hours, are more optimistic about their future income, are more likely to remarry after divorce (the classic "triumph of hope over experience"), and are more prone to bet on individual stocks. Of course, the blessings of optimism are offered only to individuals who are only mildly biased and who are able to "accentuate the positive" without losing track of reality.

Optimistic individuals play a disproportionate role in shaping our lives. Their decisions make a difference; they are the inventors, the entrepreneurs, the political and military leaders—not average people. They got to where they are by seeking challenges and taking risks. They are talented and they have been lucky, almost certainly luckier than they acknowledge. They are probably optimistic by temperament; a survey of founders of small businesses concluded that entrepreneurs are more sanguine than midlevel managers about life in general. Their experiences of success have confirmed their faith in their judgment and in their ability to control events. Their self-confidence is reinforced by the admiration of others. This reasoning leads to a hypothesis: the people who have the greatest influence on the lives of others are likely to be optimistic and overconfident, and to take more risks than they realize.

The evidence suggests that an optimistic bias plays a role—sometimes the dominant role—whenever individuals or institutions voluntarily take on significant risks. More often than not, risk takers underestimate the odds they face, and do invest sufficient effort to find out what the odds are. Because they misread the risks, optimistic entrepreneurs often believe they are prudent, even when they are not. Their confidence in their future success sustains a positive mood that helps them obtain resources from others, raise the morale of their employees, and enhance their prospects of prevailing. When action is needed, optimism, even of the mildly delusional variety, may be a good thing.

ENTREPRENEURIAL DELUSIONS

The chances that a small business will survive for five years in the United States are about 35%. But the individuals who open such businesses do not believe that the statistics apply to them. A survey found that American entrepreneurs tend to believe they are in a promising line of business: their average estimate of the chances of success for "any business like yours" was 60%—almost double the true value. The bias was more glaring when people assessed the odds of their own venture. Fully 81% of the entrepreneurs put their personal odds of success at 7 out of 10 or higher, and 33% said their chance of failing was zero.

The direction of the bias is not surprising. If you interviewed someone who recently opened an Italian restaurant, you would not expect her to have underestimated her prospects for success or to have a poor view of her ability as a restaurateur. But you must wonder: Would she still have invested money and time if she had made a reasonable effort to learn the odds—or, if she did learn the odds (60% of new restaurants are out of business after three years), paid attention to them? The idea of adopting the outside view probably didn't occur to her.

One of the benefits of an optimistic temperament is that it encourages persistence in the face of obstacles. But persistence can be costly. An impressive series of studies by Thomas Åstebro sheds light on what happens when optimists receive bad news. He drew his data from a Canadian organization—the Inventor's Assistance Program—which collects a small fee to provide inventors with an objective assessment of the commercial prospects of their idea. The evaluations rely on careful ratings of each invention on 37 criteria, including need for the product, cost of production, and estimated trend of demand. The analysts summarize their ratings by a letter grade, where D and E predict failure—a prediction made for over 70% of the inventions they review. The forecasts of failure are remarkably accurate: only 5 of 411 projects that were given the lowest grade reached commercialization, and none was successful.

Discouraging news led about half of the inventors to quit after receiving a grade that unequivocally predicted failure. However, 47% of them continued development efforts even after being told that their project was hopeless, and on average these persistent (or obstinate) individuals doubled their initial losses before giving up. Significantly, persistence after discouraging advice was relatively common among inventors who had a high score on a personality measure of optimism—on which inventors generally scored higher than the general population. Overall, the return on private invention was small, "lower than the return on private equity and on high-risk securities." More generally, the financial benefits of self-employment are mediocre: given the same qualifications, people achieve higher average returns by selling their skills to employers than by setting out on their own. The evidence suggests that optimism is widespread, stubborn, and costly.

Psychologists have confirmed that most people genuinely believe that they are superior to most others on most desirable traits—they are willing to bet small amounts of money on these beliefs in the laboratory. In the market, of course, beliefs in one's superiority have significant consequences. Leaders of large businesses sometimes make huge bets in expensive mergers and acquisitions, acting on the mistaken belief that they can manage the assets of another company better than its current owners do. The stock market commonly responds by downgrading the value of the acquiring firm, because experience has shown that efforts to integrate large firms fail more often than they succeed. The misguided acquisitions have been explained by a "hubris hypothesis": the executives of the acquiring firm are simply less competent than they think they are.

The economists Ulrike Malmendier and Geoffrey Tate identified optimistic CEOs by the amount of company stock that they owned personally and observed that highly optimistic leaders took excessive risks. They assumed debt rather than issue equity and were more likely than others to "overpay for target companies and undertake value-destroying mergers." Remarkably, the stock of the acquiring company suffered substantially more in mergers if the CEO was overly optimistic by the authors' measure. The stock market is apparently able to identify overconfident CEOs. This observation exonerates the CEOs from one accusation even as it convicts them of another: the leaders of enterprises who make unsound bets do not do so because they are betting with other people's money. On the contrary, they take greater risks when they personally have more at stake. The damage caused by overconfident CEOs is compounded when the business press anoints them as celebrities; the evidence indicates that prestigious press awards to the CEO are costly to stockholders. The authors write, "We find that firms with award-winning CEOs subsequently underperform, in terms both of stock and of operating performance. At the same time, CEO compensation increases, CEOs spend more time on activities outside the company such as writing books and sitting on outside boards, and they are more likely to engage in earnings management."

Many years ago, my wife and I were on vacation on Vancouver Island, looking for a place to stay. We found an attractive but deserted motel on a little-traveled road in the middle of a forest. The owners were a charming young couple who needed little prompting to tell us their story. They had been schoolteachers in the province of Alberta; they had decided to change their life and used their life savings to buy this motel, which had been built a dozen years earlier. They told us without irony or self-consciousness that they had been able to buy it cheap, "because six or seven previous owners had failed to make a go of it." They also told us about plans to seek a loan to make the establishment more attractive by building a restaurant next to it. They felt no need to explain why they expected to succeed where six or seven others had failed. A common thread of boldness and optimism links businesspeople, from motel owners to superstar CEOs.

The optimistic risk taking of entrepreneurs surely contributes to the economic dynamism of a capitalistic society, even if most risk takers end up disappointed. However, Marta Coelho of the London School of Economics has pointed out the difficult policy issues that arise when founders of small businesses ask the government to support them in decisions that are most likely to end badly. Should the government provide loans to would-be entrepreneurs who probably will bankrupt themselves in a few years? Many behavioral economists are comfortable with the "libertarian paternalistic" procedures that help people increase their savings rate beyond what they would do on their own. The question of whether and how government should support small business does not have an equally satisfying answer.

COMPETITION NEGLECT

It is tempting to explain entrepreneurial optimism by wishful thinking, but emotion is only part of the story. Cognitive biases play an important role, notably the System 1 feature WYSIATI.

- We focus on our goal, anchor on our plan, and neglect relevant base rates, exposing ourselves to the planning fallacy.
- We focus on what we want to do and can do, neglecting the plans and skills of others.
- Both in explaining the past and in predicting the future, we focus on the causal role of skill and neglect the role of luck. We are therefore prone to an *illusion of control*.
- We focus on what we know and neglect what we do not know, which makes us overly confident in our beliefs.

The observation that "90% of drivers believe they are better than average" is a well-established psychological finding that has become part of the culture, and it often comes up as a prime example of a more general above-average effect. However, the interpretation of the finding has changed in recent years, from self-aggrandizement to a cognitive bias. Consider these two questions:

> Are you a good driver?
> Are you better than average as a driver?

The first question is easy and the answer comes quickly: most drivers say yes. The second question is much harder and for most respondents almost impossible to answer seriously and correctly, because it requires an assessment of the average quality of drivers. At this point in the book it comes as no surprise that people respond to a difficult question by answering an easier one. They compare themselves to the average without ever thinking about the average. The evidence for the cognitive interpretation of the above-average effect is that when people are asked about a task they find difficult (for many of us this could be "Are you better than average in starting conversations with strangers?"), they readily rate themselves as below average. The upshot is that people tend to be overly optimistic about their relative standing on any activity in which they do moderately well.

I have had several occasions to ask founders and participants in innovative start-ups a question: To what extent will the outcome of your effort depend on what you do in your firm? This is evidently an easy question; the answer comes quickly and in my small sample it has never been less than 80%. Even when they are not sure they will succeed, these bold people think their fate is almost entirely in their own hands. They are surely wrong: the outcome of a start-up depends as much on the achievements of its competitors and on changes in the market as on its own efforts. However, WYSIATI plays its part, and entrepreneurs naturally focus on what they know best— their plans and actions and the most immediate threats and opportunities, such as the availability of funding. They know less about their competitors and therefore find it natural to imagine a future in which the competition plays little part.

Colin Camerer and Dan Lovallo, who coined the concept of competition neglect, illustrated it with a quote from the then chairman of Disney Studios. Asked why so many expensive big-budget movies are released on the same days (such as Memorial Day and Independence Day), he replied:

> Hubris. Hubris. If you only think about your own business, you think, "I've got a good story department, I've got a good marketing department, we're

going to go out and do this." And you don't think that everybody else is thinking the same way. In a given weekend in a year you'll have five movies open, and there's certainly not enough people to go around.

The candid answer refers to hubris, but it displays no arrogance, no conceit of superiority to competing studios. The competition is simply not part of the decision, in which a difficult question has again been replaced by an easier one. The question that needs an answer is this: Considering what others will do, how many people will see our film? The question the studio executives considered is simpler and refers to knowledge that is most easily available to them: Do we have a good film and a good organization to market it? The familiar System 1 processes of WYSIATI and substitution produce both competition neglect and the above-average effect. The consequence of competition neglect is excess entry: more competitors enter the market than the market can profitably sustain, so their average outcome is a loss. The outcome is disappointing for the typical entrant in the market, but the effect on the economy as a whole could well be positive. In fact, Giovanni Dosi and Dan Lovallo call entrepreneurial firms that fail but signal new markets to more qualified competitors "optimistic martyrs"— good for the economy but bad for their investors.

OVERCONFIDENCE

For a number of years, professors at Duke University conducted a survey in which the chief financial officers of large corporations estimated the returns of the Standard & Poor's index over the following year. The Duke scholars collected 11,600 such forecasts and examined their accuracy. The conclusion was straightforward: financial officers of large corporations had no clue about the short-term future of the stock market; the correlation between their estimates and the true value was slightly less than zero! When they said the market would go down, it was slightly more likely than not that it would go up. These findings are not surprising. The truly bad news is that the CFOs did not appear to know that their forecasts were worthless.

In addition to their best guess about S&P returns, the participants provided two other estimates: a value that they were 90% sure would be too high, and one that they were 90% sure would be too low. The range between the two values is called an "80% confidence interval" and outcomes that fall outside the interval are labeled "surprises." An individual who sets confidence intervals on multiple occasions expects about 20% of the outcomes to be surprises. As frequently happens in such exercises, there were far too many surprises; their incidence was 67%, more than 3 times higher than expected. This shows that CFOs were grossly overconfident about their ability to forecast the market. *Overconfidence* is another manifestation of WYSIATI: when we estimate a quantity, we rely on information that comes to mind and construct a coherent story in which the estimate makes sense. Allowing for the information that does not come to mind—perhaps because one never knew it—is impossible.

The authors calculated the confidence intervals that would have reduced the incidence of surprises to 20%. The results were striking. To maintain the rate of surprises at the desired level, the CFOs should have said, year after year, "There is an 80% chance that the S&P return next year will be between −10% and +30%." The confidence interval that properly reflects the CFOs' knowledge (more precisely, their ignorance) is more than 4 times wider than the intervals they actually stated.

Social psychology comes into the picture here, because the answer that a truthful CFO would offer is plainly ridiculous. A CFO who informs his colleagues that "there is a good chance that the S&P returns will be between −10% and +30%" can expect to be laughed out of the room. The wide confidence interval is a confession of ignorance, which is not socially acceptable for someone who is paid to be knowledgeable in financial matters. Even if they knew how little they know, the executives would be penalized for admitting it. President Truman famously asked for a "one-armed economist" who would take a clear stand; he was sick and tired of economists who kept saying, "On the other hand . . ."

Organizations that take the word of overconfident experts can expect costly consequences. The study of CFOs showed that those who were most confident and optimistic about the S&P index were also overconfident and optimistic about the prospects of their own firm, which went on to take more risk than others. As Nassim Taleb has argued, inadequate appreciation of the uncertainty of the environment inevitably leads economic agents to take risks they should avoid. However, optimism is highly valued, socially and in the market; people and firms reward the providers of dangerously misleading information more than they reward truth tellers. One of the lessons of the financial crisis that led to the Great Recession is that there are periods in which competition, among experts and among organizations, creates powerful forces that favor a collective blindness to risk and uncertainty.

The social and economic pressures that favor overconfidence are not restricted to financial forecasting. Other professionals must deal with the fact that an expert worthy of the name is expected to display high confidence. Philip Tetlock observed that the most overconfident experts were the most likely to be invited to strut their stuff in news shows. Overconfidence also appears to be endemic in medicine. A study of patients who died in the ICU compared autopsy results with the diagnosis that physicians had provided while the patients were still alive. Physicians also reported their confidence. The result: "clinicians who were 'completely certain' of the diagnosis antemortem were wrong 40% of the time." Here again, expert overconfidence is encouraged by their clients: "Generally, it is considered a weakness and a sign of vulnerability for clinicians to appear unsure. Confidence is valued over uncertainty and there is a prevailing censure against disclosing uncertainty to patients." Experts who acknowledge the full extent of their ignorance may expect to be replaced by more confident competitors, who are better able to gain the trust of clients. An unbiased appreciation of uncertainty is a cornerstone of rationality—but it is not what people and organizations want. Extreme uncertainty is paralyzing under dangerous circumstances, and the admission that one is merely guessing is especially unacceptable when the stakes are high. Acting on pretended knowledge is often the preferred solution.

When they come together, the emotional, cognitive, and social factors that support exaggerated optimism are a heady brew, which sometimes leads people to take risks that they would avoid if they knew the odds. There is no evidence that risk takers in the economic domain have an unusual appetite for gambles on high stakes; they are merely less aware of risks than more timid people are. Dan Lovallo and I coined the phrase "bold forecasts and timid decisions" to describe the background of risk taking.

The effects of high optimism on decision making are, at best, a mixed blessing, but the contribution of optimism to good implementation is certainly positive. The main benefit of optimism is resilience in the face of setbacks. According to Martin Seligman, the founder of positive psychology, an "optimistic explanation style" contributes to resilience by defending one's self-image. In essence, the optimistic style involves taking credit for successes but little blame for failures. This style can be taught, at least to some extent, and Seligman has documented the effects of training on various occupations that are characterized by a high rate of failures, such as cold-call sales of insurance (a common pursuit in pre-Internet days). When one has just had a door slammed in one's face by an angry homemaker, the thought that "she was an awful woman" is clearly superior to "I am an inept salesperson." I have always believed that scientific research is another domain where a form of optimism is essential to success: I have yet to meet a successful scientist who lacks the ability to exaggerate the importance of what he or she is doing, and I believe that someone who lacks a delusional sense of significance will wilt in the face of repeated experiences of multiple small failures and rare successes, the fate of most researchers.

THE PREMORTEM: A PARTIAL REMEDY

Can overconfident optimism be overcome by training? I am not optimistic. There have been numerous attempts to train people to state confidence intervals that reflect the imprecision of their judgments, with only a few reports of modest success. An often cited example is that geologists at Royal Dutch Shell became less overconfident in their assessments of possible drilling sites after training with multiple past cases for which the outcome was known. In other situations, overconfidence was mitigated (but not eliminated) when judges were encouraged to consider competing hypotheses. However, overconfidence is a direct consequence of features of System 1 that can be tamed—but not vanquished. The main obstacle is that subjective confidence is determined by the coherence of the story one has constructed, not by the quality and amount of the information that supports it.

Organizations may be better able to tame optimism and individuals than individuals are. The best idea for doing so was contributed by Gary Klein, my "adversarial collaborator" who generally defends intuitive decision making against claims of bias and is typically hostile to algorithms. He labels his proposal the *premortem*. The procedure is simple: when the organization has almost come to an important decision but has not formally committed itself, Klein proposes gathering for a brief session a group of individuals who are knowledgeable about the decision. The premise of the session is a short speech: "Imagine that we are a year into the future. We implemented the plan as it now exists. The outcome was a disaster. Please take 5 to 10 minutes to write a brief history of that disaster."

Gary Klein's idea of the premortem usually evokes immediate enthusiasm. After I described it casually at a session in Davos, someone behind me muttered, "It was worth coming to Davos just for this!" (I later noticed that the speaker was the CEO of a major international corporation.) The premortem has two main advantages: it overcomes the groupthink that affects many teams once a decision appears to have been made, and it unleashes the imagination of knowledgeable individuals in a much-needed direction.

As a team converges on a decision—and especially when the leader tips her hand—public doubts about the wisdom of the planned move are gradually suppressed and eventually come to be treated as evidence of flawed loyalty to the team and its leaders. The suppression of doubt contributes to overconfidence in a group where only supporters of the decision have a voice. The main virtue of the premortem is that it legitimizes doubts. Furthermore, it encourages even supporters of the decision to search for possible threats that they had not considered earlier. The premortem is not a panacea and does not provide complete protection against nasty surprises, but it goes some way toward reducing the damage of plans that are subject to the biases of WYSIATI and uncritical optimism.

SPEAKING OF OPTIMISM

"They have an illusion of control. They seriously underestimate the obstacles."

"They seem to suffer from an acute case of competitor neglect."

"This is a case of overconfidence. They seem to believe they know more than they actually do know."

"We should conduct a premortem session. Someone may come up with a threat we have neglected."

PART 4

CHOICES

25

BERNOULLI'S ERRORS

One day in the early 1970s, Amos handed me a mimeographed essay by a Swiss economist named Bruno Frey, which discussed the psychological assumptions of economic theory. I vividly remember the color of the cover: dark red. Bruno Frey barely recalls writing the piece, but I can still recite its first sentence: "The agent of economic theory is rational, selfish, and his tastes do not change."

I was astonished. My economist colleagues worked in the building next door, but I had not appreciated the profound difference between our intellectual worlds. To a psychologist, it is self-evident that people are neither fully rational nor completely selfish, and that their tastes are anything but stable. Our two disciplines seemed to be studying different species, which the behavioral economist Richard Thaler later dubbed Econs and Humans.

Unlike Econs, the Humans that psychologists know have a System 1. Their view of the world is limited by the information that is available at a given moment (WYSIATI), and therefore they cannot be as consistent and logical as Econs. They are sometimes generous and often willing to contribute to the group to which they are attached. And they often have little idea of what they will like next year or even tomorrow. Here was an opportunity for an interesting conversation across the boundaries of the disciplines. I did not anticipate that my career would be defined by that conversation.

Soon after he showed me Frey's article, Amos suggested that we make the study of decision making our next project. I knew next to nothing about the topic, but Amos was an expert and a star of the field, and he said he would coach me. While still a graduate student he had coauthored a text-book, *Mathematical Psychology*, and he directed me to a few chapters that he thought would be a good introduction.

I soon learned that our subject matter would be people's attitudes to risky options and that we would seek to answer a specific question: What rules govern people's choices between different simple gambles and be-tween gambles and sure things?

Simple gambles (such as "40% chance to win $300") are to students of decision making what the fruit fly is to geneticists. Choices between such gambles provide a simple model that shares important features with the more complex decisions that researchers actually aim to understand. Gam-bles represent the fact that the consequences of choices are never certain. Even ostensibly sure outcomes are uncertain: when you sign the contract to buy an apartment, you do not know the price at which you later may have to sell it, nor do you know that your neighbor's son will soon take up the tuba. Every significant choice we make in life comes with some uncer-tainty—which is why students of decision making hope that some of the lessons learned in the model situation will be applicable to more interesting everyday problems. But of course the main reason that decision theorists study simple gambles is that this is what other decision theorists do.

The field had a theory, expected utility theory, which was the founda-tion of the rational-agent model and is to this day the most important theory in the social sciences. Expected utility theory was not intended as a psycho-logical model; it was a logic of choice, based on elementary rules (axioms) of rationality. Consider this example:

> If you prefer an apple to a banana,
> then
> you also prefer a 10% chance to win an apple to a 10% chance to win a banana.

The apple and the banana stand for any objects of choice (including gambles), and the 10% chance stands for any probability. The mathematician John von Neumann, one of the giant intellectual figures of the twentieth century, and the economist Oskar Morgenstern had derived their theory of rational choice between gambles from a few axioms. Economists adopted expected utility theory in a dual role: as a logic that prescribes how decisions should be made, and as a description of how Econs make choices. Amos and I were psychologists, however, and we set out to understand how Humans actually make risky choices, without assuming anything about their rationality.

We maintained our routine of spending many hours each day in conversation, sometimes in our offices, sometimes at restaurants, often on long walks through the quiet streets of beautiful Jerusalem. As we had done when we studied judgment, we engaged in a careful examination of our own intuitive preferences. We spent our time inventing simple decision problems and asking ourselves how we would choose. For example:

Which do you prefer?
A. Toss a coin. If it comes up heads you win $100, and if it comes up tails you win nothing.
B. Get $46 for sure.

We were not trying to figure out the most rational or advantageous choice; we wanted to find the intuitive choice, the one that appeared immediately tempting. We almost always selected the same option. In this example, both of us would have picked the sure thing, and you probably would do the same. When we confidently agreed on a choice, we believed—almost always correctly, as it turned out—that most people would share our preference, and we moved on as if we had solid evidence. We knew, of course, that we would need to verify our hunches later, but by playing the roles of both experimenters and subjects we were able to move quickly.

Five years after we began our study of gambles, we finally completed an essay that we titled "Prospect Theory: An Analysis of Decision under Risk." Our theory was closely modeled on utility theory but departed from it in fundamental ways. Most important, our model was purely descriptive, and its goal was to document and explain systematic violations of the axioms of rationality in choices between gambles. We submitted our essay to *Econometrica*, a journal that publishes significant theoretical articles in economics and in decision theory. The choice of venue turned out to be important; if we had published the identical paper in a psychological journal, it would likely have had little impact on economics. However, our decision was not guided by a wish to influence economics; *Econometrica* just happened to be where the best papers on decision making had been published in the past, and we were aspiring to be in that company. In this choice as in many others, we were lucky. Prospect theory turned out to be the most significant work we ever did, and our article is among the most often cited in the social sciences. Two years later, we published in *Science* an account of framing effects: the large changes of preferences that are sometimes caused by inconsequential variations in the wording of a choice problem.

During the first five years we spent looking at how people make decisions, we established a dozen facts about choices between risky options. Several of these facts were in flat contradiction to expected utility theory. Some had been observed before, a few were new. Then we constructed a theory that modified expected utility theory just enough to explain our collection of observations. That was prospect theory.

Our approach to the problem was in the spirit of a field of psychology called psychophysics, which was founded and named by the German psychologist and mystic Gustav Fechner (1801–1887). Fechner was obsessed with the relation of mind and matter. On one side there is a physical quantity that can vary, such as the energy of a light, the frequency of a tone, or an amount of money. On the other side there is a subjective experience of brightness, pitch, or value. Mysteriously, variations of the physical quantity cause variations in the intensity or quality of the subjective experience. Fechner's project was to find the psychophysical laws that relate the subjective quantity in the observer's mind to the objective quantity in the material world. He proposed that for many dimensions, the function is logarithmic— which simply means that an increase of stimulus intensity by a given factor (say, times 1.5 or times 10) always yields the same increment on the psychological scale. If raising the energy of the sound from 10 to 100 units of physical energy increases psychological intensity by 4 units, then a further increase of stimulus intensity from 100 to 1,000 will also increase psychological intensity by 4 units.

BERNOULLI'S ERROR

As Fechner well knew, he was not the first to look for a function that relates psychological intensity to the physical magnitude of the stimulus. In 1738, the Swiss scientist Daniel Bernoulli anticipated Fechner's reasoning and applied it to the relationship between the psychological value or desirability of money (now called *utility*) and the actual amount of money. He argued that a gift of 10 ducats has the same utility to someone who already has 100 ducats as a gift of 20 ducats to someone whose current wealth is 200 ducats. Bernoulli was right, of course: we normally speak of changes of income in terms of percentages, as when we say "she got a 30% raise." The idea is that a 30% raise may evoke a fairly similar psychological response for the rich and for the poor, which an increase of $100 will not do. As in Fechner's law, the psychological response to a change of wealth is inversely proportional to the initial amount of wealth, leading to the conclusion that utility is a logarithmic function of wealth. If this function is accurate, the same psychological distance separates $100,000 from $1 million, and $10 million from $100 million.

Bernoulli drew on his psychological insight into the utility of wealth to propose a radically new approach to the evaluation of gambles, an important topic for the mathematicians of his day. Prior to Bernoulli, mathematicians had assumed that gambles are assessed by their expected value: a weighted average of the possible outcomes, where each outcome is weighted by its probability. For example, the expected value of:

80% chance to win $100 and 20% chance to win $10
is $82 (0.8 x 100 + 0.2 x 10).

Now ask yourself this question: Which would you prefer to receive as a gift, this gamble or $80 for sure? Almost everyone prefers the sure thing. If people valued uncertain prospects by their expected value, they would prefer the gamble, because $82 is more than $80. Bernoulli pointed out that people do not in fact evaluate gambles in this way.

Bernoulli observed that most people dislike risk (the chance of receiving the lowest possible outcome), and if they are offered a choice between a gamble and an amount equal to its expected value they will pick the sure thing. In fact a risk-averse decision maker will choose a sure thing that is less than expected value, in effect paying a premium to avoid the uncertainty. One hundred years before Fechner, Bernoulli invented psychophysics to explain this aversion to risk. His idea was straightforward: people's choices are based not on dollar values but on the psychological values of outcomes, their utilities. The psychological value of a gamble is therefore not the weighted average of its possible dollar outcomes; it is the average of the utilities of these outcomes, each weighted by its probability.

Table 3 shows a version of the utility function that Bernoulli calculated; it presents the utility of different levels of wealth, from 1 million to 10 million. You can see that adding 1 million to a wealth of 1 million yields an

Wealth (millions)	1	2	3	4	5	6	7	8	9	10
Utility units	10	30	48	60	70	78	84	90	96	100

Table 3

increment of 20 utility points, but adding 1 million to a wealth of 9 million adds only 4 points. Bernoulli proposed that the diminishing marginal value of wealth (in the modern jargon) is what explains risk aversion—the common preference that people generally show for a sure thing over a favorable gamble of equal or slightly higher expected value. Consider this choice:

Equal chances to have 1 million or 7 million	Utility: $(10 + 84)/2 = 47$
OR	
Have 4 million with certainty	Utility: 60

The expected value of the gamble and the "sure thing" are equal in ducats (4 million), but the psychological utilities of the two options are different, because of the diminishing utility of wealth: the increment of utility from 1 million to 4 million is 50 units, but an equal increment, from 4 to 7 million, increases the utility of wealth by only 24 units. The utility of the gamble is $94/2 = 47$ (the utility of its two outcomes, each weighted by its probability of 1/2). The utility of 4 million is 60. Because 60 is more than 47, an individual with this utility function will prefer the sure thing. Bernoulli's insight was that a decision maker with diminishing marginal utility for wealth will be risk averse.

Bernoulli's essay is a marvel of concise brilliance. He applied his new concept of expected utility (which he called "moral expectation") to compute how much a merchant in St. Petersburg would be willing to pay to insure a shipment of spice from Amsterdam if "he is well aware of the fact that at this time of year of one hundred ships which sail from Amsterdam to Petersburg, five are usually lost." His utility function explained why poor people buy insurance and why richer people sell it to them. As you can see in the table, the loss of 1 million causes a loss of 4 points of utility (from 100 to 96) to someone who has 10 million and a much larger loss of 18 points (from 48 to 30) to someone who starts off with 3 million. The poorer man will happily pay a premium to transfer the risk to the richer one, which is what insurance is about. Bernoulli also offered a solution to the famous "St. Petersburg paradox," in which people who are offered a gamble that has infinite expected value (in ducats) are willing to spend only a few ducats for it. Most impressive, his analysis of risk attitudes in terms of preferences for wealth has stood the test of time: it is still current in economic analysis almost 300 years later.

The longevity of the theory is all the more remarkable because it is seriously flawed. The errors of a theory are rarely found in what it asserts explicitly; they hide in what it ignores or tacitly assumes. For an example, take the following scenarios:

> Today Jack and Jill each have a wealth of 5 million.
> Yesterday, Jack had 1 million and Jill had 9 million.
> Are they equally happy? (Do they have the same utility?)

Bernoulli's theory assumes that the utility of their wealth is what makes people more or less happy. Jack and Jill have the same wealth, and the theory therefore asserts that they should be equally happy, but you do not need a degree in psychology to know that today Jack is elated and Jill despondent. Indeed, we know that Jack would be a great deal happier than Jill even if he had only 2 million today while she has 5. So Bernoulli's theory must be wrong.

The happiness that Jack and Jill experience is determined by the recent *change* in their wealth, relative to the different states of wealth that define their reference points (1 million for Jack, 9 million for Jill). This reference dependence is ubiquitous in sensation and perception. The same sound will be experienced as very loud or quite faint, depending on whether it was preceded by a whisper or by a roar. To predict the subjective experience of loudness, it is not enough to know its absolute energy; you also need to know the reference sound to which it is automatically compared. Similarly, you need to know about the background before you can predict whether a gray patch on a page will appear dark or light. And you need to know the reference before you can predict the utility of an amount of wealth.

For another example of what Bernoulli's theory misses, consider Anthony and Betty:

> Anthony's current wealth is 1 million.
> Betty's current wealth is 4 million.

They are both offered a choice between a gamble and a sure thing.

> The gamble: equal chances to end up owning 1 million or 4 million
> OR
> The sure thing: own 2 million for sure

In Bernoulli's account, Anthony and Betty face the same choice: their expected wealth will be 2.5 million if they take the gamble and 2 million if they prefer the sure-thing option. Bernoulli would therefore expect An-thony and Betty to make the same choice, but this prediction is incorrect. Here again, the theory fails because it does not allow for the different *refer-ence points* from which Anthony and Betty consider their options. If you imagine yourself in Anthony's and Betty's shoes, you will quickly see that current wealth matters a great deal. Here is how they may think:

Anthony (who currently owns 1 million): "If I choose the sure thing, my wealth will double with certainty. This is very attractive. Alternatively, I can take a gamble with equal chances to quadruple my wealth or to gain nothing."

Betty (who currently owns 4 million): "If I choose the sure thing, I lose half of my wealth with certainty, which is awful. Alternatively, I can take a gamble with equal chances to lose three-quarters of my wealth or to lose nothing."

You can sense that Anthony and Betty are likely to make different choices because the sure-thing option of owning 2 million makes Anthony happy and makes Betty miserable. Note also how the *sure* outcome differs from the *worst* outcome of the gamble: for Anthony, it is the difference be-tween doubling his wealth and gaining nothing; for Betty, it is the difference between losing half her wealth and losing three-quarters of it. Betty is much more likely to take her chances, as others do when faced with very bad op-tions. As I have told their story, neither Anthony nor Betty thinks in terms of states of wealth: Anthony thinks of gains and Betty thinks of losses. The psychological outcomes they assess are entirely different, although the pos-sible states of wealth they face are the same.

Because Bernoulli's model lacks the idea of a reference point, expected utility theory does not represent the obvious fact that the outcome that is good for Anthony is bad for Betty. His model could explain Anthony's risk aversion, but it cannot explain Betty's risk-seeking preference for the gamble, a behavior that is often observed in entrepreneurs and in generals when all their options are bad.

All this is rather obvious, isn't it? One could easily imagine Bernoulli himself constructing similar examples and developing a more complex theory to accommodate them; for some reason, he did not. One could also imagine colleagues of his time disagreeing with him, or later scholars ob-jecting as they read his essay; for some reason, they did not either.

The mystery is how a conception of the utility of outcomes that is vul-nerable to such obvious counterexamples survived for so long. I can explain it only by a weakness of the scholarly mind that I have often observed in myself. I call it theory-induced blindness: once you have accepted a theory and used it as a tool in your thinking, it is extraordinarily difficult to notice its flaws. If you come upon an observation that does not seem to fit the model, you assume that there must be a perfectly good explanation that you are somehow missing. You give the theory the benefit of the doubt, trusting the community of experts who have accepted it. Many scholars have surely thought at one time or another of stories such as those of Anthony and Betty, or Jack and Jill, and casually noted that these stories did not jibe with utility theory. But they did not pursue the idea to the point of saying, "This theory is seriously wrong because it ignores the fact that utility depends on the history of one's wealth, not only on present wealth." As the psychologist Daniel Gilbert observed, disbelieving is hard work, and System 2 is easily tired.

SPEAKING OF BERNOULLI'S ERRORS

"He was very happy with a $20,000 bonus three years ago, but his salary has gone up by 20% since, so he will need a higher bonus to get the same utility."

"Both candidates are willing to accept the salary we're offering, but they won't be equally satisfied because their reference points are different. She currently has a much higher salary."

"She's suing him for alimony. She would actually like to settle, but he prefers to go to court. That's not surprising—she can only gain, so she's risk averse. He, on the other hand, faces options that are all bad, so he'd rather take the risk."

26

PROSPECT THEORY

Amos and I stumbled on the central flaw in Bernoulli's theory by a lucky combination of skill and ignorance. At Amos's suggestion, I read a chapter in his book that described experiments in which distinguished scholars had measured the utility of money by asking people to make choices about gambles in which the participant could win or lose a few pennies. The experimenters were measuring the utility of wealth, by modifying wealth within a range of less than a dollar. This raised questions. Is it plausible to assume that people evaluate the gambles by tiny differences in wealth? How could one hope to learn about the psychophysics of wealth by studying reactions to gains and losses of pennies? Recent developments in psychophysical theory suggested that if you want to study the subjective value of wealth, you should ask direct questions about wealth, not about changes of wealth. I did not know enough about utility theory to be blinded by respect for it, and I was puzzled.

When Amos and I met the next day, I reported my difficulties as a vague thought, not as a discovery. I fully expected him to set me straight and to explain why the experiment that had puzzled me made sense after all, but he did nothing of the kind—the relevance of the modern psychophysics was immediately obvious to him. He remembered that the economist Harry Markowitz, who would later earn the Nobel Prize for his work on finance, had proposed a theory in which utilities were attached to changes of wealth rather than to states of wealth. Markowitz's idea had been around for a quarter of a century and had not attracted much attention, but we quickly concluded that this was the way to go, and that the theory we were planning to develop would define outcomes as gains and losses, not as states of wealth. Knowledge of perception and ignorance about decision theory both contributed to a large step forward in our research.

We soon knew that we had overcome a serious case of theory-induced blindness, because the idea we had rejected now seemed not only false but absurd. We were amused to realize that we were unable to assess our current wealth within tens of thousands of dollars. The idea of deriving attitudes to small changes from the utility of wealth now seemed indefensible. You know you have made a theoretical advance when you can no longer reconstruct why you failed for so long to see the obvious. Still, it took us years to explore the implications of thinking about outcomes as gains and losses.

In utility theory, the utility of a gain is assessed by comparing the utilities of two states of wealth. For example, the utility of getting an extra $500 when your wealth is $1 million is the difference between the utility of $1,000,500 and the utility of $1 million. And if you own the larger amount, the disutility of losing $500 is again the difference between the utilities of the two states of wealth. In this theory, the utilities of gains and losses are allowed to differ only in their sign (+ or –). There is no way to represent the fact that the disutility of losing $500 could be greater than the utility of winning the same amount—though of course it is. As might be expected in a situation of theory-induced blindness, possible differences between gains and losses were neither expected nor studied. The distinction between gains and losses was assumed not to matter, so there was no point in examining it.

Amos and I did not see immediately that our focus on changes of wealth opened the way to an exploration of a new topic. We were mainly concerned with differences between gambles with high or low probability of winning. One day, Amos made the casual suggestion, "How about losses?" and we quickly found that our familiar risk aversion was replaced by risk seeking when we switched our focus. Consider these two problems:

Problem 1: Which do you choose?
Get $900 for sure OR 90% chance to get $1,000

Problem 2: Which do you choose?
Lose $900 for sure OR 90% chance to lose $1,000

You were probably risk averse in problem 1, as is the great majority of people. The subjective value of a gain of $900 is certainly more than 90% of the value of a gain of $1,000. The risk-averse choice in this problem would not have surprised Bernoulli.

Now examine your preference in problem 2. If you are like most other people, you chose the gamble in this question. The explanation for this risk-seeking choice is the mirror image of the explanation of risk aversion in problem 1: the (negative) value of losing $900 is much more than 90% of the (negative) value of losing $1,000. The sure loss is very aversive, and this drives you to take the risk. Later, we will see that the evaluations of the probabilities (90% versus 100%) also contributes to both risk aversion in problem 1 and the preference for the gamble in problem 2.

We were not the first to notice that people become risk seeking when all their options are bad, but theory-induced blindness had prevailed. Because the dominant theory did not provide a plausible way to accommodate different attitudes to risk for gains and losses, the fact that the attitudes differed had to be ignored. In contrast, our decision to view outcomes as gains and losses led us to focus precisely on this discrepancy. The observation of contrasting attitudes to risk with favorable and unfavorable prospects soon yielded a significant advance: we found a way to demonstrate the central error in Bernoulli's model of choice. Have a look:

Problem 3: In addition to whatever you own, you have been given $1,000. You are now asked to choose one of these options:
50% chance to win $1,000 OR get $500 for sure

Problem 4: In addition to whatever you own, you have been given $2,000. You are now asked to choose one of these options:
50% chance to lose $1,000 OR lose $500 for sure

You can easily confirm that in terms of final states of wealth—all that matters for Bernoulli's theory—problems 3 and 4 are identical. In both cases you have a choice between the same two options: you can have the certainty of being richer than you currently are by $1,500, or accept a gamble in which you have equal chances to be richer by $1,000 or by $2,000. In Bernoulli's theory, therefore, the two problems should elicit similar preferences. Check your intuitions, and you will probably guess what other people did.

- In the first choice, a large majority of respondents preferred the sure thing.
- In the second choice, a large majority preferred the gamble.

The finding of different preferences in problems 3 and 4 was a decisive counterexample to the key idea of Bernoulli's theory. If the utility of wealth is all that matters, then transparently equivalent statements of the same problem should yield identical choices. The comparison of the problems highlights the all-important role of the reference point from which the options are evaluated. The reference point is higher than current wealth by $1,000 in problem 3, by $2,000 in problem 4. Being richer by $1,500 is therefore a gain of $500 in problem 3 and a loss in problem 4. Obviously, other examples of the same kind are easy to generate. The story of Anthony and Betty had a similar structure.

How much attention did you pay to the gift of $1,000 or $2,000 that you were "given" prior to making your choice? If you are like most people, you barely noticed it. Indeed, there was no reason for you to attend to it, because the gift is included in the reference point, and reference points are generally ignored. You know something about your preferences that utility theorists do not—that your attitudes to risk would not be different if your net worth were higher or lower by a few thousand dollars (unless you are abjectly poor). And you also know that your attitudes to gains and losses are not derived from your evaluation of your wealth. The reason you like the idea of gaining $100 and dislike the idea of losing $100 is not that these amounts change your wealth. You just like winning and dislike losing—and you almost certainly dislike losing more than you like winning.

The four problems highlight the weakness of Bernoulli's model. His theory is too simple and lacks a moving part. The missing variable is the *reference point*, the earlier state relative to which gains and losses are evaluated. In Bernoulli's theory you need to know only the state of wealth to determine its utility, but in prospect theory you also need to know the reference state. Prospect theory is therefore more complex than utility theory. In science complexity is considered a cost, which must be justified by a sufficiently rich set of new and (preferably) interesting predictions of facts that the existing theory cannot explain. This was the challenge we had to meet.

Although Amos and I were not working with the two-systems model of the mind, it's clear now that there are three cognitive features at the heart of prospect theory. They play an essential role in the evaluation of financial outcomes and are common to many automatic processes of perception, judgment, and emotion. They should be seen as operating characteristics of System 1.

- Evaluation is relative to a neutral reference point, which is sometimes referred to as an "adaptation level." You can easily set up a compelling demonstration of this principle. Place three bowls of water in front of you. Put ice water into the left-hand bowl and warm water into the right-hand bowl. The water in the middle bowl should be at room temperature. Immerse your hands in the cold and warm water for about a minute, then dip both in the middle bowl. You will experience the same temperature as heat in one hand and cold in the other. For financial outcomes, the usual reference point is the status quo, but it can also be the outcome that you expect, or perhaps the outcome to which you feel entitled, for example, the raise or bonus that your colleagues receive. Outcomes that are better than the reference points are gains. Below the reference point they are losses.
- A principle of diminishing sensitivity applies to both sensory dimensions and the evaluation of changes of wealth. Turning on a weak light has a large effect in a dark room. The same increment of light may be undetectable in a brightly illuminated room. Similarly, the subjective difference between $900 and $1,000 is much smaller than the difference between $100 and $200.
- The third principle is loss aversion. When directly compared or weighted against each other, losses loom larger than gains. This asymmetry between the power of positive and negative expectations or experiences has an evolutionary history. Organisms that treat threats as more urgent than opportunities have a better chance to survive and reproduce.

The three principles that govern the value of outcomes are illustrated by figure 10. If prospect theory had a flag, this image would be drawn on it. The graph shows the psychological value of gains and losses, which are the "carriers" of value in prospect theory (unlike Bernoulli's model, in which states of wealth are the carriers of value). The graph has two distinct parts, to the right and to the left of a neutral reference point. A salient feature is that it is S-shaped, which represents diminishing sensitivity for both gains and losses. Finally, the two curves of the S are not symmetrical. The slope of the function changes abruptly at the reference point: the response

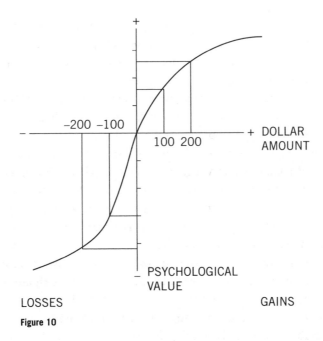

Figure 10

to losses is stronger than the response to corresponding gains. This is loss aversion.

LOSS AVERSION

Many of the options we face in life are "mixed": there is a risk of loss and an opportunity for gain, and we must decide whether to accept the gamble or reject it. Investors who evaluate a start-up, lawyers who wonder whether to file a lawsuit, wartime generals who consider an offensive, and politicians who must decide whether to run for office all face the possibilities of victory or defeat. For an elementary example of a mixed prospect, examine your reaction to the next question.

> Problem 5: You are offered a gamble on the toss of a coin.
> If the coin shows tails, you lose $100.
> If the coin shows heads, you win $150.
> Is this gamble attractive? Would you accept it?

To make this choice, you must balance the psychological benefit of getting $150 against the psychological cost of losing $100. How do you feel about it? Although the expected value of the gamble is obviously positive, because you stand to gain more than you can lose, you probably dislike it—most people do. The rejection of this gamble is an act of System 2, but the critical inputs are emotional responses that are generated by System 1. For most people, the fear of losing $100 is more intense than the hope of gaining $150. We concluded from many such observations that "losses loom larger than gains" and that people are *loss averse*.

You can measure the extent of your aversion to losses by asking yourself a question: What is the smallest gain that I need to balance an equal chance to lose $100? For many people the answer is about $200, twice as much as the loss. The "loss aversion ratio" has been estimated in several experiments and is usually in the range of 1.5 to 2.5. This is an average, of course; some people are much more loss averse than others. Professional risk takers in the financial markets are more tolerant of losses, probably because they do not respond emotionally to every fluctuation. When participants in an experiment were instructed to "think like a trader," they became less loss averse and their emotional reaction to losses (measured by a physiological index of emotional arousal) was sharply reduced.

In order to examine your loss aversion ratio for different stakes, consider the following questions. Ignore any social considerations, do not try to appear either bold or cautious, and focus only on the subjective impact of the possible loss and the offsetting gain.

- Consider a 50–50 gamble in which you can lose $10. What is the smallest gain that makes the gamble attractive? If you say $10, then you are indifferent to risk. If you give a number less than $10, you seek risk. If your answer is above $10, you are loss averse.
- What about a possible loss of $500 on a coin toss? What possible gain do you require to offset it?
- What about a loss of $2,000?

As you carried out this exercise, you probably found that your loss aversion coefficient tends to increase when the stakes rise, but not dramatically. All bets are off, of course, if the possible loss is potentially ruinous, or if your lifestyle is threatened. The loss aversion coefficient is very large in such cases and may even be infinite—there are risks that you will not accept, regardless of how many millions you might stand to win if you are lucky.

Another look at figure 10 may help prevent a common confusion. In this chapter I have made two claims, which some readers may view as contradictory:

- In mixed gambles, where both a gain and a loss are possible, loss aversion causes extremely risk-averse choices.
- In bad choices, where a sure loss is compared to a larger loss that is merely probable, diminishing sensitivity causes risk seeking.

There is no contradiction. In the mixed case, the possible loss looms twice as large as the possible gain, as you can see by comparing the slopes of the value function for losses and gains. In the bad case, the bending of the value curve (diminishing sensitivity) causes risk seeking. The pain of losing $900 is more than 90% of the pain of losing $1,000. These two insights are the essence of prospect theory.

Figure 10 shows an abrupt change in the slope of the value function where gains turn into losses, because there is considerable loss aversion even when the amount at risk is minuscule relative to your wealth. Is it plausible that attitudes to states of wealth could explain the extreme aversion to small risks? It is a striking example of theory-induced blindness that this obvious flaw in Bernoulli's theory failed to attract scholarly notice for more than 250 years. In 2000, the behavioral economist Matthew Rabin finally proved mathematically that attempts to explain loss aversion by the utility of wealth are absurd and doomed to fail, and his proof attracted attention. Rabin's theorem shows that anyone who rejects a favorable gamble with small stakes is mathematically committed to a foolish level of risk aversion for some larger gamble. For example, he notes that most Humans reject the following gamble:

   50% chance to lose $100 and 50% chance to win $200

He then shows that according to utility theory, an individual who rejects that gamble will also turn down the following gamble:

   50% chance to lose $200 and 50% chance to win $20,000

But of course no one in his or her right mind will reject this gamble! In an exuberant article they wrote about the proof, Matthew Rabin and Richard

Thaler commented that the larger gamble "has an expected return of $9,900—with exactly zero chance of losing more than $200. Even a lousy lawyer could have you declared legally insane for turning down this gamble."

Perhaps carried away by their enthusiasm, they concluded their article by recalling the famous Monty Python sketch in which a frustrated customer attempts to return a dead parrot to a pet store. The customer uses a long series of phrases to describe the state of the bird, culminating in "this is an ex-parrot." Rabin and Thaler went on to say that "it is time for economists to recognize that expected utility is an ex-hypothesis." Many economists saw this flippant statement as little short of blasphemy. However, the theory-induced blindness of accepting the utility of wealth as an explanation of attitudes to small losses is a legitimate target for humorous comment.

BLIND SPOTS OF PROSPECT THEORY

So far in this part of the book I have extolled the virtues of prospect theory and criticized the rational model and expected utility theory. It is time for some balance.

Most graduate students in economics have heard about prospect theory and loss aversion, but you are unlikely to find these terms in the index of an introductory text in economics. I am sometimes pained by this omission, but in fact it is quite reasonable, because of the central role of rationality in basic economic theory. The standard concepts and results that undergraduates are taught are most easily explained by assuming that Econs do not make foolish mistakes. This assumption is truly necessary, and it would be undermined by introducing the Humans of prospect theory, whose evaluations of outcomes are unreasonably short-sighted.

There are good reasons for keeping prospect theory out of introductory texts. The basic concepts of economics are essential intellectual tools, which are not easy to grasp even with simplified and unrealistic assumptions about the nature of the economic agents who interact in markets. Raising questions about these assumptions even as they are introduced would be confusing, and perhaps demoralizing. It is reasonable to put priority on helping students acquire the basic tools of the discipline. Furthermore, the failure of rationality that is built into prospect theory is often irrelevant to the predictions of economic theory, which work out with great precision in some situations and provide good approximations in many others. In some contexts, however, the difference becomes significant: the Humans described by prospect theory are guided by the immediate emotional impact of gains and losses, not by long-term prospects of wealth and global utility.

I emphasized theory-induced blindness in my discussion of flaws in Bernoulli's model that remained unquestioned for more than two centuries. But of course theory-induced blindness is not restricted to expected utility theory. Prospect theory has flaws of its own, and theory-induced blindness to these flaws has contributed to its acceptance as the main alternative to utility theory.

Consider the assumption of prospect theory, that the reference point, usually the status quo, has a value of zero. This assumption seems reasonable, but it leads to some absurd consequences. Have a good look at the following prospects. What would it be like to own them?

A. one chance in a million to win $1 million
B. 90% chance to win $12 and 10% chance to win nothing
C. 90% chance to win $1 million and 10% chance to win nothing

Winning nothing is a possible outcome in all three gambles, and prospect theory assigns the same value to that outcome in the three cases. Winning nothing is the reference point and its value is zero. Do these statements correspond to your experience? Of course not. Winning nothing is a nonevent in the first two cases, and assigning it a value of zero makes good sense. In contrast, failing to win in the third scenario is intensely disappointing. Like a salary increase that has been promised informally, the high probability of winning the large sum sets up a tentative new reference point. Relative to your expectations, winning nothing will be experienced as a large loss. Prospect theory cannot cope with this fact, because it does not allow the value of an outcome (in this case, winning nothing) to change when it is highly unlikely, or when the alternative is very valuable. In simple words, prospect theory cannot deal with disappointment. Disappointment and the anticipation of disappointment are real, however, and the failure to acknowledge them is as obvious a flow as the counterexamples that I invoked to criticize Bernoulli's theory.

Prospect theory and utility theory also fail to allow for regret. The two theories share the assumption that available options in a choice are evaluated separately and independently, and that the option with the highest value is selected. This assumption is certainly wrong, as the following example shows.

Problem 6: Choose between 90% chance to win $1 million OR $50 with certainty.

Problem 7: Choose between 90% chance to win $1 million OR $150,000 with certainty.

Compare the anticipated pain of choosing the gamble and *not* winning in the two cases. Failing to win is a disappointment in both, but the potential pain is compounded in problem 7 by knowing that if you choose the gamble and lose you will regret the "greedy" decision you made by spurning a sure gift of $150,000. In regret, the experience of an outcome depends on an option you could have adopted but did not.

Several economists and psychologists have proposed models of decision making that are based on the emotions of regret and disappointment. It is fair to say that these models have had less influence than prospect theory, and the reason is instructive. The emotions of regret and disappointment are real, and decision makers surely anticipate these emotions when making their choices. The problem is that regret theories make few striking predictions that would distinguish them from prospect theory, which has the advantage of being simpler. The complexity of prospect theory was more acceptable in the competition with expected utility theory because it did predict observations that expected utility theory could not explain.

Richer and more realistic assumptions do not suffice to make a theory successful. Scientists use theories as a bag of working tools, and they will not take on the burden of a heavier bag unless the new tools are very useful. Prospect theory was accepted by many scholars not because it is "true" but because the concepts that it added to utility theory, notably the reference point and loss aversion, were worth the trouble; they yielded new predictions that turned out to be true. We were lucky.

SPEAKING OF PROSPECT THEORY

"He suffers from extreme loss aversion, which makes him turn down very favorable opportunities."

"Considering her vast wealth, her emotional response to trivial gains and losses makes no sense."

"He weighs losses about twice as much as gains, which is normal."

27

THE ENDOWMENT EFFECT

You have probably seen figure 11 or a close cousin of it even if you never had a class in economics. The graph displays an individual's "indifference map" for two goods.

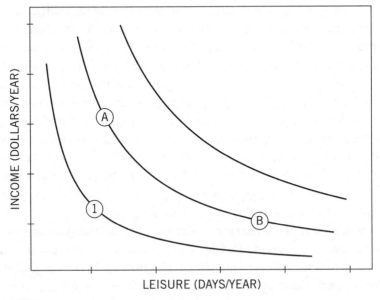

Figure 11

Students learn in introductory economics classes that each point on the map specifies a particular combination of income and vacation days. Each "indifference curve" connects the combinations of the two goods that are equally desirable—they have the same utility. The curves would turn into parallel straight lines if people were willing to "sell" vacation days for extra income at the same price regardless of how much income and how much vacation time they have. The convex shape indicates diminishing marginal utility: the more leisure you have, the less you care for an extra day of it, and each added day is worth less than the one before. Similarly, the more income you have, the less you care for an extra dollar, and the amount you are willing to give up for an extra day of leisure increases.

All locations on an indifference curve are equally attractive. This is literally what indifference means: you don't care where you are on an indifference curve. So if A and B are on the same indifference curve for you, you are indifferent between them and will need no incentive to move from one to the other, or back. Some version of this figure has appeared in every economics textbook written in the last hundred years, and many millions of students have stared at it. Few have noticed what is missing. Here again, the power and elegance of a theoretical model have blinded students and scholars to a serious deficiency.

What is missing from the figure is an indication of the individual's current income and leisure. If you are a salaried employee, the terms of your employment specify a salary and a number of vacation days, which is a point on the map. This is your reference point, your status quo, but the figure does not show it. By failing to display it, the theorists who draw this figure invite you to believe that the reference point does not matter, but by now you know that of course it does. This is Bernoulli's error all over again. The representation of indifference curves implicitly assumes that your utility at any given moment is determined entirely by your present situation, that the past is irrelevant, and that your evaluation of a possible job does not depend on the terms of your current job. These assumptions are completely unrealistic in this case and in many others.

The omission of the reference point from the indifference map is a surprising case of theory-induced blindness, because we so often encounter cases in which the reference point obviously matters. In labor negotiations, it is well understood by both sides that the reference point is the existing contract and that the negotiations will focus on mutual demands for concessions relative to that reference point. The role of loss aversion in bargaining is also well understood: making concessions hurts. You have much personal experience of the role of reference point. If you changed jobs or locations, or even considered such a change, you surely remember that the features of the new place were coded as pluses or minuses relative to where you were. You may also have noticed that disadvantages loomed larger than advantages in this evaluation—loss aversion was at work. It is difficult to accept changes for the worse. For example, the minimal wage that unemployed workers would accept for new employment averages 90% of their previous wage, and it drops by less than 10% over a period of one year.

To appreciate the power that the reference point exerts on choices, consider Albert and Ben, "hedonic twins" who have identical tastes and currently hold identical starting jobs, with little income and little leisure time. Their current circumstances correspond to the point marked 1 in figure 11. The firm offers them two improved positions, A and B, and lets them decide who will get a raise of $10,000 (position A) and who will get an extra day of paid vacation each month (position B). As they are both indifferent, they toss a coin. Albert gets the raise, Ben gets the extra leisure. Some time passes as the twins get accustomed to their positions. Now the company suggests they may switch jobs if they wish.

The standard theory represented in the figure assumes that preferences are stable over time. Positions A and B are equally attractive for both twins and they will need little or no incentive to switch. In sharp contrast, prospect theory asserts that both twins will definitely prefer to remain as they are. This preference for the status quo is a consequence of loss aversion.

Let us focus on Albert. He was initially in position 1 on the graph, and from that reference point he found these two alternatives equally attractive:

Go to A: a raise of $10,000
OR
Go to B: 12 extra days of vacation

Taking position A changes Albert's reference point, and when he considers switching to B, his choice has a new structure:

Stay at A: no gain and no loss.
OR
Move to B: 12 extra days of vacation and a $10,000 salary cut

You just had the subjective experience of loss aversion. You could feel it: a salary cut of $10,000 is very bad news. Even if a gain of 12 vacation days was as impressive as a gain of $10,000, the same improvement of leisure is not sufficient to compensate for a loss of $10,000. Albert will stay at A because the disadvantage of moving outweighs the advantage. The same reasoning applies to Ben, who will also want to keep his present job because the loss of now-precious leisure outweighs the benefit of the extra income.

This example highlights two aspects of choice that the standard model of indifference curves does not predict. First, tastes are not fixed; they vary with the reference point. Second, the disadvantages of a change loom larger than its advantages, inducing a bias that favors the status quo. Of course, loss aversion does not imply that you never prefer to change your situation; the benefits of an opportunity may exceed even overweighted losses. Loss aversion implies only that choices are strongly biased in favor of the reference situation (and generally biased to favor small rather than large changes).

Conventional indifference maps and Bernoulli's representation of outcomes as states of wealth share a mistaken assumption: that your utility for a state of affairs depends only on that state and is not affected by your history. Correcting that mistake has been one of the achievements of behavioral economics.

THE ENDOWMENT EFFECT

The question of when an approach or a movement got its start is often difficult to answer, but the origin of what is now known as behavioral economics can be specified precisely. In the early 1970s, Richard Thaler, then a graduate student in the very conservative economics department of the University of Rochester, began having heretical thoughts. Thaler always had a sharp wit and an ironic bent, and as a student he amused himself by collecting observations of behavior that the model of rational economic behavior could not explain. He took special pleasure in evidence of economic irrationality among his professors, and he found one that was particularly striking.

Professor R (now revealed to be Richard Rosett, who went on to become the dean of the University of Chicago Graduate School of Business) was a firm believer in standard economic theory as well as a sophisticated wine lover. Thaler observed that Professor R was very reluctant to sell a bottle from his collection—even at the high price of $100 (in 1975 dollars!).

Professor R bought wine at auctions, but would never pay more than $35 for a bottle of that quality. At prices between $35 and $100, he would neither buy nor sell. The large gap is inconsistent with economic theory, in which the professor is expected to have a single value for the bottle. If a particular bottle is worth $50 to him, then he should be willing to sell it for any amount in excess of $50. If he did not own the bottle, he should be willing to pay any amount up to $50 for it. The just-acceptable selling price and the just-acceptable buying price should have been identical, but in fact the minimum price to sell ($100) was much higher than the maximum buying price of $35. Owning the good appeared to increase its value.

Richard Thaler found many examples of what he called the *endowment effect*, especially for goods that are not regularly traded. You can easily imagine yourself in a similar situation. Suppose you hold a ticket to a sold-out concert by a popular band, which you bought at the regular price of $200. You are an avid fan and would have been willing to pay up to $500 for the ticket. Now you have your ticket and you learn on the Internet that richer or more desperate fans are offering $3,000. Would you sell? If you resemble most of the audience at sold-out events you do not sell. Your lowest selling price is above $3,000 and your maximum buying price is $500. This is an example of an endowment effect, and a believer in standard economic theory would be puzzled by it. Thaler was looking for an account that could explain puzzles of this kind.

Chance intervened when Thaler met one of our former students at a conference and obtained an early draft of prospect theory. He reports that he read the manuscript with considerable excitement, because he quickly realized that the loss-averse value function of prospect theory could explain the endowment effect and some other puzzles in his collection. The solution was to abandon the standard idea that Professor R had a unique utility for the state of *having* a particular bottle. Prospect theory suggested that the willingness to buy or sell the bottle depends on the reference point— whether or not the professor owns the bottle now. If he owns it, he considers the pain of *giving up* the bottle. If he does not own it, he considers the pleasure of *getting* the bottle. The values were unequal because of loss aversion: giving up a bottle of nice wine is more painful than getting an equally good bottle is pleasurable. Remember the graph of losses and gains in the previous chapter. The slope of the function is steeper in the negative domain; the response to a loss is stronger than the response to a corresponding gain. This was the explanation of the endowment effect that Thaler had been searching for. And the first application of prospect theory to an economic puzzle now appears to have been a significant milestone in the development of behavioral economics.

Thaler arranged to spend a year at Stanford when he knew that Amos and I would be there. During this productive period, we learned much from each other and became friends. Seven years later, he and I had another opportunity to spend a year together and to continue the conversation between psychology and economics. The Russell Sage Foundation, which was for a long time the main sponsor of behavioral economics, gave one of its first grants to Thaler for the purpose of spending a year with me in Vancouver. During that year, we worked closely with a local economist, Jack Knetsch, with whom we shared intense interest in the endowment effect, the rules of economic fairness, and spicy Chinese food.

The starting point for our investigation was that the endowment effect is not universal. If someone asks you to change a $5 bill for five singles, you hand over the five ones without any sense of loss. Nor is there much loss aversion when you shop for shoes. The merchant who gives up the shoes in exchange for money certainly feels no loss. Indeed, the shoes that he hands over have always been, from his point of view, a cumbersome proxy for money that he was hoping to collect from some consumer. Furthermore, you probably do not experience paying the merchant as a loss, because you were effectively holding money as a proxy for the shoes you intended to buy. These cases of routine trading are not essentially different from the exchange of a $5 bill for five singles. There is no loss aversion on either side of routine commercial exchanges.

What distinguishes these market transactions from Professor R's reluctance to sell his wine, or the reluctance of Super Bowl ticket holders to sell even at a very high price? The distinctive feature is that both the shoes the merchant sells you and the money you spend from your budget for shoes are held "for exchange." They are intended to be traded for other goods. Other goods, such as wine and Super Bowl tickets, are held "for use," to be consumed or otherwise enjoyed. Your leisure time and the standard of living that your income supports are also not intended for sale or exchange.

Knetsch, Thaler, and I set out to design an experiment that would highlight the contrast between goods that are held for use and for exchange. We borrowed one aspect of the design of our experiment from Vernon Smith, the founder of experimental economics, with whom I would share a Nobel Prize many years later. In this method, a limited number of tokens are distributed to the participants in a "market." Any participants who own a token at the end of the experiment can redeem it for cash. The redemption values differ for different individuals, to represent the fact that the goods traded in markets are more valuable to some people than to others. The same token may be worth $10 to you and $20 to me, and an exchange at any price between these values will be advantageous to both of us.

Smith created vivid demonstrations of how well the basic mechanisms of supply and demand work. Individuals would make successive public offers to buy or sell a token, and others would respond publicly to the offer. Everyone watches these exchanges and sees the price at which the tokens change hands. The results are as regular as those of a demonstration in physics. As inevitably as water flows downhill, those who own a token that is of little value to them (because their redemption values are low) end up selling their token at a profit to someone who values it more. When trading ends, the tokens are in the hands of those who can get the most money for them from the experimenter. The magic of the markets has worked! Furthermore, economic theory correctly predicts both the final price at which the market will settle and the number of tokens that will change hands. If half the participants in the market were randomly assigned tokens, the theory predicts that half of the tokens will change hands.

We used a variation on Smith's method for our experiment. Each session began with several rounds of trades for tokens, which perfectly replicated Smith's finding. The estimated number of trades was typically very close or identical to the amount predicted by the standard theory. The tokens, of course, had value only because they could be exchanged for the experimenter's cash; they had no value for use. Then we conducted a similar market for an object that we expected people to value for use: an attractive coffee mug, decorated with the university insignia of wherever we were conducting the experiments. The mug was then worth about $6 (and would be worth about double that amount today). Mugs were distributed randomly to half the participants. The Sellers had their mug in front of them, and the Buyers were invited to look at their neighbor's mug; all indicated the price at which they would trade. The Buyers had to use their own money to acquire a mug. The results were dramatic: the average selling price was about double the average buying price, and the estimated number of trades was less than half of the number predicted by standard theory. The magic of the market did not work for a good that the owners expected to use.

We conducted a series of experiments using variants of the same procedure, always with the same results. My favorite is one in which we added to the Sellers and Buyers a third group—Choosers. Unlike the Buyers, who had to spend their own money to acquire the good, the Choosers could receive either a mug or a sum of money, and they indicated the amount of money that was as desirable as receiving the good. These were the results:

Sellers	$7.12
Choosers	$3.12
Buyers	$2.87

The gap between Sellers and Choosers is remarkable, because they actually face the same choice! If you are a Seller you can go home with either a mug or money, and if you are a Chooser you have exactly the same two options. The long-term effects of the decision are identical for the two groups. The only difference is in the emotion of the moment. The high price that Sellers set reflects the reluctance to give up an object that they already own, a reluctance that can be seen in babies who hold on fiercely to a toy and show great agitation when it is taken away. Loss aversion is built into the automatic evaluations of System 1.

Buyers and Choosers set similar cash values, although the Buyers have to pay for the mug, which is free for the Choosers. This is what we would expect if Buyers do not experience spending money on the mug as a loss. Evidence from brain imaging confirms the difference. Selling goods that one would normally use activates regions of the brain that are associated with disgust and pain. Buying also activates these areas, but only when the prices are perceived as too high—when you feel that a seller is taking money that exceeds the exchange value. Brain recordings also indicate that buying at especially low prices is a pleasurable event.

The cash value that the Sellers set on the mug is a bit more than twice as high as the value set by Choosers and Buyers. The ratio is very close to the loss aversion coefficient in risky choice, as we might expect if the same value function for gains and losses of money is applied to both riskless and risky decisions. A ratio of about 2:1 has appeared in studies of diverse economic domains, including the response of households to price changes. As economists would predict, customers tend to increase their purchases of eggs, orange juice, or fish when prices drop and to reduce their purchases when prices rise; however, in contrast to the predictions of economic theory, the effect of price increases (losses relative to the reference price) is about twice as large as the effect of gains.

The mugs experiment has remained the standard demonstration of the endowment effect, along with an even simpler experiment that Jack Knetsch reported at about the same time. Knetsch asked two classes to fill out a questionnaire and rewarded them with a gift that remained in front of them for the duration of the experiment. In one session, the prize was an expensive pen; in another, a bar of Swiss chocolate. At the end of the class, the experimenter showed the alternative gift and allowed everyone to trade his or her gift for another. Only about 10% of the participants opted to exchange their gift. Most of those who had received the pen stayed with the pen, and those who had received the chocolate did not budge either.

THINKING LIKE A TRADER

The fundamental ideas of prospect theory are that reference points exist, and that losses loom larger than corresponding gains. Observations in real markets collected over the years illustrate the power of these concepts. A study of the market for condo apartments in Boston during a downturn yielded particularly clear results. The authors of that study compared the behavior of owners of similar units who had bought their dwellings at different prices. For a rational agent, the buying price is irrelevant history—the current market value is all that matters. Not so for Humans in a down market for housing. Owners who have a high reference point and thus face higher losses set a higher price on their dwelling, spend a longer time trying to sell their home, and eventually receive more money.

The original demonstration of an asymmetry between selling prices and buying prices (or, more convincingly, between selling and choosing) was very important in the initial acceptance of the ideas of reference point and loss aversion. However, it is well understood that reference points are labile, especially in unusual laboratory situations, and that the endowment effect can be eliminated by changing the reference point.

No endowment effect is expected when owners view their goods as carriers of value for future exchanges, a widespread attitude in routine commerce and in financial markets. The experimental economist John List, who has studied trading at baseball card conventions, found that novice traders were reluctant to part with the cards they owned, but that this reluctance eventually disappeared with trading experience. More surprisingly, List found a large effect of trading experience on the endowment effect for new goods.

At a convention, List displayed a notice that invited people to take part in a short survey, for which they would be compensated with a small gift: a coffee mug or a chocolate bar of equal value. The gifts were assigned at random. As the volunteers were about to leave, List said to each of them,

"We gave you a mug [or chocolate bar], but you can trade for a chocolate bar [or mug] instead, if you wish." In an exact replication of Jack Knetsch's earlier experiment, List found that only 18% of the inexperienced traders were willing to exchange their gift for the other. In sharp contrast, experienced traders showed no trace of an endowment effect: 48% of them traded! At least in a market environment in which trading was the norm, they showed no reluctance to trade.

Jack Knetsch also conducted experiments in which subtle manipulations made the endowment effect disappear. Participants displayed an endowment effect only if they had physical possession of the good for a while before the possibility of trading it was mentioned. Economists of the standard persuasion might be tempted to say that Knetsch had spent too much time with psychologists, because his experimental manipulation showed concern for the variables that social psychologists expect to be important. Indeed, the different methodological concerns of experimental economists and psychologists have been much in evidence in the ongoing debate about the endowment effect.

Veteran traders have apparently learned to ask the correct question, which is "How much do I want to *have* that mug, compared with other things I could have instead?" This is the question that Econs ask, and with this question there is no endowment effect, because the asymmetry between the pleasure of getting and the pain of giving up is irrelevant.

Recent studies of the psychology of "decision making under poverty" suggest that the poor are another group in which we do not expect to find the endowment effect. Being poor, in prospect theory, is living below one's reference point. There are goods that the poor need and cannot afford, so they are always "in the losses." Small amounts of money that they receive are therefore perceived as a reduced loss, not as a gain. The money helps one climb a little toward the reference point, but the poor always remain on the steep limb of the value function.

People who are poor think like traders, but the dynamics are quite different. Unlike traders, the poor are not indifferent to the differences between gaining and giving up. Their problem is that all their choices are between losses. Money that is spent on one good is the loss of another good that could have been purchased instead. For the poor, costs are losses.

We all know people for whom spending is painful, although they are objectively quite well-off. There may also be cultural differences in the attitude toward money, and especially toward the spending of money on whims and minor luxuries, such as the purchase of a decorated mug. Such a difference may explain the large discrepancy between the results of the "mugs study" in the United States and in the UK. Buying and selling prices diverge substantially in experiments conducted in samples of students of the United States, but the differences are much smaller among English students. Much remains to be learned about the endowment effect.

SPEAKING OF THE ENDOWMENT EFFECT

"She didn't care which of the two offices she would get, but a day after the announcement was made, she was no longer willing to trade. Endowment effect!"

"These negotiations are going nowhere because both sides find it difficult to make concessions, even when they can get something in return. Losses loom larger than gains."

"When they raised their prices, demand dried up."

"He just hates the idea of selling his house for less money than he paid for it. Loss aversion is at work."

"He is a miser, and treats any dollar he spends as a loss."

28

BAD EVENTS

The concept of loss aversion is certainly the most significant contribution of psychology to behavioral economics. This is odd, because the idea that people evaluate many outcomes as gains and losses, and that losses loom larger than gains, surprises no one. Amos and I often joked that we were engaged in studying a subject about which our grandmothers knew a great deal. In fact, however, we know more than our grandmothers did and can now embed loss aversion in the context of a broader two-systems model of the mind, and specifically a biological and psychological view in which negativity and escape dominate positivity and approach. We can also trace the consequences of loss aversion in surprisingly diverse observations: only out-of-pocket losses are compensated when goods are lost in transport; attempts at large-scale reforms very often fail; and professional golfers putt more accurately for par than for a birdie. Clever as she was, my grandmother would have been surprised by the specific predictions from a general idea she considered obvious.

NEGATIVITY DOMINANCE

Figure 12

Your heartbeat accelerated when you looked at the left-hand figure. It accelerated even before you could label what is so eerie about that picture. After some time you may have recognized the eyes of a terrified person. The eyes on the right, narrowed by the raised cheeks of a smile, express happiness— and they are not nearly as exciting. The two pictures were presented to people lying in a brain scanner. Each picture was shown for less than $^2/_{100}$ of a second and immediately masked by "visual noise," a random display of dark and bright squares. None of the observers ever consciously knew that he had seen pictures of eyes, but one part of their brain evidently knew: the amygdala, which has a primary role as the "threat center" of the brain, although it is also activated in other emotional states. Images of the brain showed an intense response of the amygdala to a threatening picture that the viewer did not recognize. The information about the threat probably traveled via a superfast neural channel that feeds directly into a part of the brain that processes emotions, bypassing the visual cortex that supports the conscious experience of "seeing." The same circuit also causes schematic angry faces (a potential threat) to be processed faster and more efficiently than schematic happy faces. Some experimenters have reported that an angry face "pops out" of a crowd of happy faces, but a single happy face does not stand out in an angry crowd. The brains of humans and other animals contain a mechanism that is designed to give priority to bad news. By shaving a few hundredths of a second from the time needed to detect a predator, this circuit improves the animal's odds of living long enough to reproduce. The automatic operations of System 1 reflect this evolutionary history. No comparably rapid mechanism for recognizing good news has been detected. Of course, we and our animal cousins are quickly alerted to signs of opportunities to mate or to feed, and advertisers design billboards accordingly. Still, threats are privileged above opportunities, as they should be.

The brain responds quickly even to purely symbolic threats. Emotionally loaded words quickly attract attention, and bad words (*war, crime*) attract attention faster than do happy words (*peace, love*). There is no real threat, but the mere reminder of a bad event is treated in System 1 as threatening. As we saw earlier with the word *vomit*, the symbolic representation associatively evokes in attenuated form many of the reactions to the real thing, including physiological indices of emotion and even fractional tendencies to avoid or approach, recoil or lean forward. The sensitivity to threats extends to the processing of statements of opinions with which we strongly disagree. For example, depending on your attitude to euthanasia, it would take your brain less than one-quarter of a second to register the "threat" in a sentence that starts with "I think euthanasia is an acceptable/ unacceptable . . ."

The psychologist Paul Rozin, an expert on disgust, observed that a single cockroach will completely wreck the appeal of a bowl of cherries, but a cherry will do nothing at all for a bowl of cockroaches. As he points out, the negative trumps the positive in many ways, and loss aversion is one of many manifestations of a broad negativity dominance. Other scholars, in a paper titled "Bad Is Stronger Than Good," summarized the evidence as follows: "Bad emotions, bad parents, and bad feedback have more impact than good ones, and bad information is processed more thoroughly than good. The self is more motivated to avoid bad self-definitions than to pursue good ones. Bad impressions and bad stereotypes are quicker to form and more resistant to disconfirmation than good ones." They cite John Gottman, the well-known expert in marital relations, who observed that the long-term success of a relationship depends far more on avoiding the negative than on seeking the positive. Gottman estimated that a stable relationship requires that good interactions outnumber bad interactions by at least 5 to 1. Other asymmetries in the social domain are even more striking. We all know that a friendship that may take years to develop can be ruined by a single action.

Some distinctions between good and bad are hardwired into our biology. Infants enter the world ready to respond to pain as bad and to sweet (up to a point) as good. In many situations, however, the boundary between good and bad is a reference point that changes over time and depends on the immediate circumstances. Imagine that you are out in the country on a cold night, inadequately dressed for the torrential rain, your clothes soaked. A stinging cold wind completes your misery. As you wander around, you find a large rock that provides some shelter from the fury of the elements. The biologist Michel Cabanac would call the experience of that moment intensely pleasurable because it functions, as pleasure normally does, to indicate the direction of a biologically significant improvement of circumstances. The pleasant relief will not last very long, of course, and you will soon be shivering behind the rock again, driven by your renewed suffering to seek better shelter.

GOALS ARE REFERENCE POINTS

Loss aversion refers to the relative strength of two motives: we are driven more strongly to avoid losses than to achieve gains. A reference point is sometimes the status quo, but it can also be a goal in the future: not achieving a goal is a loss, exceeding the goal is a gain. As we might expect from negativity dominance, the two motives are not equally powerful. The aversion to the failure of not reaching the goal is much stronger than the desire to exceed it.

People often adopt short-term goals that they strive to achieve but not necessarily to exceed. They are likely to reduce their efforts when they have reached an immediate goal, with results that sometimes violate economic logic. New York cabdrivers, for example, may have a target income for the month or the year, but the goal that controls their effort is typically a daily target of earnings. Of course, the daily goal is much easier to achieve (and exceed) on some days than on others. On rainy days, a New York cab never remains free for long, and the driver quickly achieves his target; not so in pleasant weather, when cabs often waste time cruising the streets looking for fares. Economic logic implies that cabdrivers should work many hours on rainy days and treat themselves to some leisure on mild days, when they can "buy" leisure at a lower price. The logic of loss aversion suggests the opposite: drivers who have a fixed daily target will work many more hours when the pickings are slim and go home early when rain-drenched customers are begging to be taken somewhere.

The economists Devin Pope and Maurice Schweitzer, at the University of Pennsylvania, reasoned that golf provides a perfect example of a reference point: par. Every hole on the golf course has a number of strokes associated with it; the par number provides the baseline for good—but not outstanding—performance. For a professional golfer, a birdie (one stroke under par) is a gain, and a bogey (one stroke over par) is a loss. The economists compared two situations a player might face when near the hole:

- putt to avoid a bogey
- putt to achieve a birdie

Every stroke counts in golf, and in professional golf every stroke counts a lot. According to prospect theory, however, some strokes count more than others. Failing to make par is a loss, but missing a birdie putt is a foregone gain, not a loss. Pope and Schweitzer reasoned from loss aversion that players would try a little harder when putting for par (to avoid a bogey) than when putting for a birdie. They analyzed more than 2.5 million putts in exquisite detail to test that prediction.

They were right. Whether the putt was easy or hard, at every distance from the hole, the players were more successful when putting for par than for a birdie. The difference in their rate of success when going for par (to avoid a bogey) or for a birdie was 3.6%. This difference is not trivial. Tiger Woods was one of the "participants" in their study. If in his best years Tiger Woods had managed to putt as well for birdies as he did for par, his average tournament score would have improved by one stroke and his earnings by almost $1 million per season. These fierce competitors certainly do not make a conscious decision to slack off on birdie putts, but their intense aversion to a bogey apparently contributes to extra concentration on the task at hand.

The study of putts illustrates the power of a theoretical concept as an aid to thinking. Who would have thought it worthwhile to spend months analyzing putts for par and birdie? The idea of loss aversion, which surprises no one except perhaps some economists, generated a precise and nonintuitive hypothesis and led researchers to a finding that surprised everyone— including professional golfers.

DEFENDING THE STATUS QUO

If you are set to look for it, the asymmetric intensity of the motives to avoid losses and to achieve gains shows up almost everywhere. It is an ever-present feature of negotiations, especially of renegotiations of an existing contract, the typical situation in labor negotiations and in international discussions of trade or arms limitations. The existing terms define reference points, and a proposed change in any aspect of the agreement is inevitably viewed as a concession that one side makes to the other. Loss aversion creates an asymmetry that makes agreements difficult to reach. The concessions you make to me are my gains, but they are your losses; they cause you much more pain than they give me pleasure. Inevitably, you will place a higher value on them than I do. The same is true, of course, of the very painful concessions you demand from me, which you do not appear to value sufficiently! Negotiations over a shrinking pie are especially difficult, because they require an allocation of losses. People tend to be much more easygoing when they bargain over an expanding pie.

Many of the messages that negotiators exchange in the course of bargaining are attempts to communicate a reference point and provide an anchor to the other side. The messages are not always sincere. Negotiators often pretend intense attachment to some good (perhaps missiles of a particular type in bargaining over arms reductions), although they actually view that good as a bargaining chip and intend ultimately to give it away in an exchange. Because negotiators are influenced by a norm of reciprocity, a concession that is presented as painful calls for an equally painful (and perhaps equally inauthentic) concession from the other side.

Animals, including people, fight harder to prevent losses than to achieve gains. In the world of territorial animals, this principle explains the success of defenders. A biologist observed that "when a territory holder is challenged by a rival, the owner almost always wins the contest—usually within a matter of seconds." In human affairs, the same simple rule explains much of what happens when institutions attempt to reform themselves, in "reorganizations" and "restructuring" of companies, and in efforts to rationalize a bureaucracy, simplify the tax code, or reduce medical costs. As initially conceived, plans for reform almost always produce many winners and some losers while achieving an overall improvement. If the affected parties have any political influence, however, potential losers will be more active and determined than potential winners; the outcome will be biased in their favor and inevitably more expensive and less effective than initially planned. Reforms commonly include grandfather clauses that protect current stakeholders—for example, when the existing workforce is reduced by attrition rather than by dismissals, or when cuts in salaries and benefits apply only to future workers. Loss aversion is a powerful conservative force that favors minimal changes from the status quo in the lives of both institutions and individuals. This conservatism helps keep us stable in our neighborhood, our marriage, and our job; it is the gravitational force that holds our life together near the reference point.

LOSS AVERSION IN THE LAW

During the year that we spent working together in Vancouver, Richard Thaler, Jack Knetsch, and I were drawn into a study of fairness in economic transactions, partly because we were interested in the topic but also because we had an opportunity as well as an obligation to make up a new questionnaire every week. The Canadian government's Department of Fisheries and Oceans had a program for unemployed professionals in Toronto, who were paid to administer telephone surveys. The large team of interviewers worked every night and new questions were constantly needed to keep the operation going. Through Jack Knetsch, we agreed to generate a questionnaire every week, in four color-labeled versions. We could ask about anything; the only constraint was that the questionnaire should include at least one mention of fish, to make it pertinent to the mission of the department. This went on for many months, and we treated ourselves to an orgy of data collection.

We studied public perceptions of what constitutes unfair behavior on the part of merchants, employers, and landlords. Our overarching question was whether the opprobrium attached to unfairness imposes constraints on profit seeking. We found that it does. We also found that the moral rules by which the public evaluates what firms may or may not do draw a crucial distinction between losses and gains. The basic principle is that the existing wage, price, or rent sets a reference point, which has the nature of an entitlement that must not be infringed. It is considered unfair for the firm to impose losses on its customers or workers relative to the reference transaction, unless it must do so to protect its own entitlement. Consider this example:

> A hardware store has been selling snow shovels for $15. The morning after a large snowstorm, the store raises the price to $20.
> Please rate this action as:
> Completely Fair   Acceptable   Unfair   Very Unfair

The hardware store behaves appropriately according to the standard economic model: it responds to increased demand by raising its price. The participants in the survey did not agree: 82% rated the action Unfair or Very Unfair. They evidently viewed the pre-blizzard price as a reference point and the raised price as a loss that the store imposes on its customers, not because it must but simply because it can. A basic rule of fairness, we found, is that the exploitation of market power to impose losses on others is unacceptable. The following example illustrates this rule in another context (the dollar values should be adjusted for about 100% inflation since these data were collected in 1984):

> A small photocopying shop has one employee who has worked there for six months and earns $9 per hour. Business continues to be satisfactory, but a factory in the area has closed and unemployment has increased. Other small shops have now hired reliable workers at $7 an hour to perform jobs similar to those done by the photocopy shop employee. The owner of the shop reduces the employee's wage to $7.

The respondents did not approve: 83% considered the behavior Unfair or Very Unfair. However, a slight variation on the question clarifies the nature of the employer's obligation. The background scenario of a profitable store in an area of high unemployment is the same, but now

> the current employee leaves, and the owner decides to pay a replacement $7 an hour.

A large majority (73%) considered this action Acceptable. It appears that the employer does not have a moral obligation to pay $9 an hour. The entitlement is personal: the current worker has a right to retain his wage even if market conditions would allow the employer to impose a wage cut. The replacement worker has no entitlement to the previous worker's reference wage, and the employer is therefore allowed to reduce pay without the risk of being branded unfair.

The firm has its own entitlement, which is to retain its current profit. If it faces a threat of a loss, it is allowed to transfer the loss to others. A substantial majority of respondents believed that it is not unfair for a firm to reduce its workers' wages when its profitability is falling. We described the rules as defining dual entitlements to the firm and to individuals with whom it interacts. When threatened, it is not unfair for the firm to be selfish. It is not even expected to take on part of the losses; it can pass them on.

Different rules governed what the firm could do to improve its profits or to avoid reduced profits. When a firm faced lower production costs, the rules of fairness did not require it to share the bonanza with either its customers or its workers. Of course, our respondents liked a firm better and described it as more fair if it was generous when its profits increased, but they did not brand as unfair a firm that did not share. They showed indignation only when a firm exploited its power to break informal contracts with workers or customers, and to impose a loss on others in order to increase its profit. The important task for students of economic fairness is not to identify ideal behavior but to find the line that separates acceptable conduct from actions that invite opprobrium and punishment.

We were not optimistic when we submitted our report of this research to the *American Economic Review*. Our article challenged what was then accepted wisdom among many economists that economic behavior is ruled by self-interest and that concerns for fairness are generally irrelevant. We also relied on the evidence of survey responses, for which economists generally have little respect. However, the editor of the journal sent our article for evaluation to two economists who were not bound by those conventions (we later learned their identity; they were the most friendly the editor could have found). The editor made the correct call. The article is often cited, and its conclusions have stood the test of time. More recent research has supported the observations of reference-dependent fairness and has also shown that fairness concerns are economically significant, a fact we had suspected but did not prove. Employers who violate rules of fairness are punished by reduced productivity, and merchants who follow unfair pricing policies can expect to lose sales. People who learned from a new catalog that the merchant was now charging less for a product that they had recently bought at a higher price reduced their future purchases from that supplier by 15%, an average loss of $90 per customer. The customers evidently perceived the lower price as the reference point and thought of themselves as having sustained a loss by paying more than appropriate. Moreover, the customers who reacted the most strongly were those who bought more items and at higher prices. The losses far exceeded the gains from the increased purchases produced by the lower prices in the new catalog.

Unfairly imposing losses on people can be risky if the victims are in a position to retaliate. Furthermore, experiments have shown that strangers who observe unfair behavior often join in the punishment. Neuroeconomists (scientists who combine economics with brain research) have used MRI machines to examine the brains of people who are engaged in punishing one stranger for behaving unfairly to another stranger. Remarkably, altruistic punishment is accompanied by increased activity in the "pleasure centers" of the brain. It appears that maintaining the social order and the rules of fairness in this fashion is its own reward. Altruistic punishment could well be the glue that holds societies together. However, our brains are not designed to reward generosity as reliably as they punish meanness. Here again, we find a marked asymmetry between losses and gains.

The influence of loss aversion and entitlements extends far beyond the realm of financial transactions. Jurists were quick to recognize their impact on the law and in the administration of justice. In one study, David Cohen and Jack Knetsch found many examples of a sharp distinction between actual losses and foregone gains in legal decisions. For example, a merchant whose goods were lost in transit may be compensated for costs he actually incurred, but is unlikely to be compensated for lost profits. The familiar rule that possession is nine-tenths of the law confirms the moral status of the reference point. In a more recent discussion, Eyal Zamir makes the provocative point that the distinction drawn in the law between restoring losses and compensating for foregone gains may be justified by their asymmetrical effects on individual well-being. If people who lose suffer more than people who merely fail to gain, they may also deserve more protection from the law.

SPEAKING OF LOSSES

"This reform will not pass. Those who stand to lose will fight harder than those who stand to gain."

"Each of them thinks the other's concessions are less painful. They are both wrong, of course. It's just the asymmetry of losses."

"They would find it easier to renegotiate the agreement if they realized the pie was actually expanding. They're not allocating losses; they are allocating gains."

"Rental prices around here have gone up recently, but our tenants don't think it's fair that we should raise their rent, too. They feel entitled to their current terms."

"My clients don't resent the price hike because they know my costs have gone up, too. They accept my right to stay profitable."

29

THE FOURFOLD PATTERN

Whenever you form a global evaluation of a complex object—a car you may buy, your son-in-law, or an uncertain situation—you assign weights to its characteristics. This is simply a cumbersome way of saying that some characteristics influence your assessment more than others do. The weighting occurs whether or not you are aware of it; it is an operation of System 1. Your overall evaluation of a car may put more or less weight on gas economy, comfort, or appearance. Your judgment of your son-in-law may depend more or less on how rich or handsome or reliable he is. Similarly, your assessment of an uncertain prospect assigns weights to the possible outcomes. The weights are certainly correlated with the probabilities of these outcomes: a 50% chance to win a million is much more attractive than a 1% chance to win the same amount. The assignment of weights is sometimes conscious and deliberate. Most often, however, you are just an observer to a global evaluation that your System 1 delivers.

CHANGING CHANCES

One reason for the popularity of the gambling metaphor in the study of decision making is that it provides a natural rule for the assignment of weights to the outcomes of a prospect: the more probable an outcome, the more weight it should have. The expected value of a gamble is the average of its outcomes, each weighted by its probability. For example, the expected value of "20% chance to win $1,000 and 75% chance to win $100" is $275.

In the pre-Bernoulli days, gambles were assessed by their expected value. Bernoulli retained this method for assigning weights to the outcomes, which is known as the expectation principle, but applied it to the psychological value of the outcomes. The utility of a gamble, in his theory, is the average of the utilities of its outcomes, each weighted by its probability.

The expectation principle does not correctly describe how you think about the probabilities related to risky prospects. In the four examples below, your chances of receiving $1 million improve by 5%. Is the news equally good in each case?

A. From 0 to 5%
B. From 5% to 10%
C. From 60% to 65%
D. From 95% to 100%

The expectation principle asserts that your utility increases in each case by exactly 5% of the utility of receiving $1 million. Does this prediction describe your experiences? Of course not.

Everyone agrees that $0 \rightarrow 5\%$ and $95\% \rightarrow 100\%$ are more impressive than either $5\% \rightarrow 10\%$ or $60\% \rightarrow 65\%$. Increasing the chances from 0 to 5% transforms the situation, creating a possibility that did not exist earlier, a hope of winning the prize. It is a qualitative change, where $5 \rightarrow 10\%$ is only a quantitative improvement. The change from 5% to 10% doubles the probability of winning, but there is general agreement that the psychological value of the prospect does not double. The large impact of $0 \rightarrow 5\%$ illustrates the *possibility effect*, which causes highly unlikely outcomes to be weighted disproportionately more than they "deserve." People who buy lottery tickets in vast amounts show themselves willing to pay much more than expected value for very small chances to win a large prize.

The improvement from 95% to 100% is another qualitative change that has a large impact, the *certainty effect*. Outcomes that are almost certain are given less weight than their probability justifies. To appreciate the certainty effect, imagine that you inherited $1 million, but your greedy stepsister has contested the will in court. The decision is expected tomorrow. Your lawyer assures you that you have a strong case and that you have a 95% chance to win, but he takes pains to remind you that judicial decisions are never perfectly predictable. Now you are approached by a risk-adjustment company, which offers to buy your case for $910,000 outright—take it or leave it. The offer is lower (by $40,000!) than the expected value of waiting for the judgment (which is $950,000), but are you quite sure you would want to reject it? If such an event actually happens in your life, you should know that a large industry of "structured settlements" exists to provide certainty at a hefty price, by taking advantage of the certainty effect.

Possibility and certainty have similarly powerful effects in the domain of losses. When a loved one is wheeled into surgery, a 5% risk that an amputation will be necessary is very bad—much more than half as bad as a 10% risk. Because of the possibility effect, we tend to overweight small risks and are willing to pay far more than expected value to eliminate them altogether. The psychological difference between a 95% risk of disaster and the certainty of disaster appears to be even greater; the sliver of hope that everything could still be okay looms very large. Overweighting of small probabilities increases the attractiveness of both gambles and insurance policies.

The conclusion is straightforward: the decision weights that people assign to outcomes are not identical to the probabilities of these outcomes, contrary to the expectation principle. Improbable outcomes are overweighted—this is the possibility effect. Outcomes that are almost certain are underweighted relative to actual certainty. The *expectation principle*, by which values are weighted by their probability, is poor psychology.

The plot thickens, however, because there is a powerful argument that a decision maker who wishes to be rational *must* conform to the expectation principle. This was the main point of the axiomatic version of utility theory that von Neumann and Morgenstern introduced in 1944. They proved that any weighting of uncertain outcomes that is not strictly proportional to probability leads to inconsistencies and other disasters. Their derivation of the expectation principle from axioms of rational choice was immediately recognized as a monumental achievement, which placed expected utility theory at the core of the rational agent model in economics and other social sciences. Thirty years later, when Amos introduced me to their work, he presented it as an object of awe. He also introduced me to a famous challenge to that theory.

ALLAIS'S PARADOX

In 1952, a few years after the publication of von Neumann and Morgenstern's theory, a meeting was convened in Paris to discuss the economics of risk. Many of the most renowned economists of the time were in attendance. The American guests included the future Nobel laureates Paul Samuelson, Kenneth Arrow, and Milton Friedman, as well as the leading statistician Jimmie Savage.

One of the organizers of the Paris meeting was Maurice Allais, who would also receive a Nobel Prize some years later. Allais had something up his sleeve, a couple of questions on choice that he presented to his distinguished audience. In the terms of this chapter, Allais intended to show that his guests were susceptible to a certainty effect and therefore violated expected utility theory and the axioms of rational choice on which that theory rests. The following set of choices is a simplified version of the puzzle that Allais constructed. In problems A and B, which would you choose?

A. 61% chance to win $520,000 OR 63% chance to win $500,000

B. 98% chance to win $520,000 OR 100% chance to win $500,000

If you are like most other people, you preferred the left-hand option in problem A and you preferred the right-hand option in problem B. If these were your preferences, you have just committed a logical sin and violated the rules of rational choice. The illustrious economists assembled in Paris committed similar sins in a more involved version of the "Allais paradox."

To see why these choices are problematic, imagine that the outcome will be determined by a blind draw from an urn that contains 100 marbles—you win if you draw a red marble, you lose if you draw white. In problem A, almost everybody prefers the left-hand urn, although it has fewer winning red marbles, because the difference in the size of the prize is more impressive than the difference in the chances of winning. In problem B, a large majority chooses the urn that guarantees a gain of $500,000. Furthermore, people are comfortable with both choices—until they are led through the logic of the problem.

Compare the two problems, and you will see that the two urns of problem B are more favorable versions of the urns of problem A, with 37 white marbles replaced by red winning marbles in each urn. The improvement on the left is clearly superior to the improvement on the right, since each red marble gives you a chance to win $520,000 on the left and only $500,000 on the right. So you started in the first problem with a preference for the left-hand urn, which was then improved more than the right-hand urn—but now you like the one on the right! This pattern of choices does not make logical sense, but a psychological explanation is readily available: the certainty effect is at work. The 2% difference between a 100% and a 98% chance to win in problem B is vastly more impressive than the same difference between 63% and 61% in problem A.

As Allais had anticipated, the sophisticated participants at the meeting did not notice that their preferences violated utility theory until he drew their attention to that fact as the meeting was about to end. Allais had intended this announcement to be a bombshell: the leading decision theorists in the world had preferences that were inconsistent with their own view of rationality! He apparently believed that his audience would be persuaded to give up the approach that he rather contemptuously labeled "the American school" and adopt an alternative logic of choice that he had developed. He was to be sorely disappointed.

Economists who were not aficionados of decision theory mostly ignored the Allais problem. As often happens when a theory that has been widely adopted and found useful is challenged, they noted the problem as an anomaly and continued using expected utility theory as if nothing had happened. In contrast, decision theorists—a mixed collection of statisticians, economists, philosophers, and psychologists—took Allais's challenge very seriously. When Amos and I began our work, one of our initial goals was to develop a satisfactory psychological account of Allais's paradox.

Most decision theorists, notably including Allais, maintained their belief in human rationality and tried to bend the rules of rational choice to make the Allais pattern permissible. Over the years there have been multiple attempts to find a plausible justification for the certainty effect, none very convincing. Amos had little patience for these efforts; he called the theorists who tried to rationalize violations of utility theory "lawyers for the misguided." We went in another direction. We retained utility theory as a logic of rational choice but abandoned the idea that people are perfectly rational choosers. We took on the task of developing a psychological theory that would describe the choices people make, regardless of whether they are rational. In prospect theory, decision weights would not be identical to probabilities.

DECISION WEIGHTS

Many years after we published prospect theory, Amos and I carried out a study in which we measured the decision weights that explained people's preferences for gambles with modest monetary stakes. The estimates for gains are shown in table 4.

Probability (%)	0	1	2	5	10	20	50	80	90	95	98	99	100
Decision weight	0	5.5	8.1	13.2	18.6	26.1	42.1	60.1	71.2	79.3	87.1	91.2	100

Table 4

You can see that the decision weights are identical to the corresponding probabilities at the extremes: both equal to 0 when the outcome is impossible, and both equal to 100 when the outcome is a sure thing. However, decision weights depart sharply from probabilities near these points. At the low end, we find the possibility effect: unlikely events are considerably overweighted. For example, the decision weight that corresponds to a 2% chance is 8.1. If people conformed to the axioms of rational choice, the decision weight would be 2—so the rare event is overweighted by a factor of 4. The certainty effect at the other end of the probability scale is even more striking. A 2% risk of *not* winning the prize reduces the utility of the gamble by 13%, from 100 to 87.1.

To appreciate the asymmetry between the possibility effect and the certainty effect, imagine first that you have a 1% chance to win $1 million. You will know the outcome tomorrow. Now, imagine that you are almost certain to win $1 million, but there is a 1% chance that you will not. Again, you will learn the outcome tomorrow. The anxiety of the second situation appears to be more salient than the hope in the first. The certainty effect is also more striking than the possibility effect if the outcome is a surgical disaster rather than a financial gain. Compare the intensity with which you focus on the faint sliver of hope in an operation that is almost certain to be fatal, compared to the fear of a 1% risk.

The combination of the certainty effect and possibility effects at the two ends of the probability scale is inevitably accompanied by inadequate sensitivity to intermediate probabilities. You can see that the range of probabilities between 5% and 95% is associated with a much smaller range of decision weights (from 13.2 to 79.3), about two-thirds as much as rationally expected. Neuroscientists have confirmed these observations, finding regions of the brain that respond to changes in the probability of winning a prize. The brain's response to variations of probabilities is strikingly similar to the decision weights estimated from choices.

Probabilities that are extremely low or high (below 1% or above 99%) are a special case. It is difficult to assign a unique decision weight to very rare events, because they are sometimes ignored altogether, effectively assigned a decision weight of zero. On the other hand, when you do not ignore the very rare events, you will certainly overweight them. Most of us spend very little time worrying about nuclear meltdowns or fantasizing about large inheritances from unknown relatives. However, when an unlikely event becomes the focus of attention, we will assign it much more weight than its probability deserves. Furthermore, people are almost completely insensitive to variations of risk among small probabilities. A cancer risk of 0.001% is not easily distinguished from a risk of 0.00001%, although the former would translate to 3,000 cancers for the population of the United States, and the latter to 30.

When you pay attention to a threat, you worry—and the decision weights reflect how much you worry. Because of the possibility effect, the worry is not proportional to the probability of the threat. Reducing or mitigating the risk is not adequate; to eliminate the worry the probability must be brought down to zero.

The question below is adapted from a study of the rationality of consumer valuations of health risks, which was published by a team of economists in the 1980s. The survey was addressed to parents of small children.

> Suppose that you currently use an insect spray that costs you $10 per bottle and it results in 15 inhalation poisonings and 15 child poisonings for every 10,000 bottles of insect spray that are used.
>
> You learn of a more expensive insecticide that reduces each of the risks to 5 for every 10,000 bottles. How much would you be willing to pay for it?

The parents were willing to pay an additional $2.38, on average, to reduce the risks by two-thirds from 15 per 10,000 bottles to 5. They were willing to pay $8.09, more than three times as much, to eliminate it completely. Other questions showed that the parents treated the two risks (inhalation and child poisoning) as separate worries and were willing to pay a certainty premium for the complete elimination of either one. This premium is compatible with the psychology of worry but not with the rational model.

THE FOURFOLD PATTERN

When Amos and I began our work on prospect theory, we quickly reached two conclusions: people attach values to gains and losses rather than to wealth, and the decision weights that they assign to outcomes are different from probabilities. Neither idea was completely new, but in combination they explained a distinctive pattern of preferences that we called the four-fold pattern. The name has stuck. The scenarios are illustrated below.

	GAINS	LOSSES
HIGH PROBABILITY Certainty Effect	95% chance to win $10,000 Fear of disappointment RISK AVERSE Accept unfavorable settlement	95% chance to lose $10,000 Hope to avoid loss RISK SEEKING Reject favorable settlement
LOW PROBABILITY Possibility Effect	5% chance to win $10,000 Hope of large gain RISK SEEKING Reject favorable settlement	5% chance to lose $10,000 Fear of large loss RISK AVERSE Accept unfavorable settlement

Figure 13

- The top row in each cell shows an illustrative prospect.
- The second row characterizes the focal emotion that the prospect evokes.
- The third row indicates how most people behave when offered a choice between a gamble and a sure gain (or loss) that corresponds to its expected value (for example, between "95% chance to win $10,000" and "$9,500 with certainty"). Choices are said to be risk averse if the sure thing is preferred, risk seeking if the gamble is preferred.
- The fourth row describes the expected attitudes of a defendant and a plaintiff as they discuss a settlement of a civil suit.

The *fourfold pattern* of preferences is considered one of the core achievements of prospect theory. Three of the four cells are familiar; the fourth (top right) was new and unexpected.

- The top left is the one that Bernoulli discussed: people are averse to risk when they consider prospects with a substantial chance to achieve a large gain. They are willing to accept less than the expected value of a gamble to lock in a sure gain.
- The possibility effect in the bottom left cell explains why lotteries are popular. When the top prize is very large, ticket buyers appear indifferent to the fact that their chance of winning is minuscule. A lottery

ticket is the ultimate example of the possibility effect. Without a ticket you cannot win, with a ticket you have a chance, and whether the chance is tiny or merely small matters little. Of course, what people acquire with a ticket is more than a chance to win; it is the right to dream pleasantly of winning.

- The bottom right cell is where insurance is bought. People are willing to pay much more for insurance than expected value—which is how insurance companies cover their costs and make their profits. Here again, people buy more than protection against an unlikely disaster; they eliminate a worry and purchase peace of mind.

The results for the top right cell initially surprised us. We were accustomed to think in terms of risk aversion except for the bottom left cell, where lotteries are preferred. When we looked at our choices for bad options, we quickly realized that we were just as risk seeking in the domain of losses as we were risk averse in the domain of gains. We were not the first to observe risk seeking with negative prospects—at least two authors had reported that fact, but they had not made much of it. However, we were fortunate to have a framework that made the finding of risk seeking easy to interpret, and that was a milestone in our thinking. Indeed, we identified two reasons for this effect.

First, there is diminishing sensitivity. The sure loss is very aversive because the reaction to a loss of $900 is more than 90% as intense as the reaction to a loss of $1,000. The second factor may be even more powerful: the decision weight that corresponds to a probability of 90% is only about 71, much lower than the probability. The result is that when you consider a choice between a sure loss and a gamble with a high probability of a larger loss, diminishing sensitivity makes the sure loss more aversive, and the certainty effect reduces the aversiveness of the gamble. The same two factors enhance the attractiveness of the sure thing and reduce the attractiveness of the gamble when the outcomes are positive.

The shape of the value function and the decision weights both contribute to the pattern observed in the top row of table 13. In the bottom row, however, the two factors operate in opposite directions: diminishing sensitivity continues to favor risk aversion for gains and risk seeking for losses, but the overweighting of low probabilities overcomes this effect and produces the observed pattern of gambling for gains and caution for losses.

Many unfortunate human situations unfold in the top right cell. This is where people who face very bad options take desperate gambles, accepting a high probability of making things worse in exchange for a small hope of avoiding a large loss. Risk taking of this kind often turns manageable failures into disasters. The thought of accepting the large sure loss is too painful, and the hope of complete relief too enticing, to make the sensible decision that it is time to cut one's losses. This is where businesses that are losing ground to a superior technology waste their remaining assets in futile attempts to catch up. Because defeat is so difficult to accept, the losing side in wars often fights long past the point at which the victory of the other side is certain, and only a matter of time.

GAMBLING IN THE SHADOW OF THE LAW

The legal scholar Chris Guthrie has offered a compelling application of the fourfold pattern to two situations in which the plaintiff and the defendant in a civil suit consider a possible settlement. The situations differ in the strength of the plaintiff's case.

As in a scenario we saw earlier, you are the plaintiff in a civil suit in which you have made a claim for a large sum in damages. The trial is going very well and your lawyer cites expert opinion that you have a 95% chance to win outright, but adds the caution, "You never really know the outcome until the jury comes in." Your lawyer urges you to accept a settlement in which you might get only 90% of your claim. You are in the top left cell of the fourfold pattern, and the question on your mind is, "Am I willing to take even a small chance of getting nothing at all? Even 90% of the claim is a great deal of money, and I can walk away with it now." Two emotions are evoked, both driving in the same direction: the attraction of a sure (and substantial) gain and the fear of intense disappointment and regret if you reject a settlement and lose in court. You can feel the pressure that typically leads to cautious behavior in this situation. The plaintiff with a strong case is likely to be risk averse.

Now step into the shoes of the defendant in the same case. Although you have not completely given up hope of a decision in your favor, you realize that the trial is going poorly. The plaintiff's lawyers have proposed a settlement in which you would have to pay 90% of their original claim, and it is clear they will not accept less. Will you settle, or will you pursue the case? Because you face a high probability of a loss, your situation belongs in the top right cell. The temptation to fight on is strong: the settlement that the plaintiff has offered is almost as painful as the worst outcome you face, and there is still hope of prevailing in court. Here again, two emotions are involved: the sure loss is repugnant and the possibility of winning in court is highly attractive. A defendant with a weak case is likely to be risk seeking, prepared to gamble rather than accept a very unfavorable settlement. In the face-off between a risk-averse plaintiff and a risk-seeking defendant, the defendant holds the stronger hand. The superior bargaining position of the defendant should be reflected in negotiated settlements, with the plaintiff settling for less than the statistically expected outcome of the trial. This prediction from the fourfold pattern was confirmed by experiments conducted with law students and practicing judges, and also by analyses of actual negotiations in the shadow of civil trials.

Now consider "frivolous litigation," when a plaintiff with a flimsy case files a large claim that is most likely to fail in court. Both sides are aware of the probabilities, and both know that in a negotiated settlement the plaintiff will get only a small fraction of the amount of the claim. The negotiation is conducted in the bottom row of the fourfold pattern. The plaintiff is in the left-hand cell, with a small chance to win a very large amount; the frivolous claim is a lottery ticket for a large prize. Overweighting the small chance of success is natural in this situation, leading the plaintiff to be bold and aggressive in the negotiation. For the defendant, the suit is a nuisance with a small risk of a very bad outcome. Overweighting the small chance of a large loss favors risk aversion, and settling for a modest amount is equivalent to purchasing insurance against the unlikely event of a bad verdict. The shoe is now on the other foot: the plaintiff is willing to gamble and the defendant wants to be safe. Plaintiffs with frivolous claims are likely to obtain a more generous settlement than the statistics of the situation justify.

The decisions described by the fourfold pattern are not obviously unreasonable. You can empathize in each case with the feelings of the plaintiff and the defendant that lead them to adopt a combative or an accommodating posture. In the long run, however, deviations from expected value are likely to be costly. Consider a large organization, the City of New York, and suppose it faces 200 "frivolous" suits each year, each with a 5% chance to cost the city $1 million. Suppose further that in each case the city could settle the lawsuit for a payment of $100,000. The city considers two alternative policies that it will apply to all such cases: settle or go to trial. (For simplicity, I ignore legal costs.)

- If the city litigates all 200 cases, it will lose 10, for a total loss of $10 million.

- If the city settles every case for $100,000, its total loss will be $20 million.

When you take the long view of many similar decisions, you can see that paying a premium to avoid a small risk of a large loss is costly. A similar analysis applies to each of the cells of the fourfold pattern: systematic deviations from expected value are costly in the long run—and this rule applies to both risk aversion and risk seeking. Consistent overweighting of improbable outcomes—a feature of intuitive decision making—eventually leads to inferior outcomes.

SPEAKING OF THE FOURFOLD PATTERN

"He is tempted to settle this frivolous claim to avoid a freak loss, however unlikely. That's overweighting of small probabilities. Since he is likely to face many similar problems, he would be better off not yielding."

"We never let our vacations hang on a last-minute deal. We're willing to pay a lot for certainty."

"They will not cut their losses so long as there is a chance of breaking even. This is risk-seeking in the losses."

"They know the risk of a gas explosion is minuscule, but they want it mitigated. It's a possibility effect, and they want peace of mind."

30

RARE EVENTS

I visited Israel several times during a period in which suicide bombings in buses were relatively common—though of course quite rare in absolute terms. There were altogether 23 bombings between December 2001 and September 2004, which had caused a total of 236 fatalities. The number of daily bus riders in Israel was approximately 1.3 million at that time. For any traveler, the risks were tiny, but that was not how the public felt about it. People avoided buses as much as they could, and many travelers spent their time on the bus anxiously scanning their neighbors for packages or bulky clothes that might hide a bomb.

I did not have much occasion to travel on buses, as I was driving a rented car, but I was chagrined to discover that my behavior was also affected. I found that I did not like to stop next to a bus at a red light, and I drove away more quickly than usual when the light changed. I was ashamed of myself, because of course I knew better. I knew that the risk was truly negligible, and that any effect at all on my actions would assign an inordinately high "decision weight" to a minuscule probability. In fact, I was more likely to be injured in a driving accident than by stopping near a bus. But my avoidance of buses was not motivated by a rational concern for survival. What drove me was the experience of the moment: being next to a bus made me think of bombs, and these thoughts were unpleasant. I was avoiding buses because I wanted to think of something else.

My experience illustrates how terrorism works and why it is so effective: it induces an availability cascade. An extremely vivid image of death and damage, constantly reinforced by media attention and frequent conversations, becomes highly accessible, especially if it is associated with a specific situation such as the sight of a bus. The emotional arousal is associative, automatic, and uncontrolled, and it produces an impulse for protective action. System 2 may "know" that the probability is low, but this knowledge does not eliminate the self-generated discomfort and the wish to avoid it. System 1 cannot be turned off. The emotion is not only disproportionate to the probability, it is also insensitive to the exact level of probability. Suppose that two cities have been warned about the presence of suicide bombers. Residents of one city are told that two bombers are ready to strike. Residents of another city are told of a single bomber. Their risk is lower by half, but do they feel much safer?

Many stores in New York City sell lottery tickets, and business is good. The psychology of high-prize lotteries is similar to the psychology of terrorism. The thrilling possibility of winning the big prize is shared by the community and reinforced by conversations at work and at home. Buying a ticket is immediately rewarded by pleasant fantasies, just as avoiding a bus was immediately rewarded by relief from fear. In both cases, the actual probability is inconsequential; only possibility matters. The original formulation of prospect theory included the argument that "highly unlikely events are either ignored or overweighted," but it did not specify the conditions under which one or the other will occur, nor did it propose a psychological interpretation of it. My current view of decision weights has been strongly influenced by recent research on the role of emotions and vividness in decision making. Overweighting of unlikely outcomes is rooted in System 1 features that are familiar by now. Emotion and vividness influence fluency, availability, and judgments of probability—and thus account for our excessive response to the few rare events that we do not ignore.

OVERESTIMATION AND OVERWEIGHTING

What is your judgment of the probability that the next president of the United States will be a third-party candidate?

How much will you pay for a bet in which you receive $1,000 if the next president of the United States is a third-party candidate, and no money otherwise?

The two questions are different but obviously related. The first asks you to assess the probability of an unlikely event. The second invites you to put a decision weight on the same event, by placing a bet on it.

How do people make the judgments and how do they assign decision weights? We start from two simple answers, then qualify them. Here are the oversimplified answers:

- People overestimate the probabilities of unlikely events.
- People overweight unlikely events in their decisions.

Although overestimation and overweighting are distinct phenomena, the same psychological mechanisms are involved in both: focused attention, confirmation bias, and cognitive ease.

Specific descriptions trigger the associative machinery of System 1. When you thought about the unlikely victory of a third-party candidate, your associative system worked in its usual confirmatory mode, selectively retrieving evidence, instances, and images that would make the statement true. The process was biased, but it was not an exercise in fantasy. You looked for a plausible scenario that conforms to the constraints of reality; you did not simply imagine the Fairy of the West installing a third-party president. Your judgment of probability was ultimately determined by the cognitive ease, or fluency, with which a plausible scenario came to mind.

You do not always focus on the event you are asked to estimate. If the target event is very likely, you focus on its alternative. Consider this example:

What is the probability that a baby born in your local hospital will be released within three days?

You were asked to estimate the probability of the baby going home, but you almost certainly focused on the events that might cause a baby *not* to be released within the normal period. Our mind has a useful capability to focus spontaneously on whatever is odd, different, or unusual. You quickly realized that it is normal for babies in the United States (not all countries have the same standards) to be released within two or three days of birth, so your attention turned to the abnormal alternative. The unlikely event became focal. The availability heuristic is likely to be evoked: your judgment was probably determined by the number of scenarios of medical problems you produced and by the ease with which they came to mind. Because you were in confirmatory mode, there is a good chance that your estimate of the frequency of problems was too high.

The probability of a rare event is most likely to be overestimated when the alternative is not fully specified. My favorite example comes from a study that the psychologist Craig Fox conducted while he was Amos's student. Fox recruited fans of professional basketball and elicited several judgments and decisions concerning the winner of the NBA playoffs. In particular, he asked them to estimate the probability that each of the eight participating teams would win the playoff; the victory of each team in turn was the focal event.

You can surely guess what happened, but the magnitude of the effect that Fox observed may surprise you. Imagine a fan who has been asked to estimate the chances that the Chicago Bulls will win the tournament. The focal event is well defined, but its alternative—one of the other seven teams winning—is diffuse and less evocative. The fan's memory and imagination, operating in confirmatory mode, are trying to construct a victory for the Bulls. When the same person is next asked to assess the chances of the Lakers, the same selective activation will work in favor of that team. The eight best professional basketball teams in the United States are all very good, and it is possible to imagine even a relatively weak team among them emerging as champion. The result: the probability judgments generated successively for the eight teams added up to 240%! This pattern is absurd, of course, because the sum of the chances of the eight events *must* add up to 100%. The absurdity disappeared when the same judges were asked whether the winner would be from the Eastern or the Western conference. The focal event and its alternative were equally specific in that question and the judgments of their probabilities added up to 100%.

To assess decision weights, Fox also invited the basketball fans to bet on the tournament result. They assigned a cash equivalent to each bet (a cash amount that was just as attractive as playing the bet). Winning the bet would earn a payoff of $160. The sum of the cash equivalents for the eight individual teams was $287. An average participant who took all eight bets would be guaranteed a loss of $127! The participants surely knew that there were eight teams in the tournament and that the average payoff for betting on all of them could not exceed $160, but they overweighted nonetheless. The fans not only overestimated the probability of the events they focused on—they were also much too willing to bet on them.

These findings shed new light on the planning fallacy and other manifestations of optimism. The successful execution of a plan is specific and easy to imagine when one tries to forecast the outcome of a project. In contrast, the alternative of failure is diffuse, because there are innumerable ways for things to go wrong. Entrepreneurs and the investors who evaluate their prospects are prone both to overestimate their chances and to overweight their estimates.

VIVID OUTCOMES

As we have seen, prospect theory differs from utility theory in the relationship it suggests between probability and decision weight. In utility theory, decision weights and probabilities are the same. The decision weight of a sure thing is 100, and the weight that corresponds to a 90% chance is exactly 90, which is 9 times more than the decision weight for a 10% chance. In prospect theory, variations of probability have less effect on decision weights. An experiment that I mentioned earlier found that the decision weight for a 90% chance was 71.2 and the decision weight for a 10% chance was 18.6. The ratio of the probabilities was 9.0, but the ratio of the decision weights was only 3.83, indicating insufficient sensitivity to probability in that range. In both theories, the decision weights depend only on probability, not on the outcome. Both theories predict that the decision weight for a 90% chance is the same for winning $100, receiving a dozen roses, or getting an electric shock. This theoretical prediction turns out to be wrong.

Psychologists at the University of Chicago published an article with the attractive title "Money, Kisses, and Electric Shocks: On the Affective Psychology of Risk." Their finding was that the valuation of gambles was much less sensitive to probability when the (fictitious) outcomes were emotional ("meeting and kissing your favorite movie star" or "getting a painful, but not dangerous, electric shock") than when the outcomes were gains or losses of cash. This was not an isolated finding. Other researchers had found, using physiological measures such as heart rate, that the fear of an impending electric shock was essentially uncorrelated with the probability of receiving the shock. The mere possibility of a shock triggered the full-blown fear response. The Chicago team proposed that "affect-laden imagery" overwhelmed the response to probability. Ten years later, a team of psychologists at Princeton challenged that conclusion.

The Princeton team argued that the low sensitivity to probability that had been observed for emotional outcomes is normal. Gambles on money are the exception. The sensitivity to probability is relatively high for these gambles, because they have a definite expected value.

What amount of cash is as attractive as each of these gambles?

A. 84% chance to win $59

B. 84% chance to receive one dozen red roses in a glass vase

What do you notice? The salient difference is that question A is much easier than question B. You did not stop to compute the expected value of the bet, but you probably knew quickly that it is not far from $50 (in fact it is $49.56), and the vague estimate was sufficient to provide a helpful anchor as you searched for an equally attractive cash gift. No such anchor is available for question B, which is therefore much harder to answer. Respondents also assessed the cash equivalent of gambles with a 21% chance to win the two outcomes. As expected, the difference between the high-probability and low-probability gambles was much more pronounced for the money than for the roses.

To bolster their argument that insensitivity to probability is not caused by emotion, the Princeton team compared willingness to pay to avoid gambles:

21% chance (or 84% chance) to spend a weekend painting someone's three-bedroom apartment

21% chance (or 84% chance) to clean three stalls in a dormitory bathroom after a weekend of use

The second outcome is surely much more emotional than the first, but the decision weights for the two outcomes did not differ. Evidently, the intensity of emotion is not the answer.

Another experiment yielded a surprising result. The participants received explicit price information along with the verbal description of the prize. An example could be:

84% chance to win: A dozen red roses in a glass vase. Value $59.

21% chance to win: A dozen red roses in a glass vase. Value $59.

It is easy to assess the expected monetary value of these gambles, but adding a specific monetary value did not alter the results: evaluations remained insensitive to probability even in that condition. People who thought of the gift as a chance to get roses did not use price information as an anchor in

evaluating the gamble. As scientists sometimes say, this is a surprising finding that is trying to tell us something. What story is it trying to tell us?

The story, I believe, is that a rich and vivid representation of the outcome, whether or not it is emotional, reduces the role of probability in the
evaluation of an uncertain prospect. This hypothesis suggests a prediction,
in which I have reasonably high confidence: adding irrelevant but vivid
details to a monetary outcome also disrupts calculation. Compare your
cash equivalents for the following outcomes:

21% (or 84%) chance to receive $59 next Monday

21% (or 84%) chance to receive a large blue cardboard envelope containing
$59 next Monday morning

The new hypothesis is that there will be less sensitivity to probability in the
second case, because the blue envelope evokes a richer and more fluent representation than the abstract notion of a sum of money. You constructed
the event in your mind, and the vivid image of the outcome exists there
even if you know that its probability is low. Cognitive ease contributes to
the certainty effect as well: when you hold a vivid image of an event, the
possibility of its not occurring is also represented vividly, and overweighted.
The combination of an enhanced possibility effect with an enhanced certainty effect leaves little room for decision weights to change between
chances of 21% and 84%.

VIVID PROBABILITIES

The idea that fluency, vividness, and the ease of imagining contribute to
decision weights gains support from many other observations. Participants
in a well-known experiment are given a choice of drawing a marble from
one of two urns, in which red marbles win a prize:

Urn A contains 10 marbles, of which 1 is red.
Urn B contains 100 marbles, of which 8 are red.

Which urn would you choose? The chances of winning are 10% in urn A
and 8% in urn B, so making the right choice should be easy, but it is not:
about 30%–40% of students choose the urn with the larger *number* of winning marbles, rather than the urn that provides a better chance of winning.

Seymour Epstein has argued that the results illustrate the superficial processing characteristic of System 1 (which he calls the experiential system).

As you might expect, the remarkably foolish choices that people make in this situation have attracted the attention of many researchers. The bias has been given several names; following Paul Slovic I will call it *denominator neglect*. If your attention is drawn to the winning marbles, you do not assess the number of nonwinning marbles with the same care. Vivid imagery contributes to denominator neglect, at least as I experience it. When I think of the small urn, I see a single red marble on a vaguely defined background of white marbles. When I think of the larger urn, I see eight winning red marbles on an indistinct background of white marbles, which creates a more hopeful feeling. The distinctive vividness of the winning marbles increases the decision weight of that event, enhancing the possibility effect. Of course, the same will be true of the certainty effect. If I have a 90% chance of winning a prize, the event of not winning will be more salient if 10 of 100 marbles are "losers" than if 1 of 10 marbles yields the same outcome.

The idea of denominator neglect helps explain why different ways of communicating risks vary so much in their effects. You read that "a vaccine that protects children from a fatal disease carries a 0.001% risk of permanent disability." The risk appears small. Now consider another description of the same risk: "One of 100,000 vaccinated children will be permanently disabled." The second statement does something to your mind that the first does not: it calls up the image of an individual child who is permanently disabled by a vaccine; the 999,999 safely vaccinated children have faded into the background. As predicted by denominator neglect, low-probability events are much more heavily weighted when described in terms of relative frequencies (how many) than when stated in more abstract terms of "chances," "risk," or "probability" (how likely). As we have seen, System 1 is much better at dealing with individuals than categories.

The effect of the frequency format is large. In one study, people who saw information about "a disease that kills 1,286 people out of every 10,000" judged it as more dangerous than people who were told about "a disease that kills 24.14% of the population." The first disease appears more threatening than the second, although the former risk is only half as large as the latter! In an even more direct demonstration of denominator neglect, "a disease that kills 1,286 people out of every 10,000" was judged more dangerous than a disease that "kills 24.4 out of 100." The effect would surely be reduced or eliminated if participants were asked for a direct comparison of the two formulations, a task that explicitly calls for System 2. Life, however,

is usually a between-subjects experiment, in which you see only one formulation at a time. It would take an exceptionally active System 2 to generate
alternative formulations of the one you see and to discover that they evoke
a different response.

Experienced forensic psychologists and psychiatrists are not immune to
the effects of the format in which risks are expressed. In one experiment,
professionals evaluated whether it was safe to discharge from the psychi-
atric hospital a patient, Mr. Jones, with a history of violence. The information they received included an expert's assessment of the risk. The same
statistics were described in two ways:

> Patients similar to Mr. Jones are estimated to have a 10% probability of
> committing an act of violence against others during the first several months
> after discharge.

> Of every 100 patients similar to Mr. Jones, 10 are estimated to commit an
> act of violence against others during the first several months after discharge.

The professionals who saw the frequency format were almost twice as likely
to deny the discharge (41%, compared to 21% in the probability format).
The more vivid description produces a higher decision weight for the same
probability.

The power of format creates opportunities for manipulation, which
people with an axe to grind know how to exploit. Slovic and his colleagues
cite an article that states that "approximately 1,000 homicides a year are
committed nationwide by seriously mentally ill individuals who are not
taking their medication." Another way of expressing the same fact is that
"1,000 out of 273,000,000 Americans will die in this manner each year." Another is that "the annual likelihood of being killed by such an individual is
approximately 0.00036%." Still another: "1,000 Americans will die in this
manner each year, or less than one-thirtieth the number who will die of
suicide and about one-fourth the number who will die of laryngeal cancer."
Slovic points out that "these advocates are quite open about their motivation: they *want* to frighten the general public about violence by people with
mental disorder, in the hope that this fear will translate into increased funding for mental health services."

A good attorney who wishes to cast doubt on DNA evidence will not tell
the jury that "the chance of a false match is 0.1%." The statement that "a
false match occurs in 1 of 1,000 capital cases" is far more likely to pass the

threshold of reasonable doubt. The jurors hearing those words are invited to generate the image of the man who sits before them in the courtroom being wrongly convicted because of flawed DNA evidence. The prosecutor, of course, will favor the more abstract frame—hoping to fill the jurors' minds with decimal points.

DECISIONS FROM GLOBAL IMPRESSIONS

The evidence suggests the hypothesis that focal attention and salience contribute to both the overestimation of unlikely events and the overweighting of unlikely outcomes. Salience is enhanced by mere mention of an event, by its vividness, and by the format in which probability is described. There are exceptions, of course, in which focusing on an event does not raise its probability: cases in which an erroneous theory makes an event appear impossible even when you think about it, or cases in which an inability to imagine how an outcome might come about leaves you convinced that it will not happen. The bias toward overestimation and overweighting of salient events is not an absolute rule, but it is large and robust.

There has been much interest in recent years in studies of *choice from experience*, which follow different rules from the *choices from description* that are analyzed in prospect theory. Participants in a typical experiment face two buttons. When pressed, each button produces either a monetary reward or nothing, and the outcome is drawn randomly according to the specifications of a prospect (for example, "5% to win $12" or "95% chance to win $1"). The process is truly random, so there is no guarantee that the sample a participant sees exactly represents the statistical setup. The expected values associated with the two buttons are approximately equal, but one is riskier (more variable) than the other. (For example, one button may produce $10 on 5% of the trials and the other $1 on 50% of the trials). Choice from experience is implemented by exposing the participant to many trials in which she can observe the consequences of pressing one button or another. On the critical trial, she chooses one of the two buttons, and she earns the outcome on that trial. Choice from description is realized by showing the subject the verbal description of the risky prospect associated with each button (such as "5% to win $12") and asking her to choose one. As expected from prospect theory, choice from description yields a possibility effect—rare outcomes are overweighted relative to their probability. In sharp contrast, overweighting is never observed in choice from experience, and underweighting is common.

The experimental situation of choice by experience is intended to represent many situations in which we are exposed to variable outcomes from the same source. A restaurant that is usually good may occasionally serve a brilliant or an awful meal. Your friend is usually good company, but he sometimes turns moody and aggressive. California is prone to earthquakes, but they happen rarely. The results of many experiments suggest that rare events are not overweighted when we make decisions such as choosing a restaurant or tying down the boiler to reduce earthquake damage.

The interpretation of choice from experience is not yet settled, but there is general agreement on one major cause of underweighting of rare events, both in experiments and in the real world: many participants never experience the rare event! Most Californians have never experienced a major earthquake, and in 2007 no banker had personally experienced a devastating financial crisis. Ralph Hertwig and Ido Erev note that "chances of rare events (such as the burst of housing bubbles) receive less impact than they deserve according to their objective probabilities." They point to the public's tepid response to long-term environmental threats as an example.

These examples of neglect are both important and easily explained, but underweighting also occurs when people have actually experienced the rare event. Suppose you have a complicated question that two colleagues on your floor could probably answer. You have known them both for years and have had many occasions to observe and experience their character. Adele is fairly consistent and generally helpful, though not exceptional on that dimension. Brian is not quite as friendly and helpful as Adele most of the time, but on some occasions he has been extremely generous with his time and advice. Whom will you approach?

Consider two possible views of this decision:

- It is a choice between two gambles. Adele is closer to a sure thing; the prospect of Brian is more likely to yield a slightly inferior outcome, with a low probability of a very good one. The rare event will be overweighted by a possibility effect, favoring Brian.
- It is a choice between your global impressions of Adele and Brian. The good and the bad experiences you have had are pooled in your representation of their normal behavior. Unless the rare event is so extreme that it comes to mind separately (Brian once verbally abused a colleague who asked for his help), the norm will be biased toward typical and recent instances, favoring Adele.

In a two-system mind, the second interpretation appears far more plausible. System 1 generates global representations of Adele and Brian, which include an emotional attitude and a tendency to approach or avoid. Nothing beyond a comparison of these tendencies is needed to determine the door on which you will knock. Unless the rare event comes to your mind explicitly, it will not be overweighted. Applying the same idea to the experiments on choice from experience is straightforward. As they are observed generating outcomes over time, the two buttons develop integrated "personalities" to which emotional responses are attached.

The conditions under which rare events are ignored or overweighted are better understood now than they were when prospect theory was formulated. The probability of a rare event will (often, not always) be overestimated, because of the confirmatory bias of memory. Thinking about that event, you try to make it true in your mind. A rare event will be overweighted if it specifically attracts attention. Separate attention is effectively guaranteed when prospects are described explicitly ("99% chance to win $1,000, and 1% chance to win nothing"). Obsessive concerns (the bus in Jerusalem), vivid images (the roses), concrete representations (1 of 1,000), and explicit reminders (as in choice from description) all contribute to overweighting. And when there is no overweighting, there will be neglect. When it comes to rare probabilities, our mind is not designed to get things quite right. For the residents of a planet that may be exposed to events no one has yet experienced, this is not good news.

SPEAKING OF RARE EVENTS

"Tsunamis are very rare even in Japan, but the image is so vivid and compelling that tourists are bound to overestimate their probability."

"It's the familiar disaster cycle. Begin by exaggeration and overweighting, then neglect sets in."

"We shouldn't focus on a single scenario, or we will overestimate its probability. Let's set up specific alternatives and make the probabilities add up to 100%."

"They want people to be worried by the risk. That's why they describe it as 1 death per 1,000. They're counting on denominator neglect."

31

RISK POLICIES

Imagine that you face the following pair of concurrent decisions. First examine both decisions, then make your choices.

Decision (i): Choose between
A. sure gain of $240
B. 25% chance to gain $1,000 and 75% chance to gain nothing

Decision (ii): Choose between
C. sure loss of $750
D. 75% chance to lose $1,000 and 25% chance to lose nothing

This pair of choice problems has an important place in the history of prospect theory, and it has new things to tell us about rationality. As you skimmed the two problems, your initial reaction to the sure things (A and C) was attraction to the first and aversion to the second. The emotional evaluation of "sure gain" and "sure loss" is an automatic reaction of System 1, which certainly occurs before the more effortful (and optional) computation of the expected values of the two gambles (respectively, a gain of $250 and a loss of $750). Most people's choices correspond to the predilections of System 1, and large majorities prefer A to B and D to C. As in many other choices that involve moderate or high probabilities, people tend to be risk averse in the domain of gains and risk seeking in the domain of losses.

In the original experiment that Amos and I carried out, 73% of respondents chose A in decision i and D in decision ii and only 3% favored the combination of B and C.

You were asked to examine both options before making your first choice, and you probably did so. But one thing you surely did not do: you did not compute the possible results of the four combinations of choices (A and C, A and D, B and C, B and D) to determine which combination you like best. Your separate preferences for the two problems were intuitively compelling and there was no reason to expect that they could lead to trouble. Furthermore, combining the two decision problems is a laborious exercise that you would need paper and pencil to complete. You did not do it. Now consider the following choice problem:

> AD. 25% chance to win $240 and 75% chance to lose $760
> BC. 25% chance to win $250 and 75% chance to lose $750

This choice is easy! Option BC actually *dominates* option AD (the technical term for one option being unequivocally better than another). You already know what comes next. The dominant option in AD is the combination of the two rejected options in the first pair of decision problems, the one that only 3% of respondents favored in our original study. The inferior option BC was preferred by 73% of respondents.

BROAD OR NARROW?

This set of choices has a lot to tell us about the limits of human rationality. For one thing, it helps us see the logical consistency of Human preferences for what it is—a hopeless mirage. Have another look at the last problem, the easy one. Would you have imagined the possibility of decomposing this obvious choice problem into a pair of problems that would lead a large majority of people to choose an inferior option? This is generally true: every simple choice formulated in terms of gains and losses can be deconstructed in innumerable ways into a combination of choices, yielding preferences that are likely to be inconsistent.

The example also shows that it is costly to be risk averse for gains and risk seeking for losses. These attitudes make you willing to pay a premium to obtain a sure gain rather than face a gamble, and also willing to pay a premium (in expected value) to avoid a sure loss. Both payments come out of the same pocket, and when you face both kinds of problems at once, the discrepant attitudes are unlikely to be optimal.

There were two ways of construing decisions i and ii:

- narrow framing: a sequence of two simple decisions, considered separately
- broad framing: a single comprehensive decision, with four options

Broad framing was obviously superior in this case. Indeed, it will be superior (or at least not inferior) in every case in which several decisions are to be contemplated together. Imagine a longer list of 5 simple (binary) decisions to be considered simultaneously. The broad (comprehensive) frame consists of a single choice with 32 options. Narrow framing will yield a sequence of 5 simple choices. The sequence of 5 choices will be one of the 32 options of the broad frame. Will it be the best? Perhaps, but not very likely. A rational agent will of course engage in broad framing, but Humans are by nature narrow framers.

The ideal of logical consistency, as this example shows, is not achievable by our limited mind. Because we are susceptible to WYSIATI and averse to mental effort, we tend to make decisions as problems arise, even when we are specifically instructed to consider them jointly. We have neither the inclination nor the mental resources to enforce consistency on our preferences, and our preferences are not magically set to be coherent, as they are in the rational-agent model.

SAMUELSON'S PROBLEM

The great Paul Samuelson—a giant among the economists of the twentieth century—famously asked a friend whether he would accept a gamble on the toss of a coin in which he could lose $100 or win $200. His friend responded, "I won't bet because I would feel the $100 loss more than the $200 gain. But I'll take you on if you promise to let me make 100 such bets." Unless you are a decision theorist, you probably share the intuition of Samuelson's friend, that playing a very favorable but risky gamble multiple times reduces the subjective risk. Samuelson found his friend's answer interesting and went on to analyze it. He proved that under some very specific conditions, a utility maximizer who rejects a single gamble should also reject the offer of many.

Remarkably, Samuelson did not seem to mind the fact that his proof, which is of course valid, led to a conclusion that violates common sense, if not rationality: the offer of a hundred gambles is so attractive that no sane person would reject it. Matthew Rabin and Richard Thaler pointed out that "the aggregated gamble of one hundred 50–50 lose $100/gain $200 bets has an expected return of $5,000, with only a 1/2,300 chance of losing any money and merely a 1/62,000 chance of losing more than $1,000." Their point, of course, is that if utility theory can be consistent with such a foolish preference under any circumstances, then something must be wrong with it as a model of rational choice. Samuelson had not seen Rabin's proof of the absurd consequences of severe loss aversion for small bets, but he would surely not have been surprised by it. His willingness even to consider the possibility that it could be rational to reject the package testifies to the powerful hold of the rational model.

Let us assume that a very simple value function describes the preferences of Samuelson's friend (call him Sam). To express his aversion to losses Sam first rewrites the bet, *after multiplying each loss by a factor of 2*. He then computes the expected value of the rewritten bet. Here are the results, for one, two, or three tosses. They are sufficiently instructive to deserve some pupil-dilating effort.

		Expected Value
One toss	(50% lose 100; 50% win 200)	50
Losses doubled	(50% lose 200; 50% win 200)	0
Two tosses	(25% lose 200; 50% win 100; 25% win 400)	100
Losses doubled	(25% lose 400; 50% win 100; 25% win 400)	50
Three tosses	(12.5% lose 300; 37.5% win 0; 37.5% win 300; 12.5% win 600)	150
Losses doubled	(12.5% lose 600; 37.5% win 0; 37.5% win 300; 12.5% win 600)	112.5

You can see in the display that the gamble has an expected value of 50. However, one toss is worth nothing to Sam because he feels that the pain of losing a dollar is twice as intense as the pleasure of winning a dollar. After rewriting the gamble to reflect his loss aversion, Sam will find that the value of the gamble is 0.

Now consider two tosses. The chances of losing have gone down to 25%. The two extreme outcomes (lose 200 or win 400) cancel out in value; they are equally likely, and the losses are weighted twice as much as the gain. But the intermediate outcome (one loss, one gain) is positive, and so is the compound gamble as a whole. Now you can see the cost of narrow framing and the magic of aggregating gambles. Here are two favorable gambles, which individually are worth nothing to Sam. If he encounters the offer on two separate occasions, he will turn it down both times. However, if he bundles the two offers together, they are jointly worth $50!

Things get even better when three gambles are bundled. The extreme outcomes still cancel out, but they have become less significant. The third toss, although worthless if evaluated on its own, has added $62.50 to the total value of the package. By the time Sam is offered five gambles, the expected value of the offer will be $250, his probability of losing anything will be 18.75%, and his cash equivalent will be $203.125. The notable aspect of this story is that Sam never wavers in his aversion to losses. However, the aggregation of favorable gambles rapidly reduces the probability of losing, and the impact of loss aversion on his preferences diminishes accordingly.

Now I have a sermon ready for Sam if he rejects the offer of a single highly favorable gamble played once, and for you if you share his unreasonable aversion to losses:

> I sympathize with your aversion to losing any gamble, but it is costing you a lot of money. Please consider this question: Are you on your deathbed? Is this the last offer of a small favorable gamble that you will ever consider? Of course, you are unlikely to be offered exactly this gamble again, but you will have many opportunities to consider attractive gambles with stakes that are very small relative to your wealth. You will do yourself a large financial favor if you are able to see each of these gambles as part of a bundle of small gambles and rehearse the mantra that will get you significantly closer to economic rationality: you win a few, you lose a few. The main purpose of the mantra is to control your emotional response when you do lose. If you can trust it to be effective, you should remind yourself of it when deciding whether or not to accept a small risk with positive expected value. Remember these qualifications when using the mantra:
>
> - It works when the gambles are genuinely independent of each other; it does not apply to multiple investments in the same industry, which would all go bad together.

- It works only when the possible loss does not cause you to worry about your total wealth. If you would take the loss as significant bad news about your economic future, watch it!
- It should not be applied to long shots, where the probability of winning is very small for each bet.

> If you have the emotional discipline that this rule requires, you will never consider a small gamble in isolation or be loss averse for a small gamble until you are actually on your deathbed—and not even then.

This advice is not impossible to follow. Experienced traders in financial markets live by it every day, shielding themselves from the pain of losses by *broad framing*. As was mentioned earlier, we now know that experimental subjects could be almost cured of their loss aversion (in a particular context) by inducing them to "think like a trader," just as experienced baseball card traders are not as susceptible to the endowment effect as novices are. Students made risky decisions (to accept or reject gambles in which they could lose) under different instructions. In the narrow-framing condition, they were told to "make each decision as if it were the only one" and to accept their emotions. The instructions for broad framing of a decision included the phrases "imagine yourself as a trader," "you do this all the time," and "treat it as one of many monetary decisions, which will sum together to produce a 'portfolio.'" The experimenters assessed the subjects' emotional response to gains and losses by physiological measures, including changes in the electrical conductance of the skin that are used in lie detection. As expected, broad framing blunted the emotional reaction to losses and increased the willingness to take risks.

The combination of loss aversion and narrow framing is a costly curse. Individual investors can avoid that curse, achieving the emotional benefits of broad framing while also saving time and agony, by reducing the frequency with which they check how well their investments are doing. Closely following daily fluctuations is a losing proposition, because the pain of the frequent small losses exceeds the pleasure of the equally frequent small gains. Once a quarter is enough, and may be more than enough for individual investors. In addition to improving the emotional quality of life, the deliberate avoidance of exposure to short-term outcomes improves the quality of both decisions and outcomes. The typical short-term reaction to bad news is increased loss aversion. Investors who get aggregated feedback receive such news much less often and are likely to be less risk averse and to end up richer. You are also less prone to useless churning of your portfolio if you don't know how every stock in it is doing every day (or every week or even every month). A commitment not to change one's position for several periods (the equivalent of "locking in" an investment) improves financial performance.

RISK POLICIES

Decision makers who are prone to narrow framing construct a preference every time they face a risky choice. They would do better by having a *risk policy* that they routinely apply whenever a relevant problem arises. Familiar examples of risk policies are "always take the highest possible deductible when purchasing insurance" and "never buy extended warranties." A risk policy is a broad frame. In the insurance examples, you expect the occasional loss of the entire deductible, or the occasional failure of an uninsured product. The relevant issue is your ability to reduce or eliminate the pain of the occasional loss by the thought that the policy that left you exposed to it will almost certainly be financially advantageous over the long run.

A risk policy that aggregates decisions is analogous to the outside view of planning problems that I discussed earlier. The outside view shifts the focus from the specifics of the current situation to the statistics of outcomes in similar situations. The outside view is a broad frame for thinking about plans. A risk policy is a broad frame that embeds a particular risky choice in a set of similar choices.

The outside view and the risk policy are remedies against two distinct biases that affect many decisions: the exaggerated optimism of the planning fallacy and the exaggerated caution induced by loss aversion. The two biases oppose each other. Exaggerated optimism protects individuals and organizations from the paralyzing effects of loss aversion; loss aversion protects them from the follies of overconfident optimism. The upshot is rather comfortable for the decision maker. Optimists believe that the decisions they make are more prudent than they really are, and loss-averse decision makers correctly reject marginal propositions that they might otherwise accept. There is no guarantee, of course, that the biases cancel out in every situation. An organization that could eliminate both excessive optimism and excessive loss aversion should do so. The combination of the outside view with a risk policy should be the goal.

Richard Thaler tells of a discussion about decision making he had with the top managers of the 25 divisions of a large company. He asked them to consider a risky option in which, with equal probabilities, they could lose a large amount of the capital they controlled or earn double that amount. None of the executives was willing to take such a dangerous gamble. Thaler then turned to the CEO of the company, who was also present, and asked for his opinion. Without hesitation, the CEO answered, "I would like all of them to accept their risks." In the context of that conversation, it was natural for the CEO to adopt a broad frame that encompassed all 25 bets. Like Sam facing 100 coin tosses, he could count on statistical aggregation to mitigate the overall risk.

SPEAKING OF RISK POLICIES

"Tell her to think like a trader! You win a few, you lose a few."

"I decided to evaluate my portfolio only once a quarter. I am too loss averse to make sensible decisions in the face of daily price fluctuations."

"They never buy extended warranties. That's their risk policy."

"Each of our executives is loss averse in his or her domain. That's perfectly natural, but the result is that the organization is not taking enough risk."

32

KEEPING SCORE

Except for the very poor, for whom income coincides with survival, the main motivators of money-seeking are not necessarily economic. For the billionaire looking for the extra billion, and indeed for the participant in an experimental economics project looking for the extra dollar, money is a proxy for points on a scale of self-regard and achievement. These rewards and punishments, promises and threats, are all in our heads. We carefully keep score of them. They shape our preferences and motivate our actions, like the incentives provided in the social environment. As a result, we refuse to cut losses when doing so would admit failure, we are biased against actions that could lead to regret, and we draw an illusory but sharp distinction between omission and commission, not doing and doing, because the sense of responsibility is greater for one than for the other. The ultimate currency that rewards or punishes is often emotional, a form of mental self-dealing that inevitably creates conflicts of interest when the individual acts as an agent on behalf of an organization.

MENTAL ACCOUNTS

Richard Thaler has been fascinated for many years by analogies between the world of accounting and the mental accounts that we use to organize and run our lives, with results that are sometimes foolish and sometimes very helpful. Mental accounts come in several varieties. We hold our money in different accounts, which are sometimes physical, sometimes only mental.

We have spending money, general savings, earmarked savings for our children's education or for medical emergencies. There is a clear hierarchy in our willingness to draw on these accounts to cover current needs. We use accounts for self-control purposes, as in making a household budget, limiting the daily consumption of espressos, or increasing the time spent exercising. Often we pay for self-control, for instance simultaneously putting money in a savings account and maintaining debt on credit cards. The Econs of the rational-agent model do not resort to mental accounting: they have a comprehensive view of outcomes and are driven by external incentives. For Humans, mental accounts are a form of narrow framing; they keep things under control and manageable by a finite mind.

Mental accounts are used extensively to keep score. Recall that professional golfers putt more successfully when working to avoid a bogey than to achieve a birdie. One conclusion we can draw is that the best golfers create a separate account for each hole; they do not only maintain a single account for their overall success. An ironic example that Thaler related in an early article remains one of the best illustrations of how mental accounting affects behavior:

> Two avid sports fans plan to travel 40 miles to see a basketball game. One of them paid for his ticket; the other was on his way to purchase a ticket when he got one free from a friend. A blizzard is announced for the night of the game. Which of the two ticket holders is more likely to brave the blizzard to see the game?

The answer is immediate: we know that the fan who paid for his ticket is more likely to drive. Mental accounting provides the explanation. We assume that both fans set up an account for the game they hoped to see. Missing the game will close the accounts with a negative balance. Regardless of how they came by their ticket, both will be disappointed—but the closing balance is distinctly more negative for the one who bought a ticket and is now out of pocket as well as deprived of the game. Because staying home is worse for this individual, he is more motivated to see the game and therefore more likely to make the attempt to drive into a blizzard. These are tacit calculations of emotional balance, of the kind that System 1 performs without deliberation. The emotions that people attach to the state of their mental accounts are not acknowledged in standard economic theory. An Econ would realize that the ticket has already been paid for and cannot be returned. Its cost is "sunk" and the Econ would not care whether he had bought the ticket to the game or got it from a friend (if Econs have friends). To implement this rational behavior, System 2 would have to be aware of the counterfactual possibility: "Would I still drive into this snowstorm if I had gotten the ticket free from a friend?" It takes an active and disciplined mind to raise such a difficult question.

A related mistake afflicts individual investors when they sell stocks from their portfolio:

> You need money to cover the costs of your daughter's wedding and will have to sell some stock. You remember the price at which you bought each stock and can identify it as a "winner," currently worth more than you paid for it, or as a loser. Among the stocks you own, Blueberry Tiles is a winner; if you sell it today you will have achieved a gain of $5,000. You hold an equal investment in Tiffany Motors, which is currently worth $5,000 less than you paid for it. The value of both stocks has been stable in recent weeks. Which are you more likely to sell?

A plausible way to formulate the choice is this: "I could close the Blueberry Tiles account and score a success for my record as an investor. Alternatively, I could close the Tiffany Motors account and add a failure to my record. Which would I rather do?" If the problem is framed as a choice between giving yourself pleasure and causing yourself pain, you will certainly sell Blueberry Tiles and enjoy your investment prowess. As might be expected, finance research has documented a massive preference for selling winners rather than losers—a bias that has been given an opaque label: the *disposition effect*.

The disposition effect is an instance of *narrow framing*. The investor has set up an account for each share that she bought, and she wants to close every account as a gain. A rational agent would have a comprehensive view of the portfolio and sell the stock that is least likely to do well in the future, without considering whether it is a winner or a loser. Amos told me of a conversation with a financial adviser, who asked him for a complete list of the stocks in his portfolio, including the price at which each had been purchased. When Amos asked mildly, "Isn't it supposed not to matter?" the adviser looked astonished. He had apparently always believed that the state of the mental account was a valid consideration.

Amos's guess about the financial adviser's beliefs was probably right, but he was wrong to dismiss the buying price as irrelevant. The purchase price does matter and should be considered, even by Econs. The disposition effect is a costly bias because the question of whether to sell winners or losers has a clear answer, and it is not that it makes no difference. If you care about your wealth rather than your immediate emotions, you will sell the loser Tiffany Motors and hang on to the winning Blueberry Tiles. At least in the United States, taxes provide a strong incentive: realizing losses reduces your taxes, while selling winners exposes you to taxes. This elementary fact of financial life is actually known to all American investors, and it determines the decisions they make during one month of the year—investors sell more losers in December, when taxes are on their mind. The tax advantage is available all year, of course, but for 11 months of the year mental accounting prevails over financial common sense. Another argument against selling winners is the well-documented market anomaly that stocks that recently gained in value are likely to go on gaining at least for a short while. The net effect is large: the expected after-tax extra return of selling Tiffany rather than Blueberry is 3.4% over the next year. Closing a mental account with a gain is a pleasure, but it is a pleasure you pay for. The mistake is not one that an Econ would ever make, and experienced investors, who are using their System 2, are less susceptible to it than are novices.

A rational decision maker is interested only in the future consequences of current investments. Justifying earlier mistakes is not among the Econ's concerns. The decision to invest additional resources in a losing account, when better investments are available, is known as the *sunk-cost fallacy*, a costly mistake that is observed in decisions large and small. Driving into the blizzard because one paid for tickets is a sunk-cost error.

Imagine a company that has already spent $50 million on a project. The project is now behind schedule and the forecasts of its ultimate returns are less favorable than at the initial planning stage. An additional investment of $60 million is required to give the project a chance. An alternative proposal is to invest the same amount in a new project that currently looks likely to bring higher returns. What will the company do? All too often a company afflicted by sunk costs drives into the blizzard, throwing good money after bad rather than accepting the humiliation of closing the account of a costly failure. This situation is in the top-right cell of the fourfold pattern (page 317), where the choice is between a sure loss and an unfavorable gamble, which is often unwisely preferred.

The escalation of commitment to failing endeavors is a mistake from the perspective of the firm but not necessarily from the perspective of the executive who "owns" a floundering project. Canceling the project will leave a permanent stain on the executive's record, and his personal interests are perhaps best served by gambling further with the organization's resources in the hope of recouping the original investment—or at least in an attempt to postpone the day of reckoning. In the presence of sunk costs, the manager's incentives are misaligned with the objectives of the firm and its shareholders, a familiar type of what is known as the agency problem. Boards of directors are well aware of these conflicts and often replace a CEO who is encumbered by prior decisions and reluctant to cut losses. The members of the board do not necessarily believe that the new CEO is more competent than the one she replaces. They do know that she does not carry the same mental accounts and is therefore better able to ignore the sunk costs of past investments in evaluating current opportunities.

The sunk-cost fallacy keeps people for too long in poor jobs, unhappy marriages, and unpromising research projects. I have often observed young scientists struggling to salvage a doomed project when they would be better advised to drop it and start a new one. Fortunately, research suggests that at least in some contexts the fallacy can be overcome. The sunk-cost fallacy is identified and taught as a mistake in both economics and business courses, apparently to good effect: there is evidence that graduate students in these fields are more willing than others to walk away from a failing project.

REGRET

Regret is an emotion, and it is also a punishment that we administer to ourselves. The fear of regret is a factor in many of the decisions that people make ("Don't do this, you will regret it" is a common warning), and the actual experience of regret is familiar. The emotional state has been well described by two Dutch psychologists, who noted that regret is "accompanied by feelings that one should have known better, by a sinking feeling, by thoughts about the mistake one has made and the opportunities lost, by a tendency to kick oneself and to correct one's mistake, and by wanting to undo the event and to get a second chance." Intense regret is what you experience when you can most easily imagine yourself doing something other than what you did.

Regret is one of the counterfactual emotions that are triggered by the availability of alternatives to reality. After every plane crash there are special stories about passengers who "should not" have been on the plane—they got a seat at the last moment, they were transferred from another airline, they were supposed to fly a day earlier but had had to postpone. The common feature of these poignant stories is that they involve unusual events—and unusual events are easier than normal events to undo in imagination. Associative memory contains a representation of the normal world and its rules. An abnormal event attracts attention, and it also activates the idea of the event that would have been normal under the same circumstances.

To appreciate the link of regret to normality, consider the following scenario:

Mr. Brown almost never picks up hitchhikers. Yesterday he gave a man a ride and was robbed.

Mr. Smith frequently picks up hitchhikers. Yesterday he gave a man a ride and was robbed.

Who of the two will experience greater regret over the episode?

The results are not surprising: 88% of respondents said Mr. Brown, 12% said Mr. Smith.

Regret is not the same as blame. Other participants were asked this question about the same incident:

Who will be criticized most severely by others?

The results: Mr. Brown 23%, Mr. Smith 77%.

Regret and blame are both evoked by a comparison to a norm, but the relevant norms are different. The emotions experienced by Mr. Brown and Mr. Smith are dominated by what they usually do about hitchhikers. Taking a hitchhiker is an abnormal event for Mr. Brown, and most people therefore expect him to experience more intense regret. A judgmental observer, however, will compare both men to conventional norms of reasonable behavior and is likely to blame Mr. Smith for habitually taking unreasonable risks. We are tempted to say that Mr. Smith deserved his fate and that Mr. Brown was unlucky. But Mr. Brown is the one who is more likely to be kicking himself, because he acted out of character in this one instance.

Decision makers know that they are prone to regret, and the anticipation of that painful emotion plays a part in many decisions. Intuitions about regret are remarkably uniform and compelling, as the next example illustrates.

> Paul owns shares in company A. During the past year he considered switching to stock in company B, but he decided against it. He now learns that he would have been better off by $1,200 if he had switched to the stock of company B.

> George owned shares in company B. During the past year he switched to stock in company A. He now learns that he would have been better off by $1,200 if he had kept his stock in company B.
> Who feels greater regret?

The results are clear-cut: 8% of respondents say Paul, 92% say George.

This is curious, because the situations of the two investors are objectively identical. They both now own stock A and both would have been better off by the same amount if they owned stock B. The only difference is that George got to where he is by acting, whereas Paul got to the same place by failing to act. This short example illustrates a broad story: people expect to have stronger emotional reactions (including regret) to an outcome that is produced by action than to the same outcome when it is produced by inaction. This has been verified in the context of gambling: people expect to be happier if they gamble and win than if they refrain from gambling and get the same amount. The asymmetry is at least as strong for losses, and it applies to blame as well as to regret. The key is not the difference between commission and omission but the distinction between default options and actions that deviate from the default. When you deviate from the default, you can easily imagine the norm—and if the default is associated with bad consequences, the discrepancy between the two can be the source of painful emotions. The default option when you own a stock is not to sell it, but the default option when you meet your colleague in the morning is to greet him. Selling a stock and failing to greet your coworker are both departures from the default option and natural candidates for regret or blame.

In a compelling demonstration of the power of default options, participants played a computer simulation of blackjack. Some players were asked "Do you wish to hit?" while others were asked "Do you wish to stand?" Regardless of the question, saying yes was associated with much more regret than saying no if the outcome was bad! The question evidently suggests a default response, which is, "I don't have a strong wish to do it." It is the departure from the default that produces regret. Another situation in which action is the default is that of a coach whose team lost badly in their last game. The coach is expected to make a change of personnel or strategy, and a failure to do so will produce blame and regret.

The asymmetry in the risk of regret favors conventional and risk-averse choices. The bias appears in many contexts. Consumers who are reminded that they may feel regret as a result of their choices show an increased preference for conventional options, favoring brand names over generics. The behavior of the managers of financial funds as the year approaches its end also shows an effect of anticipated evaluation: they tend to clean up their portfolios of unconventional and otherwise questionable stocks. Even life-or-death decisions can be affected. Imagine a physician with a gravely ill patient. One treatment fits the normal standard of care; another is unusual. The physician has some reason to believe that the unconventional treatment improves the patient's chances, but the evidence is inconclusive. The physician who prescribes the unusual treatment faces a substantial risk of regret, blame, and perhaps litigation. In hindsight, it will be easier to imagine the normal choice; the abnormal choice will be easy to undo. True, a good outcome will contribute to the reputation of the physician who dared, but the potential benefit is smaller than the potential cost because success is generally a more normal outcome than is failure.

RESPONSIBILITY

Losses are weighted about twice as much as gains in several contexts: choice between gambles, the endowment effect, and reactions to price changes. The loss-aversion coefficient is much higher in some situations. In particular, you may be more loss averse for aspects of your life that are more important than money, such as health. Furthermore, your reluctance to "sell" important endowments increases dramatically when doing so might make you responsible for an awful outcome. Richard Thaler's early classic on consumer behavior included a compelling example, slightly modified in the following question:

> You have been exposed to a disease which if contracted leads to a quick and painless death within a week. The probability that you have the disease is 1/1,000. There is a vaccine that is effective only before any symptoms appear. What is the maximum you would be willing to pay for the vaccine?

Most people are willing to pay a significant but limited amount. Facing the possibility of death is unpleasant, but the risk is small and it seems unreasonable to ruin yourself to avoid it. Now consider a slight variation:

Volunteers are needed for research on the above disease. All that is required is that you expose yourself to a 1/1,000 chance of contracting the disease. What is the minimum you would ask to be paid in order to volunteer for this program? (You would not be allowed to purchase the vaccine.)

As you might expect, the fee that volunteers set is far higher than the price they were willing to pay for the vaccine. Thaler reported informally that a typical ratio is about 50:1. The extremely high selling price reflects two features of this problem. In the first place, you are not supposed to sell your health; the transaction is not considered legitimate and the reluctance to engage in it is expressed in a higher price. Perhaps most important, you will be responsible for the outcome if it is bad. You know that if you wake up one morning with symptoms indicating that you will soon be dead, you will feel more regret in the second case than in the first, because you could have rejected the idea of selling your health without even stopping to consider the price. You could have stayed with the default option and done nothing, and now this counterfactual will haunt you for the rest of your life.

The survey of parents' reactions to a potentially hazardous insecticide mentioned earlier also included a question about the willingness to accept increased risk. The respondents were told to imagine that they used an insecticide where the risk of inhalation and child poisoning was 15 per 10,000 bottles. A less expensive insecticide was available, for which the risk rose from 15 to 16 per 10,000 bottles. The parents were asked for the discount that would induce them to switch to the less expensive (and less safe) product. More than two-thirds of the parents in the survey responded that they would not purchase the new product at any price! They were evidently revolted by the very idea of trading the safety of their child for money. The minority who found a discount they could accept demanded an amount that was significantly higher than the amount they were willing to pay for a far larger improvement in the safety of the product.

Anyone can understand and sympathize with the reluctance of parents to trade even a minute increase of risk to their child for money. It is worth noting, however, that this attitude is incoherent and potentially damaging to the safety of those we wish to protect. Even the most loving parents have finite resources of time and money to protect their child (the keeping-my-child-safe mental account has a limited budget), and it seems reasonable to deploy these resources in a way that puts them to best use. Money that could be saved by accepting a minute increase in the risk of harm from a pesticide could certainly be put to better use in reducing the child's exposure to other harms, perhaps by purchasing a safer car seat or covers for electric sockets. The *taboo tradeoff* against accepting any increase in risk is not an efficient way to use the safety budget. In fact, the resistance may be motivated by a selfish fear of regret more than by a wish to optimize the child's safety. The what-if? thought that occurs to any parent who deliberately makes such a trade is an image of the regret and shame he or she would feel in the event the pesticide caused harm.

The intense aversion to trading increased risk for some other advantage plays out on a grand scale in the laws and regulations governing risk. This trend is especially strong in Europe, where the precautionary principle, which prohibits any action that might cause harm, is a widely accepted doctrine. In the regulatory context, the precautionary principle imposes the entire burden of proving safety on anyone who undertakes actions that might harm people or the environment. Multiple international bodies have specified that the absence of scientific evidence of potential damage is not sufficient justification for taking risks. As the jurist Cass Sunstein points out, the precautionary principle is costly, and when interpreted strictly it can be paralyzing. He mentions an impressive list of innovations that would not have passed the test, including "airplanes, air conditioning, antibiotics, automobiles, chlorine, the measles vaccine, open-heart surgery, radio, refrigeration, smallpox vaccine, and X-rays." The strong version of the precautionary principle is obviously untenable. But *enhanced loss aversion* is embedded in a strong and widely shared moral intuition; it originates in System 1. The dilemma between intensely loss-averse moral attitudes and efficient risk management does not have a simple and compelling solution.

We spend much of our day anticipating, and trying to avoid, the emotional pains we inflict on ourselves. How seriously should we take these intangible outcomes, the self-administered punishments (and occasional rewards) that we experience as we score our lives? Econs are not supposed to have them, and they are costly to Humans. They lead to actions that are detrimental to the wealth of individuals, to the soundness of policy, and to the welfare of society. But the emotions of regret and moral responsibility are real, and the fact that Econs do not have them may not be relevant.

Is it reasonable, in particular, to let your choices be influenced by the anticipation of regret? Susceptibility to regret, like susceptibility to fainting spells, is a fact of life to which one must adjust. If you are an investor, sufficiently rich and cautious at heart, you may be able to afford the luxury of a portfolio that minimizes the expectation of regret even if it does not maximize the accrual of wealth.

You can also take precautions that will inoculate you against regret. Perhaps the most useful is to be explicit about the anticipation of regret. If you can remember when things go badly that you considered the possibility of regret carefully before deciding, you are likely to experience less of it. You should also know that regret and hindsight bias will come together, so anything you can do to preclude hindsight is likely to be helpful. My personal hindsight-avoiding policy is to be either very thorough or completely casual when making a decision with long-term consequences. Hindsight is worse when you think a little, just enough to tell yourself later, "I almost made a better choice."

Daniel Gilbert and his colleagues provocatively claim that people generally anticipate more regret than they will actually experience, because they underestimate the efficacy of the psychological defenses they will deploy— which they label the "psychological immune system." Their recommendation is that you should not put too much weight on regret; even if you have some, it will hurt less than you now think.

SPEAKING OF KEEPING SCORE

"He has separate mental accounts for cash and credit purchases. I constantly remind him that money is money."

"We are hanging on to that stock just to avoid closing our mental account at a loss. It's the disposition effect."

"We discovered an excellent dish at that restaurant and we never try anything else, to avoid regret."

"The salesperson showed me the most expensive car seat and said it was the safest, and I could not bring myself to buy the cheaper model. It felt like a taboo tradeoff."

33

REVERSALS

You have the task of setting compensation for victims of violent crimes. You consider the case of a man who lost the use of his right arm as a result of a gunshot wound. He was shot when he walked in on a robbery occurring in a convenience store in his neighborhood.

Two stores were located near the victim's home, one of which he frequented more regularly than the other. Consider two scenarios:
(i)   The burglary happened in the man's regular store.
(ii) The man's regular store was closed for a funeral, so he did his shopping in the other store, where he was shot.

Should the store in which the man was shot make a difference to his compensation?

You made your judgment in joint evaluation, where you consider two scenarios at the same time and make a comparison. You can apply a rule. If you think that the second scenario deserves higher compensation, you should assign it a higher dollar value.

There is almost universal agreement on the answer: compensation should be the same in both situations. The compensation is for the crippling injury, so why should the location in which it occurred make any difference? The joint evaluation of the two scenarios gave you a chance to examine your moral principles about the factors that are relevant to victim compensation. For most people, location is not one of these factors. As in other situations that require an explicit comparison, thinking was slow and System 2 was involved.

The psychologists Dale Miller and Cathy McFarland, who originally designed the two scenarios, presented them to different people for single evaluation. In their between-subjects experiment, each participant saw only one scenario and assigned a dollar value to it. They found, as you surely guessed, that the victim was awarded a much larger sum if he was shot in a store he rarely visited than if he was shot in his regular store. Poignancy (a close cousin of regret) is a counterfactual feeling, which is evoked because the thought "if only he had shopped at his regular store . . ." comes readily to mind. The familiar System 1 mechanisms of substitution and intensity matching translate the strength of the emotional reaction to the story onto a monetary scale, creating a large difference in dollar awards.

The comparison of the two experiments reveals a sharp contrast. Almost everyone who sees both scenarios together (within-subject) endorses the principle that poignancy is not a legitimate consideration. Unfortunately, the principle becomes relevant only when the two scenarios are seen together, and this is not how life usually works. We normally experience life in the between-subjects mode, in which contrasting alternatives that might change your mind are absent, and of course WYSIATI. As a consequence, the beliefs that you endorse when you reflect about morality do not necessarily govern your emotional reactions, and the moral intuitions that come to your mind in different situations are not internally consistent.

The discrepancy between single and joint evaluation of the burglary scenario belongs to a broad family of reversals of judgment and choice. The first preference reversals were discovered in the early 1970s, and many reversals of other kinds were reported over the years.

CHALLENGING ECONOMICS

Preference reversals have an important place in the history of the conversation between psychologists and economists. The reversals that attracted attention were reported by Sarah Lichtenstein and Paul Slovic, two psychologists who had done their graduate work at the University of Michigan at the same time as Amos. They conducted an experiment on preferences between bets, which I show in a slightly simplified version.

You are offered a choice between two bets, which are to be played on a roulette wheel with 36 sectors.

Bet A: 11/36 to win $160, 25/36 to lose $15

Bet B: 35/36 to win $40, 1/36 to lose $10

You are asked to choose between a safe bet and a riskier one: an almost certain win of a modest amount, or a small chance to win a substantially larger amount and a high probability of losing. Safety prevails, and B is clearly the more popular choice.

Now consider each bet separately: If you owned that bet, what is the lowest price at which you would sell it? Remember that you are not negotiating with anyone—your task is to determine the lowest price at which you would truly be willing to give up the bet. Try it. You may find that the prize that can be won is salient in this task, and that your evaluation of what the bet is worth is anchored on that value. The results support this conjecture, and the selling price is higher for bet A than for bet B. This is a preference reversal: people choose B over A, but if they imagine owning only one of them, they set a higher value on A than on B. As in the burglary scenarios, the preference reversal occurs because joint evaluation focuses attention on an aspect of the situation—the fact that bet A is much less safe than bet B—which was less salient in single evaluation. The features that caused the difference between the judgments of the options in single evaluation—the poignancy of the victim being in the wrong grocery store and the anchoring on the prize—are suppressed or irrelevant when the options are evaluated jointly. The emotional reactions of System 1 are much more likely to determine single evaluation; the comparison that occurs in joint evaluation always involves a more careful and effortful assessment, which calls for System 2.

The preference reversal can be confirmed in a within-subject experiment, in which subjects set prices on both sets as part of a long list, and also choose between them. Participants are unaware of the inconsistency, and their reactions when confronted with it can be entertaining. A 1968 interview of a participant in the experiment, conducted by Sarah Lichtenstein, is an enduring classic of the field. The experimenter talks at length with a bewildered participant, who chooses one bet over another but is then willing to pay money to exchange the item he just chose for the one he just rejected, and goes through the cycle repeatedly.

Rational Econs would surely not be susceptible to preference reversals, and the phenomenon was therefore a challenge to the rational-agent model and to the economic theory that is built on this model. The challenge could have been ignored, but it was not. A few years after the preference reversals were reported, two respected economists, David Grether and Charles Plott, published an article in the prestigious *American Economic Review*, in which they reported their own studies of the phenomenon that Lichtenstein and Slovic had described. This was probably the first finding by experimental psychologists that ever attracted the attention of economists. The introductory paragraph of Grether and Plott's article was unusually dramatic for a scholarly paper, and their intent was clear: "A body of data and theory has been developing within psychology which should be of interest to economists. Taken at face value the data are simply inconsistent with preference theory and have broad implications about research priorities within economics. . . . This paper reports the results of a series of experiments designed to discredit the psychologists' works as applied to economics."

Grether and Plott listed thirteen theories that could explain the original findings and reported carefully designed experiments that tested these theories. One of their hypotheses, which—needless to say—psychologists found patronizing, was that the results were due to the experiment being carried out by psychologists! Eventually, only one hypothesis was left standing: the psychologists were right. Grether and Plott acknowledged that this hypothesis is the least satisfactory from the point of view of standard preference theory, because "it allows individual choice to depend on the context in which the choices are made"—a clear violation of the coherence doctrine.

You might think that this surprising outcome would cause much anguished soul-searching among economists, as a basic assumption of their theory had been successfully challenged. But this is not the way things work in social science, including both psychology and economics. Theoretical beliefs are robust, and it takes much more than one embarrassing finding for established theories to be seriously questioned. In fact, Grether and Plott's admirably forthright report had little direct effect on the convictions of economists, probably including Grether and Plott. It contributed, however, to a greater willingness of the community of economists to take psychological research seriously and thereby greatly advanced the conversation across the boundaries of the disciplines.

CATEGORIES

"How tall is John?" If John is 5' tall, your answer will depend on his age; he is very tall if he is 6 years old, very short if he is 16. Your System 1 automatically retrieves the relevant norm, and the meaning of the scale of tallness is adjusted automatically. You are also able to match intensities across categories and answer the question, "How expensive is a restaurant meal that matches John's height?" Your answer will depend on John's age: a much less expensive meal if he is 16 than if he is 6.

But now look at this:

John is 6. He is 5′ tall.
Jim is 16. He is 5′1″ tall.

In single evaluations, everyone will agree that John is very tall and Jim is not, because they are compared to different norms. If you are asked a directly comparative question, "Is John as tall as Jim?" you will answer that he is not. There is no surprise here and little ambiguity. In other situations, however, the process by which objects and events recruit their own context of comparison can lead to incoherent choices on serious matters.

You should not form the impression that single and joint evaluations are always inconsistent, or that judgments are completely chaotic. Our world is broken into categories for which we have norms, such as six-year-old boys or tables. Judgments and preferences are coherent within categories but potentially incoherent when the objects that are evaluated belong to different categories. For an example, answer the following three questions:

Which do you like more, apples or peaches?
Which do you like more, steak or stew?
Which do you like more, apples or steak?

The first and the second questions refer to items that belong to the same category, and you know immediately which you like more. Furthermore, you would have recovered the same ranking from single evaluation ("How much do you like apples?" and "How much do you like peaches?") because apples and peaches both evoke fruit. There will be no preference reversal because different fruits are compared to the same norm and implicitly compared to each other in single as well as in joint evaluation. In contrast to the within-category questions, there is no stable answer for the comparison of apples and steak. Unlike apples and peaches, apples and steak are not natural substitutes and they do not fill the same need. You sometimes want steak and sometimes an apple, but you rarely say that either one will do just as well as the other.

Imagine receiving an e-mail from an organization that you generally trust, requesting a contribution to a cause:

> Dolphins in many breeding locations are threatened by pollution, which is expected to result in a decline of the dolphin population. A special fund supported by private contributions has been set up to provide pollution-free breeding locations for dolphins.

What associations did this question evoke? Whether or not you were fully aware of them, ideas and memories of related causes came to your mind. Projects intended to preserve endangered species were especially likely to be recalled. Evaluation on the GOOD–BAD dimension is an automatic operation of System 1, and you formed a crude impression of the ranking of the dolphin among the species that came to mind. The dolphin is much more charming than, say, ferrets, snails, or carp—it has a highly favorable rank in the set of species to which it is spontaneously compared.

The question you must answer is not whether you like dolphins more than carp; you have been asked to come up with a dollar value. Of course, you may know from the experience of previous solicitations that you never respond to requests of this kind. For a few minutes, imagine yourself as someone who does contribute to such appeals.

Like many other difficult questions, the assessment of dollar value can be solved by substitution and intensity matching. The dollar question is difficult, but an easier question is readily available. Because you like dolphins, you will probably feel that saving them is a good cause. The next step, which is also automatic, generates a dollar number by translating the intensity of your liking of dolphins onto a scale of contributions. You have a sense of your scale of previous contributions to environmental causes, which may differ from the scale of your contributions to politics or to the football team of your alma mater. You know what amount would be a "very large" contribution for you and what amounts are "large," "modest," and "small." You also have scales for your attitude to species (from "like very much" to "not at all"). You are therefore able to translate your attitude onto the dollar scale, moving automatically from "like a lot" to "fairly large contribution" and from there to a number of dollars.

On another occasion, you are approached with a different appeal:

> Farmworkers, who are exposed to the sun for many hours, have a higher rate of skin cancer than the general population. Frequent medical check-ups can

reduce the risk. A fund will be set up to support medical check-ups for threatened groups.

Is this an urgent problem? Which category did it evoke as a norm when you assessed urgency? If you automatically categorized the problem as a public-health issue, you probably found that the threat of skin cancer in farmwork-ers does not rank very high among these issues—almost certainly lower than the rank of dolphins among endangered species. As you translated your impression of the relative importance of the skin cancer issue into a dollar amount, you might well have come up with a smaller contribution than you offered to protect an endearing animal. In experiments, the dol-phins attracted somewhat larger contributions in single evaluation than did the farmworkers.

Next, consider the two causes in joint evaluation. Which of the two, dolphins or farmworkers, deserves a larger dollar contribution? Joint eval-uation highlights a feature that was not noticeable in single evaluation but is recognized as decisive when detected: farmers are human, dolphins are not. You knew that, of course, but it was not relevant to the judgment that you made in single evaluation. The fact that dolphins are not human did not arise because all the issues that were activated in your memory shared that feature. The fact that farmworkers are human did not come to mind because all public-health issues involve humans. The narrow framing of single evaluation allowed dolphins to have a higher intensity score, leading to a high rate of contributions by intensity matching. Joint evaluation changes the representation of the issues: the "human vs. animal" feature becomes salient only when the two are seen together. In joint evaluation people show a solid preference for the farmworkers and a willingness to contribute substantially more to their welfare than to the protection of a likable non-human species. Here again, as in the cases of the bets and the burglary shooting, the judgments made in single and in joint evaluation will not be consistent.

Christopher Hsee, of the University of Chicago, has contributed the fol-lowing example of preference reversal, among many others of the same type. The objects to be evaluated are secondhand music dictionaries.

	Dictionary A	Dictionary B
Year of publication	1993	1993
Number of entries	10,000	20,000
Condition	Like new	Cover torn, otherwise like new

When the dictionaries are presented in single evaluation, dictionary A is valued more highly, but of course the preference changes in joint evaluation. The result illustrates Hsee's *evaluability hypothesis*: The number of entries is given no weight in single evaluation, because the numbers are not "evaluable" on their own. In joint evaluation, in contrast, it is immediately obvious that dictionary B is superior on this attribute, and it is also apparent that the number of entries is far more important than the condition of the cover.

UNJUST REVERSALS

There is good reason to believe that the administration of justice is infected by predictable incoherence in several domains. The evidence is drawn in part from experiments, including studies of mock juries, and in part from observation of patterns in legislation, regulation, and litigation.

In one experiment, mock jurors recruited from jury rolls in Texas were asked to assess punitive damages in several civil cases. The cases came in pairs, each consisting of one claim for physical injury and one for financial loss. The mock jurors first assessed one of the scenarios and then they were shown the case with which it was paired and were asked to compare the two. The following are summaries of one pair of cases:

Case 1: A child suffered moderate burns when his pajamas caught fire as he was playing with matches. The firm that produced the pajamas had not made them adequately fire resistant.

Case 2: The unscrupulous dealings of a bank caused another bank a loss of $10 million.

Half of the participants judged case 1 first (in single evaluation) before comparing the two cases in joint evaluation. The sequence was reversed for the other participants. In single evaluation, the jurors awarded higher punitive damages to the defrauded bank than to the burned child, presumably because the size of the financial loss provided a high anchor.

When the cases were considered together, however, sympathy for the individual victim prevailed over the anchoring effect and the jurors increased the award to the child to surpass the award to the bank. Averaging over several such pairs of cases, awards to victims of personal injury were more than twice as large in joint than in single evaluation. The jurors who saw the case of the burned child on its own made an offer that matched the intensity of their feelings. They could not anticipate that the award to the child would appear inadequate in the context of a large award to a financial institution. In joint evaluation, the punitive award to the bank remained anchored on the loss it had sustained, but the award to the burned child increased, reflecting the outrage evoked by negligence that causes injury to a child.

As we have seen, rationality is generally served by broader and more comprehensive frames, and joint evaluation is obviously broader than single evaluation. Of course, you should be wary of joint evaluation when someone who controls what you see has a vested interest in what you choose. Salespeople quickly learn that manipulation of the context in which customers see a good can profoundly influence preferences. Except for such cases of deliberate manipulation, there is a presumption that the comparative judgment, which necessarily involves System 2, is more likely to be stable than single evaluations, which often reflect the intensity of emotional responses of System 1. We would expect that any institution that wishes to elicit thoughtful judgments would seek to provide the judges with a broad context for the assessments of individual cases. I was surprised to learn from Cass Sunstein that jurors who are to assess punitive damages are explicitly prohibited from considering other cases. The legal system, contrary to psychological common sense, favors single evaluation.

In another study of incoherence in the legal system, Sunstein compared the administrative punishments that can be imposed by different U.S. government agencies including the Occupational Safety and Health Administration and the Environmental Protection Agency. He concluded that "within categories, penalties seem extremely sensible, at least in the sense that the more serious harms are punished more severely. For occupational safety and health violations, the largest penalties are for repeated violations, the next largest for violations that are both willful and serious, and the least serious for failures to engage in the requisite record-keeping." It should not surprise you, however, that the size of penalties varied greatly across agencies, in a manner that reflected politics and history more than any global concern for fairness. The fine for a "serious violation" of the regulations concerning worker safety is capped at $7,000, while a violation of the Wild Bird Conservation Act can result in a fine of up to $25,000. The fines are sensible in the context of other penalties set by each agency, but they appear odd when compared to each other. As in the other examples in this chapter, you can see the absurdity only when the two cases are viewed together in a broad frame. The system of administrative penalties is coherent within agencies but incoherent globally.

SPEAKING OF REVERSALS

"The BTU units meant nothing to me until I saw how much air-conditioning units vary. Joint evaluation was essential."

"You say this was an outstanding speech because you compared it to her other speeches. Compared to others, she was still inferior."

"It is often the case that when you broaden the frame, you reach more reasonable decisions."

"When you see cases in isolation, you are likely to be guided by an emotional reaction of System 1."

34

FRAMES AND REALITY

Italy and France competed in the 2006 final of the World Cup. The next two sentences both describe the outcome: "Italy won." "France lost." Do those statements have the same meaning? The answer depends entirely on what you mean by *meaning*.

For the purpose of logical reasoning, the two descriptions of the outcome of the match are interchangeable because they designate the same state of the world. As philosophers say, their truth conditions are identical: if one of these sentences is true, then the other is true as well. This is how Econs understand things. Their beliefs and preferences are reality-bound. In particular, the objects of their choices are states of the world, which are not affected by the words chosen to describe them.

There is another sense of *meaning*, in which "Italy won" and "France lost" do not have the same meaning at all. In this sense, the meaning of a sentence is what happens in your associative machinery while you understand it. The two sentences evoke markedly different associations. "Italy won" evokes thoughts of the Italian team and what it did to win. "France lost" evokes thoughts of the French team and what it did that caused it to lose, including the memorable head butt of an Italian player by the French star Zidane. In terms of the associations they bring to mind—how System 1 reacts to them—the two sentences really "mean" different things. The fact that logically equivalent statements evoke different reactions makes it impossible for Humans to be as reliably rational as Econs.

EMOTIONAL FRAMING

Amos and I applied the label of framing effects to the unjustified influences of formulation on beliefs and preferences. This is one of the examples we used:

> Would you accept a gamble that offers a 10% chance to win $95 and a 90% chance to lose $5?

> Would you pay $5 to participate in a lottery that offers a 10% chance to win $100 and a 90% chance to win nothing?

First, take a moment to convince yourself that the two problems are identical. In both of them you must decide whether to accept an uncertain prospect that will leave you either richer by $95 or poorer by $5. Someone whose preferences are reality-bound would give the same answer to both questions, but such individuals are rare. In fact, one version attracts many more positive answers: the second. A bad outcome is much more acceptable if it is framed as the cost of a lottery ticket that did not win than if it is simply described as losing a gamble. We should not be surprised: *losses* evokes stronger negative feelings than *costs*. Choices are not reality-bound because System 1 is not reality-bound.

The problem we constructed was influenced by what we had learned from Richard Thaler, who told us that when he was a graduate student he had pinned on his board a card that said COSTS ARE NOT LOSSES. In his early essay on consumer behavior, Thaler described the debate about whether gas stations would be allowed to charge different prices for purchases paid with cash or on credit. The credit-card lobby pushed hard to make differential pricing illegal, but it had a fallback position: the difference, if allowed, would be labeled a cash discount, not a credit surcharge. Their psychology was sound: people will more readily forgo a discount than pay a surcharge. The two may be economically equivalent, but they are not emotionally equivalent.

In an elegant experiment, a team of neuroscientists at University College London combined a study of framing effects with recordings of activity in different areas of the brain. In order to provide reliable measures of the brain response, the experiment consisted of many trials. Figure 14 illustrates the two stages of one of these trials.

First, the subject is asked to imagine that she received an amount of money, in this example £50.

The subject is then asked to choose between a sure outcome and a

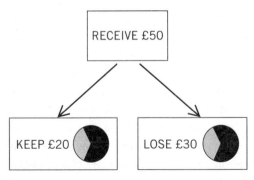

Figure 14

gamble on a wheel of chance. If the wheel stops on white she "receives" the entire amount; if it stops on black she gets nothing. The sure outcome is simply the expected value of the gamble, in this case a gain of £20.

As shown, the same sure outcome can be framed in two different ways: as KEEP £20 or as LOSE £30. The objective outcomes are precisely identical in the two frames, and a reality-bound Econ would respond to both in the same way—selecting either the sure thing or the gamble regardless of the frame—but we already know that the Human mind is not bound to reality. Tendencies to approach or avoid are evoked by the words, and we expect System 1 to be biased in favor of the sure option when it is designated as KEEP and against that same option when it is designated as LOSE.

The experiment consisted of many trials, and each participant encountered several choice problems in both the KEEP and the LOSE frames. As expected, every one of the 20 subjects showed a framing effect: they were more likely to choose the sure thing in the KEEP frame and more likely to accept the gamble in the LOSE frame. But the subjects were not all alike. Some were highly susceptible to the framing of the problem. Others mostly made the same choice regardless of the frame—as a reality-bound individual should do. The authors ranked the 20 subjects accordingly and gave the ranking a striking label: the rationality index.

The activity of the brain was recorded as the subjects made each decision. Later, the trials were separated into two categories:

1. Trials on which the subject's choice conformed to the frame
   - preferred the sure thing in the KEEP version
   - preferred the gamble in the LOSS version
2. Trials in which the choice did not conform to the frame.

The remarkable results illustrate the potential of the new discipline of neu-roeconomics—the study of what a person's brain does while he makes deci-sions. Neuroscientists have run thousands of such experiments, and they have learned to expect particular regions of the brain to "light up"—indicating increased flow of oxygen, which suggests heightened neural activity—depending on the nature of the task. Different regions are active when the individual attends to a visual object, imagines kicking a ball, recognizes a face, or thinks of a house. Other regions light up when the individual is emotionally aroused, is in conflict, or concentrates on solving a problem. Although neuroscientists carefully avoid the language of "this part of the brain does such and such . . . ," they have learned a great deal about the "personalities" of different brain regions, and the contribution of analyses of brain activity to psychological interpretation has greatly im-proved. The framing study yielded three main findings:

- A region that is commonly associated with emotional arousal (the amygdala) was most likely to be active when subjects' choices con-formed to the frame. This is just as we would expect if the emotion-ally loaded words KEEP and LOSE produce an immediate tendency to approach the sure thing (when it is framed as a gain) or avoid it (when it is framed as a loss). The amygdala is accessed very rapidly by emotional stimuli—and it is a likely suspect for involvement in System 1.
- A brain region known to be associated with conflict and self-control (the anterior cingulate) was more active when subjects did not do what comes naturally—when they chose the sure thing in spite of its being labeled LOSE. Resisting the inclination of System 1 apparently involves conflict.
- The most "rational" subjects—those who were the least susceptible to framing effects—showed enhanced activity in a frontal area of the brain that is implicated in combining emotion and reasoning to guide decisions. Remarkably, the "rational" individuals were not those who showed the strongest neural evidence of conflict. It appears that these elite participants were (often, not always) reality-bound with little conflict.

By joining observations of actual choices with a mapping of neural activity, this study provides a good illustration of how the emotion evoked by a word can "leak" into the final choice.

An experiment that Amos carried out with colleagues at Harvard Medical School is the classic example of emotional framing. Physician participants were given statistics about the outcomes of two treatments for lung cancer: surgery and radiation. The five-year survival rates clearly favor surgery, but in the short term surgery is riskier than radiation. Half the participants read statistics about survival rates, the others received the same information in terms of mortality rates. The two descriptions of the short-term outcomes of surgery were:

> The one-month survival rate is 90%.
> There is 10% mortality in the first month.

You already know the results: surgery was much more popular in the former frame (84% of physicians chose it) than in the latter (where 50% favored radiation). The logical equivalence of the two descriptions is transparent, and a reality-bound decision maker would make the same choice regardless of which version she saw. But System 1, as we have gotten to know it, is rarely indifferent to emotional words: mortality is bad, survival is good, and 90% survival sounds encouraging whereas 10% mortality is frightening. An important finding of the study is that physicians were just as susceptible to the framing effect as medically unsophisticated people (hospital patients and graduate students in a business school). Medical training is, evidently, no defense against the power of framing.

The KEEP–LOSE study and the survival–mortality experiment differed in one important respect. The participants in the brain-imaging study had many trials in which they encountered the different frames. They had an opportunity to recognize the distracting effects of the frames and to simplify their task by adopting a common frame, perhaps by translating the LOSE amount into its KEEP equivalent. It would take an intelligent person (and an alert System 2) to learn to do this, and the few participants who managed the feat were probably among the "rational" agents that the experimenters identified. In contrast, the physicians who read the statistics about the two therapies in the survival frame had no reason to suspect that they would have made a different choice if they had heard the same statistics framed in terms of mortality. Reframing is effortful and System 2 is normally lazy. Unless there is an obvious reason to do otherwise, most of us passively accept decision problems as they are framed and therefore rarely have an opportunity to discover the extent to which our preferences are *frame-bound* rather than *reality-bound*.

EMPTY INTUITIONS

Amos and I introduced our discussion of framing by an example that has become known as the "Asian disease problem":

> Imagine that the United States is preparing for the outbreak of an unusual Asian disease, which is expected to kill 600 people. Two alternative programs to combat the disease have been proposed. Assume that the exact scientific estimates of the consequences of the programs are as follows:
>
> If program A is adopted, 200 people will be saved.
>
> If program B is adopted, there is a one-third probability that 600 people will be saved and a two-thirds probability that no people will be saved.

A substantial majority of respondents choose program A: they prefer the certain option over the gamble.

The outcomes of the programs are framed differently in a second version:

> If program A' is adopted, 400 people will die.
>
> If program B' is adopted, there is a one-third probability that nobody will die and a two-thirds probability that 600 people will die.

Look closely and compare the two versions: the consequences of programs A and A' are identical; so are the consequences of programs B and B'. In the second frame, however, a large majority of people choose the gamble.

The different choices in the two frames fit prospect theory, in which choices between gambles and sure things are resolved differently, depending on whether the outcomes are good or bad. Decision makers tend to prefer the sure thing over the gamble (they are risk averse) when the outcomes are good. They tend to reject the sure thing and accept the gamble (they are risk seeking) when both outcomes are negative. These conclusions were well established for choices about gambles and sure things in the domain of money. The disease problem shows that the same rule applies when the outcomes are measured in lives saved or lost. In this context, as well, the framing experiment reveals that risk-averse and risk-seeking preferences are not reality-bound. Preferences between the same objective outcomes reverse with different formulations.

An experience that Amos shared with me adds a grim note to the story.

Amos was invited to give a speech to a group of public-health profession-als—the people who make decisions about vaccines and other programs. He took the opportunity to present them with the Asian disease problem: half saw the "lives-saved" version, the others answered the "lives-lost" ques-tion. Like other people, these professionals were susceptible to the framing effects. It is somewhat worrying that the officials who make decisions that affect everyone's health can be swayed by such a superficial manipulation—but we must get used to the idea that even important decisions are influ-enced, if not governed, by System 1.

Even more troubling is what happens when people are confronted with their inconsistency: "You chose to save 200 lives for sure in one formu-lation and you chose to gamble rather than accept 400 deaths in the other. Now that you know these choices were inconsistent, how do you de-cide?" The answer is usually embarrassed silence. The intuitions that deter-mined the original choice came from System 1 and had no more moral basis than did the preference for keeping £20 or the aversion to losing £30. Saving lives with certainty is good, deaths are bad. Most people find that their System 2 has no moral intuitions of its own to answer the question.

I am grateful to the great economist Thomas Schelling for my favorite example of a framing effect, which he described in his book *Choice and Consequence*. Schelling's book was written before our work on framing was published, and framing was not his main concern. He reported on his expe-rience teaching a class at the Kennedy School at Harvard, in which the topic was child exemptions in the tax code. Schelling told his students that a stan-dard exemption is allowed for each child, and that the amount of the ex-emption is independent of the taxpayer's income. He asked their opinion of the following proposition:

Should the child exemption be larger for the rich than for the poor?

Your own intuitions are very likely the same as those of Schelling's students: they found the idea of favoring the rich by a larger exemption completely unacceptable.

Schelling then pointed out that the tax law is arbitrary. It assumes a childless family as the default case and reduces the tax by the amount of the exemption for each child. The tax law could of course be rewritten with another default case: a family with two children. In this formulation, families with fewer than the default number of children would pay a surcharge. Schelling now asked his students to report their view of another proposition:

Should the childless poor pay as large a surcharge as the childless rich?

Here again you probably agree with the students' reaction to this idea, which they rejected with as much vehemence as the first. But Schelling showed his class that they could not logically reject both proposals. Set the two formulations next to each other. The difference between the tax due by a childless family and by a family with two children is described as a reduction of tax in the first version and as an increase in the second. If in the first version you want the poor to receive the same (or greater) benefit as the rich for having children, then you must want the poor to pay at least the same penalty as the rich for being childless.

We can recognize System 1 at work. It delivers an immediate response to any question about rich and poor: when in doubt, favor the poor. The surprising aspect of Schelling's problem is that this apparently simple moral rule does not work reliably. It generates contradictory answers to the same problem, depending on how that problem is framed. And of course you already know the question that comes next. Now that you have seen that your reactions to the problem are influenced by the frame, what is your answer to the question: How should the tax code treat the children of the rich and the poor?

Here again, you will probably find yourself dumbfounded. You have moral intuitions about differences between the rich and the poor, but these intuitions depend on an arbitrary reference point, and they are not about the real problem. This problem—the question about actual states of the world—is how much tax individual families should pay, how to fill the cells in the matrix of the tax code. You have no compelling moral intuitions to guide you in solving that problem. Your moral feelings are attached to frames, to descriptions of reality rather than to reality itself. The message about the nature of framing is stark: framing should not be viewed as an intervention that masks or distorts an underlying preference. At least in this instance—and also in the problems of the Asian disease and of surgery versus radiation for lung cancer—there is no underlying preference that is masked or distorted by the frame. Our preferences are about framed problems, and our moral intuitions are about descriptions, not about substance.

GOOD FRAMES

Not all frames are equal, and some frames are clearly better than alternative ways to describe (or to think about) the same thing. Consider the following pair of problems:

> A woman has bought two $80 tickets to the theater. When she arrives at the theater, she opens her wallet and discovers that the tickets are missing. Will she buy two more tickets to see the play?

> A woman goes to the theater, intending to buy two tickets that cost $80 each. She arrives at the theater, opens her wallet, and discovers to her dismay that the $160 with which she was going to make the purchase is missing. She could use her credit card. Will she buy the tickets?

Respondents who see only one version of this problem reach different conclusions, depending on the frame. Most believe that the woman in the first story will go home without seeing the show if she has lost tickets, and most believe that she will charge tickets for the show if she has lost money.

The explanation should already be familiar—this problem involves mental accounting and the sunk-cost fallacy. The different frames evoke different mental accounts, and the significance of the loss depends on the account to which it is posted. When tickets to a particular show are lost, it is natural to post them to the account associated with that play. The cost appears to have doubled and may now be more than the experience is worth. In contrast, a loss of cash is charged to a "general revenue" account— the theater patron is slightly poorer than she had thought she was, and the question she is likely to ask herself is whether the small reduction in her disposable wealth will change her decision about paying for tickets. Most respondents thought it would not.

The version in which cash was lost leads to more reasonable decisions. It is a better frame because the loss, even if tickets were lost, is "sunk," and sunk costs should be ignored. History is irrelevant and the only issue that matters is the set of options the theater patron has now, and their likely consequences. Whatever she lost, the relevant fact is that she is less wealthy than she was before she opened her wallet. If the person who lost tickets were to ask for my advice, this is what I would say: "Would you have bought tickets if you had lost the equivalent amount of cash? If yes, go ahead and buy new ones." Broader frames and inclusive accounts generally lead to more rational decisions.

In the next example, two alternative frames evoke different mathematical intuitions, and one is much superior to the other. In an article titled "The MPG Illusion," which appeared in *Science* magazine in 2008, the psychologists Richard Larrick and Jack Soll identified a case in which passive acceptance of a misleading frame has substantial costs and serious policy consequences. Most car buyers list gas mileage as one of the factors that determine their choice; they know that high-mileage cars have lower operating costs. But the frame that has traditionally been used in the United States—miles per gallon—provides very poor guidance to the decisions of both individuals and policy makers. Consider two car owners who seek to reduce their costs:

> Adam switches from a gas-guzzler of 12 mpg to a slightly less voracious guzzler that runs at 14 mpg.

> The environmentally virtuous Beth switches from a 30 mpg car to one that runs at 40 mpg.

Suppose both drivers travel equal distances over a year. Who will save more gas by switching? You almost certainly share the widespread intuition that Beth's action is more significant than Adam's: she reduced mpg by 10 miles rather than 2, and by a third (from 30 to 40) rather than a sixth (from 12 to 14). Now engage your System 2 and work it out. If the two car owners both drive 10,000 miles, Adam will reduce his consumption from a scandalous 833 gallons to a still shocking 714 gallons, for a saving of 119 gallons. Beth's use of fuel will drop from 333 gallons to 250, saving only 83 gallons. The mpg frame is wrong, and it should be replaced by the gallons-per-mile frame (or liters-per-100 kilometers, which is used in most other countries). As Larrick and Soll point out, the misleading intuitions fostered by the mpg frame are likely to mislead policy makers as well as car buyers.

Under President Obama, Cass Sunstein served as administrator of the Office of Information and Regulatory Affairs. With Richard Thaler, Sunstein coauthored *Nudge*, which is the basic manual for applying behavioral economics to policy. It was no accident that the "fuel economy and environment" sticker that will be displayed on every new car starting in 2013 will for the first time in the United States include the gallons-per-mile information. Unfortunately, the correct formulation will be in small print, along with the more familiar mpg information in large print, but the move is in the right direction. The five-year interval between the publication of "The MPG Illusion" and the implementation of a partial correction is probably a speed record for a significant application of psychological science to public policy.

A directive about organ donation in case of accidental death is noted on an individual's driver license in many countries. The formulation of that directive is another case in which one frame is clearly superior to the other. Few people would argue that the decision of whether or not to donate one's organs is unimportant, but there is strong evidence that most people make their choice thoughtlessly. The evidence comes from a comparison of the rate of organ donation in European countries, which reveals startling differences between neighboring and culturally similar countries. An article published in 2003 noted that the rate of organ donation was close to 100% in Austria but only 12% in Germany, 86% in Sweden but only 4% in Denmark.

These enormous differences are a framing effect, which is caused by the format of the critical question. The high-donation countries have an opt-out form, where individuals who wish not to donate must check an appropriate box. Unless they take this simple action, they are considered willing donors. The low-contribution countries have an opt-in form: you must check a box to become a donor. That is all. The best single predictor of whether or not people will donate their organs is the designation of the default option that will be adopted without having to check a box.

Unlike other framing effects that have been traced to features of System 1, the organ donation effect is best explained by the laziness of System 2. People will check the box if they have already decided what they wish to do. If they are unprepared for the question, they have to make the effort of thinking whether they want to check the box. I imagine an organ donation form in which people are required to solve a mathematical problem in the box that corresponds to their decision. One of the boxes contains the problem $2 + 2 = ?$ The problem in the other box is $13 \times 37 = ?$ The rate of donations would surely be swayed.

When the role of formulation is acknowledged, a policy question arises: Which formulation should be adopted? In this case, the answer is straightforward. If you believe that a large supply of donated organs is good for society, you will not be neutral between a formulation that yields almost 100% donations and another formulation that elicits donations from 4% of drivers.

As we have seen again and again, an important choice is controlled by an utterly inconsequential feature of the situation. This is embarrassing—it is not how we would wish to make important decisions. Furthermore, it is not how we experience the workings of our mind, but the evidence for these cognitive illusions is undeniable.

Count that as a point against the rational-agent theory. A theory that is worthy of the name asserts that certain events are impossible—they will not happen if the theory is true. When an "impossible" event is observed, the theory is falsified. Theories can survive for a long time after conclusive evidence falsifies them, and the rational-agent model certainly survived the evidence we have seen, and much other evidence as well.

The case of organ donation shows that the debate about human rationality can have a large effect in the real world. A significant difference between believers in the rational-agent model and the skeptics who question it is that the believers simply take it for granted that the formulation of a choice cannot determine preferences on significant problems. They will not even be interested in investigating the problem—and so we are often left with inferior outcomes.

Skeptics about rationality are not surprised. They are trained to be sensitive to the power of inconsequential factors as determinants of preference—my hope is that readers of this book have acquired this sensitivity.

SPEAKING OF FRAMES AND REALITY

"They will feel better about what happened if they manage to frame the outcome in terms of how much money they kept rather than how much they lost."

"Let's reframe the problem by changing the reference point. Imagine we did not own it; how much would we think it is worth?"

"Charge the loss to your mental account of 'general revenue'—you will feel better!"

"They ask you to check the box to opt out of their mailing list. Their list would shrink if they asked you to check a box to opt in!"

PART 5

TWO SELVES

35

TWO SELVES

The term *utility* has had two distinct meanings in its long history. Jeremy Bentham opened his *Introduction to the Principles of Morals and Legislation* with the famous sentence "Nature has placed mankind under the governance of two sovereign masters, *pain* and *pleasure*. It is for them alone to point out what we ought to do, as well as to determine what we shall do." In an awkward footnote, Bentham apologized for applying the word *utility* to these experiences, saying that he had been unable to find a better word. To distinguish Bentham's interpretation of the term, I will call it *experienced utility*.

For the last 100 years, economists have used the same word to mean something else. As economists and decision theorists apply the term, it means "wantability"—and I have called it *decision utility*. Expected utility theory, for example, is entirely about the rules of rationality that should govern decision utilities; it has nothing at all to say about hedonic experiences. Of course, the two concepts of utility will coincide if people want what they will enjoy, and enjoy what they chose for themselves—and this assumption of coincidence is implicit in the general idea that economic agents are rational. Rational agents are expected to know their tastes, both present and future, and they are supposed to make good decisions that will maximize these interests.

EXPERIENCED UTILITY

My fascination with the possible discrepancies between experienced utility and decision utility goes back a long way. While Amos and I were still working on prospect theory, I formulated a puzzle, which went like this: imagine an individual who receives one painful injection every day. There is no adaptation; the pain is the same day to day. Will people attach the same value to reducing the number of planned injections from 20 to 18 as from 6 to 4? Is there any justification for a distinction?

I did not collect data, because the outcome was evident. You can verify for yourself that you would pay more to reduce the number of injections by a third (from 6 to 4) than by one tenth (from 20 to 18). The decision utility of avoiding two injections is higher in the first case than in the second, and everyone will pay more for the first reduction than for the second. But this difference is absurd. If the pain does not change from day to day, what could justify assigning different utilities to a reduction of the total amount of pain by two injections, depending on the number of previous injections? In the terms we would use today, the puzzle introduced the idea that experienced utility could be measured by the number of injections. It also suggested that, at least in some cases, experienced utility is the criterion by which a decision should be assessed. A decision maker who pays different amounts to achieve the same gain of experienced utility (or be spared the same loss) is making a mistake. You may find this observation obvious, but in decision theory the only basis for judging that a decision is wrong is inconsistency with other preferences. Amos and I discussed the problem but we did not pursue it. Many years later, I returned to it.

EXPERIENCE AND MEMORY

How can experienced utility be measured? How should we answer questions such as "How much pain did Helen suffer during the medical procedure?" or "How much enjoyment did she get from her 20 minutes on the beach?" The British economist Francis Edgeworth speculated about this topic in the nineteenth century and proposed the idea of a "hedonimeter," an imaginary instrument analogous to the devices used in weather-recording stations, which would measure the level of pleasure or pain that an individual experiences at any moment.

Experienced utility would vary, much as daily temperature or barometric pressure do, and the results would be plotted as a function of time.

The answer to the question of how much pain or pleasure Helen experienced during her medical procedure or vacation would be the "area under the curve." Time plays a critical role in Edgeworth's conception. If Helen stays on the beach for 40 minutes instead of 20, and her enjoyment remains as intense, then the total experienced utility of that episode doubles, just as doubling the number of injections makes a course of injections twice as bad. This was Edgeworth's theory, and we now have a precise understanding of the conditions under which his theory holds.

The graphs in figure 15 show profiles of the experiences of two patients undergoing a painful colonoscopy, drawn from a study that Don Redelmeier and I designed together. Redelmeier, a physician and researcher at the University of Toronto, carried it out in the early 1990s. This procedure is now routinely administered with an anesthetic as well as an amnesic drug, but these drugs were not as widespread when our data were collected. The patients were prompted every 60 seconds to indicate the level of pain they experienced at the moment. The data shown are on a scale where zero is "no pain at all" and 10 is "intolerable pain." As you can see, the experience of each patient varied considerably during the procedure, which lasted 8 minutes for patient A and 24 minutes for patient B (the last reading of zero pain was recorded after the end of the procedure). A total of 154 patients participated in the experiment; the shortest procedure lasted 4 minutes, the longest 69 minutes.

Next, consider an easy question: Assuming that the two patients used the scale of pain similarly, which patient suffered more? No contest. There is general agreement that patient B had the worse time. Patient B spent at least as much time as patient A at any level of pain, and the "area under the curve" is clearly larger for B than for A. The key factor, of course, is that B's

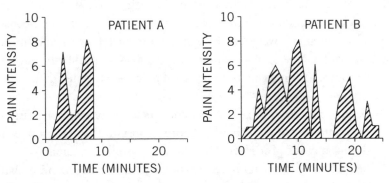

Figure 15

procedure lasted much longer. I will call the measures based on reports of momentary pain hedonimeter totals.

When the procedure was over, all participants were asked to rate "the total amount of pain" they had experienced during the procedure. The wording was intended to encourage them to think of the integral of the pain they had reported, reproducing the hedonimeter totals. Surprisingly, the patients did nothing of the kind. The statistical analysis revealed two findings, which illustrate a pattern we have observed in other experiments:

- Peak-end rule: The global retrospective rating was well predicted by the average of the level of pain reported at the worst moment of the experience and at its end.
- Duration neglect: The duration of the procedure had no effect whatsoever on the ratings of total pain.

You can now apply these rules to the profiles of patients A and B. The worst rating (8 on the 10-point scale) was the same for both patients, but the last rating before the end of the procedure was 7 for patient A and only 1 for patient B. The peak-end average was therefore 7.5 for patient A and only 4.5 for patient B. As expected, patient A retained a much worse memory of the episode than patient B. It was the bad luck of patient A that the procedure ended at a bad moment, leaving him with an unpleasant memory.

We now have an embarrassment of riches: two measures of experienced utility—the hedonimeter total and the retrospective assessment—that are systematically different. The hedonimeter totals are computed by an observer from an individual's report of the experience of moments. We call these judgments duration-weighted, because the computation of the "area under the curve" assigns equal weights to all moments: two minutes of pain at level 9 is twice as bad as one minute at the same level of pain. However, the findings of this experiment and others show that the retrospective assessments are insensitive to duration and weight two singular moments, the peak and the end, much more than others. So which should matter? What should the physician do? The choice has implications for medical practice. We noted that:

- If the objective is to reduce patients' memory of pain, lowering the peak intensity of pain could be more important than minimizing the duration of the procedure. By the same reasoning, gradual relief may be preferable to abrupt relief if patients retain a better memory when the pain at the end of the procedure is relatively mild.

- If the objective is to reduce the amount of pain actually experienced, conducting the procedure swiftly may be appropriate even if doing so increases the peak pain intensity and leaves patients with an awful memory.

Which of the two objectives did you find most compelling? I have not conducted a proper survey, but my impression is that a strong majority will come down in favor of reducing the memory of pain. I find it helpful to think of this dilemma as a conflict of interests between two selves (which do *not* correspond to the two familiar systems). The *experiencing self* is the one that answers the question: "Does it hurt now?" The *remembering self* is the one that answers the question: "How was it, on the whole?" Memories are all we get to keep from our experience of living, and the only perspective that we can adopt as we think about our lives is therefore that of the remembering self.

A comment I heard from a member of the audience after a lecture illustrates the difficulty of distinguishing memories from experiences. He told of listening raptly to a long symphony on a disc that was scratched near the end, producing a shocking sound, and he reported that the bad ending "ruined the whole experience." But the experience was not actually ruined, only the memory of it. The experiencing self had had an experience that was almost entirely good, and the bad end could not undo it, because it had already happened. My questioner had assigned the entire episode a failing grade because it had ended very badly, but that grade effectively ignored 40 minutes of musical bliss. Does the actual experience count for nothing?

Confusing experience with the memory of it is a compelling cognitive illusion—and it is the substitution that makes us believe a past experience can be ruined. The experiencing self does not have a voice. The remembering self is sometimes wrong, but it is the one that keeps score and governs what we learn from living, and it is the one that makes decisions. What we learn from the past is to maximize the qualities of our future memories, not necessarily of our future experience. This is the tyranny of the remembering self.

WHICH SELF SHOULD COUNT?

To demonstrate the decision-making power of the remembering self, my colleagues and I designed an experiment, using a mild form of torture that I will call the cold-hand situation (its ugly technical name is cold-pressor).

Participants are asked to hold their hand up to the wrist in painfully cold water until they are invited to remove it and are offered a warm towel. The subjects in our experiment used their free hand to control arrows on a keyboard to provide a continuous record of the pain they were enduring, a direct communication from their experiencing self. We chose a temperature that caused moderate but tolerable pain: the volunteer participants were of course free to remove their hand at any time, but none chose to do so.

Each participant endured two cold-hand episodes:

> The short episode consisted of 60 seconds of immersion in water at 14° Celsius, which is experienced as painfully cold, but not intolerable. At the end of the 60 seconds, the experimenter instructed the participant to remove his hand from the water and offered a warm towel.

> The long episode lasted 90 seconds. Its first 60 seconds were identical to the short episode. The experimenter said nothing at all at the end of the 60 seconds. Instead he opened a valve that allowed slightly warmer water to flow into the tub. During the additional 30 seconds, the temperature of the water rose by roughly 1°, just enough for most subjects to detect a slight decrease in the intensity of pain.

Our participants were told that they would have three cold-hand trials, but in fact they experienced only the short and the long episodes, each with a different hand. The trials were separated by seven minutes. Seven minutes after the second trial, the participants were given a choice about the third trial. They were told that one of their experiences would be repeated exactly, and were free to choose whether to repeat the experience they had had with their left hand or with their right hand. Of course, half the participants had the short trial with the left hand, half with the right; half had the short trial first, half began with the long, etc. This was a carefully controlled experiment.

The experiment was designed to create a conflict between the interests of the experiencing and the remembering selves, and also between experienced utility and decision utility. From the perspective of the experiencing self, the long trial was obviously worse. We expected the remembering self to have another opinion. The peak-end rule predicts a worse memory for the short than for the long trial, and duration neglect predicts that the difference between 90 seconds and 60 seconds of pain will be ignored. We therefore predicted that the participants would have a more favorable (or less unfavorable) memory of the long trial and choose to repeat it. They did. Fully 80% of the participants who reported that their pain diminished during the final phase of the longer episode opted to repeat it, thereby declaring themselves willing to suffer 30 seconds of needless pain in the anticipated third trial.

The subjects who preferred the long episode were not masochists and did not deliberately choose to expose themselves to the worse experience; they simply made a mistake. If we had asked them, "Would you prefer a 90-second immersion or only the first part of it?" they would certainly have selected the short option. We did not use these words, however, and the subjects did what came naturally: they chose to repeat the episode of which they had the less aversive memory. The subjects knew quite well which of the two exposures was longer—we asked them—but they did not use that knowledge. Their decision was governed by a simple rule of intuitive choice: pick the option you like the most, or dislike the least. Rules of memory determined how much they disliked the two options, which in turn determined their choice. The cold-hand experiment, like my old injections puzzle, revealed a discrepancy between decision utility and experienced utility.

The preferences we observed in this experiment are another example of the less-is-more effect that we have encountered on previous occasions. One was Christopher Hsee's study in which adding dishes to a set of 24 dishes lowered the total value because some of the added dishes were broken. Another was Linda, the activist woman who is judged more likely to be a feminist bank teller than a bank teller. The similarity is not accidental. The same operating feature of System 1 accounts for all three situations: System 1 represents sets by averages, norms, and prototypes, not by sums. Each cold-hand episode is a set of moments, which the remembering self stores as a prototypical moment. This leads to a conflict. For an objective observer evaluating the episode from the reports of the experiencing self, what counts is the "area under the curve" that integrates pain over time; it has the nature of a sum. The memory that the remembering self keeps, in contrast, is a representative moment, strongly influenced by the peak and the end.

Of course, evolution could have designed animals' memory to store integrals, as it surely does in some cases. It is important for a squirrel to "know" the total amount of food it has stored, and a representation of the average size of the nuts would not be a good substitute. However, the integral of pain or pleasure over time may be less biologically significant.

We know, for example, that rats show duration neglect for both pleasure and pain. In one experiment, rats were consistently exposed to a sequence in which the onset of a light signals that an electric shock will soon be delivered. The rats quickly learned to fear the light, and the intensity of their fear could be measured by several physiological responses. The main finding was that the duration of the shock has little or no effect on fear—all that matters is the painful intensity of the stimulus.

Other classic studies showed that electrical stimulation of specific areas in the rat brain (and of corresponding areas in the human brain) produce a sensation of intense pleasure, so intense in some cases that rats who can stimulate their brain by pressing a lever will die of starvation without taking a break to feed themselves. Pleasurable electric stimulation can be delivered in bursts that vary in intensity and duration. Here again, only intensity matters. Up to a point, increasing the duration of a burst of stimulation does not appear to increase the eagerness of the animal to obtain it. The rules that govern the remembering self of humans have a long evolutionary history.

BIOLOGY VS. RATIONALITY

The most useful idea in the injections puzzle that preoccupied me years ago was that the experienced utility of a series of equally painful injections can be measured, by simply counting the injections. If all injections are equally aversive, then 20 of them are twice as bad as 10, and a reduction from 20 to 18 and a reduction from 6 to 4 are equally valuable. If the decision utility does not correspond to the experienced utility, then something is wrong with the decision. The same logic played out in the cold-hand experiment: an episode of pain that lasts 90 seconds is worse than the first 60 seconds of that episode. If people willingly choose to endure the longer episode, something is wrong with their decision. In my early puzzle, the discrepancy between the decision and the experience originated from diminishing sensitivity: the difference between 18 and 20 is less impressive, and appears to be worth less, than the difference between 6 and 4 injections. In the cold-hand experiment, the error reflects two principles of memory: duration neglect and the peak-end rule. The mechanisms are different but the outcome is the same: a decision that is not correctly attuned to the experience.

Decisions that do not produce the best possible experience and erroneous forecasts of future feelings—both are bad news for believers in the rationality of choice. The cold-hand study showed that we cannot fully trust our preferences to reflect our interests, even if they are based on personal experience, and even if the memory of that experience was laid down within the last quarter of an hour! Tastes and decisions are shaped by memories, and the memories can be wrong. The evidence presents a profound challenge to the idea that humans have consistent preferences and know how to maximize them, a cornerstone of the rational-agent model. An inconsistency is built into the design of our minds. We have strong preferences about the duration of our experiences of pain and pleasure. We want pain to be brief and pleasure to last. But our memory, a function of System 1, has evolved to represent the most intense moment of an episode of pain or pleasure (the peak) and the feelings when the episode was at its end. A memory that neglects duration will not serve our preference for long pleasure and short pains.

SPEAKING OF TWO SELVES

"You are thinking of your failed marriage entirely from the perspective of the remembering self. A divorce is like a symphony with a screeching sound at the end—the fact that it ended badly does not mean it was all bad."

"This is a bad case of duration neglect. You are giving the good and the bad part of your experience equal weight, although the good part lasted ten times as long as the other."

36

LIFE AS A STORY

Early in the days of my work on the measurement of experience, I saw Verdi's opera *La Traviata*. Known for its gorgeous music, it is also a moving story of the love between a young aristocrat and Violetta, a woman of the demimonde. The young man's father approaches Violetta and convinces her to give up her lover, to protect the honor of the family and the marriage prospects of the young man's sister. In an act of supreme self-sacrifice, Violetta pretends to reject the man she adores. She soon relapses into consumption (the nineteenth-century term for tuberculosis). In the final act, Violetta lies dying, surrounded by a few friends. Her beloved has been alerted and is rushing to Paris to see her. Hearing the news, she is transformed with hope and joy, but she is also deteriorating quickly.

No matter how many times you have seen the opera, you are gripped by the tension and fear of the moment: Will the young lover arrive in time? There is a sense that it is immensely important for him to join his beloved before she dies. He does, of course, some marvelous love duets are sung, and after 10 minutes of glorious music Violetta dies.

On my way home from the opera, I wondered: Why do we care so much about those last 10 minutes? I quickly realized that I did not care at all about the length of Violetta's life. If I had been told that she died at age 27, not age 28 as I believed, the news that she had missed a year of happy life would not have moved me at all, but the possibility of missing the last 10 minutes mattered a great deal. Furthermore, the emotion I felt about the lovers' reunion would not have changed if I had learned that they actually had a week together, rather than 10 minutes. If the lover had come too late, however, *La Traviata* would have been an altogether different story. A story is about significant events and memorable moments, not about time passing. Duration neglect is normal in a story, and the ending often defines its character. The same core features appear in the rules of narratives and in the memories of colonoscopies, vacations, and films. This is how the remembering self works: it composes stories and keeps them for future reference.

It is not only at the opera that we think of life as a story and wish it to end well. When we hear about the death of a woman who had been estranged from her daughter for many years, we want to know whether they were reconciled as death approached. We do not care only about the daughter's feelings—it is the narrative of the mother's life that we wish to improve. Caring for people often takes the form of concern for the quality of their stories, not for their feelings. Indeed, we can be deeply moved even by events that change the stories of people who are already dead. We feel pity for a man who died believing in his wife's love for him, when we hear that she had a lover for many years and stayed with her husband only for his money. We pity the husband although he had lived a happy life. We feel the humiliation of a scientist who made an important discovery that was proved false after she died, although she did not experience the humiliation. Most important, of course, we all care intensely for the narrative of our own life and very much want it to be a good story, with a decent hero.

The psychologist Ed Diener and his students wondered whether duration neglect and the peak-end rule would govern evaluations of entire lives. They used a short description of the life of a fictitious character called Jen, a never-married woman with no children, who died instantly and painlessly in an automobile accident. In one version of Jen's story, she was extremely happy throughout her life (which lasted either 30 or 60 years), enjoying her work, taking vacations, spending time with her friends and on her hobbies. Another version added 5 extra years to Jen's life, who now died either when she was 35 or 65. The extra years were described as pleasant but less so than before. After reading a schematic biography of Jen, each participant answered two questions: "Taking her life as a whole, how desirable do you think Jen's life was?" and "How much total happiness or unhappiness would you say that Jen experienced in her life?"

The results provided clear evidence of both duration neglect and a peak-end effect. In a between-subjects experiment (different participants saw different forms), doubling the duration of Jen's life had no effect whatsoever on the desirability of her life, or on judgments of the total happiness that Jen experienced. Clearly, her life was represented by a prototypical slice of time, not as a sequence of time slices. As a consequence, her "total happiness" was the happiness of a typical period in her lifetime, not the sum (or integral) of happiness over the duration of her life.

As expected from this idea, Diener and his students also found a less-is-more effect, a strong indication that an average (prototype) has been substituted for a sum. Adding 5 "slightly happy" years to a very happy life caused a substantial drop in evaluations of the total happiness of that life.

At my urging, they also collected data on the effect of the extra 5 years in a within-subject experiment; each participant made both judgments in immediate succession. In spite of my long experience with judgment errors, I did not believe that reasonable people could say that adding 5 slightly happy years to a life would make it substantially worse. I was wrong. The intuition that the disappointing extra 5 years made the whole life worse was overwhelming.

The pattern of judgments seemed so absurd that Diener and his students initially thought that it represented the folly of the young people who participated in their experiments. However, the pattern did not change when the parents and older friends of students answered the same questions. In intuitive evaluation of entire lives as well as brief episodes, peaks and ends matter but duration does not.

The pains of labor and the benefits of vacations always come up as objections to the idea of duration neglect: we all share the intuition that it is much worse for labor to last 24 than 6 hours, and that 6 days at a good resort is better than 3. Duration appears to matter in these situations, but this is only because the quality of the end changes with the length of the episode. The mother is more depleted and helpless after 24 hours than after 6, and the vacationer is more refreshed and rested after 6 days than after 3. What truly matters when we intuitively assess such episodes is the progressive deterioration or improvement of the ongoing experience, and how the person feels at the end.

AMNESIC VACATIONS

Consider the choice of a vacation. Do you prefer to enjoy a relaxing week at the familiar beach to which you went last year? Or do you hope to enrich your store of memories? Distinct industries have developed to cater to these alternatives: resorts offer restorative relaxation; tourism is about helping people construct stories and collect memories. The frenetic picture taking of many tourists suggests that storing memories is often an important goal, which shapes both the plans for the vacation and the experience of it. The photographer does not view the scene as a moment to be savored but as a future memory to be designed. Pictures may be useful to the remembering self—though we rarely look at them for very long, or as often as we expected, or even at all—but picture taking is not necessarily the best way for the tourist's experiencing self to enjoy a view.

In many cases we evaluate touristic vacations by the story and the memories that we expect to store. The word *memorable* is often used to describe vacation highlights, explicitly revealing the goal of the experience. In other situations—love comes to mind—the declaration that the present moment will never be forgotten, though not always accurate, changes the character of the moment. A self-consciously memorable experience gains a weight and a significance that it would not otherwise have.

Ed Diener and his team provided evidence that it is the remembering self that chooses vacations. They asked students to maintain daily diaries and record a daily evaluation of their experiences during spring break. The students also provided a global rating of the vacation when it had ended. Finally, they indicated whether or not they intended to repeat or not to repeat the vacation they had just had. Statistical analysis established that the intentions for future vacations were entirely determined by the final evaluation—even when that score did not accurately represent the quality of the experience that was described in the diaries. As in the cold-hand experiment, right or wrong, people *choose by memory* when they decide whether or not to repeat an experience.

A thought experiment about your next vacation will allow you to observe your attitude to your experiencing self.

> At the end of the vacation, all pictures and videos will be destroyed. Furthermore, you will swallow a potion that will wipe out all your memories of the vacation.
>
> How would this prospect affect your vacation plans? How much would you be willing to pay for it, relative to a normally memorable vacation?

While I have not formally studied the reactions to this scenario, my impression from discussing it with people is that the elimination of memories greatly reduces the value of the experience. In some cases, people treat themselves as they would treat another amnesic, choosing to maximize overall pleasure by returning to a place where they have been happy in the past. However, some people say that they would not bother to go at all, revealing that they care only about their remembering self, and care less about their amnesic experiencing self than about an amnesic stranger. Many point out that they would not send either themselves or another amnesic to climb mountains or trek through the jungle—because these experiences are mostly painful in real time and gain value from the expectation that both the pain and the joy of reaching the goal will be memorable.

For another thought experiment, imagine you face a painful operation during which you will remain conscious. You are told you will scream in pain and beg the surgeon to stop. However, you are promised an amnesia-inducing drug that will completely wipe out any memory of the episode. How do you feel about such a prospect? Here again, my informal observation is that most people are remarkably indifferent to the pains of their experiencing self. Some say they don't care at all. Others share my feeling, which is that I feel pity for my suffering self but not more than I would feel for a stranger in pain. Odd as it may seem, I am my remembering self, and the experiencing self, who does my living, is like a stranger to me.

SPEAKING OF LIFE AS A STORY

"He is desperately trying to protect the narrative of a life of integrity, which is endangered by the latest episode."

"The length to which he was willing to go for a one-night encounter is a sign of total duration neglect."

"You seem to be devoting your entire vacation to the construction of memories. Perhaps you should put away the camera and enjoy the moment, even if it is not very memorable?"

"She is an Alzheimer's patient. She no longer maintains a narrative of her life, but her experiencing self is still sensitive to beauty and gentleness."

37

EXPERIENCED WELL-BEING

When I became interested in the study of well-being about fifteen years ago, I quickly found out that almost everything that was known about the subject drew on the answers of millions of people to minor variations of a survey question, which was generally accepted as a measure of happiness. The question is clearly addressed to your remembering self, which is invited to think about your life:

> All things considered, how satisfied are you with your life as a whole these days?

Having come to the topic of well-being from the study of the mistaken memories of colonoscopies and painfully cold hands, I was naturally suspicious of global satisfaction with life as a valid measure of well-being. As the remembering self had not proved to be a good witness in my experiments, I focused on the well-being of the experiencing self. I proposed that it made sense to say that "Helen was happy in the month of March" if

> she spent most of her time engaged in activities that she would rather continue than stop, little time in situations she wished to escape, and—very important because life is short—not too much time in a neutral state in which she would not care either way.

There are many different experiences we would rather continue than stop, including both mental and physical pleasures. One of the examples I had in mind for a situation that Helen would wish to continue is total absorption in a task, which Mihaly Csikszentmihalyi calls *flow*—a state that some artists experience in their creative moments and that many other people achieve when enthralled by a film, a book, or a crossword puzzle: interruptions are not welcome in any of these situations. I also had memories of a happy early childhood in which I always cried when my mother came to tear me away from my toys to take me to the park, and cried again when she took me away from the swings and the slide. The resistance to interruption was a sign I had been having a good time, both with my toys and with the swings.

I proposed to measure Helen's objective happiness precisely as we assessed the experience of the two colonoscopy patients, by evaluating a profile of the well-being she experienced over successive moments of her life. In this I was following Edgeworth's hedonimeter method of a century earlier. In my initial enthusiasm for this approach, I was inclined to dismiss Helen's remembering self as an error-prone witness to the actual well-being of her experiencing self. I suspected this position was too extreme, which it turned out to be, but it was a good start.

EXPERIENCED WELL-BEING

I assembled "a dream team" that included three other psychologists of different specialties and one economist, and we set out together to develop a measure of the well-being of the experiencing self. A continuous record of experience was unfortunately impossible—a person cannot live normally while constantly reporting her experiences. The closest alternative was experience sampling, a method that Csikszentmihalyi had invented. Technology has advanced since its first uses. Experience sampling is now implemented by programming an individual's cell phone to beep or vibrate at random intervals during the day. The phone then presents a brief menu of questions about what the respondent was doing and who was with her when she was interrupted. The participant is also shown rating scales to report the intensity of various feelings: happiness, tension, anger, worry, engagement, physical pain, and others.

Experience sampling is expensive and burdensome (although less disturbing than most people initially expect; answering the questions takes very little time). A more practical alternative was needed, so we developed a method that we called the Day Reconstruction Method (DRM). We hoped it would approximate the results of experience sampling and provide additional information about the way people spend their time. Participants (all women, in the early studies) were invited to a two-hour session. We first asked them to relive the previous day in detail, breaking it up into episodes like scenes in a film. Later, they answered menus of questions about each episode, based on the experience-sampling method. They selected activities in which they were engaged from a list and indicated the one to which they paid most attention. They also listed the individuals they had been with, and rated the intensity of several feelings on separate 0–6 scales (0 = the absence of the feeling; 6 = most intense feeling). Our method drew on evidence that people who are able to retrieve a past situation in detail are also able to relive the feelings that accompanied it, even experiencing their earlier physiological indications of emotion.

We assumed that our participants would fairly accurately recover the feeling of a prototypical moment of the episode. Several comparisons with experience sampling confirmed the validity of the DRM. Because the participants also reported the times at which episodes began and ended, we were able to compute a duration-weighted measure of their feeling during the entire waking day. Longer episodes counted more than short episodes in our summary measure of daily affect. Our questionnaire also included measures of life satisfaction, which we interpreted as the satisfaction of the remembering self. We used the DRM to study the determinants of both emotional well-being and life satisfaction in several thousand women in the United States, France, and Denmark.

The experience of a moment or an episode is not easily represented by a single happiness value. There are many variants of positive feelings, including love, joy, engagement, hope, amusement, and many others. Negative emotions also come in many varieties, including anger, shame, depression, and loneliness. Although positive and negative emotions exist at the same time, it is possible to classify most moments of life as ultimately positive or negative. We could identify unpleasant episodes by comparing the ratings of positive and negative adjectives. We called an episode unpleasant if a negative feeling was assigned a higher rating than all the positive feelings. We found that American women spent about 19% of the time in an unpleasant state, somewhat higher than French women (16%) or Danish women (14%).

We called the percentage of time that an individual spends in an unpleasant state the U-index. For example, an individual who spent 4 hours of a 16-hour waking day in an unpleasant state would have a U-index of 25%. The appeal of the U-index is that it is based not on a rating scale but on an objective measurement of time. If the U-index for a population drops from 20% to 18%, you can infer that the total time that the population spent in emotional discomfort or pain has diminished by a tenth.

A striking observation was the extent of inequality in the distribution of emotional pain. About half our participants reported going through an entire day without experiencing an unpleasant episode. On the other hand, a significant minority of the population experienced considerable emotional distress for much of the day. It appears that a small fraction of the population does most of the suffering—whether because of physical or mental illness, an unhappy temperament, or the misfortunes and personal tragedies in their life.

A U-index can also be computed for activities. For example, we can measure the proportion of time that people spend in a negative emotional state while commuting, working, or interacting with their parents, spouses, or children. For 1,000 American women in a Midwestern city, the U-index was 29% for the morning commute, 27% for work, 24% for child care, 18% for housework, 12% for socializing, 12% for TV watching, and 5% for sex. The U-index was higher by about 6% on weekdays than it was on weekends, mostly because on weekends people spend less time in activities they dislike and do not suffer the tension and stress associated with work. The biggest surprise was the emotional experience of the time spent with one's children, which for American women was slightly less enjoyable than doing housework. Here we found one of the few contrasts between French and American women: Frenchwomen spend less time with their children but enjoy it more, perhaps because they have more access to child care and spend less of the afternoon driving children to various activities.

An individual's mood at any moment depends on her temperament and overall happiness, but emotional well-being also fluctuates considerably over the day and the week. The mood of the moment depends primarily on the current situation. Mood at work, for example, is largely unaffected by the factors that influence general job satisfaction, including benefits and status. More important are situational factors such as an opportunity to socialize with coworkers, exposure to loud noise, time pressure (a significant source of negative affect), and the immediate presence of a boss (in our first study, the only thing that was worse than being alone). Attention is key. Our emotional state is largely determined by what we attend to, and we are normally focused on our current activity and immediate environment. There are exceptions, where the quality of subjective experience is dominated by recurrent thoughts rather than by the events of the moment. When happily in love, we may feel joy even when caught in traffic, and if grieving, we may remain depressed when watching a funny movie. In normal circumstances, however, we draw pleasure and pain from what is happening at the moment, if we attend to it. To get pleasure from eating, for example, you must notice that you are doing it. We found that French and American women spent about the same amount of time eating, but for Frenchwomen, eating was twice as likely to be focal as it was for American women. The Americans were far more prone to combine eating with other activities, and their pleasure from eating was correspondingly diluted.

These observations have implications for both individuals and society. The use of time is one of the areas of life over which people have some control. Few individuals can will themselves to have a sunnier disposition, but some may be able to arrange their lives to spend less of their day commuting, and more time doing things they enjoy with people they like. The feelings associated with different activities suggest that another way to improve experience is to switch time from passive leisure, such as TV watching, to more active forms of leisure, including socializing and exercise. From the social perspective, improved transportation for the labor force, availability of child care for working women, and improved socializing opportunities for the elderly may be relatively efficient ways to reduce the U-index of society—even a reduction by 1% would be a significant achievement, amounting to millions of hours of avoided suffering. Combined national surveys of time use and of experienced well-being can inform social policy in multiple ways. The economist on our team, Alan Krueger, took the lead in an effort to introduce elements of this method into national statistics.

Measures of experienced well-being are now routinely used in large-scale national surveys in the United States, Canada, and Europe, and the Gallup World Poll has extended these measurements to millions of respondents in the United States and in more than 150 countries. The polls elicit reports of the emotions experienced during the previous day, though in less detail than the DRM. The gigantic samples allow extremely fine analyses, which have confirmed the importance of situational factors, physical health, and social contact in experienced well-being. Not surprisingly, a headache will make a person miserable, and the second best predictor of the feelings of a day is whether a person did or did not have contacts with friends or relatives. It is only a slight exaggeration to say that happiness is the experience of spending time with people you love and who love you.

The Gallup data permit a comparison of two aspects of well-being:

- the well-being that people experience as they live their lives
- the judgment they make when they evaluate their life

Gallup's life evaluation is measured by a question known as the Cantril Self-Anchoring Striving Scale:

> Please imagine a ladder with steps numbered from zero at the bottom to
> 10 at the top. The top of the ladder represents the best possible life for you
> and the bottom of the ladder represents the worst possible life for you.
> On which step of the ladder would you say you personally feel you stand at
> this time?

Some aspects of life have more effect on the evaluation of one's life than on the experience of living. Educational attainment is an example. More education is associated with higher evaluation of one's life, but not with greater experienced well-being. Indeed, at least in the United States, the more educated tend to report higher stress. On the other hand, ill health has a much stronger adverse effect on experienced well-being than on life evaluation. Living with children also imposes a significant cost in the currency of daily feelings—reports of stress and anger are common among parents, but the adverse effects on life evaluation are smaller. Religious participation also has relatively greater favorable impact on both positive affect and stress reduction than on life evaluation. Surprisingly, however, religion provides no reduction of feelings of depression or worry.

An analysis of more than 450,000 responses to the Gallup-Healthways Well-Being Index, a daily survey of 1,000 Americans, provides a surprisingly definite answer to the most frequently asked question in well-being research: Can money buy happiness? The conclusion is that being poor makes one miserable, and that being rich may enhance one's life satisfaction, but does not (on average) improve experienced well-being.

Severe poverty amplifies the experienced effects of other misfortunes of life. In particular, illness is much worse for the very poor than for those who are more comfortable. A headache increases the proportion reporting sadness and worry from 19% to 38% for individuals in the top two-thirds of the income distribution. The corresponding numbers for the poorest tenth are 38% and 70%—a higher baseline level and a much larger increase. Significant differences between the very poor and others are also found for the effects of divorce and loneliness. Furthermore, the beneficial effects of the weekend on experienced well-being are significantly smaller for the very poor than for most everyone else.

The satiation level beyond which experienced well-being no longer increases was a household income of about $75,000 in high-cost areas (it could be less in areas where the cost of living is lower). The average increase of experienced well-being associated with incomes beyond that level was precisely zero. This is surprising because higher income undoubtedly permits the purchase of many pleasures, including vacations in interesting places and opera tickets, as well as an improved living environment. Why do these added pleasures not show up in reports of emotional experience? A plausible interpretation is that higher income is associated with a reduced ability to enjoy the small pleasures of life. There is suggestive evidence in favor of this idea: priming students with the idea of wealth reduces the pleasure their face expresses as they eat a bar of chocolate!

There is a clear contrast between the effects of income on experienced well-being and on life satisfaction. Higher income brings with it higher satisfaction, well beyond the point at which it ceases to have any positive effect on experience. The general conclusion is as clear for well-being as it was for colonoscopies: people's evaluations of their lives and their actual experience may be related, but they are also different. Life satisfaction is not a flawed measure of their experienced well-being, as I thought some years ago. It is something else entirely.

SPEAKING OF EXPERIENCED WELL-BEING

"The objective of policy should be to reduce human suffering. We aim for a lower U-index in society. Dealing with depression and extreme poverty should be a priority."

"The easiest way to increase happiness is to control your use of time. Can you find more time to do the things you enjoy doing?"

"Beyond the satiation level of income, you can buy more pleasurable experiences, but you will lose some of your ability to enjoy the less expensive ones."

38

THINKING ABOUT LIFE

Figure 16 is taken from an analysis by Andrew Clark, Ed Diener, and Yannis Georgellis of the German Socio-Economic Panel, in which the same respondents were asked every year about their satisfaction with their life. Respondents also reported major changes that had occurred in their circumstances during the preceding year. The graph shows the level of satisfaction reported by people around the time they got married.

Figure 16

The graph reliably evokes nervous laughter from audiences, and the nervousness is easy to understand: after all, people who decide to get married do so either because they expect it will make them happier or because they hope that making a tie permanent will maintain the present state of bliss. In the useful term introduced by Daniel Gilbert and Timothy Wilson, the decision to get married reflects, for many people, a massive error of *affective forecasting*. On their wedding day, the bride and the groom know that the rate of divorce is high and that the incidence of marital disappointment is even higher, but they do not believe that these statistics apply to them.

The startling news of figure 16 is the steep decline of life satisfaction. The graph is commonly interpreted as tracing a process of adaptation, in which the early joys of marriage quickly disappear as the experiences become routine. However, another approach is possible, which focuses on heuristics of judgment. Here we ask what happens in people's minds when they are asked to evaluate their life. The questions "How satisfied are you with your life as a whole?" and "How happy are you these days?" are not as simple as "What is your telephone number?" How do survey participants manage to answer such questions in a few seconds, as all do? It will help to think of this as another judgment. As is also the case for other questions, some people may have a ready-made answer, which they had produced on another occasion in which they evaluated their life. Others, probably the majority, do not quickly find a response to the exact question they were asked, and automatically make their task easier by substituting the answer to another question. System 1 is at work. When we look at figure 16 in this light, it takes on a different meaning.

The answers to many simple questions can be substituted for a global evaluation of life. You remember the study in which students who had just been asked how many dates they had in the previous month reported their "happiness these days" as if dating was the only significant fact in their life. In another well-known experiment in the same vein, Norbert Schwarz and his colleagues invited subjects to the lab to complete a questionnaire on life satisfaction. Before they began that task, however, he asked them to photocopy a sheet of paper for him. Half the respondents found a dime on the copying machine, planted there by the experimenter. The minor lucky incident caused a marked improvement in subjects' reported satisfaction with their life as a whole! A mood heuristic is one way to answer life-satisfaction questions.

The dating survey and the coin-on-the-machine experiment demonstrated, as intended, that the responses to global well-being questions should be taken with a grain of salt. But of course your current mood is not the only thing that comes to mind when you are asked to evaluate your life. You are likely to be reminded of significant events in your recent past or near future; of recurrent concerns, such as the health of a spouse or the bad company that your teenager keeps; of important achievements and painful failures. A few ideas that are relevant to the question will occur to you; many others will not. Even when it is not influenced by completely irrelevant accidents such as the coin on the machine, the score that you quickly assign to your life is determined by a small sample of highly available ideas, not by a careful weighting of the domains of your life.

People who recently married, or are expecting to marry in the near future, are likely to retrieve that fact when asked a general question about their life. Because marriage is almost always voluntary in the United States, almost everyone who is reminded of his or her recent or forthcoming marriage will be happy with the idea. Attention is the key to the puzzle. Figure 16 can be read as a graph of the likelihood that people will think of their recent or forthcoming marriage when asked about their life. The salience of this thought is bound to diminish with the passage of time, as its novelty wanes.

The figure shows an unusually high level of life satisfaction that lasts two or three years around the event of marriage. However, if this apparent surge reflects the time course of a heuristic for answering the question, there is little we can learn from it about either happiness or about the process of adaptation to marriage. We cannot infer from it that a tide of raised happiness lasts for several years and gradually recedes. Even people who are happy to be reminded of their marriage when asked a question about their life are not necessarily happier the rest of the time. Unless they think happy thoughts about their marriage during much of their day, it will not directly influence their happiness. Even newlyweds who are lucky enough to enjoy a state of happy preoccupation with their love will eventually return to earth, and their experienced well-being will again depend, as it does for the rest of us, on the environment and activities of the present moment.

In the DRM studies, there was no overall difference in experienced well-being between women who lived with a mate and women who did not. The details of how the two groups used their time explained the finding. Women who have a mate spend less time alone, but also much less time with friends. They spend more time making love, which is wonderful, but also more time doing housework, preparing food, and caring for children, all relatively unpopular activities. And of course, the large amount of time married women spend with their husband is much more pleasant for some than for others. Experienced well-being is on average unaffected by marriage, not because marriage makes no difference to happiness but because it changes some aspects of life for the better and others for the worse.

One reason for the low correlations between individuals' circumstances and their satisfaction with life is that both experienced happiness and life satisfaction are largely determined by the genetics of temperament. A disposition for well-being is as heritable as height or intelligence, as demonstrated by studies of twins separated at birth. People who appear equally fortunate vary greatly in how happy they are. In some instances, as in the case of marriage, the correlations with well-being are low because of balancing effects. The same situation may be good for some people and bad for others, and new circumstances have both benefits and costs. In other cases, such as high income, the effects on life satisfaction are generally positive, but the picture is complicated by the fact that some people care much more about money than others do.

A large-scale study of the impact of higher education, which was conducted for another purpose, revealed striking evidence of the lifelong effects of the goals that young people set for themselves. The relevant data were drawn from questionnaires collected in 1995–1997 from approximately 12,000 people who had started their higher education in elite schools in 1976. When they were 17 or 18, the participants had filled out a questionnaire in which they rated the goal of "being very well-off financially" on a 4-point scale ranging from "not important" to "essential." The questionnaire they completed twenty years later included measures of their income in 1995, as well as a global measure of life satisfaction.

Goals make a large difference. Nineteen years after they stated their financial aspirations, many of the people who wanted a high income had achieved it. Among the 597 physicians and other medical professionals in the sample, for example, each additional point on the money-importance scale was associated with an increment of over $14,000 of job income in 1995 dollars! Nonworking married women were also likely to have satisfied their financial ambitions. Each point on the scale translated into more than $12,000 of added household income for these women, evidently through the earnings of their spouse.

The importance that people attached to income at age 18 also anticipated their satisfaction with their income as adults. We compared life satisfaction in a high-income group (more than $200,000 household income) to a low- to moderate-income group (less than $50,000). The effect of income on life satisfaction was larger for those who had listed being well-off financially as an essential goal: .57 point on a 5-point scale. The corresponding difference for those who had indicated that money was not important was only .12. The people who wanted money and got it were significantly more satisfied than average; those who wanted money and didn't get it were significantly more dissatisfied. The same principle applies to other goals—one recipe for a dissatisfied adulthood is setting goals that are especially difficult to attain. Measured by life satisfaction 20 years later, the least promising goal that a young person could have was "becoming accomplished in a performing art." Teenagers' goals influence what happens to them, where they end up, and how satisfied they are.

In part because of these findings I have changed my mind about the definition of well-being. The goals that people set for themselves are so important to what they do and how they feel about it that an exclusive focus on experienced well-being is not tenable. We cannot hold a concept of well-being that ignores what people want. On the other hand, it is also true that a concept of well-being that ignores how people feel as they live and focuses only on how they feel when they think about their life is also untenable. We must accept the complexities of a hybrid view, in which the well-being of both selves is considered.

THE FOCUSING ILLUSION

We can infer from the speed with which people respond to questions about their life, and from the effects of current mood on their responses, that they do not engage in a careful examination when they evaluate their life. They must be using heuristics, which are examples of both substitution and WYSIATI. Although their view of their life was influenced by a question about dating or by a coin on the copying machine, the participants in these studies did not forget that there is more to life than dating or feeling lucky. The concept of happiness is not suddenly changed by finding a dime, but System 1 readily substitutes a small part of it for the whole of it. Any aspect of life to which attention is directed will loom large in a global evaluation. This is the essence of the *focusing illusion*, which can be described in a single sentence:

> Nothing in life is as important as you think it is when you are thinking about it.

The origin of this idea was a family debate about moving from California to Princeton, in which my wife claimed that people are happier in California than on the East Coast. I argued that climate is demonstrably not an important determinant of well-being—the Scandinavian countries are probably the happiest in the world. I observed that permanent life circumstances have little effect on well-being and tried in vain to convince my wife that her intuitions about the happiness of Californians were an error of affective forecasting.

A short time later, with this debate still on my mind, I participated in a workshop about the social science of global warming. A colleague made an argument that was based on his view of the well-being of the population of planet Earth in the next century. I argued that it was preposterous to forecast what it would be like to live on a warmer planet when we did not even know what it is like to live in California. Soon after that exchange, my colleague David Schkade and I were granted research funds to study two questions: Are people who live in California happier than others? and What are the popular beliefs about the relative happiness of Californians?

We recruited large samples of students at major state universities in California, Ohio, and Michigan. From some of them we obtained a detailed report of their satisfaction with various aspects of their lives. From others we obtained a prediction of how someone "with your interests and values" who lived elsewhere would complete the same questionnaire.

As we analyzed the data, it became obvious that I had won the family argument. As expected, the students in the two regions differed greatly in their attitude to their climate: the Californians enjoyed their climate and the Midwesterners despised theirs. But climate was not an important determinant of well-being. Indeed, there was no difference whatsoever between the life satisfaction of students in California and in the Midwest. We also found that my wife was not alone in her belief that Californians enjoy greater well-being than others. The students in both regions shared the same mistaken view, and we were able to trace their error to an exaggerated belief in the importance of climate. We described the error as a *focusing illusion*.

The essence of the focusing illusion is WYSIATI, giving too much weight to the climate, too little to all the other determinants of well-being. To appreciate how strong this illusion is, take a few seconds to consider the question:

How much pleasure do you get from your car?

An answer came to your mind immediately; you know how much you like and enjoy your car. Now examine a different question: "*When* do you get pleasure from your car?" The answer to this question may surprise you, but it is straightforward: you get pleasure (or displeasure) from your car when you think about your car, which is probably not very often. Under normal circumstances, you do not spend much time thinking about your car when you are driving it. You think of other things as you drive, and your mood is determined by whatever you think about. Here again, when you tried to rate how much you enjoyed your car, you actually answered a much narrower question: "How much pleasure do you get from your car *when you think about it*?" The substitution caused you to ignore the fact that you rarely think about your car, a form of duration neglect. The upshot is a focusing illusion. If you like your car, you are likely to exaggerate the pleasure you derive from it, which will mislead you when you think of the virtues of your current vehicle as well as when you contemplate buying a new one.

A similar bias distorts judgments of the happiness of Californians. When asked about the happiness of Californians, you probably conjure an image of someone attending to a distinctive aspect of the California experience, such as hiking in the summer or admiring the mild winter weather. The focusing illusion arises because Californians actually spend little time attending to these aspects of their life. Moreover, long-term Californians are unlikely to be reminded of the climate when asked for a global evaluation of their life. If you have been there all your life and do not travel much, living in California is like having ten toes: nice, but not something one thinks much about. Thoughts of any aspect of life are more likely to be salient if a contrasting alternative is highly available.

People who recently moved to California will respond differently. Consider an enterprising soul who moved from Ohio to seek happiness in a better climate. For a few years following the move, a question about his satisfaction with life will probably remind him of the move and also evoke thoughts of the contrasting climates in the two states. The comparison will surely favor California, and the attention to that aspect of life may distort its true weight in experience. However, the focusing illusion can also bring comfort. Whether or not the individual is actually happier after the move, he will report himself happier, because thoughts of the climate will make him believe that he is. The focusing illusion can cause people to be wrong about their present state of well-being as well as about the happiness of others, and about their own happiness in the future.

What proportion of the day do paraplegics spend in a bad mood?

This question almost certainly made you think of a paraplegic who is currently thinking about some aspect of his condition. Your guess about a paraplegic's mood is therefore likely to be accurate in the early days after a crippling accident; for some time after the event, accident victims think of little else. But over time, with few exceptions, attention is withdrawn from a new situation as it becomes more familiar. The main exceptions are chronic pain, constant exposure to loud noise, and severe depression. Pain and noise are biologically set to be signals that attract attention, and depression involves a self-reinforcing cycle of miserable thoughts. There is therefore no adaptation to these conditions. Paraplegia, however, is not one of the exceptions: detailed observations show that paraplegics are in a fairly good mood more than half of the time as early as one month following their accident—though their mood is certainly somber when they think about their situation. Most of the time, however, paraplegics work, read, enjoy jokes and friends, and get angry when they read about politics in the newspaper. When they are involved in any of these activities, they are not much different from anyone else, and we can expect the experienced well-being of paraplegics to be near normal much of the time. Adaptation to a new situation, whether good or bad, consists in large part of thinking less and less about it. In that sense, most long-term circumstances of life, including paraplegia and marriage, are part-time states that one inhabits only when one attends to them.

One of the privileges of teaching at Princeton is the opportunity to guide bright undergraduates through a research thesis. And one of my favorite experiences in this vein was a project in which Beruria Cohn collected and analyzed data from a survey firm that asked respondents to estimate the proportion of time that paraplegics spend in a bad mood. She split her respondents into two groups: some were told that the crippling accident had occurred a month earlier, some a year earlier. In addition, each respondent indicated whether he or she knew a paraplegic personally. The two groups agreed closely in their judgment about the recent paraplegics: those who knew a paraplegic estimated 75% bad mood; those who had to imagine a paraplegic said 70%. In contrast, the two groups differed sharply in their estimates of the mood of paraplegics a year after the accidents: those who knew a paraplegic offered 41% as their estimate of the time in that bad mood. The estimates of those who were not personally acquainted with a paraplegic averaged 68%. Evidently, those who knew a paraplegic had observed the gradual withdrawal of attention from the condition, but others did not forecast that this adaptation would occur. Judgments about the mood of lottery winners one month and one year after the event showed exactly the same pattern.

We can expect the life satisfaction of paraplegics and those afflicted by other chronic and burdensome conditions to be low relative to their experienced well-being, because the request to evaluate their lives will inevitably remind them of the life of others and of the life they used to lead. Consistent with this idea, recent studies of colostomy patients have produced dramatic inconsistencies between the patients' experienced well-being and their evaluations of their lives. Experience sampling shows no difference in experienced happiness between these patients and a healthy population. Yet colostomy patients would be willing to trade away years of their life for a shorter life without the colostomy. Furthermore, patients whose colostomy has been reversed remember their time in this condition as awful, and they would give up even more of their remaining life not to have to return to it. Here it appears that the remembering self is subject to a massive focusing illusion about the life that the experiencing self endures quite comfortably.

Daniel Gilbert and Timothy Wilson introduced the word *miswanting* to describe bad choices that arise from errors of affective forecasting. This word deserves to be in everyday language. The focusing illusion (which Gilbert and Wilson call focalism) is a rich source of miswanting. In particular, it makes us prone to exaggerate the effect of significant purchases or changed circumstances on our future well-being.

Compare two commitments that will change some aspects of your life: buying a comfortable new car and joining a group that meets weekly, perhaps a poker or book club. Both experiences will be novel and exciting at the start. The crucial difference is that you will eventually pay little attention to the car as you drive it, but you will always attend to the social interaction to which you committed yourself. By WYSIATI, you are likely to exaggerate the long-term benefits of the car, but you are not likely to make the same mistake for a social gathering or for inherently attention-demanding activities such as playing tennis or learning to play the cello. The focusing illusion creates a bias in favor of goods and experiences that are initially exciting, even if they will eventually lose their appeal. Time is neglected, causing experiences that will retain their attention value in the long term to be appreciated less than they deserve to be.

TIME AND TIME AGAIN

The role of time has been a refrain in this part of the book. It is logical to describe the life of the experiencing self as a series of moments, each with a value. The value of an episode—I have called it a hedonimeter total—is simply the sum of the values of its moments. But this is not how the mind represents episodes. The remembering self, as I have described it, also tells stories and makes choices, and neither the stories nor the choices properly represent time. In storytelling mode, an episode is represented by a few critical moments, especially the beginning, the peak, and the end. Duration is neglected. We saw this focus on singular moments both in the cold-hand situation and in Violetta's story.

We saw a different form of duration neglect in prospect theory, in which a state is represented by the transition to it. Winning a lottery yields a new state of wealth that will endure for some time, but decision utility corresponds to the anticipated intensity of the reaction to the news that one has won. The withdrawal of attention and other adaptations to the new state are neglected, as only that thin slice of time is considered. The same focus on the transition to the new state and the same neglect of time and adaptation are found in forecasts of the reaction to chronic diseases, and of course in the focusing illusion. The mistake that people make in the focusing illusion involves attention to selected moments and neglect of what happens at other times. The mind is good with stories, but it does not appear to be well designed for the processing of time.

During the last ten years we have learned many new facts about happiness. But we have also learned that the word *happiness* does not have a simple meaning and should not be used as if it does. Sometimes scientific progress leaves us more puzzled than we were before.

SPEAKING OF THINKING ABOUT LIFE

"She thought that buying a fancy car would make her happier, but it turned out to be an error of affective forecasting."

"His car broke down on the way to work this morning and he's in a foul mood. This is not a good day to ask him about his job satisfaction!"

"She looks quite cheerful most of the time, but when she is asked she says she is very unhappy. The question must make her think of her recent divorce."

"Buying a larger house may not make us happier in the long term. We could be suffering from a focusing illusion."

"He has chosen to split his time between two cities. Probably a serious case of miswanting."

CONCLUSIONS

I began this book by introducing two fictitious characters, spent some time discussing two species, and ended with two selves. The two characters were the intuitive System 1, which does the fast thinking, and the effortful and slower System 2, which does the slow thinking, monitors System 1, and maintains control as best it can within its limited resources. The two species were the fictitious Econs, who live in the land of theory, and the Humans, who act in the real world. The two selves are the experiencing self, which does the living, and the remembering self, which keeps score and makes the choices. In this final chapter I consider some applications of the three distinctions, taking them in reverse order.

TWO SELVES

The possibility of conflicts between the remembering self and the interests of the experiencing self turned out to be a harder problem than I initially thought. In an early experiment, the cold-hand study, the combination of duration neglect and the peak-end rule led to choices that were manifestly absurd. Why would people willingly expose themselves to unnecessary pain? Our subjects left the choice to their remembering self, preferring to repeat the trial that left the better memory, although it involved more pain. Choosing by the quality of the memory may be justified in extreme cases, for example when post-traumatic stress is a possibility, but the cold-hand experience was not traumatic. An objective observer making the choice for someone else would undoubtedly choose the short exposure, favoring the sufferer's experiencing self. The choices that people made on their own behalf are fairly described as mistakes. Duration neglect and the peak-end rule in the evaluation of stories, both at the opera and in judgments of Jen's life, are equally indefensible. It does not make sense to evaluate an entire life by its last moments, or to give no weight to duration in deciding which life is more desirable.

The remembering self is a construction of System 2. However, the distinctive features of the way it evaluates episodes and lives are characteristics of our memory. Duration neglect and the peak-end rule originate in System 1 and do not necessarily correspond to the values of System 2. We believe that duration is important, but our memory tells us it is not. The rules that govern the evaluation of the past are poor guides for decision making, because time does matter. The central fact of our existence is that time is the ultimate finite resource, but the remembering self ignores that reality. The neglect of duration combined with the peak-end rule causes a bias that favors a short period of intense joy over a long period of moderate happiness. The mirror image of the same bias makes us fear a short period of intense but tolerable suffering more than we fear a much longer period of moderate pain. Duration neglect also makes us prone to accept a long period of mild unpleasantness because the end will be better, and it favors giving up an opportunity for a long happy period if it is likely to have a poor ending. To drive the same idea to the point of discomfort, consider the common admonition, "Don't do it, you will regret it." The advice sounds wise because anticipated regret is the verdict of the remembering self and we are inclined to accept such judgments as final and conclusive. We should not forget, however, that the perspective of the remembering self is not always correct. An objective observer of the hedonimeter profile, with the interests of the experiencing self in mind, might well offer different advice. The remembering self's neglect of duration, its exaggerated emphasis on peaks and ends, and its susceptibility to hindsight combine to yield distorted reflections of our actual experience.

In contrast, the duration-weighted conception of well-being treats all moments of life alike, memorable or not. Some moments end up weighted more than others, either because they are memorable or because they are important. The time that people spend dwelling on a memorable moment should be included in its duration, adding to its weight. A moment can also gain importance by altering the experience of subsequent moments. For example, an hour spent practicing the violin may enhance the experience of many hours of playing or listening to music years later. Similarly, a brief awful event that causes PTSD should be weighted by the total duration of the long-term misery it causes. In the duration-weighted perspective, we can determine only after the fact that a moment is memorable or meaningful. The statements "I will always remember . . ." or "this is a meaningful moment" should be taken as promises or predictions, which can be false—and often are—even when uttered with complete sincerity. It is a good bet that many of the things we say we will always remember will be long forgotten ten years later.

The logic of duration weighting is compelling, but it cannot be considered a complete theory of well-being because individuals identify with their remembering self and care about their story. A theory of well-being that ignores what people want cannot be sustained. On the other hand, a theory that ignores what actually happens in people's lives and focuses exclusively on what they think about their life is not tenable either. The remembering self and the experiencing self must both be considered, because their interests do not always coincide. Philosophers could struggle with these questions for a long time.

The issue of which of the two selves matters more is not a question only for philosophers; it has implications for policies in several domains, notably medicine and welfare. Consider the investment that should be made in the treatment of various medical conditions, including blindness, deafness, or kidney failure. Should the investments be determined by how much people fear these conditions? Should investments be guided by the suffering that patients actually experience? Or should they follow the intensity of the patients' desire to be relieved from their condition and by the sacrifices that they would be willing to make to achieve that relief? The ranking of blindness and deafness, or of colostomy and dialysis, might well be different depending on which measure of the severity of suffering is used. No easy solution is in sight, but the issue is too important to be ignored.

The possibility of using measures of well-being as indicators to guide government policies has attracted considerable recent interest, both among academics and in several governments in Europe. It is now conceivable, as it was not even a few years ago, that an index of the amount of suffering in society will someday be included in national statistics, along with measures of unemployment, physical disability, and income. This project has come a long way.

ECONS AND HUMANS

In everyday speech, we call people reasonable if it is possible to reason with them, if their beliefs are generally in tune with reality, and if their preferences are in line with their interests and their values. The word *rational* conveys an image of greater deliberation, more calculation, and less warmth, but in common language a rational person is certainly reasonable. For economists and decision theorists, the adjective has an altogether different meaning. The only test of rationality is not whether a person's beliefs and preferences are reasonable, but whether they are internally consistent. A rational person can believe in ghosts so long as all her other beliefs are consistent with the existence of ghosts. A rational person can prefer being hated over being loved, so long as his preferences are consistent. Rationality is logical coherence—reasonable or not. Econs are rational by this definition, but there is overwhelming evidence that Humans cannot be. An Econ would not be susceptible to priming, WYSIATI, narrow framing, the inside view, or preference reversals, which Humans cannot consistently avoid.

The definition of rationality as coherence is impossibly restrictive; it demands adherence to rules of logic that a finite mind is not able to implement. Reasonable people cannot be rational by that definition, but they should not be branded as irrational for that reason. *Irrational* is a strong word, which connotes impulsivity, emotionality, and a stubborn resistance to reasonable argument. I often cringe when my work with Amos is credited with demonstrating that human choices are irrational, when in fact our research only showed that Humans are not well described by the rational-agent model.

Although Humans are not irrational, they often need help to make more accurate judgments and better decisions, and in some cases policies and institutions can provide that help. These claims may seem innocuous, but they are in fact quite controversial. As interpreted by the important Chicago school of economics, faith in human rationality is closely linked to an ideology in which it is unnecessary and even immoral to protect people against their choices. Rational people should be free, and they should be responsible for taking care of themselves. Milton Friedman, the leading figure in that school, expressed this view in the title of one of his popular books: *Free to Choose*.

The assumption that agents are rational provides the intellectual foundation for the libertarian approach to public policy: do not interfere with the individual's right to choose, unless the choices harm others. Libertarian policies are further bolstered by admiration for the efficiency of markets in allocating goods to the people who are willing to pay the most for them. A famous example of the Chicago approach is titled *A Theory of Rational Addiction*; it explains how a rational agent with a strong preference for intense and immediate gratification may make the rational decision to accept future addiction as a consequence. I once heard Gary Becker, one of the authors of that article, who is also a Nobel laureate of the Chicago school, argue in a lighter vein, but not entirely as a joke, that we should consider the possibility of explaining the so-called obesity epidemic by people's belief that a cure for diabetes will soon become available. He was making a valuable point: when we observe people acting in ways that seem odd, we should first examine the possibility that they have a good reason to do what they do. Psychological interpretations should only be invoked when the reasons become implausible—which Becker's explanation of obesity probably is.

In a nation of Econs, government should keep out of the way, allowing the Econs to act as they choose, so long as they do not harm others. If a motorcycle rider chooses to ride without a helmet, a libertarian will support his right to do so. Citizens know what they are doing, even when they choose not to save for their old age, or when they expose themselves to addictive substances. There is sometimes a hard edge to this position: elderly people who did not save enough for retirement get little more sympathy than someone who complains about the bill after consuming a large meal at a restaurant. Much is therefore at stake in the debate between the Chicago school and the behavioral economists, who reject the extreme form of the rational-agent model. Freedom is not a contested value; all the participants in the debate are in favor of it. But life is more complex for behavioral economists than for true believers in human rationality. No behavioral economist favors a state that will force its citizens to eat a balanced diet and to watch only television programs that are good for the soul. For behavioral economists, however, freedom has a cost, which is borne by individuals who make bad choices, and by a society that feels obligated to help them. The decision of whether or not to protect individuals against their mistakes therefore presents a dilemma for behavioral economists. The economists of the Chicago school do not face that problem, because rational agents do not make mistakes. For adherents of this school, freedom is free of charge.

In 2008 the economist Richard Thaler and the jurist Cass Sunstein teamed up to write a book, *Nudge*, which quickly became an international bestseller and the bible of behavioral economics. Their book introduced several new words into the language, including Econs and Humans. It also presented a set of solutions to the dilemma of how to help people make good decisions without curtailing their freedom. Thaler and Sunstein advocate a position of libertarian paternalism, in which the state and other institutions are allowed to *nudge* people to make decisions that serve their own long-term interests. The designation of joining a pension plan as the default option is an example of a nudge. It is difficult to argue that anyone's freedom is diminished by being automatically enrolled in the plan, when they merely have to check a box to opt out. As we saw earlier, the framing of the individual's decision—Thaler and Sunstein call it choice architecture—has a huge effect on the outcome. The nudge is based on sound psychology, which I described earlier. The default option is naturally perceived as the normal choice. Deviating from the normal choice is an act of commission, which requires more effortful deliberation, takes on more responsibility, and is more likely to evoke regret than doing nothing. These are powerful forces that may guide the decision of someone who is otherwise unsure of what to do.

Humans, more than Econs, also need protection from others who deliberately exploit their weaknesses—and especially the quirks of System 1 and the laziness of System 2. Rational agents are assumed to make important decisions carefully, and to use all the information that is provided to them. An Econ will read and understand the fine print of a contract before signing it, but Humans usually do not. An unscrupulous firm that designs contracts that customers will routinely sign without reading has considerable legal leeway in hiding important information in plain sight. A pernicious implication of the rational-agent model in its extreme form is that customers are assumed to need no protection beyond ensuring that the relevant information is disclosed. The size of the print and the complexity of the language in the disclosure are not considered relevant—an Econ knows how to deal with small print when it matters. In contrast, the recommendations of *Nudge* require firms to offer contracts that are sufficiently simple to be read and understood by Human customers. It is a good sign that some of these recommendations have encountered significant opposition from firms whose profits might suffer if their customers were better informed. A world in which firms compete by offering better products is preferable to one in which the winner is the firm that is best at obfuscation.

A remarkable feature of libertarian paternalism is its appeal across a broad political spectrum. The flagship example of behavioral policy, called Save More Tomorrow, was sponsored in Congress by an unusual coalition that included extreme conservatives as well as liberals. Save More Tomorrow is a financial plan that firms can offer their employees. Those who sign on allow the employer to increase their contribution to their saving plan by a fixed proportion whenever they receive a raise. The increased saving rate is implemented automatically until the employee gives notice that she wants to opt out of it. This brilliant innovation, proposed by Richard Thaler and Shlomo Benartzi in 2003, has now improved the savings rate and brightened the future prospects of millions of workers. It is soundly based in the psychological principles that readers of this book will recognize. It avoids the resistance to an immediate loss by requiring no immediate change; by tying increased saving to pay raises, it turns losses into foregone gains, which are much easier to bear; and the feature of automaticity aligns the laziness of System 2 with the long-term interests of the workers. All this, of course, without compelling anyone to do anything he does not wish to do and without any misdirection or artifice.

The appeal of libertarian paternalism has been recognized in many countries, including the UK and South Korea, and by politicians of many stripes, including Tories and the Democratic administration of President Obama. Indeed, Britain's government has created a new small unit whose mission is to apply the principles of behavioral science to help the government better accomplish its goals. The official name for this group is the Behavioural Insight Team, but it is known both in and out of government simply as the Nudge Unit. Thaler is an adviser to this team.

In a storybook sequel to the writing of *Nudge*, Sunstein was invited by President Obama to serve as administrator of the Office of Information and Regulatory Affairs, a position that gave him considerable opportunity to encourage the application of the lessons of psychology and behavioral economics in government agencies. The mission is described in the 2010 Report of the Office of Management and Budget. Readers of this book will appreciate the logic behind specific recommendations, including encouraging "clear, simple, salient, and meaningful disclosures." They will also recognize background statements such as "presentation greatly matters; if, for example, a potential outcome is framed as a loss, it may have more impact than if it is presented as a gain."

The example of a regulation about the framing of disclosures concerning fuel consumption was mentioned earlier. Additional applications that have been implemented include automatic enrollment in health insurance, a new version of the dietary guidelines that replaces the incomprehensible Food Pyramid with the powerful image of a Food Plate loaded with a balanced diet, and a rule formulated by the USDA that permits the inclusion of messages such as "90% fat-free" on the label of meat products, provided that the statement "10% fat" is also displayed "contiguous to, in lettering of the same color, size, and type as, and on the same color background as, the statement of lean percentage." Humans, unlike Econs, need help to make good decisions, and there are informed and unintrusive ways to provide that help.

TWO SYSTEMS

This book has described the workings of the mind as an uneasy interaction between two fictitious characters: the automatic System 1 and the effortful System 2. You are now quite familiar with the personalities of the two systems and able to anticipate how they might respond in different situations. And of course you also remember that the two systems do not really exist in the brain or anywhere else. "System 1 does X" is a shortcut for "X occurs automatically." And "System 2 is mobilized to do Y" is a shortcut for "arousal increases, pupils dilate, attention is focused, and activity Y is performed." I hope you find the language of systems as helpful as I do, and that you have acquired an intuitive sense of how they work without getting confused by the question of whether they exist. Having delivered this necessary warning, I will continue to use the language to the end.

The attentive System 2 is who we think we are. System 2 articulates judgments and makes choices, but it often endorses or rationalizes ideas and feelings that were generated by System 1. You may not know that you are optimistic about a project because something about its leader reminds you of your beloved sister, or that you dislike a person who looks vaguely like your dentist. If asked for an explanation, however, you will search your memory for presentable reasons and will certainly find some. Moreover, you will believe the story you make up. But System 2 is not merely an apologist for System 1; it also prevents many foolish thoughts and inappropriate impulses from overt expression. The investment of attention improves performance in numerous activities—think of the risks of driving through a narrow space while your mind is wandering—and is essential to some tasks, including comparison, choice, and ordered reasoning. However, System 2 is not a paragon of rationality. Its abilities are limited and so is the knowledge to which it has access. We do not always think straight when we reason, and the errors are not always due to intrusive and incorrect intuitions. Often we make mistakes because we (our System 2) do not know any better.

I have spent more time describing System 1, and have devoted many pages to errors of intuitive judgment and choice that I attribute to it. However, the relative number of pages is a poor indicator of the balance between the marvels and the flaws of intuitive thinking. System 1 is indeed the origin of much that we do wrong, but it is also the origin of most of what we do right—which is most of what we do. Our thoughts and actions are routinely guided by System 1 and generally are on the mark. One of the marvels is the rich and detailed model of our world that is maintained in associative memory: it distinguishes surprising from normal events in a fraction of a second, immediately generates an idea of what was expected instead of a surprise, and automatically searches for some causal interpretation of surprises and of events as they take place.

Memory also holds the vast repertory of skills we have acquired in a lifetime of practice, which automatically produce adequate solutions to challenges as they arise, from walking around a large stone on the path to averting the incipient outburst of a customer. The acquisition of skills requires a regular environment, an adequate opportunity to practice, and rapid and unequivocal feedback about the correctness of thoughts and actions. When these conditions are fulfilled, skill eventually develops, and the intuitive judgments and choices that quickly come to mind will mostly be accurate. All this is the work of System 1, which means it occurs automatically and fast. A marker of skilled performance is the ability to deal with vast amounts of information swiftly and efficiently.

When a challenge is encountered to which a skilled response is available, that response is evoked. What happens in the absence of skill? Sometimes, as in the problem $17 \times 24 = ?$, which calls for a specific answer, it is immediately apparent that System 2 must be called in. But it is rare for System 1 to be dumbfounded. System 1 is not constrained by capacity limits and is profligate in its computations. When engaged in searching for an answer to one question, it simultaneously generates the answers to related questions, and it may substitute a response that more easily comes to mind for the one that was requested. In this conception of heuristics, the heuristic answer is not necessarily simpler or more frugal than the original question—it is only more accessible, computed more quickly and easily. The heuristic answers are not random, and they are often approximately correct. And sometimes they are quite wrong.

System 1 registers the cognitive ease with which it processes information, but it does not generate a warning signal when it becomes unreliable. Intuitive answers come to mind quickly and confidently, whether they originate from skills or from heuristics. There is no simple way for System 2 to distinguish between a skilled and a heuristic response. Its only recourse is to slow down and attempt to construct an answer on its own, which it is reluctant to do because it is indolent. Many suggestions of System 1 are casually endorsed with minimal checking, as in the bat-and-ball problem. This is how System 1 acquires its bad reputation as the source of errors and biases. Its operative features, which include WYSIATI, intensity matching, and associative coherence, among others, give rise to predictable biases and to cognitive illusions such as anchoring, nonregressive predictions, over-confidence, and numerous others.

What can be done about biases? How can we improve judgments and decisions, both our own and those of the institutions that we serve and that serve us? The short answer is that little can be achieved without a considerable investment of effort. As I know from experience, System 1 is not readily educable. Except for some effects that I attribute mostly to age, my intuitive thinking is just as prone to overconfidence, extreme predictions, and the planning fallacy as it was before I made a study of these issues. I have improved only in my ability to recognize situations in which errors are likely: "This number will be an anchor . . . ," "The decision could change if the problem is reframed . . ." And I have made much more progress in recognizing the errors of others than my own.

The way to block errors that originate in System 1 is simple in principle: recognize the signs that you are in a cognitive minefield, slow down, and ask for reinforcement from System 2. This is how you will proceed when you next encounter the Müller-Lyer illusion. When you see lines with fins pointing in different directions, you will recognize the situation as one in which you should not trust your impressions of length. Unfortunately, this sensible procedure is least likely to be applied when it is needed most. We would all like to have a warning bell that rings loudly whenever we are about to make a serious error, but no such bell is available, and cognitive illusions are generally more difficult to recognize than perceptual illusions. The voice of reason may be much fainter than the loud and clear voice of an erroneous intuition, and questioning your intuitions is unpleasant when you face the stress of a big decision. More doubt is the last thing you want when you are in trouble. The upshot is that it is much easier to identify a minefield when you observe others wandering into it than when you are about to do so. Observers are less cognitively busy and more open to information than actors. That was my reason for writing a book that is oriented to critics and gossipers rather than to decision makers.

Organizations are better than individuals when it comes to avoiding errors, because they naturally think more slowly and have the power to impose orderly procedures. Organizations can institute and enforce the application of useful checklists, as well as more elaborate exercises, such as reference-class forecasting and the premortem. At least in part by providing a distinctive vocabulary, organizations can also encourage a culture in which people watch out for one another as they approach minefields. Whatever else it produces, an organization is a factory that manufactures judgments and decisions. Every factory must have ways to ensure the quality of its products in the initial design, in fabrication, and in final inspections. The corresponding stages in the production of decisions are the framing of the problem that is to be solved, the collection of relevant information leading to a decision, and reflection and review. An organization that seeks to improve its decision product should routinely look for efficiency improvements at each of these stages. The operative concept is routine. Constant quality control is an alternative to the wholesale reviews of processes that organizations commonly undertake in the wake of disasters. There is much to be done to improve decision making. One example out of many is the remarkable absence of systematic training for the essential skill of conducting efficient meetings.

Ultimately, a richer language is essential to the skill of constructive criticism. Much like medicine, the identification of judgment errors is a diagnostic task, which requires a precise vocabulary. The name of a disease is a hook to which all that is known about the disease is attached, including vulnerabilities, environmental factors, symptoms, prognosis, and care. Similarly, labels such as "anchoring effects," "narrow framing," or "excessive coherence" bring together in memory everything we know about a bias, its causes, its effects, and what can be done about it.

There is a direct link from more precise gossip at the watercooler to better decisions. Decision makers are sometimes better able to imagine the voices of present gossipers and future critics than to hear the hesitant voice of their own doubts. They will make better choices when they trust their critics to be sophisticated and fair, and when they expect their decision to be judged by how it was made, not only by how it turned out.

APPENDIX A: JUDGMENT UNDER UNCERTAINTY: HEURISTICS AND BIASES*

Amos Tversky and Daniel Kahneman

Many decisions are based on beliefs concerning the likelihood of uncertain events such as the outcome of an election, the guilt of a defendant, or the future value of the dollar. These beliefs are usually expressed in statements such as "I think that . . . ," "chances are . . . ," "it is unlikely that . . . ," and so forth. Occasionally, beliefs concerning uncertain events are expressed in numerical form as odds or subjective probabilities. What determines such beliefs? How do people assess the probability of an uncertain event or the value of an uncertain quantity? This article shows that people rely on a limited number of heuristic principles which reduce the complex tasks of assessing probabilities and predicting values to simpler judgmental operations. In general, these heuristics are quite useful, but sometimes they lead to severe and systematic errors.

The subjective assessment of probability resembles the subjective assessment of physical quantities such as distance or size. These judgments are all based on data of limited validity, which are processed according to heuristic rules. For example, the apparent distance of an object is determined in part by its clarity. The more sharply the object is seen, the closer it appears to be. This rule has some validity, because in any given scene the more distant objects are seen less sharply than nearer objects. However, the reliance on this rule leads to systematic errors in the estimation of distance. Specifically, distances are often overestimated when visibility is poor because the contours of objects are blurred. On the other hand, distances are often underestimated when visibility is good because the objects are seen sharply. Thus, the reliance on clarity as an indication of distance leads to common biases. Such biases are also found in the intuitive judgment of probability. This article describes three heuristics that are employed to assess probabilities and to predict values. Biases to which these heuristics

*This article originally appeared in *Science*, vol. 185, 1974. The research was supported by the Advanced Research Projects Agency of the Department of Defense and was monitored by the Office of Naval Research under contract N00014-73-C-0438 to the Oregon Research Institute, Eugene. Additional support for this research was provided by the Research and Development Authority of the Hebrew University, Jerusalem, Israel.

lead are enumerated, and the applied and theoretical implications of these observations are discussed.

REPRESENTATIVENESS

Many of the probabilistic questions with which people are concerned belong to one of the following types: What is the probability that object A belongs to class B? What is the probability that event A originates from process B? What is the probability that process B will generate event A? In answering such questions, people typically rely on the representativeness heuristic, in which probabilities are evaluated by the degree to which A is representative of B, that is, by the degree to which A resembles B. For example, when A is highly representative of B, the probability that A originates from B is judged to be high. On the other hand, if A is not similar to B, the probability that A originates from B is judged to be low.

For an illustration of judgment by representativeness, consider an individual who has been described by a former neighbor as follows: "Steve is very shy and withdrawn, invariably helpful, but with little interest in people, or in the world of reality. A meek and tidy soul, he has a need for order and structure, and a passion for detail." How do people assess the probability that Steve is engaged in a particular occupation from a list of possibilities (for example, farmer, salesman, airline pilot, librarian, or physician)? How do people order these occupations from most to least likely? In the representativeness heuristic, the probability that Steve is a librarian, for example, is assessed by the degree to which he is representative of, or similar to, the stereotype of a librarian. Indeed, research with problems of this type has shown that people order the occupations by probability and by similarity in exactly the same way.[1] This approach to the judgment of probability leads to serious errors, because similarity, or representativeness, is not influenced by several factors that should affect judgments of probability.

Insensitivity to prior probability of outcomes. One of the factors that have no effect on representativeness but should have a major effect on probability is the prior probability, or base-rate frequency, of the outcomes. In the case of Steve, for example, the fact that there are many more farmers than librarians in the population should enter into any reasonable estimate of the probability that Steve is a librarian rather than a farmer. Considerations of base-rate frequency, however, do not affect the similarity of Steve to the stereotypes of librarians and farmers. If people evaluate probability by representativeness, therefore, prior probabilities will be neglected. This hypothesis was tested in an experiment where prior probabilities were manipulated.[2] Subjects were shown brief personality descriptions of several individuals, allegedly sampled at random from a group of 100 professionals—engineers and lawyers. The subjects were asked to assess, for each description, the probability that it belonged to an engineer rather than to a lawyer. In one experimental condition, subjects were told that the group from which the descriptions had been drawn consisted of 70 engineers and 30 lawyers. In another condition, subjects were told that the group consisted of 30 engineers and 70 lawyers. The odds that any particular description belongs to an engineer rather than to a lawyer should be higher in the first condition, where there is a majority of engineers, than in the second condition, where there is a majority of lawyers. Specifically, it can be shown by applying Bayes' rule that the ratio of these odds should be $(.7/.3)^2$, or 5.44, for each description. In a sharp violation of Bayes' rule, the subjects in the two conditions produced essentially the same probability judgments. Apparently, subjects evaluated the likelihood that a particular description belonged to an engineer rather than to a lawyer by the degree to which this description was representative of the two stereotypes, with little or no regard for the prior probabilities of the categories.

The subjects used prior probabilities correctly when they had no other information. In the absence of a personality sketch, they judged the probability that an unknown individual is an engineer to be .7 and .3, respectively, in the two base-rate conditions. However, prior probabilities were effectively ignored when a description was introduced, even when this description was totally uninformative. The responses to the following description illustrate this phenomenon:

> Dick is a 30-year-old man. He is married with no children. A man of high ability and high motivation, he promises to be quite successful in his field. He is well liked by his colleagues.

This description was intended to convey no information relevant to the question of whether Dick is an engineer or a lawyer. Consequently, the probability that Dick is an engineer should equal the proportion of engineers in the group, as if no description had been given. The subjects, however, judged the probability of Dick being an engineer to be .5 regardless of whether the stated proportion of engineers in the group was .7 or .3. Evidently, people respond differently when given no evidence and when given worthless evidence. When no specific evidence is given, prior probabilities are properly utilized; when worthless evidence is given, prior probabilities are ignored.[3]

Insensitivity to sample size. To evaluate the probability of obtaining a particular result in a sample drawn from a specified population, people typically apply the representativeness heuristic. That is, they assess the likelihood of a sample result, for example, that the average height in a random sample of ten men will be 6 feet, by the similarity of this result to the corresponding parameter (that is, to the average height in the population of men). The similarity of a sample statistic to a population parameter does not depend on the size of the sample. Consequently, if probabilities are assessed by representativeness, then the judged probability of a sample statistic will be essentially independent of sample size. Indeed, when subjects assessed the distributions of average height for samples of various sizes, they produced identical distributions. For example, the probability of obtaining an average height greater than 6 feet was assigned the same value for samples of 1,000, 100, and 10 men.[4] Moreover, subjects failed to appreciate the role of sample size even when it was emphasized in the formulation of the problem. Consider the following question:

> A certain town is served by two hospitals. In the larger hospital about 45 babies are born each day, and in the smaller hospital about 15 babies are born each day. As you know, about 50% of all babies are boys. However, the exact percentage varies from day to day. Sometimes it may be higher than 50%, sometimes lower.
>
> For a period of 1 year, each hospital recorded the days on which more than 60% of the babies born were boys. Which hospital do you think recorded more such days?
>
> The larger hospital (21)
>
> The smaller hospital (21)
>
> About the same (that is, within 5% of each other) (53)

The values in parentheses are the number of undergraduate students who chose each answer.

Most subjects judged the probability of obtaining more than 60% boys to be the same in the small and in the large hospital, presumably because these events are described by the same statistic and are therefore equally representative of the general population. In contrast, sampling theory entails that the expected number of days on which more than 60% of the babies are boys is much greater in the small hospital than in the large one, because a large sample is less likely to stray from 50%. This fundamental notion of statistics is evidently not part of people's repertoire of intuitions.

A similar insensitivity to sample size has been reported in judgments of posterior probability, that is, of the probability that a sample has been drawn from one population rather than from another. Consider the following example:

> Imagine an urn filled with balls, of which ⅔ are of one color and ⅓ of another. One individual has drawn 5 balls from the urn, and found that 4 were red and 1 was white. Another individual has drawn 20 balls and found that 12 were red and 8 were white. Which of the two individuals should feel more confident that the urn contains ⅔ red balls and ⅓ white balls, rather than the opposite? What odds should each individual give?

In this problem, the correct posterior odds are 8 to 1 for the 4:1 sample and 16 to 1 for the 12:8 sample, assuming equal prior probabilities. However, most people feel that the first sample provides much stronger evidence for the hypothesis that the urn is predominantly red, because the proportion of red balls is larger in the first than in the second sample. Here again, intuitive judgments are dominated by the sample proportion and are essentially unaffected by the size of the sample, which plays a crucial role in the determination of the actual posterior odds.[5] In addition, intuitive estimates of posterior odds are far less extreme than the correct values. The underestimation of the impact of evidence has been observed repeatedly in problems of this type.[6] It has been labeled "conservatism."

Misconceptions of chance. People expect that a sequence of events generated by a random process will represent the essential characteristics of that process even when the sequence is short. In considering tosses of a coin for heads or tails, for example, people regard the sequence H-T-H-T-T-H to be more likely than the sequence H-H-H-T-T-T, which does not appear random, and also more likely than the sequence H-H-H-H-T-H, which does not represent the fairness of the coin.[7] Thus, people expect that the essential characteristics of the process will be represented, not only globally in the entire sequence, but also locally in each of its parts. A locally representative sequence, however, deviates systematically from chance expectation: it contains too many alternations and too few runs. Another consequence of the belief in local representativeness is the well-known gambler's fallacy. After observing a long run of red on the roulette wheel, for example, most people erroneously believe that black is now due, presumably because the occurrence of black will result in a more representative sequence than the occurrence of an additional red. Chance is commonly viewed as a self-correcting process in which a deviation in one direction induces a deviation in the opposite direction to restore the equilibrium. In fact, deviations are not "corrected" as a chance process unfolds, they are merely diluted.

Misconceptions of chance are not limited to naive subjects. A study of the statistical intuitions of experienced research psychologists[8] revealed a lingering belief in what may be called the "law of small numbers," according to which even small samples are highly representative of the populations from which they are drawn. The responses of these investigators reflected the expectation that a valid hypothesis about a population will be represented by a statistically significant result in a sample with little regard for its size. As a consequence, the researchers put too much faith in the results of small samples and grossly overestimated the replicability of such results. In the actual conduct of research, this bias leads to the selection of samples of inadequate size and to overinterpretation of findings.

Insensitivity to predictability. People are sometimes called upon to make such numerical predictions as the future value of a stock, the demand for a commodity, or the outcome of a football game. Such predictions are often made by representativeness. For example, suppose one is given a description of a company and is asked to predict its future profit. If the description of the company is very favorable, a very high profit will appear most representative of that description; if the description is mediocre, a mediocre performance will appear most representative. The degree to which the description is favorable is unaffected by the reliability of that description or by the degree to which it permits accurate prediction. Hence, if people predict solely in terms of the favorableness of the description, their predictions will be insensitive to the reliability of the evidence and to the expected accuracy of the prediction.

This mode of judgment violates the normative statistical theory in which the extremeness and the range of predictions are controlled by considerations of predictability. When predictability is nil, the same prediction should be made in all cases. For example, if the descriptions of companies provide no information relevant to profit, then the same value (such as average profit) should be predicted for all companies. If predictability is perfect, of course, the values predicted will match the actual values and the range of predictions will equal the range of outcomes. In general, the higher the predictability, the wider the range of predicted values.

Several studies of numerical prediction have demonstrated that intuitive predictions violate this rule, and that subjects show little or no regard for considerations of predictability.[9] In one of these studies, subjects were presented with several paragraphs, each describing the performance of a student teacher during a particular practice lesson. Some subjects were asked to evaluate the quality of the lesson described in the paragraph in percentile scores, relative to a specified population. Other subjects were asked to predict, also in percentile scores, the standing of each student teacher 5 years after the practice lesson. The judgments made under the two conditions were identical. That is, the prediction of a remote criterion (success of a teacher after 5 years) was identical to the evaluation of the information on which the prediction was based (the quality of the practice lesson). The students who made these predictions were undoubtedly aware of the limited predictability of teaching competence on the basis of a single trial lesson 5 years earlier; nevertheless, their predictions were as extreme as their evaluations.

The illusion of validity. As we have seen, people often predict by selecting the outcome (for example, an occupation) that is most representative of the input (for example, the description of a person). The confidence they have in their prediction depends primarily on the degree of representativeness (that is, on the quality of the match between the selected outcome and the input) with little or no regard for the factors that limit predictive accuracy. Thus, people express great confidence in the prediction that a person is a librarian when given a description of his personality which matches the stereotype of librarians, even if the description is scanty, unreliable, or outdated. The unwarranted confidence which is produced by a good fit between the predicted outcome and the input information may be called the illusion of validity. This illusion persists even when the judge is aware of the factors that limit the accuracy of his predictions. It is a common observation that psychologists who conduct selection interviews often experience considerable confidence in their predictions, even when they know of the vast literature that shows selection interviews to be highly fallible. The continued reliance on the clinical interview for selection, despite repeated demonstrations of its inadequacy, amply attests to the strength of this effect.

The internal consistency of a pattern of inputs is a major determinant of one's confidence in predictions based on these inputs. For example, people express more confidence in predicting the final grade point average of a student whose first-year record consists entirely of B's than in predicting the grade point average of a student whose first-year record includes many A's and C's. Highly consistent patterns are most often observed when the input variables are highly redundant or correlated. Hence, people tend to have great confidence in predictions based on redundant input variables. However, an elementary result in the statistics of correlation asserts that, given input variables of stated validity, a prediction based on several such inputs can achieve higher accuracy when they are independent of each other than when they are redundant or correlated. Thus, redundancy among inputs decreases accuracy even as it increases confidence, and people are often confident in predictions that are quite likely to be off the mark.[10]

Misconceptions of regression. Suppose a large group of children has been examined on two equivalent versions of an aptitude test. If one selects ten children from among those who did best on one of the two versions, he will usually find their performance on the second version to be somewhat disappointing. Conversely, if one selects ten children from among those who did worst on one version, they will be found, on the average, to do somewhat better on the other version. More generally, consider two variables X and Y which have the same distribution. If one selects individuals whose average X score deviates from the mean of X by k units, then the average of their Y scores will usually deviate from the mean of Y by less than k units. These observations illustrate a general phenomenon known as regression toward the mean, which was first documented by Galton more than 100 years ago.

In the normal course of life, one encounters many instances of regression toward the mean, in the comparison of the height of fathers and sons, of the intelligence of husbands and wives, or of the performance of individuals on consecutive examinations. Nevertheless, people do not develop correct intuitions about this phenomenon. First, they do not expect regression in many contexts where it is bound to occur. Second, when they recognize the occurrence of regression, they often invent spurious causal explanations for it.[11] We suggest that the phenomenon of regression remains elusive because it is incompatible with the belief that the predicted outcome should be maximally representative of the input, and, hence, that the value of the outcome variable should be as extreme as the value of the input variable.

The failure to recognize the import of regression can have pernicious consequences, as illustrated by the following observation.[12] In a discussion of flight training, experienced instructors noted that praise for an exceptionally smooth landing is typically followed by a poorer landing on the next try, while harsh criticism after a rough landing is usually followed by an improvement on the next try. The instructors concluded that verbal rewards are detrimental to learning, while verbal punishments are beneficial, contrary to accepted psychological doctrine. This conclusion is unwarranted because of the presence of regression toward the mean. As in other cases of repeated examination, an improvement will usually follow a poor performance and a deterioration will usually follow an outstanding performance, even if the instructor does not respond to the trainee's achievement on the first attempt. Because the instructors had praised their trainees after good landings and admonished them after poor ones, they reached the erroneous and potentially harmful conclusion that punishment is more effective than reward.

Thus, the failure to understand the effect of regression leads one to overestimate the effectiveness of punishment and to underestimate the effectiveness of reward. In social interaction, as well as in training, rewards are typically administered when performance is good, and punishments are typically administered when performance is poor. By regression alone, therefore, behavior is most likely to improve after punishment and most likely to deteriorate after reward.

Consequently, the human condition is such that, by chance alone, one is most often rewarded for punishing others and most often punished for rewarding them. People are generally not aware of this contingency. In fact, the elusive role of regression in determining the apparent consequences of reward and punishment seems to have escaped the notice of students of this area.

AVAILABILITY

There are situations in which people assess the frequency of a class or the probability of an event by the ease with which instances or occurrences can be brought to mind. For example, one may assess the risk of heart attack among middle-aged people by recalling such occurrences among one's acquaintances. Similarly, one may evaluate the probability that a given business venture will fail by imagining various difficulties it could encounter. This judgmental heuristic is called availability. Availability is a useful clue for assessing frequency or probability, because instances of large classes are usually recalled better and faster than instances of less frequent classes. However, availability is affected by factors other than frequency and probability. Consequently, the reliance on availability leads to predictable biases, some of which are illustrated below.

Biases due to the retrievability of instances. When the size of a class is judged by the availability of its instances, a class whose instances are easily retrieved will appear more numerous than a class of equal frequency whose instances are less retrievable. In an elementary demonstration of this effect, subjects heard a list of well-known personalities of both sexes and were subsequently asked to judge whether the list contained more names of men than of women. Different lists were presented to different groups of subjects. In some of the lists the men were relatively more famous than the women, and in others the women were relatively more famous than the men. In each of the lists, the subjects erroneously judged that the class (sex) that had the more famous personalities was the more numerous.[13]

In addition to familiarity, there are other factors, such as salience, which affect the retrievability of instances. For example, the impact of seeing a house burning on the subjective probability of such accidents is probably greater than the impact of reading about a fire in the local paper. Furthermore, recent occurrences are likely to be relatively more available than earlier occurrences. It is a common experience that the subjective probability of traffic accidents rises temporarily when one sees a car overturned by the side of the road.

Biases due to the effectiveness of a search set. Suppose one samples a word (of three letters or more) at random from an English text. Is it more likely that the word starts with r or that r is the third letter? People approach this problem by recalling words that begin with r (*road*) and words that have r in the third position (*car*) and assess the relative frequency by the ease with which words of the two types come to mind. Because it is much easier to search for words by their first letter than by their third letter, most people judge words that begin with a given consonant to be more numerous than words in which the same consonant appears in the third position. They do so even for consonants, such as r or k, that are more frequent in the third position than in the first.[14]

Different tasks elicit different search sets. For example, suppose you are asked to rate the frequency with which abstract words (*thought, love*) and concrete words (*door, water*) appear in written English. A natural way to answer this question is to search for contexts in which the word could appear. It seems easier to think of contexts in which an abstract concept is mentioned (love in love stories) than to think of contexts in which a concrete word (such as *door*) is mentioned. If the frequency of words is judged by the availability of the contexts in which they appear, abstract words will be judged as relatively more numerous than concrete words. This bias has been observed in a recent study[15] which showed that the judged frequency of occurrence of abstract words was much higher than that of concrete words, equated in objective frequency. Abstract words were also judged to appear in a much greater variety of contexts than concrete words.

Biases of imaginability. Sometimes one has to assess the frequency of a class whose instances are not stored in memory but can be generated according to a given rule. In such situations, one typically generates several instances and evaluates frequency or probability by the ease with which the relevant instances can be constructed. However, the ease of constructing instances does not always reflect their actual frequency, and this mode of evaluation is prone to biases. To illustrate, consider a group of 10 people who form committees of k members, $2 \le k \le 8$. How many different committees of k members can be formed? The correct answer to this problem is given by the binomial coefficient $(10/k)$ which reaches a maximum of 252 for $k = 5$. Clearly, the number of committees of k members equals the number of committees of $(10 - k)$ members, because any committee of k members defines a unique group of $(10 - k)$ nonmembers.

One way to answer this question without computation is to mentally construct committees of k members and to evaluate their number by the ease with which they come to mind. Committees of few members, say 2, are more available than committees of many members, say 8. The simplest scheme for the construction of committees is a partition of the group into disjoint sets. One readily sees that it is easy to construct five disjoint committees of 2 members, while it is impossible to generate even two disjoint committees of 8 members. Consequently, if frequency is assessed by imaginability, or by availability for construction, the small committees will appear more numerous than larger committees, in contrast to the correct bell-shaped function. Indeed, when naive subjects were asked to estimate the number of distinct committees of various sizes, their estimates were a decreasing monotonic function of committee size.[16] For example, the median estimate of the number of committees of 2 members was 70, while the estimate for committees of 8 members was 20 (the correct answer is 45 in both cases).

Imaginability plays an important role in the evaluation of probabilities in real-life situations. The risk involved in an adventurous expedition, for example, is evaluated by imagining contingencies with which the expedition is not equipped to cope. If many such difficulties are vividly portrayed, the expedition can be made to appear exceedingly dangerous, although the ease with which disasters are imagined need not reflect their actual likelihood. Conversely, the risk involved in an undertaking may be grossly underestimated if some possible dangers are either difficult to conceive of, or simply do not come to mind.

Illusory correlation. Chapman and Chapman[17] have described an interesting bias in the judgment of the frequency with which two events co-occur. They presented naive judges with information concerning several hypothetical mental patients. The data for each patient consisted of a clinical diagnosis and a drawing of a person made by the patient. Later the judges estimated the frequency with which each diagnosis (such as paranoia or suspiciousness) had been accompanied by various features of the drawing (such as peculiar eyes). The subjects markedly overestimated the frequency of co-occurrence of natural associates, such as suspiciousness and peculiar eyes. This effect was labeled illusory correlation. In their erroneous judgments of the data to which they had been exposed, naive subjects "rediscovered" much of the common, but unfounded, clinical lore concerning the interpretation of the draw-a-person test. The illusory correlation effect was extremely resistant to contradictory data. It persisted even when the correlation between symptom and diagnosis was actually negative, and it prevented the judges from detecting relationships that were in fact present.

Availability provides a natural account for the illusory-correlation effect. The judgment of how frequently two events co-occur could be based on the strength of the associative bond between them. When the association is strong, one is likely to conclude that the events have been frequently paired. Consequently, strong associates will be judged to have occurred together frequently. According to this view, the illusory correlation between suspiciousness and peculiar drawing of the eyes, for example, is due to the fact that suspiciousness is more readily associated with the eyes than with any other part of the body.

Lifelong experience has taught us that, in general, instances of large classes are recalled better and faster than instances of less frequent classes; that likely occurrences are easier to imagine than unlikely ones; and that the associative connections between events are strengthened when the events frequently co-occur. As a result, man has at his disposal a procedure (the availability heuristic) for estimating the numerosity of a class, the likelihood of an event, or the frequency of co-occurrences, by the ease with which the relevant mental operations of retrieval, construction, or association can be performed. However, as the preceding examples have demonstrated, this valuable estimation procedure results in systematic errors.

ADJUSTMENT AND ANCHORING

In many situations, people make estimates by starting from an initial value that is adjusted to yield the final answer. The initial value, or starting point, may be suggested by the formulation of the problem, or it may be the result of a partial computation. In either case, adjustments are typically insufficient.[18] That is, different starting points yield different estimates, which are biased toward the initial values. We call this phenomenon anchoring.

Insufficient adjustment. In a demonstration of the anchoring effect, subjects were asked to estimate various quantities, stated in percentages (for example, the percentage of African countries in the United Nations). For each quantity, a number between 0 and 100 was determined by spinning a wheel of fortune in the subjects' presence. The subjects were instructed to indicate first whether that number was higher or lower than the value of the quantity, and then to estimate the value of the quantity by moving upward or downward from the given number. Different groups were given different numbers for each quantity, and these arbitrary numbers had a marked effect on estimates. For example, the median estimates of the percentage of African countries in the United Nations were 25 and 45 for groups that received 10 and 65, respectively, as starting points. Payoffs for accuracy did not reduce the anchoring effect.

Anchoring occurs not only when the starting point is given to the subject, but also when the subject bases his estimate on the result of some incomplete computation. A study of intuitive numerical estimation illustrates this effect. Two groups of high school students estimated, within 5 seconds, a numerical expression that was written on the blackboard. One group estimated the product

$$8 \times 7 \times 6 \times 5 \times 4 \times 3 \times 2 \times 1$$

while another group estimated the product

$$1 \times 2 \times 3 \times 4 \times 5 \times 6 \times 7 \times 8$$

To rapidly answer such questions, people may perform a few steps of computation and estimate the product by extrapolation or adjustment. Because adjustments are typically insufficient, this procedure should lead to underestimation. Furthermore, because the result of the first few steps of multiplication (performed from left to right) is higher in the descending sequence than in the ascending sequence, the former expression should be judged larger than the latter. Both predictions were confirmed. The median estimate for the ascending sequence was 512, while the median estimate for the descending sequence was 2,250. The correct answer is 40,320.

Biases in the evaluation of conjunctive and disjunctive events. In a recent study by Bar-Hillel[19] subjects were given the opportunity to bet on one of two events. Three types of events were used: (i) simple events, such as drawing a red marble from a bag containing 50% red marbles and 50% white marbles; (ii) conjunctive events, such as drawing a red marble seven times in succession, with replacement, from a bag containing 90% red marbles and 10% white marbles; and (iii) disjunctive events, such as drawing a red marble at least once in seven successive tries, with replacement, from a bag containing 10% red marbles and 9% white marbles. In this problem, a significant majority of subjects preferred to bet on the conjunctive event (the probability of which is .48) rather than on the simple event (the probability of which is .50). Subjects also preferred to bet on the simple event rather than on the disjunctive event, which has a probability of .52. Thus, most subjects bet on the less likely event in both comparisons. This pattern of choices illustrates a general finding. Studies of choice among gambles and of judgments of probability indicate that people tend to overestimate the probability of conjunctive events[20] and to underestimate the probability of disjunctive events. These biases are readily explained as effects of anchoring. The stated probability of the elementary event (success at any one stage) provides a natural starting point for the estimation of the probabilities of both conjunctive and disjunctive events. Since adjustment from the starting point is typically insufficient, the final estimates remain too close to the probabilities of the elementary events in both cases. Note that the overall probability of a conjunctive event is lower than the probability of each elementary event, whereas the overall probability of a disjunctive event is higher than the probability of each elementary event. As a consequence of anchoring, the overall probability will be overestimated in conjunctive problems and underestimated in disjunctive problems.

Biases in the evaluation of compound events are particularly significant in the context of planning. The successful completion of an undertaking, such as the development of a new product, typically has a conjunctive character: for the undertaking to succeed, each of a series of events must occur. Even when each of these events is very likely, the overall probability of success can be quite low if the number of events is large. The general tendency to overestimate the probability of conjunctive events leads to unwarranted optimism in the evaluation of the likelihood that a plan will succeed or that a project will be completed on time. Conversely, disjunctive structures are typically encountered in the evaluation of risks. A complex system, such as a nuclear reactor or a human body, will malfunction if any of its essential components fails. Even when the likelihood of failure in each component is slight, the probability of an overall failure can be high if many components are involved. Because of anchoring, people will tend to underestimate the probabilities of failure in complex systems. Thus, the direction of the anchoring bias can sometimes be inferred from the structure of the event. The chain-like structure of conjunctions leads to overestimation, the funnel-like structure of disjunctions leads to underestimation.

Anchoring in the assessment of subjective probability distributions. In decision analysis, experts are often required to express their beliefs about a quantity, such as the value of the Dow Jones average on a particular day, in the form of a probability distribution. Such a distribution is usually constructed by asking the person to select values of the quantity that correspond to specified percentiles of his subjective probability distribution. For example, the judge may be asked to select a number, X_{90}, such that his subjective probability that this number will be higher than the value of the Dow Jones average is .90. That is, he should select the value X_{90} so that he is just willing to accept 9 to 1 odds that the Dow Jones average will not exceed it. A subjective probability distribution for the value of the Dow Jones average can be constructed from several such judgments corresponding to different percentiles.

By collecting subjective probability distributions for many different quantities, it is possible to test the judge for proper calibration. A judge is properly (or externally) calibrated in a set of problems if exactly Π% of the true values of the assessed quantities falls below his stated values of X_{Π}. For example, the true values should fall below X_{01} for 1% of the quantities and above X_{99} for 1% of the quantities. Thus, the true values should fall in the confidence interval between X_{01} and X_{99} on 98% of the problems.

Several investigators[21] have obtained probability distributions for many quantities from a large number of judges. These distributions indicated large and systematic departures from proper calibration. In most studies, the actual values of the assessed quantities are either smaller than X_{01} or greater than X_{99} for about 30% of the problems. That is, the subjects state overly narrow confidence intervals which reflect more certainty than is justified by their knowledge about the assessed quantities. This bias is common to naive and to sophisticated subjects, and it is not eliminated by introducing proper scoring rules, which provide incentives for external calibration. This effect is attributable, in part at least, to anchoring.

To select X_{90} for the value of the Dow Jones average, for example, it is natural to begin by thinking about one's best estimate of the Dow Jones and to adjust this value upward. If this adjustment—like most others—is insufficient, then X_{90} will not be sufficiently extreme. A similar anchoring effect will occur in the selection of X_{10}, which is presumably obtained by adjusting one's best estimate downward. Consequently, the confidence interval between X_{10} and X_{90} will be too narrow, and the assessed probability distribution will be too tight. In support of this interpretation it can be shown that subjective probabilities are systematically altered by a procedure in which one's best estimate does not serve as an anchor.

Subjective probability distributions for a given quantity (the Dow Jones average) can be obtained in two different ways: (i) by asking the subject to select values of the Dow Jones that correspond to specified percentiles of his probability distribution and (ii) by asking the subject to assess the probabilities that the true value of the Dow Jones will exceed some specified values. The two procedures are formally equivalent and should yield identical distributions. However, they suggest different modes of adjustment from different anchors. In procedure (i), the natural starting point is one's best estimate of the quantity. In procedure (ii), on the other hand, the subject may be anchored on the value stated in the question. Alternatively, he may be anchored on even odds, or a 50–50 chance, which is a natural starting point in the estimation of likelihood. In either case, procedure (ii) should yield less extreme odds than procedure (i).

To contrast the two procedures, a set of 24 quantities (such as the air distance from New Delhi to Peking) was presented to a group of subjects who assessed either X_{10} or X_{90} for each problem. Another group of subjects received the median judgment of the first group for each of the 24 quantities. They were asked to assess the odds that each of the given values exceeded the true value of the relevant quantity. In the absence of any bias, the second group should retrieve the odds specified to the first group, that is, 9:1. However, if even odds or the stated value serve as anchors, the odds of the second group should be less extreme, that is, closer to 1:1. Indeed, the median odds stated by this group, across all problems, were 3:1. When the judgments of the two groups were tested for external calibration, it was found that subjects in the first group were too extreme, in accord with earlier studies. The events that they defined as having a probability of .10 actually obtained in 24% of the cases. In contrast, subjects in the second group were too conservative. Events to which they assigned an average probability of .34 actually obtained in 26% of the cases. These results illustrate the manner in which the degree of calibration depends on the procedure of elicitation.

DISCUSSION

This article has been concerned with cognitive biases that stem from the reliance on judgmental heuristics. These biases are not attributable to motivational effects such as wishful thinking or the distortion of judgments by payoffs and penalties. Indeed, several of the severe errors of judgment reported earlier occurred despite the fact that subjects were encouraged to be accurate and were rewarded for the correct answers.[22]

The reliance on heuristics and the prevalence of biases are not restricted to laymen. Experienced researchers are also prone to the same biases—when they think intuitively. For example, the tendency to predict the outcome that best represents the data, with insufficient regard for prior probability, has been observed in the intuitive judgments of individuals who have had extensive training in statistics.[23] Although the statistically sophisticated avoid elementary errors, such as the gambler's fallacy, their intuitive judgments are liable to similar fallacies in more intricate and less transparent problems.

It is not surprising that useful heuristics such as representativeness and availability are retained, even though they occasionally lead to errors in prediction or estimation. What is perhaps surprising is the failure of people to infer from lifelong experience such fundamental statistical rules as regression toward the mean, or the effect of sample size on sampling variability. Although everyone is exposed, in the normal course of life, to numerous examples from which these rules could have been induced, very few people discover the principles of sampling and regression on their own. Statistical principles are not learned from everyday experience because the relevant instances are not coded appropriately. For example, people do not discover that successive lines in a text differ more in average word length than do successive pages, because they simply do not attend to the average word length of individual lines or pages. Thus, people do not learn the relation between sample size and sampling variability, although the data for such learning are abundant.

The lack of an appropriate code also explains why people usually do not detect the biases in their judgments of probability. A person could conceivably learn whether his judgments are externally calibrated by keeping a tally of the proportion of events that actually occur among those to which he assigns the same probability. However, it is not natural to group events by their judged probability. In the absence of such grouping it is impossible for an individual to discover, for example, that only 50% of the predictions to which he has assigned a probability of .9 or higher actually came true.

The empirical analysis of cognitive biases has implications for the theoretical and applied role of judged probabilities. Modern decision theory[24] regards subjective probability as the quantified opinion of an idealized person. Specifically, the subjective probability of a given event is defined by the set of bets about this event that such a person is willing to accept. An internally consistent, or coherent, subjective probability measure can be derived for an individual if his choices among bets satisfy certain principles, that is, the axioms of the theory. The derived probability is subjective in the sense that different individuals are allowed to have different probabilities for the same event. The major contribution of this approach is that it provides a rigorous subjective interpretation of probability that is applicable to unique events and is embedded in a general theory of rational decision.

It should perhaps be noted that, while subjective probabilities can sometimes be inferred from preferences among bets, they are normally not formed in this fashion. A person bets on team A rather than on team B because he believes that team A is more likely to win; he does not infer this belief from his betting preferences. Thus, in reality, subjective probabilities determine preferences among bets and are not derived from them, as in the axiomatic theory of rational decision.[25]

The inherently subjective nature of probability has led many students to the belief that coherence, or internal consistency, is the only valid criterion by which judged probabilities should be evaluated. From the standpoint of the formal theory of subjective probability, any set of internally consistent probability judgments is as good as any other. This criterion is not entirely satisfactory, because an internally consistent set of subjective probabilities can be incompatible with other beliefs held by the individual. Consider a person whose subjective probabilities for all possible outcomes of a coin-tossing game reflect the gambler's fallacy. That is, his estimate of the probability of tails on a particular toss increases with the number of consecutive heads that preceded that toss. The judgments of such a person could be internally consistent and therefore acceptable as adequate subjective probabilities according to the criterion of the formal theory. These probabilities, however, are incompatible with the generally held belief that a coin has no memory and is therefore incapable of generating sequential dependencies. For judged probabilities to be considered adequate, or rational, internal consistency is not enough. The judgments must be compatible with the entire web of beliefs held by the individual. Unfortunately, there can be no simple formal procedure for assessing the compatibility of a set of probability judgments with the judge's total system of beliefs. The rational judge will nevertheless strive for compatibility, even though internal consistency is more easily achieved and assessed. In particular, he will attempt to make his probability judgments compatible with his knowledge about the subject matter, the laws of probability, and his own judgmental heuristics and biases.

SUMMARY

This article described three heuristics that are employed in making judgments under uncertainty: (i) representativeness, which is usually employed when people are asked to judge the probability that an object or event A belongs to class or process B; (ii) availability of instances or scenarios, which is often employed when people are asked to assess the frequency of a class or the plausibility of a particular development; and (iii) adjustment from an anchor, which is usually employed in numerical prediction when a relevant value is available. These heuristics are highly economical and usually effective, but they lead to systematic and predictable errors. A better understanding of these heuristics and of the biases to which they lead could improve judgments and decisions in situations of uncertainty.

NOTES

1. D. Kahneman and A. Tversky, "On the Psychology of Prediction," *Psychological Review* 80 (1973): 237–51.
2. Ibid.
3. Ibid.
4. D. Kahneman and A. Tversky, "Subjective Probability: A Judgment of Representativeness," *Cognitive Psychology* 3 (1972): 430–54.
5. Ibid.
6. W. Edwards, "Conservatism in Human Information Processing," in *Formal Representation of Human Judgment*, ed. B. Kleinmuntz (New York: Wiley, 1968), 17–52.
7. Kahneman and Tversky, "Subjective Probability."
8. A. Tversky and D. Kahneman, "Belief in the Law of Small Numbers," *Psychological Bulletin* 76 (1971): 105–10.
9. Kahneman and Tversky, "On the Psychology of Prediction."
10. Ibid.
11. Ibid.
12. Ibid.
13. A. Tversky and D. Kahneman, "Availability: A Heuristic for Judging Frequency and Probability," *Cognitive Psychology* 5 (1973): 207–32.
14. Ibid.
15. R. C. Galbraith and B. J. Underwood, "Perceived Frequency of Concrete and Abstract Words," *Memory & Cognition* 1 (1973): 56–60.
16. Tversky and Kahneman, "Availability."
17. L. J. Chapman and J. P. Chapman, "Genesis of Popular but Erroneous Psychodiagnostic Observations," *Journal of Abnormal Psychology* 73 (1967): 193–204; L. J. Chapman and J. P. Chapman, "Illusory Correlation as an Obstacle to the Use of Valid Psychodiagnostic Signs," *Journal of Abnormal Psychology* 74 (1969): 271–80.
18. P. Slovic and S. Lichtenstein, "Comparison of Bayesian and Regression Approaches to the Study of Information Processing in Judgment," *Organizational Behavior & Human Performance* 6 (1971): 649–744.
19. M. Bar-Hillel, "On the Subjective Probability of Compound Events," *Organizational Behavior & Human Performance* 9 (1973): 396–406.
20. J. Cohen, E. I. Chesnick, and D. Haran, "A Confirmation of the Inertial-Ψ Effect in Sequential Choice and Decision," *British Journal of Psychology* 63 (1972): 41–46.
21. M. Alpert and H. Raiffa, unpublished manuscript; C. A. Stael von Holstein, "Two Techniques for Assessment of Subjective Probability Distributions: An Experimental Study," *Acta Psychologica* 35 (1971): 478–94; R. L. Winkler, "The Assessment of Prior Distributions in Bayesian Analysis," *Journal of the American Statistical Association* 62 (1967): 776–800.
22. Kahneman and Tversky, "Subjective Probability"; Tversky and Kahneman, "Availability."
23. Kahneman and Tversky, "On the Psychology of Prediction"; Tversky and Kahneman, "Belief in the Law of Small Numbers."
24. L. J. Savage, *The Foundations of Statistics* (New York: Wiley, 1954).
25. Ibid.; B. de Finetti, "Probability: Interpretations," in *International Encyclopedia of the Social Sciences*, ed. D. E. Sills, vol. 12 (New York: Macmillan, 1968), 496–505.

APPENDIX B: CHOICES, VALUES, AND FRAMES*

Daniel Kahneman and Amos Tversky

ABSTRACT: *We discuss the cognitive and the psychophysical determinants of choice in risky and riskless contexts. The psychophysics of value induce risk aversion in the domain of gains and risk seeking in the domain of losses. The psychophysics of chance induce overweighting of sure things and of improbable events, relative to events of moderate probability. Decision problems can be described or framed in multiple ways that give rise to different preferences, contrary to the invariance criterion of rational choice. The process of mental accounting, in which people organize the outcomes of transactions, explains some anomalies of consumer behavior. In particular, the acceptability of an option can depend on whether a negative outcome is evaluated as a cost or as an uncompensated loss. The relation between decision values and experience values is discussed.*

Making decisions is like speaking prose—people do it all the time, knowingly or unknowingly. It is hardly surprising, then, that the topic of decision making is shared by many disciplines, from mathematics and statistics, through economics and political science, to sociology and psychology. The study of decisions addresses both normative and descriptive questions. The normative analysis is concerned with the nature of rationality and the logic of decision making. The descriptive analysis, in contrast, is concerned with people's beliefs and preferences as they are, not as they should be. The tension between normative and descriptive considerations characterizes much of the study of judgment and choice.

Analyses of decision making commonly distinguish risky and riskless choices. The paradigmatic example of decision under risk is the acceptability of a gamble that yields monetary outcomes with specified probabilities. A typical riskless decision concerns the acceptability of a transaction in which a good or a service is exchanged for money or labor. In the first part of this article we present an analysis of the cognitive and psychophysical factors that determine the value of risky prospects. In the second part we extend this analysis to transactions and trades.

*This article was originally presented as a Distinguished Scientific Contributions Award address at the American Psychological Association meeting, August 1983. This work was supported by grant NR 197-058 from the U.S. Office of Naval Research. Originally published in *American Psychologist*, vol. 34, 1984.

RISKY CHOICE

Risky choices, such as whether or not to take an umbrella and whether or not to go to war, are made without advance knowledge of their consequences. Because the consequences of such actions depend on uncertain events such as the weather or the opponent's resolve, the choice of an act may be construed as the acceptance of a gamble that can yield various outcomes with different probabilities. It is therefore natural that the study of decision making under risk has focused on choices between simple gambles with monetary outcomes and specified probabilities, in the hope that these simple problems will reveal basic attitudes toward risk and value.

We shall sketch an approach to risky choice that derives many of its hypotheses from a psychophysical analysis of responses to money and to probability. The psychophysical approach to decision making can be traced to a remarkable essay that Daniel Bernoulli published in 1738 (Bernoulli 1954) in which he attempted to explain why people are generally averse to risk and why risk aversion decreases with increasing wealth. To illustrate risk aversion and Bernoulli's analysis, consider the choice between a prospect that offers an 85% chance to win $1,000 (with a 15% chance to win nothing) and the alternative of receiving $800 for sure. A large majority of people prefer the sure thing over the gamble, although the gamble has higher (mathematical) expectation. The expectation of a monetary gamble is a weighted average, where each possible outcome is weighted by its probability of occurrence. The expectation of the gamble in this example is .85 x $1,000 + .15 x $0 = $850, which exceeds the expectation of $800 associated with the sure thing. The preference for the sure gain is an instance of risk aversion. In general, a preference for a sure outcome over a gamble that has higher or equal expectation is called risk averse, and the rejection of a sure thing in favor of a gamble of lower or equal expectation is called risk seeking.

Bernoulli suggested that people do not evaluate prospects by the expectation of their monetary outcomes, but rather by the expectation of the subjective value of these outcomes. The subjective value of a gamble is again a weighted average, but now it is the subjective value of each outcome that is weighted by its probability. To explain risk aversion within this framework, Bernoulli proposed that subjective value, or utility, is a concave function of money. In such a function, the difference between the utilities of $200 and $100, for example, is greater than the utility difference between $1,200 and $1,100. It follows from concavity that the subjective value attached to a gain of $800 is more than 80% of the value of a gain of $1,000. Consequently, the concavity of the utility function entails a risk averse preference for a sure gain of $800 over an 80% chance to win $1,000, although the two prospects have the same monetary expectation.

It is customary in decision analysis to describe the outcomes of decisions in terms of total wealth. For example, an offer to bet $20 on the toss of a fair coin is represented as a choice between an individual's current wealth W and an even chance to move to $W + $20 or to $W - $20. This representation appears psychologically unrealistic: People do not normally think of relatively small outcomes in terms of states of wealth but rather in terms of gains, losses, and neutral outcomes (such as the maintenance of the status quo). If the effective carriers of subjective value are changes of wealth rather than ultimate states of wealth, as we propose, the psychophysical analysis of outcomes should be applied to gains and losses rather than to total assets. This assumption plays a central role in a treatment of risky choice that we called prospect theory (Kahneman and Tversky 1979). Introspection as well as psychophysical measurements suggest that subjective value is a concave function of the size of a gain. The same generalization applies to losses as well. The difference in subjective value between a loss of $200 and a loss of $100 appears greater than the difference in subjective value between a loss of $1,200 and a loss of $1,100. When the value functions for gains and for losses are pieced together, we obtain an S-shaped function of the type displayed in Figure 1.

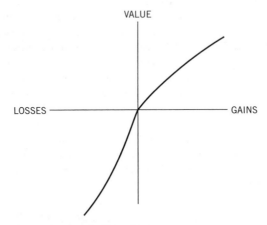

Figure 1. A Hypothetical Value Function

The value function shown in Figure 1 is (a) defined on gains and losses rather than on total wealth, (b) concave in the domain of gains and convex in the domain of losses, and (c) considerably steeper for losses than for gains. The last property, which we label *loss aversion*, expresses the intuition that a loss of $X is more aversive than a gain of $X is attractive. Loss aversion explains people's reluctance to bet on a fair coin for equal stakes: The attractiveness of the possible gain is not nearly sufficient to compensate for the aversiveness of the possible loss. For example, most respondents in a sample of undergraduates refused to stake $10 on the toss of a coin if they stood to win less than $30.

The assumption of risk aversion has played a central role in economic theory. However, just as the concavity of the value of gains entails risk aversion, the convexity of the value of losses entails risk seeking. Indeed, risk seeking in losses is a robust effect, particularly when the probabilities of loss are substantial. Consider, for example, a situation in which an individual is forced to choose between an 85% chance to lose $1,000 (with a 15% chance to lose nothing) and a sure loss of $800. A large majority of people express a preference for the gamble over the sure loss. This is a risk seeking choice because the expectation of the gamble (–$850) is inferior to the expectation of the sure loss (–$800). Risk seeking in the domain of losses has been confirmed by several investigators (Fishburn and Kochenberger 1979; Hershey and Schoemaker 1980; Payne, Laughhunn, and Crum 1980; Slovic, Fischhoff, and Lichtenstein 1982). It has also been observed with nonmonetary outcomes, such as hours of pain (Eraker and Sox 1981) and loss of human lives (Fischhoff 1983; Tversky 1977; Tversky and Kahneman 1981). Is it wrong to be risk averse in the domain of gains and risk seeking in the domain of losses? These preferences conform to compelling intuitions about the subjective value of gains and losses, and the presumption is that people should be entitled to their own values. However, we shall see that an S-shaped value function has implications that are normatively unacceptable.

To address the normative issue we turn from psychology to decision theory. Modern decision theory can be said to begin with the pioneering work of von Neumann and Morgenstern (1947), who laid down several qualitative principles, or axioms, that should govern the preferences of a rational decision maker. Their axioms included transitivity (if A is preferred to B and B is preferred to C, then A is preferred to C), and substitution (if A is preferred to B, then an even chance to get A or C is preferred to an even chance to get B or C), along with other conditions of a more technical nature. The normative and the descriptive status of the axioms of rational choice have been the subject of extensive discussions. In particular, there is convincing evidence that people do not always obey the substitution axiom, and considerable disagreement exists about the normative merit of this axiom (e.g., Allais and Hagen 1979). However, all analyses of rational choice incorporate two principles: dominance and invariance. Dominance demands that if prospect A is at least as good as prospect B in every respect and better than B in at least one respect, then A should be preferred to B. Invariance requires that the preference order between prospects should not depend on the manner in which they are described. In particular, two versions of a choice problem that are recognized to be equivalent when shown together should elicit the same preference even when shown separately. We now show that the requirement of invariance, however elementary and innocuous it may seem, cannot generally be satisfied.

FRAMING OF OUTCOMES

Risky prospects are characterized by their possible outcomes and by the probabilities of these outcomes. The same option, however, can be framed or described in different ways (Tversky and Kahneman 1981). For example, the possible outcomes of a gamble can be framed either as gains and losses relative to the status quo or as asset positions that incorporate initial wealth. Invariance requires that such changes in the description of outcomes should not alter the preference order. The following pair of problems illustrates a violation of this requirement. The total number of respondents in each problem is denoted by N, and the percentage who chose each option is indicated in parentheses.

> Problem 1 ($N = 152$): Imagine that the U.S. is preparing for the outbreak of an unusual Asian disease, which is expected to kill 600 people. Two alternative programs to combat the disease have been proposed. Assume that the exact scientific estimates of the consequences of the programs are as follows:
> If Program A is adopted, 200 people will be saved. (72%)
> If Program B is adopted, there is a one-third probability that 600 people will be saved and a two-thirds probability that no people will be saved. (28%)
> Which of the two programs would you favor?

The formulation of Problem 1 implicitly adopts as a reference point a state of affairs in which the disease is allowed to take its toll of 600 lives. The outcomes of the programs include the reference state and two possible gains, measured by the number of lives saved. As expected, preferences are risk averse: A clear majority of respondents prefer saving 200 lives for sure over a gamble that offers a one-third chance of saving 600 lives. Now consider another problem in which the same cover story is followed by a different description of the prospects associated with the two programs:

Problem 2 (*N* = 155):
If Program C is adopted, 400 people will die. (22%)
If Program D is adopted, there is a one-third probability that nobody will die
and a two-thirds probability that 600 people will die. (78%)

It is easy to verify that options C and D in Problem 2 are undistinguishable in real terms from options A and B in Problem 1, respectively. The second version, however, assumes a reference state in which no one dies of the disease. The best outcome is the maintenance of this state and the alternatives are losses measured by the number of people that will die of the disease. People who evaluate options in these terms are expected to show a risk seeking preference for the gamble (option D) over the sure loss of 400 lives. Indeed, there is more risk seeking in the second version of the problem than there is risk aversion in the first.

The failure of invariance is both pervasive and robust. It is as common among sophisticated respondents as among naive ones, and it is not eliminated even when the same respondents answer both questions within a few minutes. Respondents confronted with their conflicting answers are typically puzzled. Even after rereading the problems, they still wish to be risk averse in the "lives saved" version; they wish to be risk seeking in the "lives lost" version; and they also wish to obey invariance and give consistent answers in the two versions. In their stubborn appeal, framing effects resemble perceptual illusions more than computational errors.

The following pair of problems elicits preferences that violate the dominance requirement of rational choice.

Problem 3 (*N* = 86): Choose between:
E. 25% chance to win $240 and 75% chance to lose $760 (0%)
F. 25% chance to win $250 and 75% chance to lose $750 (100%)

It is easy to see that F dominates E. Indeed, all respondents chose accordingly.

Problem 4 (*N* = 150): Imagine that you face the following pair of concurrent decisions.
First examine both decisions, then indicate the options you prefer.
    Decision (i) Choose between:
    A. a sure gain of $240 (84%)
    B. 25% chance to gain $1,000 and 75% chance to gain nothing (16%)
    Decision (ii) Choose between:
    C. a sure loss of $750 (13%)
    D. 75% chance to lose $1,000 and 25% chance to lose nothing (87%)

As expected from the previous analysis, a large majority of subjects made a risk averse choice for the sure gain over the positive gamble in the first decision, and an even larger majority of subjects made a risk seeking choice for the gamble over the sure loss in the second decision. In fact, 73% of the respondents chose A and D and only 3% chose B and C. The same pattern of results was observed in a modified version of the problem, with reduced stakes, in which undergraduates selected gambles that they would actually play.

Because the subjects considered the two decisions in Problem 4 simultaneously, they expressed in effect a preference for A and D over B and C. The preferred conjunction, however, is actually dominated by the rejected one. Adding the sure gain of $240 (option A) to option D yields a 25% chance to win $240 and a 75% chance to lose $760. This is precisely option E in Problem 3. Similarly, adding the sure loss of $750 (option C) to option B yields a 25% chance to win $250 and a 75% chance to lose $750. This is precisely option F in Problem 3. Thus, the susceptibility to framing and the S-shaped value function produce a violation of dominance in a set of concurrent decisions.

The moral of these results is disturbing: Invariance is normatively essential, intuitively compelling, and psychologically unfeasible. Indeed, we conceive only two ways of guaranteeing invariance. The first is to adopt a procedure that will transform equivalent versions of any problem into the same canonical representation. This is the rationale for the standard admonition to students of business, that they should consider each decision problem in terms of total assets rather than in terms of gains or losses (Schlaifer 1959). Such a representation would avoid the violations of invariance illustrated in the previous problems, but the advice is easier to give than to follow. Except in the context of possible ruin, it is more natural to consider financial outcomes as gains and losses rather than as states of wealth. Furthermore, a canonical representation of risky prospects requires a compounding of all outcomes of concurrent decisions (e.g., Problem 4) that exceeds the capabilities of intuitive computation even in simple problems. Achieving a canonical representation is even more difficult in other contexts such as safety, health, or quality of life. Should we advise people to evaluate the consequence of a public health policy (e.g., Problems 1 and 2) in terms of overall mortality, mortality due to diseases, or the number of deaths associated with the particular disease under study?

Another approach that could guarantee invariance is the evaluation of options in terms of their actuarial rather than their psychological consequences. The actuarial criterion has some appeal in the context of human lives, but it is clearly inadequate for financial choices, as has been generally recognized at least since Bernoulli, and it is entirely inapplicable to outcomes that lack an objective metric. We conclude that frame invariance cannot be expected to hold and that a sense of confidence in a particular choice does not ensure that the same choice would be made in another frame. It is therefore good practice to test the robustness of preferences by deliberate attempts to frame a decision problem in more than one way (Fischhoff, Slovic, and Lichtenstein 1980).

THE PSYCHOPHYSICS OF CHANCES

Our discussion so far has assumed a Bernoullian expectation rule according to which the value, or utility, of an uncertain prospect is obtained by adding the utilities of the possible outcomes, each weighted by its probability. To examine this assumption, let us again consult psychophysical intuitions. Setting the value of the status quo at zero, imagine a cash gift, say of $300, and assign it a value of one. Now imagine that you are only given a ticket to a lottery that has a single prize of $300. How does the value of the ticket vary as a function of the probability of winning the prize? Barring utility for gambling, the value of such a prospect must vary between zero (when the chance of winning is nil) and one (when winning $300 is a certainty).

Intuition suggests that the value of the ticket is not a linear function of the probability of winning, as entailed by the expectation rule. In particular, an increase from 0% to 5% appears to have a larger effect than an increase from 30% to 35%, which also appears smaller than an increase from 95% to 100%. These considerations suggest a category-boundary effect: A change from impossibility to possibility or from possibility to certainty has a bigger impact than a comparable change in the middle of the scale. This hypothesis is incorporated into the curve displayed in Figure 2, which plots the weight attached to an event as a function of its stated numerical probability. The most salient feature of Figure 2 is that decision weights are regressive with respect to stated probabilities. Except near the endpoints, an increase of .05 in the probability of winning increases the value of the prospect by less than 5% of the value of the prize. We next investigate the implications of these psychophysical hypotheses for preferences among risky options.

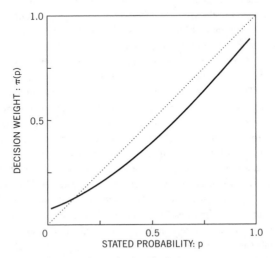

Figure 2. A Hypothetical Weighting Function

In Figure 2, decision weights are lower than the corresponding probabilities over most of the range. Underweighting of moderate and high probabilities relative to sure things contributes to risk aversion in gains by reducing the attractiveness of positive gambles. The same effect also contributes to risk seeking in losses by attenuating the aversiveness of negative gambles. Low probabilities, however, are overweighted, and very low probabilities are either overweighted quite grossly or neglected altogether, making the decision weights highly unstable in that region. The overweighting of low probabilities reverses the pattern described above: It enhances the value of long shots and amplifies the aversiveness of a small chance of a severe loss. Consequently, people are often risk seeking in dealing with improbable gains and risk averse in dealing with unlikely losses. Thus, the characteristics of decision weights contribute to the attractiveness of both lottery tickets and insurance policies.

The nonlinearity of decision weights inevitably leads to violations of invariance, as illustrated in the following pair of problems:

Problem 5 (N = 85): Consider the following two-stage game. In the first stage, there is a 75% chance to end the game without winning anything and a 25% chance to move into the second stage. If you reach the second stage you have a choice between:
    A. a sure win of $30 (74%)
    B. 80% chance to win $45 (26%)
Your choice must be made before the game starts, i.e., before the outcome of the first stage is known. Please indicate the option you prefer.

Problem 6 ($N = 81$): Which of the following options do you prefer?

C. 25% chance to win $30 (42%)

D. 20% chance to win $45 (58%)

Because there is one chance in four to move into the second stage in Problem 5, prospect A offers a .25 probability of winning $30, and prospect B offers .25 x .80 = .20 probability of winning $45. Problems 5 and 6 are therefore identical in terms of probabilities and outcomes. However, the preferences are not the same in the two versions: A clear majority favors the higher chance to win the smaller amount in Problem 5, whereas the majority goes the other way in Problem 6. This violation of invariance has been confirmed with both real and hypothetical monetary payoffs (the present results are with real money), with human lives as outcomes, and with a nonsequential representation of the chance process.

We attribute the failure of invariance to the interaction of two factors: the framing of probabilities and the nonlinearity of decision weights. More specifically, we propose that in Problem 5 people ignore the first phase, which yields the same outcome regardless of the decision that is made, and focus their attention on what happens if they do reach the second stage of the game. In that case, of course, they face a sure gain if they choose option A and an 80% chance of winning if they prefer to gamble. Indeed, people's choices in the sequential version are practically identical to the choices they make between a sure gain of $30 and an 85% chance to win $45. Because a sure thing is overweighted in comparison with events of moderate or high probability (see figure 2), the option that may lead to a gain of $30 is more attractive in the sequential version. We call this phenomenon the pseudo-certainty effect because an event that is actually uncertain is weighted as if it were certain.

A closely related phenomenon can be demonstrated at the low end of the probability range. Suppose you are undecided whether or not to purchase earthquake insurance because the premium is quite high. As you hesitate, your friendly insurance agent comes forth with an alternative offer: "For half the regular premium you can be fully covered if the quake occurs on an odd day of the month. This is a good deal because for half the price you are covered for more than half the days." Why do most people find such probabilistic insurance distinctly unattractive? Figure 2 suggests an answer. Starting anywhere in the region of low probabilities, the impact on the decision weight of a reduction of probability from p to $p/2$ is considerably smaller than the effect of a reduction from $p/2$ to 0. Reducing the risk by half, then, is not worth half the premium.

The aversion to probabilistic insurance is significant for three reasons. First, it undermines the classical explanation of insurance in terms of a concave utility function. According to expected utility theory, probabilistic insurance should be definitely preferred to normal insurance when the latter is just acceptable (see Kahneman and Tversky 1979). Second, probabilistic insurance represents many forms of protective action, such as having a medical checkup, buying new tires, or installing a burglar alarm system. Such actions typically reduce the probability of some hazard without eliminating it altogether. Third, the acceptability of insurance can be manipulated by the framing of the contingencies. An insurance policy that covers fire but not flood, for example, could be evaluated either as full protection against a specific risk (e.g., fire), or as a reduction in the overall probability of property loss. Figure 2 suggests that people greatly undervalue a reduction in the probability of a hazard in comparison to the complete elimination of that hazard. Hence, insurance should appear more attractive when it is framed as the elimination of risk than when it is described as a reduction of risk. Indeed, Slovic, Fischhoff, and Lichtenstein (1982) showed that a hypothetical vaccine that reduces the probability of contracting a disease from 20% to 10% is less attractive if it is described as effective in half of the cases than if it is presented as fully effective against one of two exclusive and equally probable virus strains that produce identical symptoms.

FORMULATION EFFECTS

So far we have discussed framing as a tool to demonstrate failures of invariance. We now turn attention to the processes that control the framing of outcomes and events. The public health problem illustrates a formulation effect in which a change of wording from "lives saved" to "lives lost" induced a marked shift of preference from risk aversion to risk seeking. Evidently, the subjects adopted the descriptions of the outcomes as given in the question and evaluated the outcomes accordingly as gains or losses. Another formulation effect was reported by McNeil, Pauker, Sox, and Tversky (1982). They found that preferences of physicians and patients between hypothetical therapies for lung cancer varied markedly when their probable outcomes were described in terms of mortality or survival. Surgery, unlike radiation therapy, entails a risk of death during treatment. As a consequence, the surgery option was relatively less attractive when the statistics of treatment outcomes were described in terms of mortality rather than in terms of survival.

A physician, and perhaps a presidential advisor as well, could influence the decision made by the patient or by the President, without distorting or suppressing information, merely by the framing of outcomes and contingencies. Formulation effects can occur fortuitously, without anyone being aware of the impact of the frame on the ultimate decision. They can also be exploited deliberately to manipulate the relative attractiveness of options. For example, Thaler (1980) noted that lobbyists for the credit card industry insisted that any price difference between cash and credit purchases be labeled a cash discount rather than a credit card surcharge. The two labels frame the price difference as a gain or as a loss by implicitly designating either the lower or the higher price as normal. Because losses loom larger than gains, consumers are less likely to accept a surcharge than to forgo a discount. As is to be expected, attempts to influence framing are common in the marketplace and in the political arena.

The evaluation of outcomes is susceptible to formulation effects because of the nonlinearity of the value function and the tendency of people to evaluate options in relation to the reference point that is suggested or implied by the statement of the problem. It is worthy of note that in other contexts people automatically transform equivalent messages into the same representation. Studies of language comprehension indicate that people quickly recode much of what they hear into an abstract representation that no longer distinguishes whether the idea was expressed in an active or in a passive form and no longer discriminates what was actually said from what was implied, presupposed, or implicated (Clark and Clark 1977). Unfortunately, the mental machinery that performs these operations silently and effortlessly is not adequate to perform the task of recoding the two versions of the public health problem or the mortality survival statistics into a common abstract form.

TRANSACTIONS AND TRADES

Our analysis of framing and of value can be extended to choices between multiattribute options, such as the acceptability of a transaction or a trade. We propose that, in order to evaluate a multiattribute option, a person sets up a mental account that specifies the advantages and the disadvantages associated with the option, relative to a multiattribute reference state. The overall value of an option is given by the balance of its advantages and its disadvantages in relation to the reference state. Thus, an option is acceptable if the value of its advantages exceeds the value of its disadvantages. This analysis assumes psychological—but not physical—separability of advantages and disadvantages. The model does not constrain the manner in which separate attributes are combined to form overall measures of advantage and of disadvantage, but it imposes on these measures assumptions of concavity and of loss aversion.

Our analysis of mental accounting owes a large debt to the stimulating work of Richard Thaler (1980, 1985), who showed the relevance of this process to consumer behavior. The following problem, based on examples of Savage (1954) and Thaler (1980), introduces some of the rules that govern the construction of mental accounts and illustrates the extension of the concavity of value to the acceptability of transactions.

> Problem 7: Imagine that you are about to purchase a jacket for $125 and a calculator for $15. The calculator salesman informs you that the calculator you wish to buy is on sale for $10 at the other branch of the store, located 20 minutes' drive away. Would you make a trip to the other store?

This problem is concerned with the acceptability of an option that combines a disadvantage of inconvenience with a financial advantage that can be framed as a minimal, topical, or comprehensive account. The minimal account includes only the differences between the two options and disregards the features that they share. In the minimal account, the advantage associated with driving to the other store is framed as a gain of $5. A topical account relates the consequences of possible choices to a reference level that is determined by the context within which the decision arises. In the preceding problem, the relevant topic is the purchase of the calculator, and the benefit of the trip is therefore framed as a reduction of the price, from $15 to $10. Because the potential saving is associated only with the calculator, the price of the jacket is not included in the topical account. The price of the jacket, as well as other expenses, could well be included in a more comprehensive account in which the saving would be evaluated in relation to, say, monthly expenses.

The formulation of the preceding problem appears neutral with respect to the adoption of a minimal, topical, or comprehensive account. We suggest, however, that people will spontaneously frame decisions in terms of topical accounts that, in the context of decision making, play a role analogous to that of "good forms" in perception and of basic-level categories in cognition. Topical organization, in conjunction with the concavity of value, entails that the willingness to travel to the other store for a saving of $5 on a calculator should be inversely related to the price of the calculator and should be independent of the price of the jacket. To test this prediction, we constructed another version of the problem in which the prices of the two items were interchanged. The price of the calculator was given as $125 in the first store and $120 in the other branch, and the price of the jacket was set at $15. As predicted, the proportions of respondents who said they would make the trip differed sharply in the two problems. The results showed that 68% of the respondents ($N = 88$) were willing to drive to the other branch to save $5 on a $15 calculator, but only 29% of 93 respondents were willing to make the same trip to save $5 on a $125 calculator. This finding supports the notion of topical organization of accounts, since the two versions are identical both in terms of a minimal and a comprehensive account.

The significance of topical accounts for consumer behavior is confirmed by the observation that the standard deviation of the prices that different stores in a city quote for the same product is roughly proportional to the average price of that product (Pratt, Wise, and Zeckhauser 1979). Since the dispersion of prices is surely controlled by shoppers' efforts to find the best buy, these results suggest that consumers hardly exert more effort to save $15 on a $150 purchase than to save $5 on a $50 purchase.

The topical organization of mental accounts leads people to evaluate gains and losses in relative rather than in absolute terms, resulting in large variations in the rate at which money is exchanged for other things, such as the number of phone calls made to find a good buy or the willingness to drive a long distance to get one. Most consumers will find it easier to buy a car stereo system or a Persian rug, respectively, in the context of buying a car or a house than separately. These observations, of course, run counter to the standard rational theory of consumer behavior, which assumes invariance and does not recognize the effects of mental accounting.

The following problems illustrate another example of mental accounting in which the posting of a cost to an account is controlled by topical organization:

Problem 8 ($N = 200$): Imagine that you have decided to see a play and paid the admission price of $10 per ticket. As you enter the theater, you discover that you have lost the ticket. The seat was not marked, and the ticket cannot be recovered.
　Would you pay $10 for another ticket?
　Yes (46%)   No (54%)

Problem 9 ($N = 183$): Imagine that you have decided to see a play where admission is $10 per ticket. As you enter the theater, you discover that you have lost a $10 bill.
　Would you still pay $10 for a ticket for the play?
　Yes (88%)   No (12%)

The difference between the responses to the two problems is intriguing. Why are so many people unwilling to spend $10 after having lost a ticket, if they would readily spend that sum after losing an equivalent amount of cash? We attribute the difference to the topical organization of mental accounts. Going to the theater is normally viewed as a transaction in which the cost of the ticket is exchanged for the experience of seeing the play. Buying a second ticket increases the cost of seeing the play to a level that many respondents apparently find unacceptable. In contrast, the loss of the cash is not posted to the account of the play, and it affects the purchase of a ticket only by making the individual feel slightly less affluent.

An interesting effect was observed when the two versions of the problem were presented to the same subjects. The willingness to replace a lost ticket increased significantly when that problem followed the lost-cash version. In contrast, the willingness to buy a ticket after losing cash was not affected by prior presentation of the other problem. The juxtaposition of the two problems apparently enabled the subjects to realize that it makes sense to think of the lost ticket as lost cash, but not vice versa.

The normative status of the effects of mental accounting is questionable. Unlike earlier examples, such as the public health problem, in which the two versions differed only in form, it can be argued that the alternative versions of the calculator and ticket problems differ also in substance. In particular, it may be more pleasurable to save $5 on a $15 purchase than on a larger purchase, and it may be more annoying to pay twice for the same ticket than to lose $10 in cash. Regret, frustration, and self-satisfaction can also be affected by framing (Kahneman and Tversky 1982). If such secondary consequences are considered legitimate, then the observed preferences do not violate the criterion of invariance and cannot readily be ruled out as inconsistent or erroneous. On the other hand, secondary consequences may change upon reflection. The satisfaction of saving $5 on a $15 item can be marred if the consumer discovers that she would not have exerted the same effort to save $10 on a $200 purchase. We do not wish to recommend that any two decision problems that have the same primary consequences should be resolved in the same way. We propose, however, that systematic examination of alternative framings offers a useful reflective device that can help decision makers assess the values that should be attached to the primary and secondary consequences of their choices.

LOSSES AND COSTS

Many decision problems take the form of a choice between retaining the status quo and accepting an alternative to it, which is advantageous in some respects and disadvantageous in others. The analysis of value that was applied earlier to unidimensional risky prospects can be extended to this case by assuming that the status quo defines the reference level for all attributes. The advantages of alternative options will then be evaluated as gains and their disadvantages as losses. Because losses loom larger than gains, the decision maker will be biased in favor of retaining the status quo.

Thaler (1980) coined the term "endowment effect" to describe the reluctance of people to part from assets that belong to their endowment. When it is more painful to give up an asset than it is pleasurable to obtain it, buying prices will be significantly lower than selling prices. That is, the highest price that an individual will pay to acquire an asset will be smaller than the minimal compensation that would induce the same individual to give up that asset, once acquired. Thaler discussed some examples of the endowment effect in the behavior of consumers and entrepreneurs. Several studies have reported substantial discrepancies between buying and selling prices in both hypothetical and real transactions (Gregory 1983; Hammack and Brown 1974; Knetsch and Sinden 1984). These results have been presented as challenges to standard economic theory, in which buying and selling prices coincide except for transaction costs and effects of wealth. We also observed reluctance to trade in a study of choices between hypothetical jobs that differed in weekly salary (S) and in the temperature (T) of the workplace. Our respondents were asked to imagine that they held a particular position (S_1, T_1) and were offered the option of moving to a different position (S_2, T_2), which was better in one respect and worse in another. We found that most subjects who were assigned to (S_1, T_1) did not wish to move to (S_2, T_2), and that most subjects who were assigned to the latter position did not wish to move to the former. Evidently, the same difference in pay or in working conditions looms larger as a disadvantage than as an advantage.

In general, loss aversion favors stability over change. Imagine two hedonically identical twins who find two alternative environments equally attractive. Imagine further that by force of circumstance the twins are separated and placed in the two environments. As soon as they adopt their new states as reference points and evaluate the advantages and disadvantages of each other's environments accordingly, the twins will no longer be indifferent between the two states, and both will prefer to stay where they happen to be. Thus, the instability of preferences produces a preference for stability. In addition to favoring stability over change, the combination of adaptation and loss aversion provides limited protection against regret and envy by reducing the attractiveness of foregone alternatives and of others' endowments.

Loss aversion and the consequent endowment effect are unlikely to play a significant role in routine economic exchanges. The owner of a store, for example, does not experience money paid to suppliers as losses and money received from customers as gains. Instead, the merchant adds costs and revenues over some period of time and only evaluates the balance. Matching debits and credits are effectively canceled prior to evaluation. Payments made by consumers are also not evaluated as losses but as alternative purchases. In accord with standard economic analysis, money is naturally viewed as a proxy for the goods and services that it could buy. This mode of evaluation is made explicit when an individual has in mind a particular alternative, such as, "I can either buy a new camera or a new tent." In this analysis, a person will buy a camera if its subjective value exceeds the value of retaining the money it would cost.

There are cases in which a disadvantage can be framed either as a cost or as a loss. In particular, the purchase of insurance can also be framed as a choice between a sure loss and the risk of a greater loss. In such cases the cost-loss discrepancy can lead to failures of invariance. Consider, for example, the choice between a sure loss of $50 and a 25% chance to lose $200. Slovic, Fischhoff, and Lichtenstein (1982) reported that 80% of their subjects expressed a risk-seeking preference for the gamble over the sure loss. However, only 35% of subjects refused to pay $50 for insurance against a 25% risk of losing $200. Similar results were also reported by Schoemaker and Kunreuther (1979) and by Hershey and Schoemaker (1980). We suggest that the same amount of money that was framed as an uncompensated loss in the first problem was framed as the cost of protection in the second. The modal preference was reversed in the two problems because losses are more aversive than costs.

We have observed a similar effect in the positive domain, as illustrated by the following pair of problems:

Problem 10: Would you accept a gamble that offers a 10% chance to win $95 and a 90% chance to lose $5?

Problem 11: Would you pay $5 to participate in a lottery that offers a 10% chance to win $100 and a 90% chance to win nothing?

A total of 132 undergraduates answered the two questions, which were separated by a short filler problem. The order of the questions was reversed for half the respondents. Although it is easily confirmed that the two problems offer objectively identical options, 55 of the respondents expressed different preferences in the two versions. Among them, 42 rejected the gamble in Problem 10 but accepted the equivalent lottery in Problem 11. The effectiveness of this seemingly inconsequential manipulation illustrates both the cost-loss discrepancy and the power of framing. Thinking of the $5 as a payment makes the venture more acceptable than thinking of the same amount as a loss.

The preceding analysis implies that an individual's subjective state can be improved by framing negative outcomes as costs rather than as losses. The possibility of such psychological manipulations may explain a paradoxical form of behavior that could be labeled the dead-loss effect. Thaler (1980) discussed the example of a man who develops tennis elbow soon after paying the membership fee in a tennis club and continues to play in agony to avoid wasting his investment. Assuming that the individual would not play if he had not paid the membership fee, the question arises: How can playing in agony improve the individual's lot? Playing in pain, we suggest, maintains the evaluation of the membership fee as a cost. If the individual were to stop playing, he would be forced to recognize the fee as a dead loss, which may be more aversive than playing in pain.

CONCLUDING REMARKS

The concepts of utility and value are commonly used in two distinct senses: (a) experience value, the degree of pleasure or pain, satisfaction or anguish in the actual experience of an outcome; and (b) decision value, the contribution of an anticipated outcome to the overall attractiveness or aversiveness of an option in a choice. The distinction is rarely explicit in decision theory because it is tacitly assumed that decision values and experience values coincide. This assumption is part of the conception of an idealized decision maker who is able to predict future experiences with perfect accuracy and evaluate options accordingly. For ordinary decision makers, however, the correspondence of decision values between experience values is far from perfect (March 1978). Some factors that affect experience are not easily anticipated, and some factors that affect decisions do not have a comparable impact on the experience of outcomes.

In contrast to the large amount of research on decision making, there has been relatively little systematic exploration of the psychophysics that relate hedonic experience to objective states. The most basic problem of hedonic psychophysics is the determination of the level of adaptation or aspiration that separates positive from negative outcomes. The hedonic reference point is largely determined by the objective status quo, but it is also affected by expectations and social comparisons. An objective improvement can be experienced as a loss, for example, when an employee receives a smaller raise than everyone else in the office. The experience of pleasure or pain associated with a change of state is also critically dependent on the dynamics of hedonic adaptation. Brickman and Campbell's (1971) concept of the hedonic treadmill suggests the radical hypothesis that rapid adaptation will cause the effects of any objective improvement to be short-lived. The complexity and subtlety of hedonic experience make it difficult for the decision maker to anticipate the actual experience that outcomes will produce. Many a person who ordered a meal when ravenously hungry has admitted to a big mistake when the fifth course arrived on the table. The common mismatch of decision values and experience values introduces an additional element of uncertainty in many decision problems.

The prevalence of framing effects and violations of invariance further complicates the relation between decision values and experience values. The framing of outcomes often induces decision values that have no counterpart in actual experience. For example, the framing of outcomes of therapies for lung cancer in terms of mortality or survival is unlikely to affect experience, although it can have a pronounced influence on choice. In other cases, however, the framing of decisions affects not only decision but experience as well. For example, the framing of an expenditure as an uncompensated loss or as the price of insurance can probably influence the experience of that outcome. In such cases, the evaluation of outcomes in the context of decisions not only anticipates experience but also molds it.

REFERENCES

Allais, M., and O. Hagen, eds. 1979. *Expected Utility Hypotheses and the Allais Paradox.* Hingham, MA: D. Reidel.

Bernoulli, D. 1954 [1738]. "Exposition of a New Theory on the Measurement of Risk." *Econometrica* 22:23–36.

Brickman, P., and D. T. Campbell. 1971. "Hedonic Relativism and Planning the Good Society." In *Adaptation Level Theory: A Symposium*, ed. M. H. Appley. New York: Academic Press, 287–302.

Clark, H. H., and E. V. Clark. 1977. *Psychology and Language.* New York: Harcourt.

Erakar, S. E., and H. C. Sox. 1981. "Assessment of Patients' Preferences for Therapeutic Outcomes." *Medical Decision Making* 1:29–39.

Fischhoff, B. 1983. "Predicting Frames." *Journal of Experimental Psychology: Learning, Memory and Cognition* 9:103–16.

Fischhoff, B., P. Slovic, and S. Lichtenstein. 1980. "Knowing What You Want: Measuring Labile Values." In *Cognitive Processes in Choice and Decision Behavior*, ed. T. Wallsten. Hillsdale, NJ: Erlbaum, 117–41.

Fishburn, P. C., and G. A. Kochenberger. 1979. "Two-Piece von Neumann–Morgenstern Utility Functions." *Decision Sciences* 10:503–18.

Gregory, R. 1983. "Measures of Consumer's Surplus: Reasons for the Disparity in Observed Values." Unpublished manuscript, Keene State College, Keene, NH.

Hammack, J., and G. M. Brown Jr. 1974. *Waterfowl and Wetlands: Toward Bioeconomic Analysis.* Baltimore: Johns Hopkins University Press.

Hershey, J. C., and P. J. H. Schoemaker. 1980. "Risk Taking and Problem Context in the Domain of Losses: An Expected-Utility Analysis." *Journal of Risk and Insurance* 47:111–32.

Kahneman, D., and A. Tversky. 1979. "Prospect Theory: An Analysis of Decision under Risk." *Econometrica* 47:263–91.

———. 1982. "The Simulation Heuristic." In *Judgment Under Uncertainty: Heuristics and Biases*, ed. D. Kahneman, P. Slovic, and A. Tversky. New York: Cambridge University Press, 201–208.

Knetsch, J., and J. Sinden. 1984. "Willingness to Pay and Compensation Demanded: Experimental Evidence of an Unexpected Disparity in Measures of Value." *Quarterly Journal of Economics* 99:507–21.

March, J. G. 1978. "Bounded Rationality, Ambiguity, and the Engineering of Choice." *Bell Journal of Economics* 9:587–608.

McNeil, B., S. Pauker, H. Sox Jr., and A. Tversky. 1982. "On the Elicitation of Preferences for Alternative Therapies." *New England Journal of Medicine* 306:1259–62.

Payne, J. W., D. J. Laughhunn, and R. Crum. 1980. "Translation of Gambles and Aspiration Level Effects in Risky Choice Behavior." *Management Science* 26:1039–60.

Pratt, J. W., D. Wise, and R. Zeckhauser. 1979. "Price Differences in Almost Competitive Markets." *Quarterly Journal of Economics* 93:189–211.

Savage, L. J. 1954. *The Foundation of Statistics.* New York: Wiley.

Schlaifer, R. 1959. *Probability and Statistics for Business Decisions.* New York: McGraw-Hill.

Schoemaker, P.J.H., and H. C. Kunreuther. 1979. "An Experimental Study of Insurance Decisions." *Journal of Risk and Insurance* 46:603–18.

Slovic, P., B. Fischhoff, and S. Lichtenstein. 1982. "Response Mode, Framing, and Information-

Processing Effects in Risk Assessment." In *New Directions for Methodology of Social and Behavioral Science: Question Framing and Response Consistency*, ed. R. Hogarth. San Francisco: Jossey-Bass, 21–36.

Thaler, R. 1980. "Toward a Positive Theory of Consumer Choice." *Journal of Economic Behavior and Organization* 1:39–60.

———. 1985. "Using Mental Accounting in a Theory of Consumer Behavior." *Marketing Science* 4:199–214.

Tversky, A. 1977. "On the Elicitation of Preferences: Descriptive and Prescriptive Considerations." In *Conflicting Objectives in Decisions*, ed. D. Bell, R. L. Kenney, and H. Raiffa. New York: Wiley, 209–22.

Tversky, A., and D. Kahneman. 1981. "The Framing of Decisions and the Psychology of Choice." *Science* 211:453–58.

von Neumann, J., and O. Morgenstern. 1947. *Theory of Games and Economic Behavior*, 2nd ed. Princeton: Princeton University Press.

NOTES

INTRODUCTION

5 *prone to collect too few observations*: We had read a book that criticized psychologists for using small samples, but did not explain their choices: Jacob Cohen, *Statistical Power Analysis for the Behavioral Sciences* (Hillsdale, NJ: Erlbaum, 1969).

7 *question about words*: I have slightly altered the original wording, which referred to letters in the first and third position of words.

9–10 *negative view of the mind*: A prominent German psychologist has been our most persistent critic. Gerd Gigerenzer, "How to Make Cognitive Illusions Disappear," *European Review of Social Psychology* 2 (1991): 83–115. Gerd Gigerenzer, "Personal Reflections on Theory and Psychology," *Theory & Psychology* 20 (2010): 733–43. Daniel Kahneman and Amos Tversky, "On the Reality of Cognitive Illusions," *Psychological Review* 103 (1996): 582–91.

10 *offered plausible alternatives*: Some examples from many are Valerie F. Reyna and Farrell J. Lloyd, "Physician Decision-Making and Cardiac Risk: Effects of Knowledge, Risk Perception, Risk Tolerance and Fuzzy-Processing," *Journal of Experimental Psychology: Applied* 12 (2006): 179–95. Nicholas Epley and Thomas Gilovich, "The Anchoring-and-Adjustment Heuristic," *Psychological Science* 17 (2006): 311–18. Norbert Schwarz et al., "Ease of Retrieval of Information: Another Look at the Availability Heuristic," *Journal of Personality and Social Psychology* 61 (1991): 195–202. Elke U. Weber et al., "Asymmetric Discounting in Intertemporal Choice," *Psychological Science* 18 (2007): 516–23. George F. Loewenstein et al., "Risk as Feelings," *Psychological Bulletin* 127 (2001): 267–86.

10 *Nobel Prize that I received*: The prize awarded in economics is named Bank of Sweden Prize in Economic Sciences in Memory of Alfred Nobel. It was first given in 1969. Some physical scientists were not pleased with the addition of a Nobel Prize in social science, and the distinctive label of the economics prize was a compromise.

11 *prolonged practice*: Herbert Simon and his students at Carnegie Mellon in the 1980s set the foundations for our understanding of expertise. For an excellent popular introduction to the subject, see Joshua Foer, *Moonwalking with Einstein: The Art and Science of Remem-*

bering (New York: Penguin Press, 2011). He presents work that is reviewed in more technical detail in K. Anders Ericsson et al., eds., *The Cambridge Handbook of Expertise and Expert Performance* (New York: Cambridge University Press, 2006.)

11 *kitchen was on fire*: Gary A. Klein, *Sources of Power* (Cambridge, MA: MIT Press, 1999).

11 *studied chess masters*: Herbert Simon was one of the great scholars of the twentieth century, whose discoveries and inventions ranged from political science (where he began his career) to economics (in which he won a Nobel Prize) to computer science (in which he was a pioneer) and to psychology.

11 *"The situation . . . recognition"*: Herbert A. Simon, "What Is an Explanation of Behavior?" *Psychological Science* 3 (1992): 150–61.

12 *affect heuristic*: The concept of the affect heuristic was developed by Paul Slovic, a classmate of Amos's at Michigan and a lifelong friend.

12 *without noticing the substitution*: See chapter 9.

1: THE CHARACTERS OF THE STORY

20 *offered many labels*: For reviews of the field, see Jonathan St. B. T. Evans and Keith Frankish, eds., *In Two Minds: Dual Processes and Beyond* (New York: Oxford University Press, 2009); Jonathan St. B. T. Evans, "Dual-Processing Accounts of Reasoning, Judgment, and Social Cognition," *Annual Review of Psychology* 59 (2008): 255–78. Among the pioneers are Seymour Epstein, Jonathan Evans, Steven Sloman, Keith Stanovich, and Richard West. I borrow the terms System 1 and System 2 from early writings of Stanovich and West that greatly influenced my thinking: Keith E. Stanovich and Richard F. West, "Individual Differences in Reasoning: Implications for the Rationality Debate," *Behavioral and Brain Sciences* 23 (2000): 645–65.

21 *subjective experience of agency*: This sense of free will is sometimes illusory, as shown in Daniel M. Wegner, *The Illusion of Conscious Will* (Cambridge, MA: Bradford Books, 2003).

25 *attention is totally focused elsewhere*: Nilli Lavie, "Attention, Distraction and Cognitive Control Under Load," *Current Directions in Psychological Science* 19 (2010): 143–48.

25 *conflict between the two systems*: In the classic Stroop task, you are shown a display of patches of different colors, or of words printed in various colors. Your task is to call out the names of the colors, ignoring the words. The task is extremely difficult when the colored words are themselves names of color (e.g., GREEN printed in red, followed by YELLOW printed in green, etc.).

28 *psychopathic charm*: Professor Hare wrote me to say, "Your teacher was right," March 16, 2011. Robert D. Hare, *Without Conscience: The Disturbing World of the Psychopaths Among Us* (New York: Guilford Press, 1999). Paul Babiak and Robert D. Hare, *Snakes in Suits: When Psychopaths Go to Work* (New York: Harper, 2007).

29 *little people*: Agents within the mind are called homunculi and are (quite properly) objects of professional derision.

29–30 *space in your working memory*: Alan D. Baddeley, "Working Memory: Looking Back and Looking Forward," *Nature Reviews: Neuroscience* 4 (2003): 829–38. Alan D. Baddeley, *Your Memory: A User's Guide* (New York: Firefly Books, 2004).

2: ATTENTION AND EFFORT

31 *Attention and Effort*: Much of the material of this chapter draws on my *Attention and Effort* (1973). It is available for free download on my website (www.princeton.edu/~kahneman/

docs/attention_and_effort/Attention_hi_quality.pdf). The main theme of that book is the idea of a limited ability to pay attention and exert mental effort. Attention and effort were considered general resources that could be used to support many mental tasks. The idea of general capacity is controversial, but it has been extended by other psychologists and neuroscientists, who found support for it in brain research. See Marcel A. Just and Patricia A. Carpenter, "A Capacity Theory of Comprehension: Individual Differences in Working Memory," *Psychological Review* 99 (1992): 122–49; Marcel A. Just et al., "Neuroindices of Cognitive Workload: Neuroimaging, Pupillometric and Event-Related Potential Studies of Brain Work," *Theoretical Issues in Ergonomics Science* 4 (2003): 56–88. There is also growing experimental evidence for general-purpose resources of attention, as in Evie Vergauwe et al., "Do Mental Processes Share a Domain-General Resource?" *Psychological Science* 21 (2010): 384–90. There is imaging evidence that the mere anticipation of a high-effort task mobilizes activity in many areas of the brain, relative to a low-effort task of the same kind. Carsten N. Boehler et al., "Task-Load-Dependent Activation of Dopaminergic Midbrain Areas in the Absence of Reward," *Journal of Neuroscience* 31 (2011): 4955–61.

32 *pupil of the eye*: Eckhard H. Hess, "Attitude and Pupil Size," *Scientific American* 212 (1965): 46–54.

33 *on the subject's mind*: The word *subject* reminds some people of subjugation and slavery, and the American Psychological Association enjoins us to use the more democratic *participant*. Unfortunately, the politically correct label is a mouthful, which occupies memory space and slows thinking. I will do my best to use *participant* whenever possible but will switch to *subject* when necessary.

33 *heart rate increases*: Daniel Kahneman et al., "Pupillary, Heart Rate, and Skin Resistance Changes During a Mental Task," *Journal of Experimental Psychology* 79 (1969): 164–67.

34 *rapidly flashing letters*: Daniel Kahneman, Jackson Beatty, and Irwin Pollack, "Perceptual Deficit During a Mental Task," *Science* 15 (1967): 218–19. We used a halfway mirror so that the observers saw the letters directly in front of them while facing the camera. In a control condition, the participants looked at the letter through a narrow aperture, to prevent any effect of the changing pupil size on their visual acuity. Their detection results showed the inverted-V pattern observed with other subjects.

34 *Much like the electricity meter*: Attempting to perform several tasks at once may run into difficulties of several kinds. For example, it is physically impossible to say two different things at exactly the same time, and it may be easier to combine an auditory and a visual task than to combine two visual or two auditory tasks. Prominent psychological theories have attempted to attribute all mutual interference between tasks to competition for separate mechanisms. See Alan D. Baddeley, *Working Memory* (New York: Oxford University Press, 1986). With practice, people's ability to multitask in specific ways may improve. However, the wide variety of very different tasks that interfere with each other supports the existence of a general resource of attention or effort that is necessary in many tasks.

35 *Studies of the brain*: Michael E. Smith, Linda K. McEvoy, and Alan Gevins, "Neurophysiological Indices of Strategy Development and Skill Acquisition," *Cognitive Brain Research* 7 (1999): 389–404. Alan Gevins et al., "High-Resolution EEG Mapping of Cortical Activation Related to Working Memory: Effects of Task Difficulty, Type of Processing and Practice," *Cerebral Cortex* 7 (1997): 374–85.

35 *less effort to solve the same problems*: For example, Sylvia K. Ahern and Jackson Beatty showed that individuals who scored higher on the SAT showed smaller pupillary dilations than low scorers in responding to the same task. "Physiological Signs of Information Processing Vary with Intelligence," *Science* 205 (1979): 1289–92.

35 *"law of least effort"*: Wouter Kool et al., "Decision Making and the Avoidance of Cognitive Demand," *Journal of Experimental Psychology—General* 139 (2010): 665–82. Joseph T. McGuire and Matthew M. Botvinick, "The Impact of Anticipated Demand on Attention and Behavioral Choice," in *Effortless Attention*, ed. Brian Bruya (Cambridge, MA: Bradford Books, 2010), 103–20.

35 *balance of benefits and costs*: Neuroscientists have identified a region of the brain that assesses the overall value of an action when it is completed. The effort that was invested counts as a cost in this neural computation. Joseph T. McGuire and Matthew M. Botvinick, "Prefrontal Cortex, Cognitive Control, and the Registration of Decision Costs," *PNAS* 107 (2010): 7922–26.

36 *read distracting words*: Bruno Laeng et al., "Pupillary Stroop Effects," *Cognitive Processing* 12 (2011): 13–21.

37 *associate with intelligence*: Michael I. Posner and Mary K. Rothbart, "Research on Attention Networks as a Model for the Integration of Psychological Science," *Annual Review of Psychology* 58 (2007): 1–23. John Duncan et al., "A Neural Basis for General Intelligence," *Science* 289 (2000): 457–60.

37 *under time pressure*: Stephen Monsell, "Task Switching," *Trends in Cognitive Sciences* 7 (2003): 134–40.

37 *working memory*: Baddeley, *Working Memory*.

37 *tests of general intelligence*: Andrew A. Conway, Michael J. Kane, and Randall W. Engle, "Working Memory Capacity and Its Relation to General Intelligence," *Trends in Cognitive Sciences* 7 (2003): 547–52.

37 *Israeli Air Force pilots*: Daniel Kahneman, Rachel Ben-Ishai, and Michael Lotan, "Relation of a Test of Attention to Road Accidents," *Journal of Applied Psychology* 58 (1973): 113–15. Daniel Gopher, "A Selective Attention Test as a Predictor of Success in Flight Training," *Human Factors* 24 (1982): 173–83.

3: THE LAZY CONTROLLER

40 *"optimal experience"*: Mihaly Csikszentmihalyi, *Flow: The Psychology of Optimal Experience* (New York: Harper, 1990).

41 *sweet tooth*: Baba Shiv and Alexander Fedorikhin, "Heart and Mind in Conflict: The Interplay of Affect and Cognition in Consumer Decision Making," *Journal of Consumer Research* 26 (1999): 278–92. Malte Friese, Wilhelm Hofmann, and Michaela Wänke, "When Impulses Take Over: Moderated Predictive Validity of Implicit and Explicit Attitude Measures in Predicting Food Choice and Consumption Behaviour," *British Journal of Social Psychology* 47 (2008): 397–419.

41 cognitively busy: Daniel T. Gilbert, "How Mental Systems Believe," *American Psychologist* 46 (1991): 107–19. C. Neil Macrae and Galen V. Bodenhausen, "Social Cognition: Thinking Categorically about Others," *Annual Review of Psychology* 51 (2000): 93–120.

41 *pointless anxious thoughts*: Sian L. Beilock and Thomas H. Carr, "When High-Powered People Fail: Working Memory and Choking Under Pressure in Math," *Psychological Science* 16 (2005): 101–105.

42 *exertion of self-control*: Martin S. Hagger et al., "Ego Depletion and the Strength Model of Self-Control: A Meta-Analysis," *Psychological Bulletin* 136 (2010): 495–525.

42 *resist the effects of ego depletion*: Mark Muraven and Elisaveta Slessareva, "Mechanisms of Self-Control Failure: Motivation and Limited Resources," *Personality and Social Psychology Bulletin* 29 (2003): 894–906. Mark Muraven, Dianne M. Tice, and Roy F. Baumeister, "Self-Control as a Limited Resource: Regulatory Depletion Patterns," *Journal of Personality and Social Psychology* 74 (1998): 774–89.

43 *more than a mere metaphor*: Matthew T. Gailliot et al., "Self-Control Relies on Glucose as a Limited Energy Source: Willpower Is More Than a Metaphor," *Journal of Personality and Social Psychology* 92 (2007): 325–36. Matthew T. Gailliot and Roy F. Baumeister, "The Physiology of Willpower: Linking Blood Glucose to Self-Control," *Personality and Social Psychology Review* 11 (2007): 303–27.

43 *ego depletion*: Gailliot, "Self-Control Relies on Glucose as a Limited Energy Source."

43 *depletion effects in judgment*: Shai Danziger, Jonathan Levav, and Liora Avnaim-Pesso, "Extraneous Factors in Judicial Decisions," *PNAS* 108 (2011): 6889–92.

45 *intuitive—incorrect—answer*: Shane Frederick, "Cognitive Reflection and Decision Making," *Journal of Economic Perspectives* 19 (2005): 25–42.

45 *syllogism as valid*: This systematic error is known as the belief bias. Evans, "Dual-Processing Accounts of Reasoning, Judgment, and Social Cognition."

46 *call them more rational*: Keith E. Stanovich, *Rationality and the Reflective Mind* (New York: Oxford University Press, 2011).

47 *cruel dilemma*: Walter Mischel and Ebbe B. Ebbesen, "Attention in Delay of Gratification," *Journal of Personality and Social Psychology* 16 (1970): 329–37.

47 *"There were no toys . . . distress"*: Inge-Marie Eigsti et al., "Predicting Cognitive Control from Preschool to Late Adolescence and Young Adulthood," *Psychological Science* 17 (2006): 478–84.

47 *higher scores on tests of intelligence*: Mischel and Ebbesen, "Attention in Delay of Gratification." Walter Mischel, "Processes in Delay of Gratification," in *Advances in Experimental Social Psychology*, Vol. 7, ed. Leonard Berkowitz (San Diego, CA: Academic Press, 1974), 249–92. Walter Mischel, Yuichi Shoda, and Monica L. Rodriguez, "Delay of Gratification in Children," *Science* 244 (1989): 933–38. Eigsti, "Predicting Cognitive Control from Preschool to Late Adolescence."

48 *improvement was maintained*: M. Rosario Rueda et al., "Training, Maturation, and Genetic Influences on the Development of Executive Attention," *PNAS* 102 (2005): 14931–36.

49 *conventional measures of intelligence*: Maggie E. Toplak, Richard F. West, and Keith E. Stanovich, "The Cognitive Reflection Test as a Predictor of Performance on Heuristics-and-Biases Tasks," *Memory & Cognition* (in press).

4: THE ASSOCIATIVE MACHINE

50 *Associative Machine*: Carey K. Morewedge and Daniel Kahneman, "Associative Processes in Intuitive Judgment," *Trends in Cognitive Sciences* 14 (2010): 435–40.

50 *beyond your control*: To avoid confusion, I did not mention in the text that the pupil also dilated. The pupil dilates both during emotional arousal and when arousal accompanies intellectual effort.

51 *think with your body*: Paula M. Niedenthal, "Embodying Emotion," *Science* 316 (2007): 1002–1005.

52 *WASH primes SOAP*: The image is drawn from the working of a pump. The first few draws on a pump do not bring up any liquid, but they enable subsequent draws to be effective.

53 *"finds he it yellow instantly"*: John A. Bargh, Mark Chen, and Lara Burrows, "Automaticity of Social Behavior: Direct Effects of Trait Construct and Stereotype Activation on Action," *Journal of Personality and Social Psychology* 71 (1996): 230–44.

54 *words related to old age*: Thomas Mussweiler, "Doing Is for Thinking! Stereotype Activation by Stereotypic Movements," *Psychological Science* 17 (2006): 17–21.

54 The Far Side: Fritz Strack, Leonard L. Martin, and Sabine Stepper, "Inhibiting and Facilitating Conditions of the Human Smile: A Nonobtrusive Test of the Facial Feedback Hypothesis," *Journal of Personality and Social Psychology* 54 (1988): 768–77.

54 *upsetting pictures*: Ulf Dimberg, Monika Thunberg, and Sara Grunedal, "Facial Reactions to Emotional Stimuli: Automatically Controlled Emotional Responses," *Cognition and Emotion* 16 (2002): 449–71.

54 *listen to messages*: Gary L. Wells and Richard E. Petty, "The Effects of Overt Head Movements on Persuasion: Compatibility and Incompatibility of Responses," *Basic and Applied Social Psychology* 1 (1980): 219–30.

55 *increase the funding of schools*: Jonah Berger, Marc Meredith, and S. Christian Wheeler, "Contextual Priming: Where People Vote Affects How They Vote," *PNAS* 105 (2008): 8846–49.

55 *Reminders of money*: Kathleen D. Vohs, "The Psychological Consequences of Money," *Science* 314 (2006): 1154–56.

56 *appeal of authoritarian ideas*: Jeff Greenberg et al., "Evidence for Terror Management Theory II: The Effect of Mortality Salience on Reactions to Those Who Threaten or Bolster the Cultural Worldview," *Journal of Personality and Social Psychology* 58 (1990): 308–18.

56 *"Lady Macbeth effect"*: Chen-Bo Zhong and Katie Liljenquist, "Washing Away Your Sins: Threatened Morality and Physical Cleansing," *Science* 313 (2006): 1451–52.

56 *preferred mouthwash over soap*: Spike Lee and Norbert Schwarz, "Dirty Hands and Dirty Mouths: Embodiment of the Moral-Purity Metaphor Is Specific to the Motor Modality Involved in Moral Transgression," *Psychological Science* 21 (2010): 1423–25.

57 *at a British university*: Melissa Bateson, Daniel Nettle, and Gilbert Roberts, "Cues of Being Watched Enhance Cooperation in a Real-World Setting," *Biology Letters* 2 (2006): 412–14.

58 *introduced to that stranger*: Timothy Wilson's *Strangers to Ourselves* (Cambridge, MA: Belknap Press, 2002) presents a concept of an "adaptive unconscious" that is similar to System 1.

5: COGNITIVE EASE

59 *"Easy" and "Strained"*: The technical term for cognitive ease is *fluency*.

59 *diverse inputs and outputs*: Adam L. Alter and Daniel M. Oppenheimer, "Uniting the Tribes of Fluency to Form a Metacognitive Nation," *Personality and Social Psychology Review* 13 (2009): 219–35.

60 *"Becoming Famous Overnight"*: Larry L. Jacoby, Colleen Kelley, Judith Brown, and Jennifer Jasechko, "Becoming Famous Overnight: Limits on the Ability to Avoid Unconscious Influences of the Past," *Journal of Personality and Social Psychology* 56 (1989): 326–38.

61 *nicely stated the problem*: Bruce W. A. Whittlesea, Larry L. Jacoby, and Krista Girard, "Illusions of Immediate Memory: Evidence of an Attributional Basis for Feelings of Familiarity and Perceptual Quality," *Journal of Memory and Language* 29 (1990): 716–32.

62 *The impression of familiarity*: Normally, when you meet a friend you can immediately place and name him; you often know where you met him last, what he was wearing, and what you said to each other. The feeling of familiarity becomes relevant only when such specific memories are not available. It is a fallback. Although its reliability is imperfect, the fallback is much better than nothing. It is the sense of familiarity that protects you from the embarrassment of being (and acting) astonished when you are greeted as an old friend by someone who only looks vaguely familiar.

62 *"body temperature of a chicken"*: Ian Begg, Victoria Armour, and Thérèse Kerr, "On Believing What We Remember," *Canadian Journal of Behavioural Science* 17 (1985): 199–214.

63 *low credibility*: Daniel M. Oppenheimer, "Consequences of Erudite Vernacular Utilized Irrespective of Necessity: Problems with Using Long Words Needlessly," *Applied Cognitive Psychology* 20 (2006): 139–56.

63 *when they rhymed*: Matthew S. McGlone and Jessica Tofighbakhsh, "Birds of a Feather Flock Conjointly (?): Rhyme as Reason in Aphorisms," *Psychological Science* 11 (2000): 424–28.

64 *fictitious Turkish companies*: Anuj K. Shah and Daniel M. Oppenheimer, "Easy Does It: The Role of Fluency in Cue Weighting," *Judgment and Decision Making Journal* 2 (2007): 371–79.

65 *engaged and analytic mode*: Adam L. Alter, Daniel M. Oppenheimer, Nicholas Epley, and Rebecca Eyre, "Overcoming Intuition: Metacognitive Difficulty Activates Analytic Reasoning," *Journal of Experimental Psychology—General* 136 (2007): 569–76.

65 *pictures of objects*: Piotr Winkielman and John T. Cacioppo, "Mind at Ease Puts a Smile on the Face: Psychophysiological Evidence That Processing Facilitation Increases Positive Affect," *Journal of Personality and Social Psychology* 81 (2001): 989–1000.

66 *small advantage*: Adam L. Alter and Daniel M. Oppenheimer, "Predicting Short-Term Stock Fluctuations by Using Processing Fluency," *PNAS* 103 (2006). Michael J. Cooper, Orlin Dimitrov, and P. Raghavendra Rau, "A Rose.com by Any Other Name," *Journal of Finance* 56 (2001): 2371–88.

66 *clunky labels*: Pascal Pensa, "Nomen Est Omen: How Company Names Influence Short- and Long-Run Stock Market Performance," *Social Science Research Network Working Paper*, September 2006.

66 mere exposure effect: Robert B. Zajonc, "Attitudinal Effects of Mere Exposure," *Journal of Personality and Social Psychology* 9 (1968): 1–27.

66 *favorite experiments*: Robert B. Zajonc and D. W. Rajecki, "Exposure and Affect: A Field Experiment," *Psychonomic Science* 17 (1969): 216–17.

67 *never consciously sees*: Jennifer L. Monahan, Sheila T. Murphy, and Robert B. Zajonc, "Subliminal Mere Exposure: Specific, General, and Diffuse Effects," *Psychological Science* 11 (2000): 462–66.

67 *inhabiting the shell*: D. W. Rajecki, "Effects of Prenatal Exposure to Auditory or Visual Stimulation on Postnatal Distress Vocalizations in Chicks," *Behavioral Biology* 11 (1974): 525–36.

67 *"The consequences . . . social stability"*: Robert B. Zajonc, "Mere Exposure: A Gateway to the Subliminal," *Current Directions in Psychological Science* 10 (2001): 227.

68 *triad of words*: Annette Bolte, Thomas Goschke, and Julius Kuhl, "Emotion and Intuition: Effects of Positive and Negative Mood on Implicit Judgments of Semantic Coherence," *Psychological Science* 14 (2003): 416–21.

68 *association is retrieved*: The analysis excludes all cases in which the subject actually found the correct solution. It shows that even subjects who will ultimately fail to find a common association have some idea of whether there is one to be found.

68 *increase cognitive ease*: Sascha Topolinski and Fritz Strack, "The Architecture of Intuition: Fluency and Affect Determine Intuitive Judgments of Semantic and Visual Coherence and Judgments of Grammaticality in Artificial Grammar Learning," *Journal of Experimental Psychology—General* 138 (2009): 39–63.

69 *doubled accuracy*: Bolte, Goschke, and Kuhl, "Emotion and Intuition."

69 *form a cluster*: Barbara Fredrickson, *Positivity: Groundbreaking Research Reveals How to Embrace the Hidden Strength of Positive Emotions, Overcome Negativity, and Thrive* (New York: Random House, 2009). Joseph P. Forgas and Rebekah East, "On Being Happy and Gullible: Mood Effects on Skepticism and the Detection of Deception," *Journal of Experimental Social Psychology* 44 (2008): 1362–67.

69 *smiling reaction*: Sascha Topolinski et al., "The Face of Fluency: Semantic Coherence Automatically Elicits a Specific Pattern of Facial Muscle Reactions," *Cognition and Emotion* 23 (2009): 260–71.

70 *"previous research . . . individuals"*: Sascha Topolinski and Fritz Strack, "The Analysis of Intuition: Processing Fluency and Affect in Judgments of Semantic Coherence," *Cognition and Emotion* 23 (2009): 1465–1503.

6: NORMS, SURPRISES, AND CAUSES

73 *An observer*: Daniel Kahneman and Dale T. Miller, "Norm Theory: Comparing Reality to Its Alternatives," *Psychological Review* 93 (1986): 136–53.

74 *"tattoo on my back"*: Jos J. A. Van Berkum, "Understanding Sentences in Context: What Brain Waves Can Tell Us," *Current Directions in Psychological Science* 17 (2008): 376–80.

75 *the word* pickpocket: Ran R. Hassin, John A. Bargh, and James S. Uleman, "Spontaneous Causal Inferences," *Journal of Experimental Social Psychology* 38 (2002): 515–22.

76 *indicate surprise*: Albert Michotte, *The Perception of Causality* (Andover, MA: Methuen, 1963). Alan M. Leslie and Stephanie Keeble, "Do Six-Month-Old Infants Perceive Causality?" *Cognition* 25 (1987): 265–88.

76 *explosive finale*: Fritz Heider and Mary-Ann Simmel, "An Experimental Study of Apparent Behavior," *American Journal of Psychology* 13 (1944): 243–59.

77 *identify bullies and victims*: Leslie and Keeble, "Do Six-Month-Old Infants Perceive Causality?"

77 *as we die*: Paul Bloom, "Is God an Accident?" *Atlantic*, December 2005.

7: A MACHINE FOR JUMPING TO CONCLUSIONS

81 *elegant experiment*: Daniel T. Gilbert, Douglas S. Krull, and Patrick S. Malone, "Unbelieving the Unbelievable: Some Problems in the Rejection of False Information," *Journal of Personality and Social Psychology* 59 (1990): 601–13.

82 *descriptions of two people*: Solomon E. Asch, "Forming Impressions of Personality," *Journal of Abnormal and Social Psychology* 41 (1946): 258–90.

83 *all six adjectives*: Ibid.

84 Wisdom of Crowds: James Surowiecki, *The Wisdom of Crowds* (New York: Anchor Books, 2005).

86 *one-sided evidence*: Lyle A. Brenner, Derek J. Koehler, and Amos Tversky, "On the Evaluation of One-Sided Evidence," *Journal of Behavioral Decision Making* 9 (1996): 59–70.

8: HOW JUDGMENTS HAPPEN

90 *biological roots*: Alexander Todorov, Sean G. Baron, and Nikolaas N. Oosterhof, "Evaluating Face Trustworthiness: A Model-Based Approach," *Social Cognitive and Affective Neuroscience* 3 (2008): 119–27.

90 *friendly or hostile*: Alexander Todorov, Chris P. Said, Andrew D. Engell, and Nikolaas N. Oosterhof, "Understanding Evaluation of Faces on Social Dimensions," *Trends in Cognitive Sciences* 12 (2008): 455–60.

90 *may spell trouble*: Alexander Todorov, Manish Pakrashi, and Nikolaas N. Oosterhof, "Evaluating Faces on Trustworthiness After Minimal Time Exposure," *Social Cognition* 27 (2009): 813–33.

91 *Australia, Germany, and Mexico*: Alexander Todorov et al., "Inference of Competence from Faces Predict Election Outcomes," *Science* 308 (2005): 1623–26. Charles C. Ballew and Alexander Todorov, "Predicting Political Elections from Rapid and Unreflective Face Judgments," *PNAS* 104 (2007): 17948–53. Christopher Y. Olivola and Alexander Todorov, "Elected in 100 Milliseconds: Appearance-Based Trait Inferences and Voting," *Journal of Nonverbal Behavior* 34 (2010): 83–110.

91 *watch less television*: Gabriel Lenz and Chappell Lawson, "Looking the Part: Television Leads Less Informed Citizens to Vote Based on Candidates' Appearance," *American Journal of Political Science* (forthcoming).

91 *absence of a specific task set*: Amos Tversky and Daniel Kahneman, "Extensional Versus Intuitive Reasoning: The Conjunction Fallacy in Probability Judgment," *Psychological Review* 90 (1983): 293–315.

93 Exxon Valdez: William H. Desvousges et al., "Measuring Natural Resource Damages with Contingent Valuation: Tests of Validity and Reliability," in *Contingent Valuation: A Critical Assessment*, ed. Jerry A. Hausman (Amsterdam: North-Holland, 1993), 91–159.

94 *sense of injustice*: Stanley S. Stevens, *Psychophysics: Introduction to Its Perceptual, Neural, and Social Prospect* (New York: Wiley, 1975).

95 *detected that the words rhymed*: Mark S. Seidenberg and Michael K. Tanenhaus, "Orthographic Effects on Rhyme Monitoring," *Journal of Experimental Psychology—Human Learning and Memory* 5 (1979): 546–54.

95–96 *sentence was literally true*: Sam Glucksberg, Patricia Gildea, and Howard G. Bookin, "On Understanding Nonliteral Speech: Can People Ignore Metaphors?" *Journal of Verbal Learning and Verbal Behavior* 21 (1982): 85–98.

9: ANSWERING AN EASIER QUESTION

99 *an intuitive answer to it came readily to mind*: An alternative approach to judgment heuristics has been proposed by Gerd Gigerenzer, Peter M. Todd, and the ABC Research Group, in *Simple Heuristics That Make Us Smart* (New York: Oxford University Press, 1999). They describe "fast and frugal" formal procedures such as "Take the best [cue]," which under some circumstances generate quite accurate judgments on the basis of little information. As Gigerenzer has emphasized, his heuristics are different from those that Amos and I studied, and he has stressed their accuracy rather than the biases to which they inevitably lead. Much of the research that supports fast and frugal heuristic uses statistical simula-

tions to show that they *could* work in some real-life situations, but the evidence for the psychological reality of these heuristics remains thin and contested. The most memorable discovery associated with this approach is the recognition heuristic, illustrated by an example that has become well-known: a subject who is asked which of two cities is larger and recognizes one of them should guess that the one she recognizes is larger. The recognition heuristic works fairly well if the subject knows that the city she recognizes is large; if she knows it to be small, however, she will quite reasonably guess that the unknown city is larger. Contrary to the theory, the subjects use more than the recognition cue: Daniel M. Oppenheimer, "Not So Fast! (and Not So Frugal!): Rethinking the Recognition Heuristic," *Cognition* 90 (2003): B1–B9. A weakness of the theory is that, from what we know of the mind, there is no need for heuristics to be frugal. The brain processes vast amounts of information in parallel, and the mind can be fast and accurate without ignoring information. Furthermore, it has been known since the early days of research on chess masters that skill need not consist of learning to use less information. On the contrary, skill is more often an ability to deal with large amounts of information quickly and efficiently.

101 *best examples of substitution*: Fritz Strack, Leonard L. Martin, and Norbert Schwarz, "Priming and Communication: Social Determinants of Information Use in Judgments of Life Satisfaction," *European Journal of Social Psychology* 18 (1988): 429–42.

102 *correlations between psychological measures*: The correlation was .66.

102 *dominates happiness reports*: Other substitution topics include marital satisfaction, job satisfaction, and leisure time satisfaction: Norbert Schwarz, Fritz Strack, and Hans-Peter Mai, "Assimilation and Contrast Effects in Part-Whole Question Sequences: A Conversational Logic Analysis," *Public Opinion Quarterly* 55 (1991): 3–23.

103 *evaluate their happiness*: A telephone survey conducted in Germany included a question about general happiness. When the self-reports of happiness were correlated with the local weather at the time of the interview, a pronounced correlation was found. Mood is known to vary with the weather, and substitution explains the effect on reported happiness. However, another version of the telephone survey yielded a somewhat different result. These respondents were asked about the current weather before they were asked the happiness question. For them, weather had no effect at all on reported happiness! The explicit priming of weather provided them with an explanation of their mood, undermining the connection that would normally be made between current mood and overall happiness.

103 *view of the benefits*: Melissa L. Finucane et al., "The Affect Heuristic in Judgments of Risks and Benefits," *Journal of Behavioral Decision Making* 13 (2000): 1–17.

10: THE LAW OF SMALL NUMBERS

109 *"It is both . . . without additives"*: Howard Wainer and Harris L. Zwerling, "Evidence That Smaller Schools Do Not Improve Student Achievement," *Phi Delta Kappan* 88 (2006): 300–303. The example was discussed by Andrew Gelman and Deborah Nolan, *Teaching Statistics: A Bag of Tricks* (New York: Oxford University Press, 2002).

112 *50% risk of failing*: Jacob Cohen, "The Statistical Power of Abnormal-Social Psychological Research: A Review," *Journal of Abnormal and Social Psychology* 65 (1962): 145–53.

113 *"Belief in the Law of Small Numbers"*: Amos Tversky and Daniel Kahneman, "Belief in the Law of Small Numbers," *Psychological Bulletin* 76 (1971): 105–10.

113 *"statistical intuitions . . . whenever possible"*: The contrast that we drew between intuition and computation seems to foreshadow the distinction between Systems 1 and 2, but we

were a long way from the perspective of this book. We used *intuition* to cover anything but a computation, any informal way to reach a conclusion.

116 *German spies*: William Feller, *Introduction to Probability Theory and Its Applications* (New York: Wiley, 1950).

116 *randomness in basketball*: Thomas Gilovich, Robert Vallone, and Amos Tversky, "The Hot Hand in Basketball: On the Misperception of Random Sequences," *Cognitive Psychology* 17 (1985): 295–314.

11: ANCHORS

121 *"'reasonable' volume"*: Robyn LeBoeuf and Eldar Shafir, "The Long and Short of It: Physical Anchoring Effects," *Journal of Behavioral Decision Making* 19 (2006): 393–406.

121 *nod their head*: Nicholas Epley and Thomas Gilovich, "Putting Adjustment Back in the Anchoring and Adjustment Heuristic: Differential Processing of Self-Generated and Experimenter-Provided Anchors," *Psychological Science* 12 (2001): 391–96.

121 *stay closer to the anchor*: Epley and Gilovich, "The Anchoring-and-Adjustment Heuristic."

123 *associative coherence*: Thomas Mussweiler, "The Use of Category and Exemplar Knowledge in the Solution of Anchoring Tasks," *Journal of Personality and Social Psychology* 78 (2000): 1038–52.

123 *San Francisco Exploratorium*: Karen E. Jacowitz and Daniel Kahneman, "Measures of Anchoring in Estimation Tasks," *Personality and Social Psychology Bulletin* 21 (1995): 1161–66.

124 *substantially lower*: Gregory B. Northcraft and Margaret A. Neale, "Experts, Amateurs, and Real Estate: An Anchoring-and-Adjustment Perspective on Property Pricing Decisions," *Organizational Behavior and Human Decision Processes* 39 (1987): 84–97. The high anchor was 12% above the listed price, the low anchor was 12% below that price.

125 *rolled a pair of dice*: Birte Englich, Thomas Mussweiler, and Fritz Strack, "Playing Dice with Criminal Sentences: The Influence of Irrelevant Anchors on Experts' Judicial Decision Making," *Personality and Social Psychology Bulletin* 32 (2006): 188–200.

126 NO LIMIT PER PERSON: Brian Wansink, Robert J. Kent, and Stephen J. Hoch, "An Anchoring and Adjustment Model of Purchase Quantity Decisions," *Journal of Marketing Research* 35 (1998): 71–81.

126 *resist the anchoring effect*: Adam D. Galinsky and Thomas Mussweiler, "First Offers as Anchors: The Role of Perspective-Taking and Negotiator Focus," *Journal of Personality and Social Psychology* 81 (2001): 657–69.

127 *otherwise be much smaller*: Greg Pogarsky and Linda Babcock, "Damage Caps, Motivated Anchoring, and Bargaining Impasse," *Journal of Legal Studies* 30 (2001): 143–59.

128 *amount of damages*: For an experimental demonstration, see Chris Guthrie, Jeffrey J. Rachlinski, and Andrew J. Wistrich, "Judging by Heuristic-Cognitive Illusions in Judicial Decision Making," *Judicature* 86 (2002): 44–50.

12: THE SCIENCE OF AVAILABILITY

129 *"the ease with which"*: Amos Tversky and Daniel Kahneman, "Availability: A Heuristic for Judging Frequency and Probability," *Cognitive Psychology* 5 (1973): 207–32.

131 *self-assessed contributions*: Michael Ross and Fiore Sicoly, "Egocentric Biases in Availability and Attribution," *Journal of Personality and Social Psychology* 37 (1979): 322–36.

131 *A major advance*: Schwarz et al., "Ease of Retrieval as Information."

132 *role of fluency*: Sabine Stepper and Fritz Strack, "Proprioceptive Determinants of Emotional and Nonemotional Feelings," *Journal of Personality and Social Psychology* 64 (1993): 211–20.

134 *experimenters dreamed up*: For a review of this area of research, see Rainer Greifeneder, Herbert Bless, and Michel T. Pham, "When Do People Rely on Affective and Cognitive Feelings in Judgment? A Review," *Personality and Social Psychology Review* 15 (2011): 107–41.

135 *affect their cardiac health*: Alexander Rotliman and Norbert Schwarz, "Constructing Perceptions of Vulnerability: Personal Relevance and the Use of Experimental Information in Health Judgments," *Personality and Social Psychology Bulletin* 24 (1998): 1053–64.

135 *effortful task at the same time*: Rainer Greifeneder and Herbert Bless, "Relying on Accessible Content Versus Accessibility Experiences: The Case of Processing Capacity," *Social Cognition* 25 (2007): 853–81.

135 *happy episode in their life*: Markus Ruder and Herbert Bless, "Mood and the Reliance on the Ease of Retrieval Heuristic," *Journal of Personality and Social Psychology* 85 (2003): 20–32.

135 *low on a depression scale*: Rainer Greifeneder and Herbert Bless, "Depression and Reliance on Ease-of-Retrieval Experiences," *European Journal of Social Psychology* 38 (2008): 213–30.

135 *knowledgeable novices*: Chezy Ofir et al., "Memory-Based Store Price Judgments: The Role of Knowledge and Shopping Experience," *Journal of Retailing* 84 (2008): 414–23.

135 *true experts*: Eugene M. Caruso, "Use of Experienced Retrieval Ease in Self and Social Judgments," *Journal of Experimental Social Psychology* 44 (2008): 148–55.

135 *faith in intuition*: Johannes Keller and Herbert Bless, "Predicting Future Affective States: How Ease of Retrieval and Faith in Intuition Moderate the Impact of Activated Content," *European Journal of Social Psychology* 38 (2008): 1–10.

135 *if they are . . . powerful*: Mario Weick and Ana Guinote, "When Subjective Experiences Matter: Power Increases Reliance on the Ease of Retrieval," *Journal of Personality and Social Psychology* 94 (2008): 956–70.

13: AVAILABILITY, EMOTION, AND RISK

139 *because of brain damage*: Damasio's idea is known as the "somatic marker hypothesis" and it has gathered substantial support: Antonio R. Damasio, *Descartes' Error: Emotion, Reason, and the Human Brain* (New York: Putnam, 1994). Antonio R. Damasio, "The Somatic Marker Hypothesis and the Possible Functions of the Prefrontal Cortex," *Philosophical Transactions: Biological Sciences* 351 (1996): 141–20.

139 *risks of each technology*: Finucane et al., "The Affect Heuristic in Judgments of Risks and Benefits." Paul Slovic, Melissa Finucane, Ellen Peters, and Donald G. MacGregor, "The Affect Heuristic," in Thomas Gilovich, Dale Griffin, and Daniel Kahneman, eds., *Heuristics and Biases* (New York: Cambridge University Press, 2002), 397–420. Paul Slovic, Melissa Finucane, Ellen Peters, and Donald G. MacGregor, "Risk as Analysis and Risk as Feelings: Some Thoughts About Affect, Reason, Risk, and Rationality," *Risk Analysis* 24 (2004): 1–12. Paul Slovic, "Trust, Emotion, Sex, Politics, and Science: Surveying the Risk-Assessment Battlefield," *Risk Analysis* 19 (1999): 689–701.

139 *British Toxicology Society*: Slovic, "Trust, Emotion, Sex, Politics, and Science." The technologies and substances used in these studies are not alternative solutions to the same problem. In realistic problems, where competitive solutions are considered, the correlation between costs and benefits must be negative; the solutions that have the largest benefits are also the most costly. Whether laypeople and even experts might fail to recognize the correct relationship even in those cases is an interesting question.

140 *"wags the rational dog"*: Jonathan Haidt, "The Emotional Dog and Its Rational Tail: A Social Institutionist Approach to Moral Judgment," *Psychological Review* 108 (2001): 814–34.

141 *"'Risk' does not exist"*: Paul Slovic, *The Perception of Risk* (Sterling, VA: EarthScan, 2000).

142 availability cascade: Timur Kuran and Cass R. Sunstein, "Availability Cascades and Risk Regulation," *Stanford Law Review* 51 (1999): 683–768. *CERCLA*, the Comprehensive Environmental Response, Compensation, and Liability Act, passed in 1980.

143 *nothing in between*: Paul Slovic, who testified for the apple growers in the Alar case, has a rather different view: "The scare was triggered by the CBS *60 Minutes* broadcast that said 4, 000 children will die of cancer (no probabilities there) along with frightening pictures of bald children in a cancer ward—and many more incorrect statements. Also the story exposed EPA's lack of competence in attending to and evaluating the safety of Alar, destroying trust in regulatory control. Given this, I think the public's response was rational." (Personal communication, May 11, 2011.)

14: TOM W'S SPECIALTY

152 *"a shy poetry lover"*: I borrowed this example from Max H. Bazerman and Don A. Moore, *Judgment in Managerial Decision Making* (New York: Wiley, 2008).

152 *always weighted more*: Jonathan St. B. T. Evans, "Heuristic and Analytic Processes in Reasoning," *British Journal of Psychology* 75 (1984): 451–68.

152 *the opposite effect*: Norbert Schwarz et al., "Base Rates, Representativeness, and the Logic of Conversation: The Contextual Relevance of 'Irrelevant' Information," *Social Cognition* 9 (1991): 67–84.

152 *told to frown*: Alter, Oppenheimer, Epley, and Eyre, "Overcoming Intuition."

154 *Bayes's rule*: The simplest form of Bayes's rule is in odds form, posterior odds = prior odds × likelihood ratio, where the posterior odds are the odds (the ratio of probabilities) for two competing hypotheses. Consider a problem of diagnosis. Your friend has tested positive for a serious disease. The disease is rare: only 1 in 600 of the cases sent in for testing actually has the disease. The test is fairly accurate. Its likelihood ratio is 25:1, which means that the probability that a person who has the disease will test positive is 25 times higher than the probability of a false positive. Testing positive is frightening news, but the odds that your friend has the disease have risen only from 1/600 to 25/600, and the probability is 4%.

    For the hypothesis that Tom W is a computer scientist, the prior odds that correspond to a base rate of 3% are (.03/.97 = .031). Assuming a likelihood ratio of 4 (the description is 4 times as likely if Tom W is a computer scientist than if he is not), the posterior odds are 4 × .031 = 12.4. From these odds you can compute that the posterior probability of Tom W being a computer scientist is now 11% (because 12.4/112.4 = .11).

15: LINDA: LESS IS MORE

156 *the role of heuristics*: Amos Tversky and Daniel Kahneman, "Extensional Versus Intuitive Reasoning: The Conjunction Fallacy in Probability Judgment," *Psychological Review* 90(1983), 293-315.

159 *"a little homunculus"*: Stephen Jay Gould, *Bully for Brontosaurus* (New York: Norton, 1991).

165 *weakened or explained*: See, among others, Ralph Hertwig and Gerd Gigerenzer, "The 'Conjunction Fallacy' Revisited: How Intelligent Inferences Look Like Reasoning Errors," *Journal of Behavioral Decision Making* 12 (1999): 275–305; Ralph Hertwig, Bjoern Benz,

NOTES

and Stefan Krauss, "The Conjunction Fallacy and the Many Meanings of And," *Cognition* 108 (2008): 740–53.

165 *settle our differences*: Barbara Mellers, Ralph Hertwig, and Daniel Kahneman, "Do Frequency Representations Eliminate Conjunction Effects? An Exercise in Adversarial Collaboration," *Psychological Science* 12 (2001): 269–75.

16: CAUSES TRUMP STATISTICS

167 *correct answer is 41%*: Applying Bayes's rule in odds form, the prior odds are the odds for the Blue cab from the base rate, and the likelihood ratio is the ratio of the probability of the witness saying the cab is Blue if it is Blue, divided by the probability of the witness saying the cab is Blue if it is Green: posterior odds = (.15/.85) × (.80/.20) = .706. The odds are the ratio of the probability that the cab is Blue, divided by the probability that the cab is Green. To obtain the probability that the cab is Blue, we compute: Probability(Blue) = .706/1.706 = .41. The probability that the cab is Blue is 41%.

167 *not too far from the Bayesian*: Amos Tversky and Daniel Kahneman, "Causal Schemas in Judgments Under Uncertainty," in *Progress in Social Psychology*, ed. Morris Fishbein (Hillsdale, NJ: Erlbaum, 1980), 49–72.

170 *University of Michigan*: Richard E. Nisbett and Eugene Borgida, "Attribution and the Psychology of Prediction," *Journal of Personality and Social Psychology* 32 (1975): 932–43.

171 *relieved of responsibility*: John M. Darley and Bibb Latane, "Bystander Intervention in Emergencies: Diffusion of Responsibility," *Journal of Personality and Social Psychology* 8 (1968): 377–83.

17: REGRESSION TO THE MEAN

180 *help of the most brilliant statisticians*: Michael Bulmer, *Francis Galton: Pioneer of Heredity and Biometry* (Baltimore: Johns Hopkins University Press, 2003).

180 standard scores: Researchers transform each original score into a standard score by subtracting the mean and dividing the result by the standard deviation. Standard scores have a mean of zero and a standard deviation of 1, can be compared across variables (especially when the statistical distributions of the original scores are similar), and have many desirable mathematical properties, which Galton had to work out to understand the nature of correlation and regression.

181 *correlation between parent and child*: This will not be true in an environment in which some children are malnourished. Differences in nutrition will become important, the proportion of shared factors will diminish, and with it the correlation between the height of parents and the height of children (unless the parents of malnourished children were also stunted by hunger in childhood).

181 *height and weight*: The correlation was computed for a very large sample of the population of the United States (the Gallup-Healthways Well-Being Index).

181 *income and education*: The correlation appears impressive, but I was surprised to learn many years ago from the sociologist Christopher Jencks that if everyone had the same education, the inequality of income (measured by standard deviation) would be reduced only by about 9%. The relevant formula is $\sqrt{(1-r^2)}$, where r is the correlation.

181 *correlation and regression*: This is true when both variables are measured in standard scores—that is, where each score is transformed by removing the mean and dividing the result by the standard deviation.

183 *confusing mere correlation with causation*: Howard Wainer, "The Most Dangerous Equation," *American Scientist* 95 (2007): 249–56.

18: TAMING INTUITIVE PREDICTIONS

190 *far more moderate*: The proof of the standard regression as the optimal solution to the prediction problem assumes that errors are weighted by the squared deviation from the correct value. This is the least-squares criterion, which is commonly accepted. Other loss functions lead to different solutions.

19: THE ILLUSION OF UNDERSTANDING

199 narrative fallacy: Nassim Nicholas Taleb, *The Black Swan: The Impact of the Highly Improbable* (New York: Random House, 2007).

199 *one attribute that is particularly significant*: See chapter 7.

199 *throwing the ball*: Michael Lewis, *Moneyball: The Art of Winning an Unfair Game* (New York: Norton, 2003).

200 *sell their company*: Seth Weintraub, "Excite Passed Up Buying Google for $750,000 in 1999," *Fortune*, September 29, 2011.

202 *ever felt differently*: Richard E. Nisbett and Timothy D. Wilson, "Telling More Than We Can Know: Verbal Reports on Mental Processes," *Psychological Review* 84 (1977): 231–59.

203 *United States and the Soviet Union*: Baruch Fischhoff and Ruth Beyth, "I Knew It Would Happen: Remembered Probabilities of Once Future Things," *Organizational Behavior and Human Performance* 13 (1975): 1–16.

203 *quality of a decision*: Jonathan Baron and John C. Hershey, "Outcome Bias in Decision Evaluation," *Journal of Personality and Social Psychology* 54 (1988): 569–79.

204 *should have hired the monitor*: Kim A. Kamin and Jeffrey Rachlinski, "Ex Post ≠ Ex Ante: Determining Liability in Hindsight," *Law and Human Behavior* 19 (1995): 89–104. Jeffrey J. Rachlinski, "A Positive Psychological Theory of Judging in Hindsight," *University of Chicago Law Review* 65 (1998): 571–625.

204 *tidbit of intelligence*: Jeffrey Goldberg, "Letter from Washington: Woodward vs. Tenet," *New Yorker*, May 21, 2007, 35–38. Also Tim Weiner, *Legacy of Ashes: The History of the CIA* (New York: Doubleday, 2007); "Espionage: Inventing the Dots," *Economist*, November 3, 2007, 100.

204 *reluctance to take risks*: Philip E. Tetlock, "Accountability: The Neglected Social Context of Judgment and Choice," *Research in Organizational Behavior* 7 (1985): 297–332.

205 *before their current appointment*: Marianne Bertrand and Antoinette Schoar, "Managing with Style: The Effect of Managers on Firm Policies," *Quarterly Journal of Economics* 118 (2003): 1169–1208. Nick Bloom and John Van Reenen, "Measuring and Explaining Management Practices Across Firms and Countries," *Quarterly Journal of Economics* 122 (2007): 1351–1408.

205 *"How often will you find . . ."*: I am indebted to Professor James H. Steiger of Vanderbilt University, who developed an algorithm that answers this question, under plausible assumptions. Steiger's analysis shows that correlations of .20 and .40 are associated, respectively, with inversion rates of 43% and 37%.

206 *his penetrating book*: *The Halo Effect* was praised as one of the best business books of the year by both the *Financial Times* and *The Wall Street Journal*: Phil Rosenzweig, *The Halo Effect: . . . and the Eight Other Business Delusions That Deceive Managers* (New York: Simon & Schuster, 2007). See also Paul Olk and Phil Rosenzweig, "The Halo Effect and the Chal-

lenge of Management Inquiry: A Dialog Between Phil Rosenzweig and Paul Olk," *Journal of Management Inquiry* 19 (2010): 48–54.

207 *"a visionary company"*: James C. Collins and Jerry I. Porras, *Built to Last: Successful Habits of Visionary Companies* (New York: Harper, 2002).

207 *flip of a coin*: In fact, even if you were the CEO yourself, your forecasts would not be impressively reliable; the extensive research on insider trading shows that executives do beat the market when they trade their own stock, but the margin of their outperformance is barely enough to cover the costs of trading. See H. Nejat Seyhun, "The Information Content of Aggregate Insider Trading," *Journal of Business* 61 (1988): 1–24; Josef Lakonishok and Inmoo Lee, "Are Insider Trades Informative?" *Review of Financial Studies* 14 (2001): 79–111; Zahid Iqbal and Shekar Shetty, "An Investigation of Causality Between Insider Transactions and Stock Returns," *Quarterly Review of Economics and Finance* 42 (2002): 41–57.

207 In Search of Excellence: Rosenzweig, *The Halo Effect*.

207 *"Most Admired Companies"*: Deniz Anginer, Kenneth L. Fisher, and Meir Statman, "Stocks of Admired Companies and Despised Ones," working paper, 2007.

207 *regression to the mean*: Jason Zweig observes that the lack of appreciation for regression has detrimental implications for the recruitment of CEOs. Struggling firms tend to turn to outsiders, recruiting CEOs from companies with high recent returns. The incoming CEO then gets credit, at least temporarily, for his new firm's subsequent improvement. (Meanwhile, his replacement at his former firm is now struggling, leading the new bosses to believe that they definitely hired "the right guy.") Anytime a CEO jumps ship, the new company must buy out his stake (in stock and options) at his old firm, setting a baseline for future compensation that has nothing to do with performance at the new firm. Tens of millions of dollars in compensation get awarded for "personal" achievements that are driven mainly by regression and halo effects (personal communication, December 29, 2009).

20: THE ILLUSION OF VALIDITY

213 *this startling conclusion*: Brad M. Barber and Terrance Odean, "Trading Is Hazardous to Your Wealth: The Common Stock Investment Performance of Individual Investors," *Journal of Finance* 55 (2002): 773–806.

214 *men acted on their useless ideas*: Brad M. Barber and Terrance Odean, "Boys Will Be Boys: Gender, Overconfidence, and Common Stock Investment," *Quarterly Journal of Economics* 116 (2006): 261–92.

214 *selling "winners"*: This "disposition effect" is discussed further in chapter 32.

214 *responding to news*: Brad M. Barber and Terrance Odean, "All That Glitters: The Effect of Attention and News on the Buying Behavior of Individual and Institutional Investors," *Review of Financial Studies* 21 (2008): 785–818.

214 *wealth from amateurs*: Research on stock trades in Taiwan concluded that the transfer of wealth from individuals to financial institutions amounts to a staggering 2.2% of GDP: Brad M. Barber, Yi-Tsung Lee, Yu-Jane Liu, and Terrance Odean, "Just How Much Do Individual Investors Lose by Trading?" *Review of Financial Studies* 22 (2009): 609–32.

215 *underperform the overall market*: John C. Bogle, *Common Sense on Mutual Funds: New Imperatives for the Intelligent Investor* (New York: Wiley, 2000), 213.

215 *persistent differences in skill*: Mark Grinblatt and Sheridan Titman, "The Persistence of Mutual Fund Performance," *Journal of Finance* 42 (1992): 1977–84. Edwin J. Elton et al., "The Persistence of Risk-Adjusted Mutual Fund Performance," *Journal of Business* 52 (1997):

1–33. Edwin Elton et al., "Efficiency With Costly Information: A Re-interpretation of Evidence from Managed Portfolios," *Review of Financial Studies* 6 (1993): 1–21.

219 *"In this age of academic hyperspecialization"*: Philip E. Tetlock, *Expert Political Judgment: How Good is It? How Can We Know?* (Princeton: Princeton University Press, 2005), 233.

21: INTUITIONS VS. FORMULAS

223 *"There is no controversy"*: Paul Meehl, "Causes and Effects of My Disturbing Little Book," *Journal of Personality Assessment* 50 (1986): 370–75.

224 *a factor of 10 or more*: During the 1990–1991 auction season, for example, the price in London of a case of 1960 Château Latour averaged $464; a case of the 1961 vintage (one of the best ever) fetched an average of $5,432.

225 *Experienced radiologists*: Paul J. Hoffman, Paul Slovic, and Leonard G. Rorer, "An Analysis-of-Variance Model for the Assessment of Configural Cue Utilization in Clinical Judgment," *Psychological Bulletin* 69 (1968): 338–39.

225 *internal corporate audits*: Paul R. Brown, "Independent Auditor Judgment in the Evaluation of Internal Audit Functions," *Journal of Accounting Research* 21 (1983): 444–55.

225 *41 separate studies*: James Shanteau, "Psychological Characteristics and Strategies of Expert Decision Makers," *Acta Psychologica* 68 (1988): 203–15.

225 *successive food breaks*: Danziger, Levav, and Avnaim-Pesso, "Extraneous Factors in Judicial Decisions."

225 *lowering validity*: Richard A. DeVaul et al., "Medical-School Performance of Initially Rejected Students," *JAMA* 257 (1987): 47–51. Jason Dana and Robyn M. Dawes, "Belief in the Unstructured Interview: The Persistence of an Illusion," working paper, Department of Psychology, University of Pennsylvania, 2011. William M. Grove et al., "Clinical Versus Mechanical Prediction: A Meta-Analysis," *Psychological Assessment* 12 (2000): 19–30.

226 *Dawes's famous article*: Robyn M. Dawes, "The Robust Beauty of Improper Linear Models in Decision Making," *American Psychologist* 34 (1979): 571–82.

226 *not affected by accidents of sampling*: Jason Dana and Robyn M. Dawes, "The Superiority of Simple Alternatives to Regression for Social Science Predictions," *Journal of Educational and Behavioral Statistics* 29 (2004): 317–31.

227 *Dr. Apgar*: Virginia Apgar, "A Proposal for a New Method of Evaluation of the Newborn Infant," *Current Researches in Anesthesia and Analgesia* 32 (1953): 260–67. Mieczyslaw Finster and Margaret Wood, "The Apgar Score Has Survived the Test of Time," *Anesthesiology* 102 (2005): 855–57.

227 *virtues of checklists*: Atul Gawande, *The Checklist Manifesto: How to Get Things Right* (New York: Metropolitan Books, 2009).

228 *organic fruit*: Paul Rozin, "The Meaning of 'Natural': Process More Important than Content," *Psychological Science* 16 (2005): 652–58.

22: EXPERT INTUITION: WHEN CAN WE TRUST IT?

234 *moderated by an arbiter*: Mellers, Hertwig, and Kahneman, "Do Frequency Representations Eliminate Conjunction Effects?"

235 *articulated this position*: Klein, *Sources of Power*.

235 *kouros*: The Getty Museum in Los Angeles brings in the world's leading experts on Greek sculpture to view a kouros—a marble statue of a striding boy—that it is about to buy. One

after another, the experts react with what one calls "intuitive repulsion"—a powerful hunch that the kouros is not 2,500 years old but a modern fake. None of the experts can immediately say why they think the sculpture is a forgery. The closest any of them could come to a rationale is an Italian art historian's complaint that something—he does not know exactly what—"seemed wrong" with the statue's fingernails. A famous American expert said that the first thought that came to his mind was the word *fresh*, and a Greek expert flatly stated, "Anyone who has ever seen a sculpture coming out of the ground could tell that that thing has never been in the ground." The lack of agreement on the reasons for the shared conclusion is striking, and rather suspect.

237 *admired as a hero*: Simon was one of the towering intellectual figures of the twentieth century. He wrote a classic on decision making in organizations while still in his twenties, and among many other achievements he went on to be one of the founders of the field of artificial intelligence, a leader in cognitive science, an influential student of the process of scientific discovery, a forerunner of behavioral economics and, almost incidentally, a Nobel laureate in economics.

237 *"nothing less than recognition"*: Simon, "What Is an Explanation of Behavior?" David G. Myers, *Intuition: Its Powers and Perils* (New Haven: Yale University Press, 2002), 56.

237 *"without knowing how he knows"*: Seymour Epstein, "Demystifying Intuition: What It Is, What It Does, How It Does It," *Psychological Inquiry* 21 (2010): 295–312.

238 *10,000 hours*: Foer, *Moonwalking with Einstein*.

23: THE OUTSIDE VIEW

247 *inside view and the outside view*: The labels are often misunderstood. Numerous authors believed that the correct terms were "insider view" and "outsider view," which are not even close to what we had in mind.

247 *very different answers*: Dan Lovallo and Daniel Kahneman, "Timid Choices and Bold Forecasts: A Cognitive Perspective on Risk Taking," *Management Science* 39 (1993): 17–31. Daniel Kahneman and Dan Lovallo, "Delusions of Success: How Optimism Undermines Executives' Decisions," *Harvard Business Review* 81 (2003): 56–63.

249 *"Pallid" statistical information*: Richard E. Nisbett and Lee D. Ross, *Human Inference: Strategies and Shortcomings of Social Judgment* (Englewood Cliffs, NJ: Prentice-Hall, 1980).

249 *impersonality of procedures*: For an example of the doubts about evidence-based medicine, see Jerome Groopman, *How Doctors Think* (New York: Mariner Books, 2008), 6.

250 *planning fallacy*: Daniel Kahneman and Amos Tversky, "Intuitive Prediction: Biases and Corrective Procedures," *Management Science* 12 (1979): 313–27.

250 *Scottish Parliament building*: Rt. Hon. The Lord Fraser of Carmyllie, "The Holyrood Inquiry, Final Report," September 8, 2004, www.holyroodinquiry.org/FINAL_report/report.htm.

250 *did not become more reliant on it*: Brent Flyvbjerg, Mette K. Skamris Holm, and Søren L. Buhl, "How (In)accurate Are Demand Forecasts in Public Works Projects?" *Journal of the American Planning Association* 71 (2005): 131–46.

250 *survey of American homeowners*: "2002 Cost vs. Value Report," *Remodeling*, November 20, 2002.

251 *completion times*: Brent Flyvbjerg, "From Nobel Prize to Project Management: Getting Risks Right," *Project Management Journal* 37 (2006): 5–15.

253 *sunk-cost fallacy*: Hal R. Arkes and Catherine Blumer, "The Psychology of Sunk Cost," *Organizational Behavior and Human Decision Processes* 35 (1985): 124–40. Hal R. Arkes and

Peter Ayton, "The Sunk Cost and Concorde Effects: Are Humans Less Rational Than Lower Animals?" *Psychological Bulletin* 125 (1998): 591–600.

24: THE ENGINE OF CAPITALISM

255 *you already feel fortunate*: Miriam A. Mosing et al., "Genetic and Environmental Influences on Optimism and Its Relationship to Mental and Self-Rated Health: A Study of Aging Twins," *Behavior Genetics* 39 (2009): 597–604. David Snowdon, *Aging with Grace: What the Nun Study Teaches Us About Leading Longer, Healthier, and More Meaningful Lives* (New York: Bantam Books, 2001).

255 *bright side of everything*: Elaine Fox, Anna Ridgewell, and Chris Ashwin, "Looking on the Bright Side: Biased Attention and the Human Serotonin Transporter Gene," *Proceedings of the Royal Society B* 276 (2009): 1747–51.

256 *"triumph of hope over experience"*: Manju Puri and David T. Robinson, "Optimism and Economic Choice," *Journal of Financial Economics* 86 (2007): 71–99.

256 *more sanguine than midlevel managers*: Lowell W. Busenitz and Jay B. Barney, "Differences Between Entrepreneurs and Managers in Large Organizations: Biases and Heuristics in Strategic Decision-Making," *Journal of Business Venturing* 12 (1997): 9–30.

256 *admiration of others*: Entrepreneurs who have failed are sustained in their confidence by the probably mistaken belief that they have learned a great deal from the experience. Gavin Cassar and Justin Craig, "An Investigation of Hindsight Bias in Nascent Venture Activity," *Journal of Business Venturing* 24 (2009): 149–64.

256 *influence on the lives of others*: Keith M. Hmieleski and Robert A. Baron, "Entrepreneurs' Optimism and New Venture Performance: A Social Cognitive Perspective," *Academy of Management Journal* 52 (2009): 473–88. Matthew L. A. Hayward, Dean A. Shepherd, and Dale Griffin, "A Hubris Theory of Entrepreneurship," *Management Science* 52 (2006): 160–72.

257 *chance of failing was zero*: Arnold C. Cooper, Carolyn Y. Woo, and William C. Dunkelberg, "Entrepreneurs' Perceived Chances for Success," *Journal of Business Venturing* 3 (1988): 97–108.

257 *given the lowest grade*: Thomas Åstebro and Samir Elhedhli, "The Effectiveness of Simple Decision Heuristics: Forecasting Commercial Success for Early-Stage Ventures," *Management Science* 52 (2006): 395–409.

257 *widespread, stubborn, and costly*: Thomas Åstebro, "The Return to Independent Invention: Evidence of Unrealistic Optimism, Risk Seeking or Skewness Loving?" *Economic Journal* 113 (2003): 226–39.

258 *bet small amounts of money*: Eleanor F. Williams and Thomas Gilovich, "Do People Really Believe They Are Above Average?" *Journal of Experimental Social Psychology* 44 (2008): 1121–28.

258 *"hubris hypothesis"*: Richard Roll, "The Hubris Hypothesis of Corporate Takeovers," *Journal of Business* 59 (1986): 197–216, part 1. This remarkable early article presented a behavioral analysis of mergers and acquisitions that abandoned the assumption of rationality, long before such analyses became popular.

258 *"value-destroying mergers"*: Ulrike Malmendier and Geoffrey Tate, "Who Makes Acquisitions? CEO Overconfidence and the Market's Reaction," *Journal of Financial Economics* 89 (2008): 20–43.

258 *"engage in earnings management"*: Ulrike Malmendier and Geoffrey Tate, "Superstar CEOs," *Quarterly Journal of Economics* 24 (2009), 1593–1638.

260 *self-aggrandizement to a cognitive bias*: Paul D. Windschitl, Jason P. Rose, Michael T. Stalk-fleet, and Andrew R. Smith, "Are People Excessive or Judicious in Their Egocentrism? A Modeling Approach to Understanding Bias and Accuracy in People's Optimism," *Journal of Personality and Social Psychology* 95 (2008): 252–73.

261 *average outcome is a loss*: A form of competition neglect has also been observed in the time of day at which sellers on eBay choose to end their auctions. The easy question is: At what time is the total number of bidders the highest? Answer: around 7:00 p.m. EST. The question sellers should answer is harder: Considering how many other sellers end their auctions during peak hours, at what time will there be the most bidders looking at my auction? The answer: around noon, when the number of bidders is large relative to the number of sellers. The sellers who remember the competition and avoid prime time get higher prices. Uri Simonsohn, "eBay's Crowded Evenings: Competition Neglect in Market Entry Decisions," *Management Science* 56 (2010): 1060–73.

263 *"diagnosis antemortem"*: Eta S. Berner and Mark L. Graber, "Overconfidence as a Cause of Diagnostic Error in Medicine," *American Journal of Medicine* 121 (2008): S2–S23.

263 *"disclosing uncertainty to patients"*: Pat Croskerry and Geoff Norman, "Overconfidence in Clinical Decision Making," *American Journal of Medicine* 121 (2008): S24–S29.

263 *background of risk taking*: Kahneman and Lovallo, "Timid Choices and Bold Forecasts."

264 *Royal Dutch Shell*: J. Edward Russo and Paul J. H. Schoemaker, "Managing Overconfidence," *Sloan Management Review* 33 (1992): 7–17.

25: BERNOULLI'S ERRORS

270 Mathematical Psychology: Clyde H. Coombs, Robyn M. Dawes, and Amos Tversky, *Mathematical Psychology: An Elementary Introduction* (Englewood Cliffs, NJ: Prentice-Hall, 1970).

272 *for the rich and for the poor*: This rule applies approximately to many dimensions of sensation and perception. It is known as Weber's law, after the German physiologist Ernst Heinrich Weber, who discovered it. Fechner drew on Weber's law to derive the logarithmic psychophysical function.

273 *$10 million from $100 million*: Bernoulli's intuition was correct, and economists still use the log of income or wealth in many contexts. For example, when Angus Deaton plotted the average life satisfaction of residents of many countries against the GDP of these countries, he used the logarithm of GDP as a measure of income. The relationship, it turns out, is extremely close: Residents of high-GDP countries are much more satisfied with the quality of their lives than are residents of poor countries, and a doubling of income yields approximately the same increment of satisfaction in rich and poor countries alike.

274 *"St. Petersburg paradox"*: Nicholas Bernoulli, a cousin of Daniel Bernoulli, asked a question that can be paraphrased as follows: "You are invited to a game in which you toss a coin repeatedly. You receive $2 if it shows heads, and the prize doubles with every successive toss that shows heads. The game ends when the coin first shows tails. How much would you pay for an opportunity to play that game?" People do not think the gamble is worth more than a few dollars, although its expected value is infinite—because the prize keeps growing, the expected value is $1 for each toss, to infinity. However, the utility of the prizes grows much more slowly, which explains why the gamble is not attractive.

277 *"history of one's wealth"*: Other factors contributed to the longevity of Bernoulli's theory. One is that it is natural to formulate choices between gambles in terms of gains, or mixed

gains and losses. Not many people thought about choices in which all options are bad, although we were by no means the first to observe risk seeking. Another fact that favors Bernoulli's theory is that thinking in terms of final states of wealth and ignoring the past is often a very reasonable thing to do. Economists were traditionally concerned with rational choices, and Bernoulli's model suited their goal.

26: PROSPECT THEORY

278 *subjective value of wealth*: Stanley S. Stevens, "To Honor Fechner and Repeal His Law," *Science* 133 (1961): 80–86. Stevens, *Psychophysics*.

282 *The three principles*: Writing this sentence reminded me that the graph of the value function has already been used as an emblem. Every Nobel laureate receives an individual certificate with a personalized drawing, which is presumably chosen by the committee. My illustration was a stylized rendition of figure 10.

284 *"loss aversion ratio"*: The loss aversion ratio is often found to be in the range of 1.5 and 2.5: Nathan Novemsky and Daniel Kahneman, "The Boundaries of Loss Aversion," *Journal of Marketing Research* 42 (2005): 119–28.

284 *emotional reaction to losses*: Peter Sokol-Hessner et al., "Thinking Like a Trader Selectively Reduces Individuals' Loss Aversion," *PNAS* 106 (2009): 5035–40.

285 *Rabin's theorem*: For several consecutive years, I gave a guest lecture in the introductory finance class of my colleague Burton Malkiel. I discussed the implausibility of Bernoulli's theory each year. I noticed a distinct change in my colleague's attitude when I first mentioned Rabin's proof. He was now prepared to take the conclusion much more seriously than in the past. Mathematical arguments have a definitive quality that is more compelling than appeals to common sense. Economists are particularly sensitive to this advantage.

285 *rejects that gamble*: The intuition of the proof can be illustrated by an example. Suppose an individual's wealth is W, and she rejects a gamble with equal probabilities to win $11 or lose $10. If the utility function for wealth is concave (bent down), the preference implies that the value of $1 has decreased by over 9% over an interval of $21! This is an extraordinarily steep decline and the effect increases steadily as the gambles become more extreme.

286 *"Even a lousy lawyer"*: Matthew Rabin, "Risk Aversion and Expected-Utility Theory: A Calibration Theorem," *Econometrica* 68 (2000): 1281–92. Matthew Rabin and Richard H. Thaler, "Anomalies: Risk Aversion," *Journal of Economic Perspectives* 15 (2001): 219–32.

288 *economists and psychologists*: Several theorists have proposed versions of regret theories that are built on the idea that people are able to anticipate how their future experiences will be affected by the options that did not materialize and/or by the choices they did not make: David E. Bell, "Regret in Decision Making Under Uncertainty," *Operations Research* 30 (1982): 961–81. Graham Loomes and Robert Sugden, "Regret Theory: An Alternative to Rational Choice Under Uncertainty," *Economic Journal* 92 (1982): 805–25. Barbara A. Mellers, "Choice and the Relative Pleasure of Consequences," *Psychological Bulletin* 126 (2000): 910–24. Barbara A. Mellers, Alan Schwartz, and Ilana Ritov, "Emotion-Based Choice," *Journal of Experimental Psychology—General* 128 (1999): 332–45. Decision makers' choices between gambles depend on whether they expect to know the outcome of the gamble they did not choose. Ilana Ritov, "Probability of Regret: Anticipation of Uncertainty Resolution in Choice," *Organizational Behavior and Human Decision Processes* 66 (1966): 228–36.

27: THE ENDOWMENT EFFECT

290 *What is missing from the figure*: A theoretical analysis that assumes loss aversion predicts a pronounced kink of the indifference curve at the reference point: Amos Tversky and Daniel Kahneman, "Loss Aversion in Riskless Choice: A Reference-Dependent Model," *Quarterly Journal of Economics* 106 (1991): 1039–61. Jack Knetsch observed these kinks in an experimental study: "Preferences and Nonreversibility of Indifference Curves," *Journal of Economic Behavior & Organization* 17 (1992): 131–39.

291 *period of one year*: Alan B. Krueger and Andreas Mueller, "Job Search and Job Finding in a Period of Mass Unemployment: Evidence from High-Frequency Longitudinal Data," working paper, Princeton University Industrial Relations Section, January 2011.

293 *did not own the bottle*: Technically, the theory allows the buying price to be slightly lower than the selling price because of what economists call an "income effect": The buyer and the seller are not equally wealthy, because the seller has an extra bottle. However, the effect in this case is negligible since $50 is a minute fraction of the professor's wealth. The theory would predict that this income effect would not change his willingness to pay by even a penny.

293 *would be puzzled by it*: The economist Alan Krueger reported on a study he conducted on the occasion of taking his father to the Super Bowl: "We asked fans who had won the right to buy a pair of tickets for $325 or $400 each in a lottery whether they would have been willing to pay $3,000 a ticket if they had lost in the lottery and whether they would have sold their tickets if someone had offered them $3,000 apiece. Ninety-four percent said they would not have bought for $3,000, and ninety-two percent said they would not have sold at that price." He concludes that "rationality was in short supply at the Super Bowl." Alan B. Krueger, "Supply and Demand: An Economist Goes to the Super Bowl," *Milken Institute Review: A Journal of Economic Policy* 3 (2001): 22–29.

293 *giving up a bottle of nice wine*: Strictly speaking, loss aversion refers to the anticipated pleasure and pain, which determine choices. These anticipations could be wrong in some cases. Deborah A. Kermer et al., "Loss Aversion Is an Affective Forecasting Error," *Psychological Science* 17 (2006): 649–53.

294 *market transactions*: Novemsky and Kahneman, "The Boundaries of Loss Aversion."

295 *half of the tokens will change hands*: Imagine that all the participants are ordered in a line by the redemption value assigned to them. Now randomly allocate tokens to half the individuals in the line. Half of the people in the front of the line will not have a token, and half of the people at the end of the line will own one. These people (half of the total) are expected to move by trading places with each other, so that in the end everyone in the first half of the line has a token, and no one behind them does.

296 *Brain recordings*: Brian Knutson et al., "Neural Antecedents of the Endowment Effect," *Neuron* 58 (2008): 814–22. Brian Knutson and Stephanie M. Greer, "Anticipatory Affect: Neural Correlates and Consequences for Choice," *Philosophical Transactions of the Royal Society B* 363 (2008): 3771–86.

296 *riskless and risky decisions*: A review of the price of risk, based on "international data from 16 different countries during over 100 years," yielded an estimate of 2.3, "in striking agreement with estimates obtained in the very different methodology of laboratory experiments of individual decision-making": Moshe Levy, "Loss Aversion and the Price of Risk," *Quantitative Finance* 10 (2010): 1009–22.

296 *effect of price increases*: Miles O. Bidwel, Bruce X. Wang, and J. Douglas Zona, "An Analysis

of Asymmetric Demand Response to Price Changes: The Case of Local Telephone Calls," *Journal of Regulatory Economics* 8 (1995): 285–98. Bruce G. S. Hardie, Eric J. Johnson, and Peter S. Fader, "Modeling Loss Aversion and Reference Dependence Effects on Brand Choice," *Marketing Science* 12 (1993): 378–94.

297 *illustrate the power of these concepts*: Colin Camerer, "Three Cheers—Psychological, Theoretical, Empirical—for Loss Aversion," *Journal of Marketing Research* 42 (2005): 129–33. Colin F. Camerer, "Prospect Theory in the Wild: Evidence from the Field," in *Choices, Values, and Frames*, ed. Daniel Kahneman and Amos Tversky (New York: Russell Sage Foundation, 2000), 288–300.

297 *condo apartments in Boston*: David Genesove and Christopher Mayer, "Loss Aversion and Seller Behavior: Evidence from the Housing Market," *Quarterly Journal of Economics* 116 (2001): 1233–60.

297 *effect of trading experience*: John A. List, "Does Market Experience Eliminate Market Anomalies?" *Quarterly Journal of Economics* 118 (2003): 47–71.

298 *Jack Knetsch also*: Jack L. Knetsch, "The Endowment Effect and Evidence of Nonreversible Indifference Curves," *American Economic Review* 79 (1989): 1277–84.

298 *ongoing debate about the endowment effect*: Charles R. Plott and Kathryn Zeiler, "The Willingness to Pay–Willingness to Accept Gap, the 'Endowment Effect,' Subject Misconceptions, and Experimental Procedures for Eliciting Valuations," *American Economic Review* 95 (2005): 530–45. Charles Plott, a leading experimental economist, has been very skeptical of the endowment effect and has attempted to show that it is not a "fundamental aspect of human preference" but rather an outcome of inferior technique. Plott and Zeiler believe that participants who show the endowment effect are under some misconception about what their true values are, and they modified the procedures of the original experiments to eliminate the misconceptions. They devised an elaborate training procedure in which the participants experienced the roles of both buyers and sellers, and were explicitly taught to assess their true values. As expected, the endowment effect disappeared. Plott and Zeiler view their method as an important improvement of technique. Psychologists would consider the method severely deficient, because it communicates to the participants a message of what the experimenters consider appropriate behavior, which happens to coincide with the experimenters' theory. Plott and Zeiler's favored version of Knetsch's exchange experiment is similarly biased: It does not allow the owner of the good to have physical possession of it, which is crucial to the effect. See Charles R. Plott and Kathryn Zeiler, "Exchange Asymmetries Incorrectly Interpreted as Evidence of Endowment Effect Theory and Prospect Theory?" *American Economic Review* 97 (2007): 1449–66. There may be an impasse here, where each side rejects the methods required by the other.

298 *People who are poor*: In their studies of decision making under poverty, Eldar Shafir, Sendhil Mullainathan, and their colleagues have observed other instances in which poverty induces economic behavior that is in some respects more realistic and more rational than that of people who are better off. The poor are more likely to respond to real outcomes than to their description. Marianne Bertrand, Sendhil Mullainathan, and Eldar Shafir, "Behavioral Economics and Marketing in Aid of Decision Making Among the Poor," *Journal of Public Policy & Marketing* 25 (2006): 8–23.

299 *in the United States and in the UK*: The conclusion that money spent on purchases is not experienced as a loss is more likely to be true for people who are relatively well-off. The key may be whether you are aware when you buy one good that you will not be unable to af-

ford another good. Novemsky and Kahneman, "The Boundaries of Loss Aversion." Ian Bateman et al., "Testing Competing Models of Loss Aversion: An Adversarial Collaboration," *Journal of Public Economics* 89 (2005): 1561–80.

28: BAD EVENTS

301 *heartbeat accelerated*: Paul J. Whalen et al., "Human Amygdala Responsivity to Masked Fearful Eye Whites," *Science* 306 (2004): 2061. Individuals with focal lesions of the amygdala showed little or no loss aversion in their risky choices: Benedetto De Martino, Colin F. Camerer, and Ralph Adolphs, "Amygdala Damage Eliminates Monetary Loss Aversion," *PNAS* 107 (2010): 3788–92.

301 *bypassing the visual cortex*: Joseph LeDoux, *The Emotional Brain: The Mysterious Underpinnings of Emotional Life* (New York: Touchstone, 1996).

301 *processed faster*: Elaine Fox et al., "Facial Expressions of Emotion: Are Angry Faces Detected More Efficiently?" *Cognition & Emotion* 14 (2000): 61–92.

301 *"pops out"*: Christine Hansen and Ranald Hansen, "Finding the Face in the Crowd: An Anger Superiority Effect," *Journal of Personality and Social Psychology* 54 (1988): 917–24.

302 *"acceptable/unacceptable"*: Jos J. A. Van Berkum et al., "Right or Wrong? The Brain's Fast Response to Morally Objectionable Statements," *Psychological Science* 20 (2009): 1092–99.

302 *negativity dominance*: Paul Rozin and Edward B. Royzman, "Negativity Bias, Negativity Dominance, and Contagion," *Personality and Social Psychology Review* 5 (2001): 296–320.

302 *resistant to disconfirmation*: Roy F. Baumeister, Ellen Bratslavsky, Catrin Finkenauer, and Kathleen D. Vohs, "Bad Is Stronger Than Good," *Review of General Psychology* 5 (2001): 323.

302 *biologically significant improvement*: Michel Cabanac, "Pleasure: The Common Currency," *Journal of Theoretical Biology* 155 (1992): 173–200.

303 *not equally powerful*: Chip Heath, Richard P. Larrick, and George Wu, "Goals as Reference Points," *Cognitive Psychology* 38 (1999): 79–109.

303 *rain-drenched customers*: Colin Camerer, Linda Babcock, George Loewenstein, and Richard Thaler, "Labor Supply of New York City Cabdrivers: One Day at a Time," *Quarterly Journal of Economics* 112 (1997): 407–41. The conclusions of this research have been questioned: Henry S. Farber, "Is Tomorrow Another Day? The Labor Supply of New York Cab Drivers," NBER Working Paper 9706, 2003. A series of studies of bicycle messengers in Zurich provides strong evidence for the effect of goals, in accord with the original study of cabdrivers: Ernst Fehr and Lorenz Goette, "Do Workers Work More if Wages Are High? Evidence from a Randomized Field Experiment," *American Economic Review* 97 (2007): 298–317.

304 *communicate a reference point*: Daniel Kahneman, "Reference Points, Anchors, Norms, and Mixed Feelings," *Organizational Behavior and Human Decision Processes* 51 (1992): 296–312.

305 *"wins the contest"*: John Alcock, *Animal Behavior: An Evolutionary Approach* (Sunderland, MA: Sinauer Associates, 2009), 278–84, cited by Eyal Zamir, "Law and Psychology: The Crucial Role of Reference Points and Loss Aversion," working paper, Hebrew University, 2011.

306 *merchants, employers, and landlords*: Daniel Kahneman, Jack L. Knetsch, and Richard H. Thaler, "Fairness as a Constraint on Profit Seeking: Entitlements in the Market," *The American Economic Review* 76 (1986): 728–41.

308 *fairness concerns are economically significant*: Ernst Fehr, Lorenz Goette, and Christian Zehnder, "A Behavioral Account of the Labor Market: The Role of Fairness Concerns," *Annual Review of Economics* 1 (2009): 355–84. Eric T. Anderson and Duncan I. Simester, "Price Stickiness and Customer Antagonism," *Quarterly Journal of Economics* 125 (2010): 729–65.

308 *altruistic punishment is accompanied*: Dominique de Quervain et al., "The Neural Basis of Altruistic Punishment," *Science* 305 (2004): 1254–58.

308 *actual losses and foregone gains*: David Cohen and Jack L. Knetsch, "Judicial Choice and Disparities Between Measures of Economic Value," *Osgoode Hall Law Review* 30 (1992): 737–70. Russell Korobkin, "The Endowment Effect and Legal Analysis," *Northwestern University Law Review* 97 (2003): 1227–93.

309 *asymmetrical effects on individual well-being*: Zamir, "Law and Psychology."

29: THE FOURFOLD PATTERN

312 *and other disasters*: Including exposure to a "Dutch book," which is a set of gambles that your incorrect preferences commit you to accept and is guaranteed to end up in a loss.

313 *puzzle that Allais constructed*: Readers who are familiar with the Allais paradoxes will recognize that this version is new. It is both much simpler and actually a stronger violation than the original paradox. The left-hand option is preferred in the first problem. The second problem is obtained by adding a more valuable prospect to the left than to the right, but the right-hand option is now preferred.

314 *sorely disappointed*: As the distinguished economist Kenneth Arrow recently described the event, the participants in the meeting paid little attention to what he called "Allais's little experiment." Personal conversation, March 16, 2011.

314 *estimates for gains*: The table shows decision weights for gains. Estimates for losses were very similar.

315 *estimated from choices*: Ming Hsu, Ian Krajbich, Chen Zhao, and Colin F. Camerer, "Neural Response to Reward Anticipation under Risk Is Nonlinear in Probabilities," *Journal of Neuroscience* 29 (2009): 2231–37.

316 *parents of small children*: W. Kip Viscusi, Wesley A. Magat, and Joel Huber, "An Investigation of the Rationality of Consumer Valuations of Multiple Health Risks," *RAND Journal of Economics* 18 (1987): 465–79.

316 *psychology of worry*: In a rational model with diminishing marginal utility, people should pay at least two-thirds as much to reduce the frequency of accidents from 15 to 5 units as they are willing to pay to eliminate the risk. Observed preferences violated this prediction.

318 *not made much of it*: C. Arthur Williams, "Attitudes Toward Speculative Risks as an Indicator of Attitudes Toward Pure Risks," *Journal of Risk and Insurance* 33 (1966): 577–86. Howard Raiffa, *Decision Analysis: Introductory Lectures on Choices under Uncertainty* (Reading, MA: Addison-Wesley, 1968).

320 *shadow of civil trials*: Chris Guthrie, "Prospect Theory, Risk Preference, and the Law," *Northwestern University Law Review* 97 (2003): 1115–63. Jeffrey J. Rachlinski, "Gains, Losses and the Psychology of Litigation," *Southern California Law Review* 70 (1996): 113–85. Samuel R. Gross and Kent D. Syverud, "Getting to No: A Study of Settlement Negotiations and the Selection of Cases for Trial," *Michigan Law Review* 90 (1991): 319–93.

320 *the frivolous claim*: Chris Guthrie, "Framing Frivolous Litigation: A Psychological Theory," *University of Chicago Law Review* 67 (2000): 163–216.

30: RARE EVENTS

323 *wish to avoid it*: George F. Loewenstein, Elke U. Weber, Christopher K. Hsee, and Ned Welch, "Risk as Feelings," *Psychological Bulletin* 127 (2001): 267–86.

323 *vividness in decision making*: Ibid. Cass R. Sunstein, "Probability Neglect: Emotions, Worst Cases, and Law," *Yale Law Journal* 112 (2002): 61–107. See notes to chapter 13: Damasio, *Descartes' Error*. Slovic, Finucane, Peters, and MacGregor, "The Affect Heuristic."

325 *Amos's student*: Craig R. Fox, "Strength of Evidence, Judged Probability, and Choice Under Uncertainty," *Cognitive Psychology* 38 (1999): 167–89.

325 *focal event and its*: Judgments of the probabilities of an event and its complement do not always add up to 100%. When people are asked about a topic they know very little about ("What is your probability that the temperature in Bangkok will exceed 100° tomorrow at noon?"), the judged probabilities of the event and its complement add up to less than 100%.

326 *receiving a dozen roses*: In cumulative prospect theory, decision weights for gains and losses are not assumed to be equal, as they were in the original version of prospect theory that I describe.

329 *superficial processing*: The question about the two urns was invented by Dale T. Miller, William Turnbull, and Cathy McFarland, "When a Coincidence Is Suspicious: The Role of Mental Simulation," *Journal of Personality and Social Psychology* 57 (1989): 581–89. Seymour Epstein and his colleagues argued for an interpretation of it in terms of two systems: Lee A. Kirkpatrick and Seymour Epstein, "Cognitive-Experiential Self-Theory and Subjective Probability: Evidence for Two Conceptual Systems," *Journal of Personality and Social Psychology* 63 (1992): 534–44.

329 *judged it as more dangerous*: Kimihiko Yamagishi, "When a 12.86% Mortality Is More Dangerous Than 24.14%: Implications for Risk Communication," *Applied Cognitive Psychology* 11 (1997): 495–506.

330 *forensic psychologists*: Slovic, Monahan, and MacGregor, "Violence Risk Assessment and Risk Communication."

330 *"1 of 1,000 capital cases"*: Jonathan J. Koehler, "When Are People Persuaded by DNA Match Statistics?" *Law and Human Behavior* 25 (2001): 493–513.

331 *studies of* choice from experience: Ralph Hertwig, Greg Barron, Elke U. Weber, and Ido Erev, "Decisions from Experience and the Effect of Rare Events in Risky Choice," *Psychological Science* 15 (2004): 534–39. Ralph Hertwig and Ido Erev, "The Description-Experience Gap in Risky Choice," *Trends in Cognitive Sciences* 13 (2009): 517–23.

332 *not yet settled*: Liat Hadar and Craig R. Fox, "Information Asymmetry in Decision from Description Versus Decision from Experience," *Judgment and Decision Making* 4 (2009): 317–25.

332 *"chances of rare events"*: Hertwig and Erev, "The Description-Experience Gap."

31: RISK POLICIES

335 *inferior option BC*: The calculation is straightforward. Each of the two combinations consists of a sure thing and a gamble. Add the sure thing to both options of the gamble and you will find AD and BC.

340 *the equivalent of "locking in"*: Thomas Langer and Martin Weber, "Myopic Prospect Theory vs. Myopic Loss Aversion: How General Is the Phenomenon?" *Journal of Economic Behavior & Organization* 56 (2005): 25–38.

32: KEEPING SCORE

343 *drive into a blizzard*: The intuition was confirmed in a field experiment in which a random selection of students who purchased season tickets to the university theater received their tickets at a much reduced price. A follow-up of attendance revealed that students who had paid the full price for their tickets were more likely to attend, especially during the first half of the season. Missing a show one has paid for involves the unpleasant experience of closing an account in the red. Arkes and Blumer, "The Psychology of Sunk Costs."

344 *the* disposition effect: Hersh Shefrin and Meir Statman, "The Disposition to Sell Winners Too Early and Ride Losers Too Long: Theory and Evidence," *Journal of Finance* 40 (1985): 777–90. Terrance Odean, "Are Investors Reluctant to Realize Their Losses?" *Journal of Finance* 53 (1998): 1775–98.

345 *less susceptible*: Ravi Dhar and Ning Zhu, "Up Close and Personal: Investor Sophistication and the Disposition Effect," *Management Science* 52 (2006): 726–40.

346 *fallacy can be overcome*: Darrin R. Lehman, Richard O. Lempert, and Richard E. Nisbett, "The Effects of Graduate Training on Reasoning: Formal Discipline and Thinking about Everyday-Life Events," *American Psychologist* 43 (1988): 431–42.

346 *"a sinking feeling"*: Marcel Zeelenberg and Rik Pieters, "A Theory of Regret Regulation 1.0," *Journal of Consumer Psychology* 17 (2007): 3–18.

347 *regret to normality*: Kahneman and Miller, "Norm Theory."

347 *habitually taking unreasonable risks*: The hitchhiker question was inspired by a famous example discussed by the legal philosophers Hart and Honoré: "A woman married to a man who suffers from an ulcerated condition of the stomach might identify eating parsnips as the cause of his indigestion. The doctor might identify the ulcerated condition as the cause and the meal as a mere occasion." Unusual events call for causal explanations and also evoke counterfactual thoughts, and the two are closely related. The same event can be compared to either a personal norm or the norm of other people, leading to different counterfactuals, different causal attributions, and different emotions (regret or blame): Herbert L. A. Hart and Tony Honoré, *Causation in the Law* (New York: Oxford University Press, 1985), 33.

347 *remarkably uniform*: Daniel Kahneman and Amos Tversky, "The Simulation Heuristic," in *Judgment Under Uncertainty: Heuristics and Biases*, ed. Daniel Kahneman, Paul Slovic, and Amos Tversky (New York: Cambridge University Press, 1982), 160–73.

348 *applies to blame*: Janet Landman, "Regret and Elation Following Action and Inaction: Affective Responses to Positive Versus Negative Outcomes," *Personality and Social Psychology Bulletin* 13 (1987): 524–36. Faith Gleicher et al., "The Role of Counterfactual Thinking in Judgment of Affect," *Personality and Social Psychology Bulletin* 16 (1990): 284–95.

348 *actions that deviate from the default*: Dale T. Miller and Brian R. Taylor, "Counterfactual Thought, Regret, and Superstition: How to Avoid Kicking Yourself," in *What Might Have Been: The Social Psychology of Counterfactual Thinking*, ed. Neal J. Roese and James M. Olson (Hillsdale, NJ: Erlbaum, 1995), 305–31.

348 *produce blame and regret*: Marcel Zeelenberg, Kees van den Bos, Eric van Dijk, and Rik Pieters, "The Inaction Effect in the Psychology of Regret," *Journal of Personality and Social Psychology* 82 (2002): 314–27.

349 *brand names over generics*: Itamar Simonson, "The Influence of Anticipating Regret and Responsibility on Purchase Decisions," *Journal of Consumer Research* 19 (1992): 105–18.

349 *clean up their portfolios*: Lilian Ng and Qinghai Wang, "Institutional Trading and the Turn-of-the-Year Effect," *Journal of Financial Economics* 74 (2004): 343–66.

349 *loss averse for aspects of your life*: Tversky and Kahneman, "Loss Aversion in Riskless Choice." Eric J. Johnson, Simon Gächter, and Andreas Herrmann, "Exploring the Nature of Loss Aversion," *Centre for Decision Research and Experimental Economics, University of Nottingham, Discussion Paper Series*, 2006. Edward J. McCaffery, Daniel Kahneman, and Matthew L. Spitzer, "Framing the Jury: Cognitive Perspectives on Pain and Suffering," *Virginia Law Review* 81 (1995): 1341–420.

349 *classic on consumer behavior*: Richard H. Thaler, "Toward a Positive Theory of Consumer Choice," *Journal of Economic Behavior and Organization* 39 (1980): 36–90.

351 taboo tradeoff: Philip E. Tetlock et al., "The Psychology of the Unthinkable: Taboo Trade-Offs, Forbidden Base Rates, and Heretical Counterfactuals," *Journal of Personality and Social Psychology* 78 (2000): 853–70.

351 *where the precautionary principle*: Cass R. Sunstein, *The Laws of Fear: Beyond the Precautionary Principle* (New York: Cambridge University Press, 2005).

352 *"psychological immune system"*: Daniel T. Gilbert et al., "Looking Forward to Looking Backward: The Misprediction of Regret," *Psychological Science* 15 (2004): 346–50.

33: REVERSALS

353 *in the man's regular store*: Dale T. Miller and Cathy McFarland, "Counterfactual Thinking and Victim Compensation: A Test of Norm Theory," *Personality and Social Psychology Bulletin* 12 (1986): 513–19.

354 *reversals of judgment and choice*: The first step toward the current interpretation was taken by Max H. Bazerman, George F. Loewenstein, and Sally B. White, "Reversals of Preference in Allocation Decisions: Judging Alternatives Versus Judging Among Alternatives," *Administrative Science Quarterly* 37 (1992): 220–40. Christopher Hsee introduced the terminology of joint and separate evaluation, and formulated the important evaluability hypothesis, which explains reversals by the idea that some attributes become evaluable only in joint evaluation: "Attribute Evaluability: Its Implications for Joint-Separate Evaluation Reversals and Beyond," in Kahneman and Tversky, *Choices, Values, and Frames*.

354 *conversation between psychologists and economists*: Sarah Lichtenstein and Paul Slovic, "Reversals of Preference Between Bids and Choices in Gambling Decisions," *Journal of Experimental Psychology* 89 (1971): 46–55. A similar result was obtained independently by Harold R. Lindman, "Inconsistent Preferences Among Gambles," *Journal of Experimental Psychology* 89 (1971): 390–97.

355 *bewildered participant*: For a transcript of the famous interview, see Sarah Lichtenstein and Paul Slovic, eds., *The Construction of Preference* (New York: Cambridge University Press, 2006).

356 *the prestigious* American Economic Review: David M. Grether and Charles R. Plott, "Economic Theory of Choice and the Preference Reversals Phenomenon," *American Economic Review* 69 (1979): 623–28.

356 *"context in which the choices are made"*: Lichtenstein and Slovic, *The Construction of Preference*, 96.

356 *one embarrassing finding*: Kuhn famously argued that the same is true of physical sciences as well: Thomas S. Kuhn, "The Function of Measurement in Modern Physical Science," *Isis* 52 (1961): 161–93.

358 *liking of dolphins*: There is evidence that questions about the emotional appeal of species and the willingness to contribute to their protection yield the same rankings: Daniel Kahneman and Ilana Ritov, "Determinants of Stated Willingness to Pay for Public Goods: A Study in the Headline Method," *Journal of Risk and Uncertainty* 9 (1994): 5–38.

360 *superior on this attribute*: Hsee, "Attribute Evaluability."

361 *"requisite record-keeping"*: Cass R. Sunstein, Daniel Kahneman, David Schkade, and Ilana Ritov, "Predictably Incoherent Judgments," *Stanford Law Review* 54 (2002): 1190.

34: FRAMES AND REALITY

364 *unjustified influences of formulation*: Amos Tversky and Daniel Kahneman, "The Framing of Decisions and the Psychology of Choice," *Science* 211 (1981): 453–58.

364 *paid with cash or on credit*: Thaler, "Toward a Positive Theory of Consumer Choice."

367 *10% mortality is frightening*: Barbara McNeil, Stephen G. Pauker, Harold C. Sox Jr., and Amos Tversky, "On the Elicitation of Preferences for Alternative Therapies," *New England Journal of Medicine* 306 (1982): 1259–62.

368 *"Asian disease problem"*: Some people have commented that the "Asian" label is unnecessary and pejorative. We probably would not use it today, but the example was written in the 1970s, when sensitivity to group labels was less developed than it is today. The word was added to make the example more concrete by reminding respondents of the Asian flu epidemic of 1957.

369 Choice and Consequence: Thomas Schelling, *Choice and Consequence* (Cambridge, MA: Harvard University Press, 1985).

372 *misleading frame*: Richard P. Larrick and Jack B. Soll, "The MPG Illusion," *Science* 320 (2008): 1593–94.

373 *rate of organ donation in European countries*: Eric J. Johnson and Daniel Goldstein, "Do Defaults Save Lives?" *Science* 302 (2003): 1338–39.

35: TWO SELVES

377 *"wantability"*: Irving Fisher, "Is 'Utility' the Most Suitable Term for the Concept It Is Used to Denote?" *American Economic Review* 8 (1918): 335.

378 *at any moment*: Francis Edgeworth, *Mathematical Psychics* (New York: Kelley, 1881).

379 *under which his theory holds*: Daniel Kahneman, Peter P. Wakker, and Rakesh Sarin, "Back to Bentham? Explorations of Experienced Utility," *Quarterly Journal of Economics* 112 (1997): 375–405. Daniel Kahneman, "Experienced Utility and Objective Happiness: A Moment-Based Approach" and "Evaluation by Moments: Past and Future," in Kahneman and Tversky, *Choices, Values, and Frames*, 673–92, 693–708.

379 *a physician and researcher*: Donald A. Redelmeier and Daniel Kahneman, "Patients' Memories of Painful Medical Treatments: Real-time and Retrospective Evaluations of Two Minimally Invasive Procedures," *Pain* 66 (1996): 3–8.

382 *free to choose*: Daniel Kahneman, Barbara L. Frederickson, Charles A. Schreiber, and Donald A. Redelmeier, "When More Pain Is Preferred to Less: Adding a Better End," *Psychological Science* 4 (1993): 401–405.

384 *duration of the shock*: Orval H. Mowrer and L. N. Solomon, "Contiguity vs. Drive-Reduction in Conditioned Fear: The Proximity and Abruptness of Drive Reduction," *American Journal of Psychology* 67 (1954): 15–25.

384 *burst of stimulation*: Peter Shizgal, "On the Neural Computation of Utility: Implications

from Studies of Brain Stimulation Reward," in *Well-Being: The Foundations of Hedonic Psychology*, ed. Daniel Kahneman, Edward Diener, and Norbert Schwarz (New York: Russell Sage Foundation, 1999), 500–24.

36: LIFE AS A STORY

387 *had a lover*: Paul Rozin and Jennifer Stellar, "Posthumous Events Affect Rated Quality and Happiness of Lives," *Judgment and Decision Making* 4 (2009): 273–79.

388 *entire lives as well as brief episodes*: Ed Diener, Derrick Wirtz, and Shigehiro Oishi, "End Effects of Rated Life Quality: The James Dean Effect," *Psychological Science* 12 (2001): 124–28. The same series of experiments also tested for the peak-end rule in an unhappy life and found similar results: Jen was not judged twice as unhappy if she lived miserably for 60 years rather than 30, but she was regarded as considerably happier if 5 mildly miserable years were added just before her death.

37: EXPERIENCED WELL-BEING

391 *life as a whole these days*: Another question that has been used frequently is, "Taken all together, how would you say things are these days? Would you say that you are very happy, pretty happy, or not too happy?" This question is included in the General Social Survey in the United States, and its correlations with other variables suggest a mix of satisfaction and experienced happiness. A pure measure of life evaluation used in the Gallup surveys is the Cantril Self-Anchoring Striving Scale, in which the respondent rates his or her current life on a ladder scale in which 0 is "the worst possible life for you" and 10 is "the best possible life for you." The language suggests that people should anchor on what they consider possible for them, but the evidence shows that people all over the world have a common standard for what a good life is, which accounts for the extraordinarily high correlation ($r = .84$) between the GDP of countries and the average ladder score of their citizens. Angus Deaton, "Income, Health, and Well-Being Around the World: Evidence from the Gallup World Poll," *Journal of Economic Perspectives* 22 (2008): 53–72.

392 *"a dream team"*: The economist was Alan Krueger of Princeton, noted for his innovative analyses of unusual data. The psychologists were David Schkade, who had methodological expertise; Arthur Stone, an expert on health psychology, experience sampling, and ecological momentary assessment; Norbert Schwarz, a social psychologist who was also an expert on survey method and had contributed experimental critiques of well-being research, including the experiment on which a dime left on a copying machine influenced subsequent reports of life satisfaction.

392 *intensity of various feelings*: In some applications, the individual also provides physiological information, such as continuous recordings of heart rate, occasional records of blood pressure, or samples of saliva for chemical analysis. The method is called Ecological Momentary Assessment: Arthur A. Stone, Saul S. Shiffman, and Marten W. DeVries, "Ecological Momentary Assessment Well-Being: The Foundations of Hedonic Psychology," in Kahneman, Diener, and Schwarz, *Well-Being*, 26–39.

393 *spend their time*: Daniel Kahneman et al., "A Survey Method for Characterizing Daily Life Experience: The Day Reconstruction Method," *Science* 306 (2004): 1776–80. Daniel Kahneman and Alan B. Krueger, "Developments in the Measurement of Subjective Well-Being," *Journal of Economic Perspectives* 20 (2006): 3–24.

393 *physiological indications of emotion*: Previous research had documented that people are able to "relive" feelings they had in a past situation when the situation is retrieved in sufficiently vivid detail. Michael D. Robinson and Gerald L. Clore, "Belief and Feeling: Evidence for an Accessibility Model of Emotional Self-Report," *Psychological Bulletin* 128 (2002): 934–60.

393 *state the U-index*: Alan B. Krueger, ed., *Measuring the Subjective Well-Being of Nations: National Accounts of Time Use and Well-Being* (Chicago: University of Chicago Press, 2009).

394 *distribution of emotional pain*: Ed Diener, "Most People Are Happy," *Psychological Science* 7 (1996): 181–85.

395 *Gallup World Poll*: For a number of years I have been one of several Senior Scientists associated with the efforts of the Gallup Organization in the domain of well-being.

396 *more than 450,000 responses*: Daniel Kahneman and Angus Deaton, "High Income Improves Evaluation of Life but Not Emotional Well-Being," *Proceedings of the National Academy of Sciences* 107 (2010): 16489–93.

396 *worse for the very poor*: Dylan M. Smith, Kenneth M. Langa, Mohammed U. Kabeto, and Peter Ubel, "Health, Wealth, and Happiness: Financial Resources Buffer Subjective Well-Being After the Onset of a Disability," *Psychological Science* 16 (2005): 663–66.

397 *$75,000 in high-cost areas*: In a TED talk I presented in February 2010 I mentioned a preliminary estimate of $60,000, which was later corrected.

397 *eat a bar of chocolate!*: Jordi Quoidbach, Elizabeth W. Dunn, K. V. Petrides, and Moïra Mikolajczak, "Money Giveth, Money Taketh Away: The Dual Effect of Wealth on Happiness," *Psychological Science* 21 (2010): 759–63.

38: THINKING ABOUT LIFE

398 *German Socio-Economic Panel*: Andrew E. Clark, Ed Diener, and Yannis Georgellis, "Lags and Leads in Life Satisfaction: A Test of the Baseline Hypothesis." Paper presented at the German Socio-Economic Panel Conference, Berlin, Germany, 2001.

399 *affective forecasting*: Daniel T. Gilbert and Timothy D. Wilson, "Why the Brain Talks to Itself: Sources of Error in Emotional Prediction," *Philosophical Transactions of the Royal Society B* 364 (2009): 1335–41.

399 *only significant fact in their life*: Strack, Martin, and Schwarz, "Priming and Communication."

399 *questionnaire on life satisfaction*: The original study was reported by Norbert Schwarz in his doctoral thesis (in German) "Mood as Information: On the Impact of Moods on the Evaluation of One's Life" (Heidelberg: Springer Verlag, 1987). It has been described in many places, notably Norbert Schwarz and Fritz Strack, "Reports of Subjective Well-Being: Judgmental Processes and Their Methodological Implications," in Kahneman, Diener, and Schwarz, *Well-Being*, 61–84.

401 *goals that young people set*: The study was described in William G. Bowen and Derek Curtis Bok, *The Shape of the River: Long-Term Consequences of Considering Race in College and University Admissions* (Princeton: Princeton University Press, 1998). Some of Bowen and Bok's findings were reported by Carol Nickerson, Norbert Schwarz, and Ed Diener, "Financial Aspirations, Financial Success, and Overall Life Satisfaction: Who? and How?" *Journal of Happiness Studies* 8 (2007): 467–515.

401 *"being very well-off financially"*: Alexander Astin, M. R. King, and G. T. Richardson, "The

American Freshman: National Norms for Fall 1976," Cooperative Institutional Research Program of the American Council on Education and the University of California at Los Angeles, Graduate School of Education, Laboratory for Research in Higher Education, 1976.

402 *money was not important*: These results were presented in a talk at the American Economic Association annual meeting in 2004. Daniel Kahneman, "Puzzles of Well-Being," paper presented at the meeting.

403 *happiness of Californians*: The question of how well people today can forecast the feelings of their descendants a hundred years from now is clearly relevant to the policy response to climate change, but it can be studied only indirectly, which is what we proposed to do.

403 *aspects of their lives*: In posing the question, I was guilty of a confusion that I now try to avoid: Happiness and life satisfaction are not synonymous. Life satisfaction refers to your thoughts and feelings when you think about your life, which happens occasionally— including in surveys of well-being. Happiness describes the feelings people have as they live their normal life.

403 *I had won the family argument*: However, my wife has never conceded. She claims that only residents of Northern California are happier.

403 *students in California and in the Midwest*: Asian students generally reported lower satisfaction with their lives, and Asian students made up a much larger proportion of the samples in California than in the Midwest. Allowing for this difference, life satisfaction in the two regions was identical.

403 *How much pleasure do you get from your car?*: Jing Xu and Norbert Schwarz have found that the quality of the car (as measured by Blue Book value) predicts the owners' answer to a general question about their enjoyment of the car, and also predicts people's pleasure during joyrides. But the quality of the car has no effect on people's mood during normal commutes. Norbert Schwarz, Daniel Kahneman, and Jing Xu, "Global and Episodic Reports of Hedonic Experience," in R. Belli, D. Alwin, and F. Stafford (eds.), *Using Calendar and Diary Methods in Life Events Research* (Newbury Park, CA: Sage), pp. 157–74.

404 *paraplegics spend in a bad mood?*: The study is described in more detail in Kahneman, "Evaluation by Moments."

405 *think about their situation*: Camille Wortman and Roxane C. Silver, "Coping with Irrevocable Loss, Cataclysms, Crises, and Catastrophes: Psychology in Action," American Psychological Association, Master Lecture Series 6 (1987): 189–235.

406 *studies of colostomy patients*: Dylan Smith et al., "Misremembering Colostomies? Former Patients Give Lower Utility Ratings than Do Current Patients," *Health Psychology* 25 (2006): 688–95. George Loewenstein and Peter A. Ubel, "Hedonic Adaptation and the Role of Decision and Experience Utility in Public Policy," *Journal of Public Economics* 92 (2008): 1795–1810.

406 *the word* miswanting: Daniel Gilbert and Timothy D. Wilson, "Miswanting: Some Problems in Affective Forecasting," in *Feeling and Thinking: The Role of Affect in Social Cognition*, ed. Joseph P. Forgas (New York: Cambridge University Press, 2000), 178–97.

CONCLUSIONS

410 *too important to be ignored*: Paul Dolan and Daniel Kahneman, "Interpretations of Utility and Their Implications for the Valuation of Health," *Economic Journal* 118 (2008): 215–234. Loewenstein and Ubel, "Hedonic Adaptation and the Role of Decision and Experience Utility in Public Policy."

410 *guide government policies*: Progress has been especially rapid in the UK, where the use of measures of well-being is now official government policy. These advances were due in good part to the influence of Lord Richard Layard's book *Happiness: Lessons from a New Science*, first published in 2005. Layard is among the prominent economists and social scientists who have been drawn into the study of well-being and its implications. Other important sources are: Derek Bok, *The Politics of Happiness: What Government Can Learn from the New Research on Well-Being* (Princeton: Princeton University Press, 2010). Ed Diener, Richard Lucus, Ulrich Schmimmack, and John F. Helliwell, *Well-Being for Public Policy* (New York: Oxford University Press, 2009). Alan B. Krueger, ed., *Measuring the Subjective Well-Being of Nations: National Account of Time Use and Well-Being* (Chicago: University of Chicago Press, 2009). Joseph E. Stiglitz, Amartya Sen, and Jean-Paul Fitoussi, *Report of the Commission on the Measurement of Economic Performance and Social Progress.* Paul Dolan, Richard Layard, and Robert Metcalfe, *Measuring Subjective Well-being for Public Policy: Recommendations on Measures* (London: Office for National Statistics, 2011).

411 *Irrational is a strong word*: The view of the mind that Dan Ariely has presented in *Predictably Irrational: The Hidden Forces That Shape Our Decisions* (New York: Harper, 2008) is not much different from mine, but we differ in our use of the term.

412 *accept future addiction*: Gary S. Becker and Kevin M. Murphy, "A Theory of Rational Addiction," *Journal of Political Economics* 96 (1988): 675–700. Nudge: Richard H. Thaler and Cass R. Sunstein, *Nudge: Improving Decisions About Health, Wealth, and Happiness* (New Haven: Yale University Press, 2008).

418 *can institute and enforce*: Atul Gawande, *The Checklist Manifesto: How to Get Things Right* (New York: Holt, 2009). Daniel Kahneman, Dan Lovallo, and Oliver Sibony, "The Big Idea: Before You Make That Big Decision . . ." *Harvard Business Review* 89 (2011): 50–60.

418 *distinctive vocabulary*: Chip Heath, Richard P. Larrick, and Joshua Klayman, "Cognitive Repairs: How Organizational Practices Can Compensate for Individual Shortcomings," *Research in Organizational Behavior* 20 (1998): 1–37.

ACKNOWLEDGMENTS

I am fortunate to have many friends and no shame about asking for help. Every one of my friends has been approached, some of them many times, with requests for information or editorial suggestions. I apologize for not listing them all. A few individuals played a major role in making the book happen. My thanks go first to Jason Zweig, who urged me into the project and patiently tried to work with me until it became clear to both of us that I am impossible to work with. Throughout, he has been generous with his editorial advice and enviable erudition, and sentences that he suggested dot the book. Roger Lewin turned transcripts of a set of lectures into chapter drafts. Mary Himmelstein provided valuable assistance throughout. John Brockman began as an agent and became a trusted friend. Ran Hassin provided advice and encouragement when it was most needed. In the final stages of a long journey I had the indispensable help of Eric Chinski, my editor at Farrar, Straus and Giroux. He knew the book better than I did and the work became an enjoyable collaboration—I had not imagined that an editor could do as much as Eric did. My daughter, Lenore Shoham, rallied round to help me through the hectic final months, providing wisdom, a sharp critical eye, and many of the sentences in the "Speaking of" sections. My wife, Anne Treisman, went through a lot and did a lot—I would have given up long ago without her steady support, wisdom, and endless patience.

INDEX